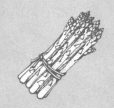

# GREAT AMERICAN

## COOKBOOK

*From Your Favorite Brand Name Companies*

Microwave ovens vary in wattage. The microwave cooking times
in this publication are approximate. Use the cooking times as
guidelines and check for doneness before adding more time.
Consult manufacturer's instructions for suitable microwave-
safe cooking dishes.

# CONTENTS

Introduction . . . . . . . . . . . . . . 6

Chicken—Delicious Creations . . . 8
Luncheon Fare                                    10
Festive Entertaining                             24
One Dish Meals                                   42
International Entrées                            56

Quick & Easy Casseroles . . . . . 76
Durkee®—The Secret to Great Casseroles 78
Minute-Wise Poultry                              80
No-Fuss Fish & Seafood                           94
Busy-Day Beef                                   102
Pronto Pork & Ham                               110
Express Veggies, Pasta & More                   118

StarKist® Sensational Tuna . . . 126
Classics Revisited                              128
Single Serving                                  138
Light 'n' Easy Suppers                          146
Entertaining Ideas                              154
Ethnic Specialties                              164
Microwave Marvels                               174

Kingsford® Best Barbecues. . . . 182
Barbecue Basics                                 184
Hot Off the Grill Meats                         188
Tempting Poultry                                204
Quick & Fabulous Seafood                        218
Spectacular Side Dishes                         228

Lawry's® New Taste of Mexico . . 236
Appetizers                                      238
Entrées
    Beef & Pork                                 248
    Poultry                                     258
    Fish & Seafood                              270
Salads & Side Dishes                            278

# GREAT AMERICAN
## C O O K B O O K

*From Your Favorite Brand Name Companies*

PUBLICATIONS INTERNATIONAL, LTD.

# Kikkoman® Oriental Cooking . . 296

Appetizers                          298
Beef                                312
Pork                                320
Poultry                             328
Seafood                             338
Side Dishes                         344

# Jell-O® Kids' Cooking Fun . . . . 352

Rules of the Kitchen                354
Cooking Tips                        355
Equipment                           356
Cooking Words to Know               358
The Real Easy Stuff                 359
JIGGLERS Mania                      369
Rainy Day Fun                       377
Family Dinners                      387

# Crisco® Cookies & Pies . . . . . 394

Tips for Cookie Success
  From the Crisco Kitchen           396
Cookie Classics                     398
Delicious Bar Cookies               412
Extra Special Cookies               420
Down-Home Pies                      432
Party-Time Pies                     446

# Hershey's® Fabulous Desserts . . 458

Cakes & Cheesecakes                 460
Cool Desserts                       476
Pies                                486
Breads, Muffins & Coffeecakes       494
Candies & Snacks                    502
Cookies & Cookie Bars               510

# Duncan Hines®
# Baking for Special Occasions . . 520

Breakfast Buffet                    522
Packed Lunch Goodies                530
Fabulous After Dinner Desserts      538
No-Cholesterol Anytime Treats       546
Special Celebrations                554
Picnic Sweets                       562
Children's Party Delights           572

# Acknowledgments . . . . . . . 582

# Index . . . . . . 583

# INTRODUCTION

The **Great American Cookbook—Collector's Edition** is the source for today's creative cook. It's full of exactly the kind of recipes you have been searching for—fresh, new ideas perfect for every occasion. We've combined ten of our most popular cookbooks in one easy-to-use volume to give you hundreds of tantalizing recipes from your favorite brand name companies. With this outstanding treasury, you'll never be at a loss for taste-tempting meal ideas.

Today's busy cooks need recipes that are not only delicious, but easy to prepare and dependable. The recipes you'll find in this volume all have easy-to-follow instructions, plus, hundreds are beautifully photographed. Each and every recipe has been kitchen-tested to ensure success time after time.

"Chicken—Delicious Creations" is filled with dozens of delicious, up-to-date chicken recipes from many of your favorite brand name companies. Whether you need a recipe for a quick, simple dinner or something spectacular for entertaining, you'll find it in this fabulous collection of chicken creations.

If you're looking for a delicious meal in a flash, turn to "Quick & Easy Casseroles." Included are recipes for simple side-dish and main-dish casseroles that make delicious one-dish meals. Look to "StarKist® Sensational Tuna" for a fabulous array of mouth-watering recipes made with healthful tuna. Everything from tempting appetizers to scrumptious entrées is included here.

How about a cookout? "Kingsford® Best Barbecues" will help you make your next barbecue the best. Filled with helpful grilling tips and terrific recipes, this section will have you grilling like an expert in no time.

For ethnic specialties, look to "Lawry's® New Taste of Mexico" and "Kikkoman® Oriental Cooking." "New Taste of Mexico" offers dozens of easy and sensational south-of-the-border dishes. Everything from nachos to enchiladas and more is here—why not have a fiesta? With "Kikkoman® Oriental Cooking," you'll find everything you need to make an authentic Oriental dinner—plus innovative ideas for contemporary meals with an Asian twist.

For the kids, there's "Jell-O® Kids' Cooking Fun." Who could resist these fun-filled recipes written with younger cooks in mind? There are instructions on kitchen safety, and the fanciful recipes have easy-to-follow instructions and illustrations. Kids from ages 5 to 105 will love to prepare these fabulous pudding and gelatin recipes.

A multitude of delicious prize-winning recipes can be found in "Crisco® Cookies & Pies." Filled with dozens of recipes for delectable cookies and delightful pies, this section also gives you tips on cookie-making success and the secrets to a perfect pie crust.

If you're a chocolate lover, look no further! "Hershey's Fabulous Desserts" is filled with recipes for a variety of luscious chocolate treats, including delightfully chocolaty cakes, cookies, pies, candies and breads. If it's chocolate, it's in here!

Looking for a knockout dessert for your next party? You'll find plenty of fantastic ideas in "Duncan Hines® Baking for Special Occasions." There are coffeecakes and breads, cakes and cookies, as well as dazzling desserts perfect for that special dinner.

Whether you're planning a romantic dinner for two, a casual family get-together or a cocktail party for 20, you'll find all you need in the **Great American Cookbook—Collector's Edition.** It's easy to create a terrific meal with help from your favorite brand name companies, and this comprehensive volume puts hundreds of magnificent recipes right at your fingertips.

# CHICKEN
## • Delicious Creations •

*From Your Favorite Brand Name Companies*

and many more

# CONTENTS

Luncheon Fare                                    10

Festive Entertaining                             24

One Dish Meals                                   42

International Entrées                            56

Caribbean Chicken Paella (*page 68*)

# LUNCHEON FARE

## CHICKEN À LA DIVAN

3 cups cooked fresh broccoli
    spears
1½ pounds sliced cooked chicken
    breasts
3 tablespoons
    FLEISCHMANN'S®
    Margarine

3 tablespoons all-purpose flour
1½ cups skim milk
½ cup EGG BEATERS® 99% Real
    Egg Product
2 tablespoons sherry cooking
    wine
Paprika

Arrange broccoli in the bottom of a 2-quart shallow baking dish or
6 individual baking dishes. Place chicken slices over broccoli; cover with foil.
Bake at 350°F for 20 minutes or until hot.

In saucepan, over low heat, melt margarine; blend in flour. Cook, stirring
until smooth and bubbly; remove from heat. Gradually stir in milk; return to
heat. Heat to a boil, stirring constantly. Gradually blend about half the hot
milk mixture into Egg Beaters®, then recombine with remaining hot mixture.
Stir in sherry. Spoon sauce over chicken and broccoli; sprinkle lightly with
paprika. Serve immediately.                          *Makes 8 servings*

## LEMON-DILLED CHICKEN

2 tablespoons olive oil
2 tablespoons lemon juice
2 cloves garlic, pressed
½ teaspoon dill weed

½ teaspoon salt
2 boneless skinless chicken
    breasts, halved

Mix oil, lemon juice, garlic, dill weed and salt in small bowl. Place chicken on
rack in broiler pan. Brush chicken with lemon mixture. Set oven temperature
at broil or 450°F. Position broiler pan about 4 inches from heat; broil 6 to
8 minutes. Turn chicken; broil about 6 to 8 minutes longer or until chicken is
golden brown and fork-tender.                        *Makes 4 servings*

Favorite recipe from **Delmarva Poultry Industry, Inc.**

Chicken à la Divan

# TANGY CHICKEN WALNUT SALAD

1 cup MJB/FARMHOUSE® Long
   Grain White Rice
2 cups chicken broth *or* 2 cups
   water and 2 chicken boullion
   cubes
1 teaspoon butter or margarine

¼ to ½ cup chopped walnuts
2 cups diced cooked chicken
½ cup sliced green onions with
   tops
½ cup sliced celery
¼ cup diced red bell pepper

**DRESSING**

3 tablespoons olive oil
3 tablespoons lemon juice
1 tablespoon soy sauce

1 teaspoon ginger powder
1 clove garlic, minced

Prepare rice as directed on package using chicken broth instead of water; cool. Heat butter in large skillet over medium-high heat. Sauté walnuts until golden brown; cool. Combine rice, chicken, walnuts, green onions, celery and red pepper in large bowl. Combine oil, lemon juice, soy sauce, ginger and garlic; toss with salad mixture. Refrigerate until ready to serve. Serve chilled.

*Makes about 6 servings*

# CHICKEN ITALIAN

1½ cups KELLOGG'S® Corn Flake
   Crumbs
1 cup (8-ounce can) tomato
   sauce
½ teaspoon garlic salt
½ teaspoon dried sweet basil
   leaves, crushed

¼ teaspoon dried oregano
   leaves, crushed
3 pounds boneless skinless
   chicken pieces, washed and
   patted dry
Vegetable cooking spray

1. Place Kellogg's® Corn Flake Crumbs in shallow dish or pan.

2. Combine tomato sauce, garlic salt, basil and oregano. Dip chicken pieces into tomato sauce mixture, then roll in Crumbs.

3. Place chicken pieces, meaty-side up, in shallow pan coated with cooking spray. Do not crowd.

4. Bake at 350°F about 1 hour or until chicken is tender and golden brown. Do not cover pan or turn chicken while baking.

*Makes 8 servings*

Grilled Chicken and Vegetable Sandwiches

# GRILLED CHICKEN AND VEGETABLE SANDWICHES

**6 tablespoons olive oil**
**3 cloves garlic**
**1½ teaspoons ground black pepper**
**1 red or yellow bell pepper, halved, cored, seeded, cut into ½-inch strips**
**1 zucchini, cut lengthwise into ¼-inch slices**
**2 COOKIN' GOOD® Boneless Skinless Chicken Breasts, halved**

**1 teaspoon salt**
**1 long loaf Italian bread, cut in half lengthwise**
**1 large tomato, sliced**
**½ cup loosely packed basil leaves _or_ 1 teaspoon dried basil leaves, crushed**
**1 package (8 ounces) mozzarella cheese, thinly sliced (optional)**

1. Prepare outdoor grill for barbecuing. Bring coals to medium heat.

2. In small bowl, combine oil, garlic and black pepper. Place vegetables in center of 12-inch square heavy aluminum foil. Place chicken on platter. Brush vegetables and chicken with olive oil mixture; sprinkle with salt. Fold foil to form packet.

3. Place vegetable packet on barbecue. Grill about 10 minutes or until tender. Remove vegetables; set aside. Grill chicken about 20 minutes, turning once, or until no longer pink.

4. To assemble sandwiches, on bottom half of bread layer peppers, zucchini, chicken, tomato, basil and cheese. Cover with hop half; cut crosswise to make 4 sandwiches. _Makes 4 sandwiches_

**Note:** For larger quantities multiply ingredients according to servings desired.

Grilled Chicken and Ziti Salad

# GRILLED CHICKEN AND ZITI SALAD

1½ pounds COOKIN' GOOD®
    Boneless Skinless Chicken
    Breasts
2 tablespoons fresh lemon juice
1 pound ziti or other tubular
    pasta
    Water
2 large red bell peppers, halved,
    cored, seeded, cut into
    ½-inch pieces
2½ cups thinly sliced celery

1 red onion, thinly sliced
1¼ cups thinly sliced pitted ripe
    olives
¼ cup minced fresh dill
3 tablespoons white wine
    vinegar
2 tablespoons mayonnaise
2 tablespoons Dijon-style
    mustard
    Salt and pepper to taste
⅔ cup olive oil

1. Heat oiled ridged grill pan over medium-high heat *or* set on rack 4 to 6 inches over glowing coals. Grill chicken in pan 8 to 10 minutes on each side until springy to touch. Transfer to clean shallow dish. Sprinkle chicken with lemon juice; let cool.

2. Boil ziti in water according to package directions until tender. Rinse ziti in colander under cold water; drain well.

3. Toss ziti, bell peppers, celery, onion, olives and dill in large bowl. Remove chicken from bowl, reserving juices. Thinly slice chicken and add to ziti salad. Add vinegar, mayonnaise, mustard, salt and pepper to juices in bowl. Whisk mixture well; add oil, whisking until dressing is thoroughly combined. Add dressing to salad; toss well. *Makes 8 to 10 servings*

# CRISPY CHICKEN DRUMMETTES

**CHICKEN DRUMMETTES**
- 2 cups Corn CHEX® brand cereal, crushed to ¾ cup
- 1 tablespoon dried parsley flakes
- ¼ teaspoon lemon pepper *or* black pepper
- 2 tablespoons teriyaki sauce
- 1½ pounds (about 18) chicken wing drummettes

**DIPPING SAUCE***
- ⅓ cup seedless raspberry jam *or* apricot jam
- ¼ cup chili sauce

To prepare Chicken Drummettes, preheat oven to 375°F. Lightly grease 13×9×2-inch baking pan. In shallow dish, combine cereal, parsley and pepper; set aside. Place teriyaki sauce in separate shallow dish. Roll drummettes in teriyaki sauce and then cereal mixture. Place drummettes in prepared pan. Bake 40 to 45 minutes until lightly browned.

To prepare Dipping Sauce, in small saucepan over low heat, combine jam and chili sauce; heat until warm.
*Makes about 18 servings*

*Substitute your favorite dipping sauce, such as honey mustard sauce, blue cheese salad dressing, ranch salad dressing, Italian salad dressing, sweet and sour sauce, hot sauce, teriyaki sauce or salsa, if desired.

**MICROWAVE DIRECTIONS:** To prepare Chicken Drummettes, lightly grease medium microwave-safe baking dish. Follow directions above to prepare Chicken Drummettes. Microwave at MEDIUM-HIGH (70% power) 18 to 20 minutes until done. To prepare Dipping Sauce, in small microwave-safe bowl, combine jam and chili sauce. Microwave on HIGH (100% power) 1 to 1½ minutes until warm.

# CHICKEN PASTA SALAD

- ¾ pound (12 ounces) spiral shape pasta
- 1¼ cups mayonnaise
- 1 can (5 fluid ounces) PET® Evaporated Milk
- ¼ cup Dijon-style mustard
- ½ teaspoon sugar
- ½ teaspoon salt
- ¼ teaspoon pepper
- ¼ teaspoon ground cumin
- 2 cups shredded cooked chicken
- ⅓ cup chopped red onion
- ½ cup diced celery
- ½ cup chopped green pepper

Prepare pasta according to package directions; rinse under cold water and drain. In a large bowl, combine mayonnaise, evaporated milk, mustard, sugar, salt, pepper and cumin; mix well. Add chicken, onion, celery, green pepper and drained pasta; mix well. Serve immediately.
*Makes 4 main-dish servings*

# MACARONI AND CHICKEN SALAD

1 (7-ounce) package
 CREAMETTES® Elbow
 Macaroni (2 cups uncooked)
2 cups cubed cooked chicken
1 large apple, cored and diced
1 cup sliced celery
1 cup seedless green grapes,
 halved

1 (15-ounce) can pineapple
 chunks, well drained
1 (11-ounce) can mandarin
 oranges, well drained
½ cup mayonnaise
½ cup sour cream
1 teaspoon sugar
⅛ teaspoon ground nutmeg

Prepare Creamettes® Elbow Macaroni according to package directions; drain. In medium bowl, combine macaroni, chicken, apple, celery, grapes, pineapple and oranges; mix well. In small bowl, blend mayonnaise, sour cream, sugar and nutmeg. Add to salad mixture; toss to coat. Cover; chill thoroughly. Refrigerate leftovers.

*Makes 8 to 10 servings*

# CILANTRO-LIME CHICKEN AND MANGO KABOBS

1 pound boneless skinless
 chicken breasts, cut into
 thin strips
1 large mango, peeled and cut
 into chunks
1 large green pepper, cut into
 1-inch squares
3 tablespoons honey

3 tablespoons lime juice
1 teaspoon grated lime peel
2 tablespoons
 FLEISCHMANN'S® Sweet
 Unsalted Margarine
2 tablespoons chopped cilantro
 or parsley

Thread chicken, mango and pepper alternately on 8 skewers; set aside.

In small saucepan, over medium heat, heat honey, lime juice, lime peel, margarine and cilatro until hot. Keep warm.

Broil or grill kabobs 4 inches from heat for 12 to 15 minutes or until chicken is cooked, turning and brushing with honey mixture often. Reheat any remaining honey mixture to a boil; serve with kabobs.

*Makes 8 appetizers or 4 main-dish servings*

Macaroni and Chicken Salad

Chicken-Apple Stuffed Pita

# CHICKEN-APPLE STUFFED PITA

¼ cup plain lowfat yogurt
2 tablespoons mayonnaise
1 tablespoon honey
2 cups chopped WASHINGTON
   Golden Delicious Apples
1 tablespoon lime juice
1 pound boneless skinless
   chicken breasts, cooked
   and diced

1 cup diced celery
¾ cup chopped unsalted
   peanuts
8 lettuce leaves
4 large pita pocket breads,
   halved

Combine yogurt, mayonnaise and honey in small bowl; set aside. Mix apples with lime juice in large bowl; add chicken, celery and peanuts. Fold yogurt mixture into apple mixture. To serve, place 1 lettuce leaf in each pita half; fill with chicken mixture and serve. *Makes 8 servings*

Favorite recipe from **Washington Apple Commission**

# ALL-AMERICAN BARBECUE SAUCE AND MARINADE

¾ cup water
⅔ cup (6-ounce can) CONTADINA® Tomato Paste
⅓ cup loosely packed parsley leaves
¼ cup chopped onion
1 large clove garlic
¼ cup firmly packed dark brown sugar
3 tablespoons apple cider vinegar
1 tablespoon vegetable oil
2 teaspoons Worcestershire sauce
1½ teaspoons prepared mustard
1½ teaspoons salt
2 pounds boneless skinless chicken breasts, halved

In blender container or food processor fitted with metal blade, combine water, tomato paste, parsley, onion, garlic, sugar, vinegar, oil, Worcestershire sauce, mustard and salt. Blend until smooth.

To use as a basting sauce, grill chicken until at least half done before brushing with sauce. Serve any remaining sauce as a table condiment.

To use as a marinade, pour into gallon-size resealable plastic bag. Place chicken in marinade; seal bag. Turn to coat all sides. Refrigerate at least 3 hours or overnight. Remaining marinade should *not* be served as a table condiment. Prepare extra sauce/marinade to serve at the table.

*Makes about 2 cups*

**Note:** Sauce may be prepared ahead and refrigerated up to 3 days before use.

**Mexican Sauce/Marinade:** Follow basic recipe, substituting cilantro leaves for parsley and lemon juice for apple cider vinegar. Add 3 tablespoons chili powder and ½ teaspoon ground cumin.

**Oriental Sauce/Marinade:** Follow basic recipe, omitting parsley and Worcestershire sauce. Reduce salt to ½ teaspoon. Add ¼ cup soy sauce and 1½ teaspoons ground ginger.

# PECAN-COATED WINGETTES

**WINGETTES**
6 tablespoons Dijon-style mustard
4 tablespoons butter, melted
2 cups pecans

⅓ cup plain bread crumbs
12 COOKIN' GOOD® Chicken Wingettes, thawed

**DIPPING SAUCE**
½ cup sour cream
½ cup plain yogurt
2 tablespoons Dijon-style mustard

2 tablespoons minced onion or minced green onions
⅛ to ¼ teaspoon hot pepper sauce

1. Preheat oven to 375°F. Combine 6 tablespoons mustard and butter in bowl; set aside.

2. Place pecans and bread crumbs in food processor bowl. Process until pecans are finely chopped. Place pecan mixture on waxed paper or in pie plate. Dip chicken in mustard mixture to coat, then in pecan mixture. Arrange Wingettes on baking sheet. Bake 25 minutes or until fork-tender.

3. While chicken is baking, whisk sour cream, yogurt, 2 tablespoons mustard, onion and hot pepper sauce in bowl. Serve Wingettes with Dipping Sauce.
*Makes 4 to 6 servings*

# ZESTY CHICKEN EN PAPILLOTE

2 boneless skinless chicken breasts, halved
1 package ALOUETTE® Light Soft Spreadable Cheese

1 red pepper, julienned
1 zucchini, julienned
4 mushrooms, sliced

1. Fold four 18×18-inch pieces of parchment paper or foil in half; cut into shape of a half heart (when unfolded whole heart is formed).

2. Cut chicken into strips; place ½ breast on 1 side of heart. Top chicken with 3 tablespoons cheese and ¼ of *each* vegetable. Fold other half of heart over to enclose chicken-cheese mixture; fold edges to seal. Repeat process with remaining chicken, cheese, vegetables and parchment.

3. Place packages on cookie sheet; bake in preheated 400°F oven 10 to 12 minutes. Place packages on plate. Serve letting diner open to release smell and flavor at table.
*Makes 4 servings*

Pecan-Coated Wingettes

# HAWAIIAN CHICKEN SALAD

4 cups chopped cooked chicken
1 can (8 ounces) crushed
     pineapple in natural juice,
     drained
1 small apple, chopped
1 rib celery, chopped
1 small onion, chopped
½ cup chopped green bell
     pepper

1 cup mayonnaise
¼ teaspoon salt
¼ teaspoon ground ginger
2 cups HONEY ALMOND
     DELIGHT® brand cereal,
     crushed to 1 cup
1 tablespoon margarine or
     butter, melted

Preheat oven to 350°F. In 1½-quart baking dish, combine chicken, pineapple, apple, celery, onion and green pepper. In small bowl, combine mayonnaise, salt and ginger. Add to chicken mixture, stirring until well combined. In separate small bowl, combine cereal and margarine. Sprinkle evenly over chicken. Bake 25 to 30 minutes until hot.        *Makes 6 servings*

**Note:** Salad is also delicious served cold, unbaked.

**MICROWAVE DIRECTIONS:** Follow directions above using 1½-quart microwave-safe baking dish; *EXCEPT* do not sprinkle cereal onto chicken mixture prior to initial cooking. Microwave on HIGH (100% power), covered, 4 minutes; stir. Sprinkle cereal evenly over chicken mixture. Microwave on HIGH 2 to 2½ minutes until hot.

# TARRAGON CHICKEN BURGERS

3 tablespoons olive oil, divided
¼ cup finely chopped onion
1 small clove garlic, finely
     chopped
1 pound WAMPLER-
     LONGACRE® Ground
     Chicken
2 tablespoons chopped fresh
     parsley

1 teaspoon dried tarragon
     leaves, crushed
¼ teaspoon dried thyme leaves,
     crushed
¼ teaspoon salt
⅛ teaspoon freshly ground
     pepper
2 tablespoons all-purpose flour

Heat 1 tablespoon olive oil in skillet over medium-low heat. Add onion and garlic; cook until tender and soft, about 3 minutes. Meanwhile, combine chicken, parsley, tarragon, thyme, salt and pepper in mixing bowl. Blend onion mixture with chicken mixture. Form into 4 patties; dust with flour. Heat remaining 2 tablespoons olive oil in clean skillet over medium heat. Cook until patties are browned on both sides, no pink remains in center and juices run clear.        *Makes 4 servings*

**Prep time:** about 7 minutes        **Cook time:** about 5 minutes

California Date-Chicken Salad

# CALIFORNIA DATE-CHICKEN SALAD

2 oranges, peeled
8 cups mixed salad greens, washed
1¾ cups shredded cooked boneless skinless chicken breast
¾ cup pitted California dates, sliced

½ cup coarsely chopped toasted walnuts
⅓ cup crumbled blue cheese
3 tablespoons olive oil
1 tablespoon balsamic or red wine vinegar
Salt and black pepper to taste

Slice oranges crosswise into ¼-inch slices; cut into quarters. Toss oranges, salad greens, chicken, dates, walnuts and blue cheese in large bowl. Whisk together olive oil and vinegar. Toss dressing in with salad until lightly coated. Season to taste with salt and pepper.

*Makes 2 servings or 4 appetizer servings*

Favorite recipe from **California Date Administrative Committee**

# FESTIVE ENTERTAINING

## GRILLED CHICKEN AND APPLE WITH FRESH ROSEMARY

½ cup apple juice
¼ cup white wine vinegar
¼ cup vegetable oil or light olive oil
1 tablespoon chopped fresh rosemary *or* 1 teaspoon dried rosemary leaves, crushed

¼ teaspoon salt
¼ teaspoon ground black pepper
3 boneless skinless chicken breasts, halved
2 WASHINGTON Golden Delicious Apples, cored and sliced into ½-inch-thick rings

1. Combine juice, vinegar, oil, rosemary, salt and pepper in shallow baking dish or bowl. Add chicken and apples; marinate in refrigerator at least 30 minutes.

2. Heat grill. Remove chicken and apples from marinade; arrange on hot grill. Discard marinade. Cook chicken 20 minutes or until cooked through, turning to grill both sides. Cook and turn apples about 6 minutes or until crisp-tender. Serve.

*Makes 6 servings*

Favorite recipe from **Washington Apple Commission**

## DIJON ALMOND CHICKEN

2 tablespoons BLUE BONNET® Spread, melted
2 tablespoons GREY POUPON® Country Dijon Mustard

2 boneless skinless chicken breasts, halved
½ cup chopped almonds

In small bowl, combine spread and mustard. Dip chicken breast in mustard mixture and then coat with chopped almonds. Place into 10×6×1¾-inch greased baking dish.

Bake at 375°F for about 30 minutes or until done.

*Makes 4 servings*

Grilled Chicken and Apple
with Fresh Rosemary

# CHICKEN ROYALE

2 boneless skinless chicken
   breasts, halved
1 package (4 ounces) Boursin or
   other herb-flavored cheese,
   quartered
½ cup English walnuts, finely
   chopped
4 large spinach leaves, steamed
   slightly

½ teaspoon salt
½ teaspoon pepper
½ cup dry white wine
½ cup bottled reduced-calorie
   raspberry vinaigrette
   dressing*
2 tablespoons margarine
   Hot cooked rice

Pound chicken breasts to ¼-inch thickness with flat side of meat mallet or chef's knife. Roll cheese in walnuts. Place 1 spinach leaf on each breast; top with a cheese quarter. Fold chicken around spinach and cheese to form a mound. Sprinkle salt and pepper over chicken. Place chicken in baking pan. Cover; bake in 350°F oven 30 minutes or until chicken is fork-tender.

Mix wine and dressing in small skillet. Cook over medium heat until sauce is reduced by one-half; stir in margarine. Pour sauce over chicken. Serve with rice.

*Makes 4 servings*

*If raspberry vinaigrette dressing is not available, substitute ¼ cup bottled reduced-calorie red wine vinegar and oil dressing and ¼ cup seedless raspberry jam. Omit margarine.

Favorite recipe from **Delmarva Poultry Industry, Inc.**

# SESAME SEED CHICKEN

1 cup KELLOGG'S® Corn Flake
   Crumbs
3 tablespoons sesame seeds
1 egg
½ cup skim milk
½ cup all-purpose flour

1½ teaspoons ground ginger
¼ teaspoon salt
3 pounds broiler chicken pieces
   (without or with skin),
   washed and patted dry
   Vegetable cooking spray

1. Combine Kellogg's® Corn Flake Crumbs and sesame seeds. Set aside in shallow dish or pan.

2. In second shallow dish or pan, beat egg and milk slightly. Add flour, ginger and salt. Mix until smooth. Dip chicken into batter. Coat with crumbs mixture. Place in single layer, meaty-side up, in shallow baking pan coated with cooking spray.

3. Bake at 350°F about 1 hour or until chicken is tender and done.

*Makes 8 servings*

Chicken Royale

Chicken Cutlets Classica® Fontina

# CHICKEN CUTLETS CLASSICA® FONTINA

4 tablespoons butter, divided
8 ounces fresh mushrooms, cut
    into slivers
4 boneless skinless chicken
    breasts, halved
Flour for coating

Ground pepper
⅓ cup dry white wine
2 tablespoons Madeira or sherry
4 ounces CLASSICA® Fontina,
    cut into 8 slices

Preheat oven to 350°F. Heat 2 tablespoons butter in large skillet over medium heat; cook mushrooms until tender. Remove mushrooms; set aside. Remove liquid from skillet; reserve.

Roll chicken in flour to coat. Season with pepper. Heat remaining 2 tablespoons butter in skillet over medium heat; brown chicken, turning once. Remove chicken; place in 9-inch square baking dish. Sprinkle with mushrooms; set aside.

Add white wine and Madeira to skillet. Bring to a boil, stirring constantly. Reduce heat to low. Cook until liquid is reduced by half, about 5 minutes. Pour wine mixture over chicken.

Bake until chicken is no longer pink, about 20 minutes. Place slice of Classica® Fontina on each chicken breast. Return to oven. Bake until cheese is melted, about 3 to 5 minutes. *Makes 6 to 8 servings*

# APRICOT GLAZED CHICKEN

1 jar (12 ounces) apricot preserves
2 tablespoons reduced-fat mayonnaise
1 tablespoon ketchup
¼ teaspoon dry mustard
8 boneless skinless chicken breasts (about 2 pounds)
2 tablespoons margarine
½ cup finely chopped onion
½ cup finely chopped celery
½ cup thinly sliced mushrooms
1¼ cups KELLOGG'S® ALL-BRAN® cereal
½ cup chicken broth
1 can (8 ounces) water chestnuts, drained and chopped
½ teaspoon salt
¼ teaspoon pepper
¼ teaspoon rubbed sage
Hot cooked rice

1. Combine preserves, mayonnaise, ketchup and dry mustard. Set aside for sauce.

2. Place each chicken breast between 2 pieces of waxed paper. Pound with flat side of meat mallet or chef's knife to ⅛-inch thickness, being careful not to tear meat. Set aside.

3. Melt margarine in medium skillet. Add onion and celery. Stirring frequently, cook over medium heat until crisp-tender. Stir in mushrooms and cook 3 to 4 minutes longer.

4. Combine Kellogg's® All-Bran® cereal and chicken broth. Let stand about 1 minute or until cereal absorbs broth. Mix in vegetables, water chestnuts, salt, pepper and sage. Top each breast with ¼ cup filling. Roll, folding in ends. Place breasts seam-side down into a 12×8-inch shallow baking dish. Cover chicken rolls with reserved sauce.

5. Bake uncovered at 350°F about 45 minutes or until chicken is tender and done. Serve over hot rice if desired.    *Makes 8 servings*

# HONEY-MUSTARD GLAZED CHICKEN

½ cup GREY POUPON® Dijon or Country Dijon Mustard
¼ cup honey
2 tablespoons lemon juice
1 clove garlic, crushed
¼ teaspoon dried tarragon leaves, crushed
1 broiler-fryer chicken, cut into serving pieces (3 pounds)
Fresh tarragon sprigs, for garnish

In small bowl, combine mustard, honey, lemon juice, garlic and tarragon. Grill or broil chicken 45 minutes or until done, turning occasionally and brushing with mustard mixture frequently. Arrange on serving platter; garnish with fresh tarragon if desired.    *Makes 4 servings*

# GRILLED ROSEMARY CHICKEN

3 large cloves garlic, quartered
3 tablespoons olive oil
3 tablespoons Dijon-style
   mustard
2 tablespoons lemon juice
2 tablespoons fresh rosemary,
   minced *or* 2 teaspoons
   dried rosemary leaves,
   crumbled

1 teaspoon ground black pepper
1 COOKIN' GOOD® Broiler
   Chicken, cut into serving
   pieces (about 3½ pounds)

1. Combine garlic, oil, mustard and lemon juice in blender. Blend until smooth and creamy. Pour mixture into bowl; stir in rosemary and pepper. Brush chicken pieces with mustard mixture. Cover; refrigerate 6 hours or overnight.

2. Prepare outdoor grill for barbecuing. Bring coals to medium heat. Place chicken, meaty-side up, on grill. Cook 12 minutes. Turn; continue to cook 20 to 25 minutes until chicken is no longer pink. Remove to clean plate.

*Makes 4 to 6 servings*

**TO BROIL:** Preheat broiler; arrange chicken on rack in broiling pan. Broil 7 to 9 inches from heat 25 minutes. Turn; continue broiling 20 minutes or until chicken is no longer pink.

# DOUBLE-COATED CHICKEN

7 cups KELLOGG'S® CORN
   FLAKES® cereal, crushed
   to 1¾ cups
1 egg
1 cup skim milk
1 cup all-purpose flour
½ teaspoon salt

¼ teaspoon black pepper
3 pounds broiler chicken pieces
   (without or with skin),
   washed and patted dry
3 tablespoons margarine,
   melted

1. Measure crushed Kellogg's® Corn Flakes cereal into shallow dish or pan. Set aside.

2. In small mixing bowl, beat egg and milk slightly. Add flour, salt and pepper. Mix until smooth. Dip chicken in batter. Coat with cereal. Place in single layer, meaty-side up, in foil-lined shallow baking pan. Drizzle with margarine.

3. Bake at 350°F about 1 hour or until chicken is tender and done. Do not cover pan or turn chicken while baking.

*Makes 8 servings*

Grilled Rosemary Chicken

Southwestern Grilled Chicken with Yogurt Salsa

# SOUTHWESTERN GRILLED CHICKEN WITH YOGURT SALSA

**1 container (8 ounces) plain lowfat yogurt**
**2 cans (4 ounces *each*) sliced mild green chilies, drained**
**¼ cup minced green onions**
**1 teaspoon ground cumin**
**1 teaspoon salt**
**1 pound boneless skinless chicken breasts, halved**
**1 *each* red, green and yellow bell pepper, *each* cut into sixths**
**1 tablespoon reduced-calorie mayonnaise**

Combine yogurt, green chilies, green onions, cumin and salt in medium bowl. Set aside ⅔ cup yogurt mixture for Yogurt Salsa; refrigerate. Pierce chicken liberally on both sides with fork tines; add to bowl with yogurt mixture, turning to coat both sides. Marinate 15 minutes.

To cook over coals, place chicken and peppers on rack 3 to 4 inches away from medium-hot coals. Grill, turning once, until chicken is cooked through and peppers are crisp-tender, about 10 minutes.

Meanwhile, prepare Yogurt Salsa by stirring mayonnaise into reserved ⅔ cup yogurt mixture; place in small serving bowl.

To serve, slice each breast into ½-inch-thick slices. Arrange chicken and peppers on individual plates. Serve with Yogurt Salsa and kidney beans with corn kernels in lettuce cups, if desired. *Makes 4 servings*

**TO BROIL:** Place chicken and peppers on rack in broiler pan 4 to 5 inches away from preheated broiler. Cook following directions for grilling.

Favorite recipe from **National Dairy Board**

# CHICKEN WITH SWEET AND SOUR GRAPE SAUCE

1 pound boneless skinless
    chicken
1 egg, beaten
½ cup corn flake crumbs
    Salt and pepper
1 tablespoon vegetable oil
½ cup sliced onion

1 cup red pepper strips
1 tablespoon *each* soy sauce,
    finely minced fresh ginger
    root
¼ cup apricot preserves
1 cup California Seedless
    Grapes

Cut chicken into bite-size pieces; dip into egg. Mix corn flake crumbs with salt and pepper; coat chicken with crumbs. Place on greased baking sheet; bake at 375°F 15 minutes or until golden. Arrange on serving platter. Heat oil in skillet over medium-high heat; cook onion until soft. Add pepper strips, soy sauce and ginger root; cook 1 minute. Stir in preserves and grapes; cook until heated through. Pour over chicken pieces.

*Makes about 4 servings*

**Tip:** Frozen prepared breaded chicken nuggets can be used instead of breading your own chicken pieces.

Favorite recipe from **California Table Grape Commission**

# APPLE & RICE-STUFFED CHICKEN

1 package LIPTON® Golden
    Sauté Rice Mix—Oriental
    Style
3 cups water, divided
1 tart cooking apple, diced
½ cup finely chopped celery

2 boneless skinless chicken
    breasts, halved (about
    1 pound), pounded to
    ¼ inch thick
Paprika

Preheat oven to 350°F.

In medium saucepan, bring Oriental style rice mix, 2½ cups water, apple and celery to a boil. Reduce heat and simmer uncovered, stirring occasionally, 10 minutes; let cool slightly.

Evenly spread each chicken breast with ¼ cup rice mixture; bring up sides to form bundles and secure with wooden toothpicks.

In 11×7-inch baking dish, combine remaining rice mixture with remaining ½ cup water. Arrange chicken bundles over rice. Sprinkle with paprika. Bake 25 minutes or until chicken is tender and done. Remove toothpicks before serving.

*Makes 4 servings*

# HOLLYWOOD CHICKEN

1 COOKIN' GOOD Roaster
   Chicken (about 5 to
   7 pounds)
1 small orange, quartered
1 small onion, quartered
4 sprigs fresh cilantro
2¾ teaspoons salt, divided
  ½ teaspoon freshly ground black
    pepper
  ¼ cup butter or margarine,
    melted, divided
1 cup orange juice

½ cup loosely packed fresh
   cilantro leaves
¼ cup orange marmalade
½ teaspoon grated orange peel
   Liquid red pepper seasoning,
    to taste
1 tablespoon flour
   Orange segments and
    avocado slices (optional)
   Fresh sprigs of cilantro
    (optional)

1. Rinse Roaster with cold water and drain well; pat dry with paper towels.
   Loosely stuff cavity of roaster with orange, onion and cilantro sprigs.
   Preheat oven to 375°F. Sprinkle bird inside and out with 2½ teaspoons
   salt and pepper. Skewer Roaster openings, truss wings underneath body
   and tie drumsticks together. Place breast side up on rack in shallow open
   roasting pan. Brush with 1 tablespoon butter; set aside.

2. Combine orange juice, cilantro leaves, orange marmalade, remaining
   3 tablespoons butter, remaining ¼ teaspoon salt, orange peel and pepper
   seasoning in container of food processor or blender. Process until well
   blended and smooth; set aside 1¼ cups. Bake Roaster in preheated oven
   2 hours or about 20 minutes per pound, basting occasionally with
   remaining orange mixture, until meat thermometer registers 185°F, leg
   moves freely or juices run clear when pierced with a fork. Let Roaster
   stand 20 minutes while completing sauce.

3. Remove 1 tablespoon drippings from roasting pan to small saucepan.
   Whisk in 1 tablespoon flour and cook over medium heat 3 minutes, stirring
   constantly. Gradually whisk in reserved basting liquid, stirring constantly
   until thickened. (If mixture is too thick, add additional orange juice until
   desired consistency.) Garnish with orange, avocado and cilantro.

*Makes 5 to 7 servings*

**Note:** If Roaster skin begins to brown too much, cover brown areas with foil.

Hollywood Chicken

# PINEAPPLE CHICKEN RICE BOWL

3 boneless skinless chicken
   breasts, cut into bite-size
   pieces
½ cup light soy sauce
¼ cup sherry
4 DOLE® Green Onions, thinly
   sliced, divided
2 tablespoons honey
1 medium DOLE® Fresh
   Pineapple
18 bamboo skewers (6 inches
   *each*), soaked in water

3 cups DOLE® Broccoli
   florettes, cooked
1 small DOLE® Red Bell Pepper,
   cut into strips
2 medium DOLE® Carrots,
   grated (1 cup)
¼ cup DOLE® Chopped
   Almonds, toasted
6 cups hot cooked brown rice
   Seasoned rice vinegar
   (optional)

• Marinate chicken in mixture of soy sauce, sherry, half the green onions and honey. Refrigerate 15 minutes or longer.

• Twist crown from pineapple. Cut pineapple in half lengthwise. Refrigerate half for another use. Cut fruit from shell. Cut into chunks. Thread pineapple and chicken onto skewers. Grill or broil 4 inches from heat source 6 to 8 minutes, turning and basting with marinade.

• Combine broccoli, red pepper, carrots, almonds and remaining 2 green onions. Spoon hot rice into individual bowls. Spoon on broccoli mixture; sprinkle with vinegar. Spoon on Celery Sauce. Serve with filled skewers.

*Makes 6 servings*

## CELERY SAUCE

½ cup minced DOLE® Celery
½ cup reduced fat mayonnaise
2 tablespoons light soy sauce

1 tablespoon seasoned rice
   vinegar

Combine celery, mayonnaise, soy sauce and vinegar.

**Prep time:** 25 minutes
**Cook time:** 15 minutes

**Marinating time:** 15 minutes

Pineapple Chicken Rice Bowl

# TANDOORI STYLE GRILLED CHICKEN

3½ pounds broiler-fryer chicken serving pieces
1 container (8 ounces) plain lowfat yogurt
1 medium onion, quartered
2 large cloves garlic
2 tablespoons curry power
1 tablespoon paprika
1½ teaspoons salt
⅛ to ¼ teaspoon ground red pepper

Pierce chicken liberally on meaty side with fork tines, then with sharp knife make ½-inch-deep diagonal cuts about 1 inch apart. Place in 12×8×2-inch glass baking dish; set aside. Combine in food processor or electric blender yogurt, onion, garlic, curry powder, paprika, salt and red pepper. Process until smooth. Set aside ¼ cup yogurt mixture; refrigerate.

Pour remaining yogurt mixture over chicken, turning to coat both sides. Marinate 15 minutes or cover and refrigerate up to 24 hours.

To cook over coals, place chicken on rack over medium-hot coals. Grill chicken, turning often and basting with reserved ¼ cup yogurt mixture. Cook chicken through, 35 to 40 minutes. *Makes 4 servings*

**TO BAKE:** Preheat oven to 400°F. Place chicken on rack in broiling pan; bake following directions for grilling. Just before serving, brush with 1 tablespoon melted butter.

Favorite recipe from **National Dairy Board**

# ROAST CHICKEN WITH SAVORY CORNBREAD STUFFING

1 package (8 to 12 ounces) corn muffin mix
Ingredients for cornbread
1 tablespoon butter or margarine
2 green onions, diagonally sliced
1 medium red pepper, seeded and diced
4 ribs celery, diced, divided
1 teaspoon grated lemon peel
½ teaspoon dried thyme leaves, crushed
½ teaspoon ground sage
1 teaspoon freshly ground pepper, divided
5 cups chicken broth, divided
1 COOKIN' GOOD® Roaster Chicken (6 pounds)
Salt
2 medium carrots, thinly sliced
1 medium potato, peeled and diced
1 small onion, thinly sliced
2 cloves garlic
1 bay leaf

Roast Chicken with Savory Cornbread Stuffing

1. Prepare corn muffin mix according to package directions for cornbread. Cool completely. Turn oven control to 350°F.

2. Melt butter in 10-inch skillet over medium heat. Cook green onions, red pepper and half the celery 10 minutes or until tender. Stir in lemon peel, thyme, sage and ½ teaspoon pepper; set aside.

3. Coarsely crumble cornbread into medium bowl. Stir in celery mixture and 1 cup chicken broth.

4. Rinse Roaster with cold water and drain well; pat dry with paper towels. Spoon stuffing into body cavity. Close by folding skin over opening; skewer if necessary. With cotton strings, tie legs and tail together. Sprinkle Roaster with salt and remaining ½ teaspoon pepper.

5. Place chicken into large roasting pan. Add carrots, potato, onion, garlic, bay leaf, remaining 4 cups chicken broth and remaining celery. Insert meat thermometer into thickest part of thigh, being careful pointed end of thermometer does not touch bone. Bake roaster about 2½ hours, checking often during last half hour of roasting. Roaster is done when temperature reaches 180°F or when juices run clear when pierced with fork.

6. Remove Roaster to serving platter; keep warm. Pour broth mixture into large measuring cup or bowl; discard bay leaf. Let stand a few seconds until fat separates from broth. Skim fat; blend mixture in food processor or blender until smooth. Reheat sauce before serving.

*Makes 6 servings*

# CHICKEN WITH SNOW PEAS AND WALNUTS

## SAUCE

1 tablespoon butter or
   margarine
1 tablespoon all-purpose flour
2 teaspoons dried basil leaves,
   crushed
1 teaspoon lemon pepper
½ teaspoon salt

½ teaspoon garlic powder
1½ cups (12-ounce can) *undiluted*
   CARNATION® Evaporated
   Milk
¼ cup dry vermouth or chicken
   broth

## CHICKEN AND VEGETABLES

2 tablespoons olive oil, divided
1 pound boneless skinless
   chicken breasts, cut into
   strips
1 cup (4½ ounces) *thinly* sliced
   or julienned carrots

2 cups (5 ounces) Chinese snow
   peas, ends removed
1 cup (3 ounces) sliced fresh
   mushrooms
Cooked rice or pasta (optional)
¼ cup chopped walnuts, toasted

For sauce, in medium saucepan, melt butter; whisk in flour, basil, lemon pepper, salt, garlic powder, and evaporated milk. Stir constantly over medium heat until thickened. Stir in vermouth. Cover; keep warm.

For chicken and vegetables, in large skillet over medium heat, heat *1 tablespoon* oil. Add chicken; cook 5 to 6 minutes, stirring frequently until cooked. Remove and set aside. Add *remaining* 1 tablespoon oil to skillet; stir-fry carrots over high heat for 1 minute. Add snow peas and mushrooms; cook until crisp-tender. Combine chicken pieces with vegetables in skillet. Serve over hot cooked rice, if desired. Pour sauce over top; sprinkle with walnuts. *Makes 4 servings*

# GOLDEN GLAZED CHICKEN BREASTS

1 envelope LIPTON® Recipe
   Secrets™ Onion Recipe
   Soup Mix
⅔ cup apricot preserves or
   peach-apricot sauce
½ cup water

1 pound boneless skinless
   chicken breasts
2 large red or green peppers,
   sliced
Hot cooked rice

In small bowl, thoroughly combine onion recipe soup mix, apricot preserves and water; set aside.

In foil-lined broiler pan, arrange chicken breasts and peppers; top with soup mixture. Broil 10 minutes or until chicken is tender and done, turning once. Serve over hot rice. *Makes about 4 servings*

Chicken with Snow Peas and Walnuts

# ONE DISH MEALS

## CITRUS CHICKEN

1 tablespoon vegetable oil
2 boneless skinless chicken
   breasts, halved (about
   1 pound)
1 cup orange juice
4 teaspoons sugar
1 clove garlic, minced

1 teaspoon dried rosemary
   leaves, crushed
2 teaspoons cornstarch
¼ cup dry white wine
   Salt and pepper
2 pink grapefruit, sectioned

Heat oil in large skillet over medium heat; add chicken. Cook about
8 minutes, turning once or until no longer pink in center. Remove chicken
from skillet; keep warm.

Add orange juice, sugar, garlic and rosemary to skillet; bring to a boil.
Combine cornstarch and wine in cup until smooth. Add to skillet; cook,
stirring constantly, until sauce is clear and thickened. Season with salt and
pepper to taste. Add grapefruit; heat through, stirring occasionally. Serve
over chicken. *Makes 4 servings*

## CHICKEN, BROCCOLI & RICE SOUP

4½ cups water
  2 cups cubed cooked chicken
  1 package LIPTON® Golden
     Sauté Rice Mix—Chicken &
     Broccoli

1 cup shredded Cheddar
   cheese (about 4 ounces)

In large saucepan, combine all ingredients except cheese; bring to a boil.
Reduce heat and simmer, uncovered, stirring occasionally, 10 minutes. To
serve, evenly pour into 4 bowls, then top each with ¼ cup cheese.
*Makes 4 (1½ cup) servings*

Citrus Chicken

Artichoke Chicken Pilaf

## ARTICHOKE CHICKEN PILAF

2 tablespoons butter or
   margarine
12 ounces boneless skinless
   chicken breasts, cut into
   strips
1 clove garlic, minced
1¾ cups water
1 package (6 ounces) MJB/
   FARMHOUSE® Rice Pilaf Mix

½ teaspoon basil leaves,
   crushed
1 jar (6 ounces) marinated
   artichokes, drained, rinsed
   and cut into halves
3 green onions, cut into ½-inch
   lengths
¼ cup toasted sliced almonds

Heat butter in large skillet over medium-high heat. Cook and stir chicken and
garlic in butter 5 to 7 minutes or until browned. Add water, seasoning mix,
rice and basil. Bring to a boil. Reduce heat to low. Cover and simmer
15 minutes. Stir in artichokes and green onions; cook 5 minutes more.
Garnish with almonds. *Makes about 4 servings*

## CHICKEN CUTLETS PARMESAN

2 boneless skinless chicken
   breasts, halved
   Salt and pepper to taste
2 tablespoons olive oil
1 jar (14 ounces) spaghetti
   sauce with mushrooms

¼ cup sliced pitted ripe olives
2 tablespoons grated Parmesan
   cheese
   Hot cooked spaghetti

Pound chicken breasts to ½-inch thickness with flat side of meat mallet or chef's knife. Sprinkle salt and pepper over chicken. Heat oil in large skillet over medium-high heat. Add chicken and cook, turning to brown on both sides, about 8 minutes. Drain off excess fat.

Spoon spaghetti sauce over chicken; top with olives. Cook over medium heat about 5 minutes or until chicken is fork-tender and sauce is bubbly. Sprinkle cheese over all. Cover; let stand 2 minutes or until cheese melts. Serve with cooked spaghetti. *Makes 4 servings*

Favorite recipe from **Delmarva Poultry Industry, Inc.**

# HEARTY LANCASTER CHICKEN, VEGETABLE AND DUMPLING SOUP

**6 cups chicken stock or broth**
**2 cups diced cooked PERDUE® Chicken**
**1 package (10 ounces) frozen corn *or* kernels from 2 ears fresh corn**
**1 cup thinly sliced leek, white and tender green parts only *or* 1 medium onion, thinly sliced**

**½ cup parboiled potatoes, cut into ½-inch cubes**
**½ cup parboiled carrots, cut into ½-inch pieces**
**½ cup shredded green cabbage**
**1 teaspoon salt**
**⅛ teaspoon freshly ground pepper**
**Knepp (recipe follows)**

Heat broth to boiling in large saucepan over high heat. Add all remaining ingredients except Knepp. Reduce heat to low. Cover and simmer 3 minutes while making dumplings.

Drop dumpling batter by half teaspoons into simmering soup. Stir in parsley when dumplings rise to top; serve. *Makes 4 servings*

## KNEPP (LITTLE DUMPLINGS)

**1 egg**
**¾ cup all-purpose flour**
**⅓ cup water**
**¼ teaspoon salt**

**⅛ teaspoon baking powder**
**Pinch ground nutmeg**
**1 teaspoon chopped fresh parsley (optional)**

Beat egg in small bowl; stir in flour, water, salt, baking powder, nutmeg and parsley.

**Chicken Spinach Stracciatella:** Omit dumplings. Clean and stem ½ pound fresh spinach; stack and cut into ½-inch strips. Whisk together 2 eggs with ½ cup grated Parmesan cheese. Stir in spinach with chicken, then heat soup to boiling. Stir soup constantly while pouring in egg mixture in thin stream. Cook until soup simmers again; stir gently just before serving.

# CREAMY HERBED CHICKEN

1 package (9 ounces) fresh bow-tie pasta or fusilli*
1 tablespoon vegetable oil
2 boneless skinless chicken breasts, halved (about 1 pound) cut into ½-inch strips
1 small red onion, cut into slices
1 package (10 ounces) frozen green peas, thawed, drained
1 yellow or red pepper, cut into strips
½ cup chicken broth
1 container (8 ounces) soft cream cheese with garlic and herbs
Salt and black pepper

Cook pasta in lightly salted boiling water according to package directions, about 5 minutes; drain.

Meanwhile, heat oil in large skillet or wok over medium-high heat. Add chicken and onion; stir-fry 3 minutes or until chicken is no longer pink in center. Add peas and yellow pepper; stir-fry 4 minutes. Reduce heat to medium.

Stir in broth and cream cheese. Cook, stirring constantly, until cream cheese is melted. Combine pasta and chicken mixture in serving bowl; mix lightly. Season with salt and black pepper to taste. Garnish as desired.

*Makes 4 servings*

*Substitute dried bow-tie pasta or fusilli for fresh pasta. Cooking time will be longer; follow package directions.

# NO-PEEK CHICKEN AND RICE

2 tablespoons vegetable oil
1 broiler-fryer chicken, cut into serving pieces (2½ to 3 pounds)
2½ cups water
1 envelope LIPTON® Recipe Secrets™ Vegetable Recipe Soup Mix
½ teaspoon dried basil leaves, crushed
¾ cup uncooked regular rice

In large skillet, heat oil over medium heat and add chicken, browning 2 minutes on each side; drain. Stir in water, vegetable recipe soup mix and basil. Bring to a boil, then stir in uncooked rice. Simmer, covered, 45 minutes or until chicken and rice are done.

*Makes about 4 servings*

Creamy Herbed Chicken

# CHICKEN WITH SHERRY SAUCE

3 boneless skinless chicken
  breasts, halved (about
  1¾ pounds)
⅛ teaspoon salt
⅛ teaspoon pepper
2 tablespoons margarine or
  butter
½ cup dry sherry

1 can (4 ounces) button
  mushrooms, undrained
*Undiluted* CARNATION®
  Evaporated Milk
1 package (.87 ounce) chicken
  gravy mix
1 cup (8 ounces) sour cream

Lightly sprinkle chicken breasts with salt and pepper. In 10 or 12-inch skillet over medium-high heat, melt margarine; brown chicken on both sides. Add sherry, mushrooms, and mushroom liquid. Reduce heat; cover and cook for 20 to 25 minutes or until chicken is cooked through.

With slotted spoon, remove chicken and mushrooms to serving dish; cover and keep warm. Measure pan juices; if necessary, add evaporated milk to make 1¼ cups liquid. In same skillet, combine liquid and chicken gravy mix. Bring to a boil; reduce heat and simmer uncovered for 5 minutes, stirring constantly. Cool slightly. Stir in ½ cup undiluted evaporated milk and sour cream; heat gently, stirring until warmed through. Do not boil. Pour over chicken.

*Makes 6 servings*

# CHICKEN THIGHS AND VEGETABLES LYONNAISE

2 medium-size baking potatoes,
  peeled and thinly sliced
  (about 2 cups)
1 package (2 pounds) PERDUE®
  Chicken Thighs (6 thighs)
½ teaspoon ground thyme,
  divided
Salt to taste
Ground pepper to taste

4 medium-size carrots, peeled
  and thinly sliced (about
  2 cups)
1 medium-size onion, peeled
  and thinly sliced (about
  1 cup)
4 teaspoons butter or margarine
1 cup milk or heavy cream
¼ teaspoon hot pepper sauce
  Paprika

Soak sliced potatoes in large bowl in cold water for at least 10 minutes. Preheat oven to 350°F. Sprinkle thighs with ¼ teaspoon thyme, salt and pepper. Drain potatoes well in a colander. Layer with carrots and onion in buttered 11×8-inch baking dish. Season each layer with remaining ¼ teaspoon thyme, salt and pepper. Dot lightly with butter. Arrange chicken, skin side up, on top of vegetables. Combine milk and hot pepper sauce and pour over chicken; sprinkle generously with paprika.

Bake 60 to 70 minutes until chicken and vegetables are tender.

*Makes 4 servings*

Quick Arroz con Pollo

## QUICK ARROZ CON POLLO

2 tablespoons olive or
  vegetable oil
¾ pound boneless chicken
  breasts, cut into 1-inch
  cubes
½ cup chopped onion
1 clove garlic, minced
1¾ cups water

1 medium tomato, chopped
1 package (6 ounces) MJB/
  FARMHOUSE® Savory
  Chicken Rice Mix
⅓ cup frozen peas, thawed
⅓ cup sliced pimento-stuffed
  green olives or sliced pitted
  ripe olives

Heat oil in large skillet over medium-high heat. Cook and stir chicken, onion and garlic in oil 5 to 7 minutes or until chicken is no longer pink. Add water and tomato. Bring to a boil over high heat. Add rice and seasoning mix. Reduce heat to low. Cover and simmer 15 minutes. Add peas and olives; cook 5 to 10 minutes longer or until liquid is absorbed.

*Makes 4 to 6 servings*

# SWEET 'N SOUR CHICKEN

1 can (20 ounces) DOLE®
    Pineapple Chunks in Juice
2 boneless skinless chicken
    breasts
    Salt and pepper to taste
1 teaspoon vegetable oil
2 DOLE® Carrots, thinly sliced
1 DOLE® Green Bell Pepper,
    seeded, chunked
1 medium onion, chunked

1 clove garlic, pressed
½ cup catsup
⅓ cup light brown sugar, packed
1 tablespoon cornstarch
1 tablespoon soy sauce
1 teaspoon ground ginger
    Grated peel and juice from
    1 DOLE® Lemon
2 cups hot cooked rice

• Drain pineapple; reserve juice.

• Cut chicken into bite-size pieces. Season with salt and pepper.

• In large nonstick skillet heat oil over medium-high heat; brown chicken, turning once. Reduce heat. Add carrots, bell pepper, onion and garlic to skillet. Cover; simmer 5 minutes.

• Combine reserved juice, catsup, brown sugar, constarch, soy sauce, ginger, lemon peel and lemon juice in small bowl until blended. Stir into same skillet. Cover; simmer 10 minutes longer. Stir in pineapple; heat through. Serve with rice.

*Makes 4 servings*

**Prep time:** 15 minutes     **Cook time:** 15 minutes

# NEW ENGLAND CHICKEN 'N' CORN CHOWDER

¼ pound bacon or salt pork,
    diced
1 cup chopped onion
½ cup chopped celery
4 cups chicken stock or broth
2 cups, ½-inch cubed, peeled
    potatoes
1 package (10 ounces) frozen
    corn

1 teaspoon salt
⅛ teaspoon freshly ground
    pepper
2 cups diced cooked PERDUE®
    Chicken
1 cup (½ pint) heavy cream
    Oyster crackers (optional)

Cook and stir bacon in large saucepan over medium-high heat, 3 minutes, until bacon is light brown. Add onion and celery; cook 3 minutes longer. Stir in stock. Bring to a boil over high heat. Add potatoes, corn, salt and pepper; cook 5 to 10 minutes until potatoes are tender. Stir in chicken and cream. Reduce heat to low. Cover and simmer 3 minutes. Serve with oyster crackers.

*Makes 4 to 6 servings*

Sweet 'n Sour Chicken

# SPICY FRUITED CHICKEN

1 medium DOLE® Fresh
  Pineapple
2 teaspoons margarine, divided
2 boneless skinless chicken
  breasts, halved
1 teaspoon garlic powder
  Salt to taste
½ large DOLE® Red Bell Pepper,
  cut into strips
1 cup *each* chunked green and
  red onion
1 teaspoon minced serrano or
  jalapeño chile

1 head DOLE® Cabbage, cut
  into 8 wedges
⅔ cup chicken broth
  Grated peel and juice from
  1 DOLE® Orange
¼ cup chutney, chopped
1 tablespoon red wine vinegar
½ teaspoon *each* ground cumin,
  allspice
1½ teaspoons *each* cornstarch,
  water

• Twist crown from pineapple. Cut pineapple in half lengthwise. Refrigerate half for another use. Cut fruit from shell; cut crosswise into slices. In nonstick skillet heat 1 teaspoon margarine over medium-high heat; brown pineapple, turning once. Remove to plate.

• Pound chicken breasts lightly until even thickness with flat side of meat mallet or chef's knife. Sprinkle with garlic powder and salt. Heat remaining 1 teaspoon margarine over medium-high heat; brown chicken, turning once. Reduce heat. Cover; cook 10 minutes. Remove to plate.

• Cook and stir bell pepper, onions and chile in pan drippings 2 minutes. Arrange cabbage in skillet. Add chicken broth, orange peel, ⅓ cup orange juice, chutney, vinegar, cumin and allspice. Bring to a boil. Reduce heat. Cover; simmer 6 minutes. Remove cabbage with slotted spoon to platter. Blend cornstarch and water in skillet. Cook, stirring, until sauce boils and thickens.

• Slice chicken; serve with cabbage, pineapple and sauce.

*Makes 4 servings*

**Prep time:** 25 minutes          **Cook time:** 30 minutes

Spicy Fruited Chicken

Chicken to the Macs

# CHICKEN TO THE MACS

1 (7-ounce) package
   CREAMETTES® Elbow
   Macaroni (2 cups uncooked)
2 cups broccoli flowerets
¼ cup margarine or butter
1 small red bell pepper, sliced
1 small onion, chopped
1 cup sliced fresh mushrooms

2 cups milk
1 (10¾-ounce) can cream of
   mushroom soup
1 teaspoon salt
¼ teaspoon black pepper
2 cups (8 ounces) shredded
   Cheddar cheese, divided
2 cups cubed cooked chicken

Prepare Creamettes® Elbow Macaroni according to package directions, adding broccoli the last 4 minutes of cooking time; drain. In large skillet heat margarine; add red pepper, onion and mushrooms and cook until onion is tender. Add milk, soup, salt and black pepper. Cook and stir for 5 minutes. Stir in 1 cup cheese and chicken. Combine macaroni and broccoli with soup mixture. Pour into a 2½-quart baking dish; top with remaining cheese. Cover; bake in 350°F oven 20 to 30 minutes, until hot and bubbly. Refrigerate leftovers.

*Makes 4 to 6 servings*

# BRUNSWICK STEW

1 broiler-fryer chicken, cut into
    8 serving pieces (2½ to
    3 pounds)
1 (13¾-fluid-ounce) can
    COLLEGE INN® Chicken
    Broth
2 (6-ounce) cans tomato paste
2 tablespoons REGINA® Red
    Wine Vinegar

2 tablespoons Worcestershire
    sauce
¼ teaspoon ground red pepper
2 cups cubed cooked pork
1 (17-ounce) can lima beans,
    undrained
1 (16-ounce) can peeled
    tomatoes, undrained and
    coarsely chopped

In large heavy saucepan, over medium-high heat, heat chicken, broth, tomato paste, vinegar, Worcestershire sauce and red pepper to a boil. Cover; reduce heat and simmer 20 minutes. Add pork, lima beans and tomatoes. Cover; simmer 20 to 25 minutes longer or until chicken is done.

*Makes 6 servings*

**MICROWAVE DIRECTIONS:** In 5-quart microwavable casserole, combine first 6 ingredients as above. Cover with waxed paper. Microwave on MEDIUM (50% power) for 28 to 30 minutes, stirring twice during cooking time. Add pork, lima beans and tomatoes; cover. Microwave on LOW (30% power) for 18 to 20 minutes or until chicken is done. Let stand, covered, 10 minutes before serving.

# PINEAPPLE CHICKEN PACKETS

1 can (8 ounces) DOLE®
    Pineapple Slices in Juice
1 cup slivered DOLE® Carrots
1 boneless skinless chicken
    breast, quartered
    lengthwise
    Salt and pepper to taste

½ teaspoon dried tarragon
    leaves, crushed
    Grated peel and juice from
    1 DOLE® Lemon
1 DOLE® Green Onion, thinly
    sliced

• Drain pineapple; reserve juice for another use.

• For each packet, arrange ½ cup carrots in center of 12-inch square heavy aluminum foil. Layer 2 pineapple slices, 2 pieces chicken, salt, pepper, tarragon, ½ teaspoon lemon peel, 1 teaspoon lemon juice and ½ onion on each. Fold foil to form packet.

• Place packets on baking sheet. Bake in 450°F oven 15 minutes. Remove from oven. Let stand 5 minutes.

*Makes 2 servings*

**Prep time:** 20 minutes    **Cook time:** 15 minutes

# INTERNATIONAL ENTRÉES

## CHICKEN AND VEGETABLE COUSCOUS

3 boneless skinless chicken
    breasts (3 ounces *each*)
1 tablespoon vegetable oil
½ cup chopped green onions
3 garlic cloves, minced
1¼ cups tomato sauce
¼ cup water
1¼ cups chopped carrots
1 cup canned small white
    beans, drained and rinsed
1 large potato, cut into cubes

1 yellow squash, chopped
1 medium tomato, chopped
¼ cup chopped seeded red
    pepper
¼ cup raisins
2 tablespoons brown sugar
2 teaspoons ground cumin
¾ teaspoon ground cinnamon
3 to 4 drops hot pepper sauce
1½ cups water
1 cup dry couscous

Cut chicken into 3-inch cubes; set aside. Heat oil in skillet over medium heat. Add chicken and cook, turning to brown on all sides. Add green onions and garlic; cook and stir 1 minute. Stir in tomato sauce and ¼ cup water. Add remaining ingredients except 1½ cups water and couscous. Reduce heat to low. Cover and simmer 15 minutes. Meanwhile bring remaining 1½ cups water to a boil over high heat; add couscous. Cover; remove from heat. Let stand 5 minutes. Serve chicken and vegetables over couscous.

*Makes 6 servings*

Favorite recipe from **The Sugar Association, Inc.**

Chicken and Vegetable Couscous

Surprisingly Simple Chicken Cacciatore

## SURPRISINGLY SIMPLE CHICKEN CACCIATORE

4 boneless skinless chicken
    breasts (4 ounces *each*),
    chunked
  Salt and pepper
  Flour
  Paprika
4 tablespoons olive oil, divided
2 cloves garlic, minced
1 (26-ounce) jar CLASSICO®
    Di Napoli Tomato and Basil
    Pasta Sauce

1 small green bell pepper, cut
    into thin strips
1 small red bell pepper, cut into
    thin strips
½ of a (1-pound) package
    CREAMETTE® Thin
    Spaghetti, uncooked
1 cup (4 ounces) shredded
    Provolone cheese

Season chicken with salt and pepper, then coat with flour and sprinkle with paprika. In large skillet, heat 3 tablespoons oil. Brown chicken and garlic; drain. Stir in Classico® Pasta Sauce. Bring to a boil; reduce heat. Cover; simmer 20 minutes, adding green and red bell peppers last 5 minutes. Prepare Creamette® Thin Spaghetti according to package directions; drain and toss with remaining 1 tablespoon oil. Arrange on warm serving platter; top with hot chicken, sauce and cheese. Serve immediately. Refrigerate leftovers.
*Makes 4 servings*

# NEW YEAR CHICKEN

¾ cup (3 ounces) shredded
    Cheddar cheese
4 strips bacon, cooked and
    finely crumbled
2 tablespoons finely chopped
    onion
1 teaspoon hot pepper sauce
2 boneless skinless chicken
    breasts, halved

2 tablespoons all-purpose flour
½ teaspoon seasoned salt
1 egg, beaten
2 cups Corn CHEX® brand
    cereal, crushed to ¾ cup
1 teaspoon dried thyme leaves,
    crushed

Preheat oven to 350°F. In small bowl combine cheese, bacon, onion and pepper sauce. Pound chicken breasts flat to ¼-inch thickness with flat side of meat mallet or chef's knife. Spread ¼ cup cheese mixture onto each chicken breast. Roll up chicken breasts securing all ends with wooden picks.

In shallow bowl combine flour and seasoned salt. In separate shallow bowl place egg. In third shallow bowl combine cereal and thyme. Dip each chicken breast first into flour mixture, then egg and then cereal mixture. Place in ungreased 9-inch square baking pan. Bake 35 to 40 minutes or until chicken is no longer pink. Remove toothpicks before serving.

*Makes 4 servings*

# CHICKEN CORDON DOUX®

3 boneless skinless chicken
    breasts, halved
6 slices DOUX DE MONTAGNE®
    cheese
6 paper-thin slices prosciutto or
    ham
  Dry mustard
1½ cups fine, dry bread crumbs
½ teaspoon salt

½ teaspoon pepper
½ teaspoon mixed herbs (sage,
    parsley, thyme, rosemary,
    bay leaves)
2 eggs, lightly beaten
¼ cup olive oil
¼ cup butter
1 cup dry white wine
  Cooked brown rice

Pound chicken breasts until paper thin, between 2 pieces of waxed paper, with flat side of meat mallet or chef's knife. Place slice of cheese and slice of ham on each piece of chicken; sprinkle with a little dry mustard. Roll up and fasten with wooden toothpicks.

Combine bread crumbs, salt, pepper and herb mixture. Dip each roll into eggs and then into bread crumb mixture. Refrigerate until ready to use (up to 8 hours). Heat oil and butter in skillet. Brown chicken rolls 10 to 12 minutes on each side; remove from pan. Remove toothpicks before serving. Add wine to pan; simmer, stirring in all brown bits from bottom and sides. Pour sauce over chicken rolls. Serve with brown rice.

*Makes 6 servings*

# COLD LIME CHICKEN AND COUSCOUS

¼ cup olive oil, divided
1 medium onion, chopped
(½ cup)
1¾ cups chicken broth, divided
1 cup couscous
⅓ cup fresh lime juice, divided
2 small cloves garlic, pressed,
divided
1 teaspoon grated lime peel,
divided
¾ teaspoon salt, divided
¼ teaspoon freshly ground black
pepper, divided
5 green onions, trimmed, cut on
diagonal into 1-inch pieces
1 small green bell pepper, cut
into ½-inch pieces
1 small red bell pepper, cut into
½-inch pieces
4 COOKIN' GOOD® Whole
Broiler or Roaster Chicken
Legs *or* 4 Thighs and
4 Drumsticks
Leaf lettuce greens

Heat 1 tablespoon oil in 10-inch heavy skillet over medium-high heat. Add onion; cook, stirring occasionally about 5 minutes, or until onion is tender. Add 1½ cups broth, couscous, 3 tablespoons lime juice, 1 clove garlic, ½ teaspoon lime peel, ¼ teaspoon salt and ⅛ teaspoon pepper. Bring to a boil over medium-high heat; cook about 2 minutes. Remove skillet from heat; cover and let stand 5 minutes. Remove lid; transfer mixture to large bowl. Cover; refrigerate for several hours.

Meanwhile, heat 1 tablespoon remaining oil in same skillet over medium heat. Add green onions, green and red peppers; cook, stirring occasionally about 2 minutes, or until vegetables are just tender. Add cooked onions and peppers along with remaining ½ teaspoon grated lime peel to mixture in refrigerator.

Heat remaining 2 tablespoons oil in skillet over medium-high heat. Sprinkle chicken with remaining ½ teaspoon salt and ⅛ teaspoon pepper and add to skillet. Cook 5 to 7 minutes on each side until golden. Add remaining ¼ cup chicken broth, lime juice and garlic clove; bring to a boil. Reduce heat to low. Simmer 15 to 20 minutes for broiler legs, thighs and drumsticks and 20 to 25 minutes for roaster legs, thighs and drumsticks, or until chicken is tender when pierced with a fork.

To serve, spoon couscous mixture onto lettuce-lined platter. Arrange chicken over couscous mixture. *Makes 4 servings*

Italian Vegetable Chicken

# ITALIAN VEGETABLE CHICKEN

**1 pound boneless skinless chicken breasts, halved**
**2 cloves garlic, pressed**
**2 teaspoons Italian herb seasoning**
**Salt and pepper to taste**
**1 egg white**
**½ cup all-purpose flour, divided**

**1 pound Italian sausage, cut into 1-inch chunks**
**2 teaspoons olive oil (optional)**
**2 cups sliced mushrooms**
**1 large onion, chopped**
**1 DOLE® Red Bell Pepper, slivered**
**1 cup water**
**2 cups DOLE® Broccoli florettes**

• Pound chicken to ¼-inch thickness with flat side of meat mallet or chef's knife. Rub chicken with garlic; sprinkle with herbs, salt and pepper. Dip into egg white; coat with flour.

• In large skillet over medium-high heat, brown sausage. Remove and drain; set aside.

• Add chicken to same skillet, turning to brown both sides. Remove to platter. Add sausage to chicken. Keep warm.

• Add olive oil to skillet if needed. Add mushrooms, onion and red pepper; cook and stir until onion is soft. Add any remaining flour or 1 additional teaspoon flour to skillet. Stir to blend. Continue cooking to brown slightly. Stir in water. Cook and stir until slightly thickened, 3 to 5 minutes. Add broccoli; heat through until crisp-tender. Spoon over chicken.

*Makes 6 servings*

**Prep time:** 20 minutes    **Cook time:** 15 minutes

# FIESTA CHICKEN SANDWICHES

1 pound COOKIN' GOOD®
   Chicken Tenders
   Water
½ teaspoon salt
1½ tablespoons olive oil
2 tablespoons finely chopped
   onion
¼ cup molasses
2 tablespoons catsup
1½ tablespoons prepared
   mustard

1½ tablespoons white vinegar
8 flour tortillas* (6 to 7 inches
   each)
1 carrot, shredded
1 small green pepper, halved,
   cored, seeded and finely
   chopped
1 cup shredded lettuce
1 medium tomato, chopped
1 cup (4 ounces) shredded
   Monterey Jack cheese

1. Preheat oven to 325°F.

2. Place chicken in 10-inch skillet. Add water to cover and salt. Bring to a boil over high heat. Reduce heat to low; cover and simmer 10 to 15 minutes, or until chicken is tender and juices run clear when pierced with a fork. Remove to warm platter and cut into 2¼×1-inch strips when cool enough to handle.

3. For barbecue sauce, heat oil in small saucepan over medium heat. Add onion; cook, stirring occasionally, 3 to 5 minutes. Add molasses, catsup, mustard and vinegar; heat to boiling. Reduce heat to low and simmer 10 minutes.

4. Meanwhile, wrap tortillas securely in foil. Warm in preheated oven 5 to 10 minutes.

5. Drain chicken tenders and add to barbecue sauce. Toss together until well-coated and heated through.

6. To assemble sandwiches, place small portion of chicken across center of 1 tortilla. Keep remaining tortillas wrapped in foil. Top with about 1 tablespoon *each* carrot, green pepper, lettuce, tomato and cheese. Fold in sides and secure with wooden pick. Repeat with remaining ingredients to make 7 more sandwiches. Remove toothpicks before serving.

*Makes 4 to 6 servings*

*Corn tortillas may be substituted for flour tortillas; however, flour tortillas seem more readily available in larger sizes than corn tortillas. Larger-size tortillas are easier to fill and they hold together better.

Fiesta Chicken Sandwiches

# SZECHUAN CHICKEN

2 tablespoons reduced-sodium
  soy sauce, divided
1 tablespoon cornstarch
1 pound boneless skinless
  chicken breasts, cut into
  1-inch pieces
1 tablespoon dry sherry
½ to 1 teaspoon crushed red
  pepper

2 tablespoons
  FLEISHCHMANN'S®
  Margarine
1 large red pepper, diced
⅓ cup sliced green onions
1 teaspoon grated ginger root
2 cups cooked regular long-
  grain rice, prepared in
  unsalted water

In small bowl, combine 1 tablespoon soy sauce and cornstarch; add chicken, tossing to coat well. Blend remaining 1 tablespoon soy sauce and sherry; set aside.

In large skillet, over medium-high heat, cook crushed red pepper in margarine until pepper turns black. Add chicken mixture; stir-fry for 3 minutes or until no longer pink. Remove chicken from skillet; set aside. In same skillet, stir-fry red pepper, green onions and ginger root for 2 minutes or until tender-crisp. Return chicken to skillet with sherry mixture; cook 2 to 3 minutes more, stirring constantly until chicken is cooked. Serve over rice.

*Makes 4 servings*

# CHICKEN ENCHILADA CASSEROLE

4 uncooked corn tortillas
4 cups cubed, cooked chicken
1 cup KELLOGG'S® ALL-BRAN®
  cereal
1 cup (4 ounces) shredded
  mozzarella cheese
1 jar (10 ounces) enchilada
  sauce

1 can (8 ounces) tomato sauce
1 cup (8 ounces) plain, nonfat
  yogurt
4 cups shredded lettuce
½ cup chopped tomato
⅓ cup sliced green onions

1. Place tortillas on baking sheet. Bake at 350°F about 10 minutes or until crisp. Cool; break into small pieces. Set aside.

2. Combine chicken, Kellogg's® All-Bran® cereal, cheese and sauces. Pour into 1½-quart casserole dish.

3. Bake at 350°F about 30 minutes or until heated through. Remove from oven.

4. Layer yogurt, lettuce, tomato and green onions on top of casserole. Sprinkle with tortilla pieces and serve immediately.   *Makes 6 servings*

Paella

# PAELLA

2 tablespoons olive or
   vegetable oil
½ pound boneless skinless
   chicken breasts, cut into
   ½-inch cubes
1 cup chopped onion
¾ cup chopped green bell
   pepper
½ cup smoked ham cubes,
   ¼ inch each
1 clove garlic, minced
1 cup MJB/FARMHOUSE®
   Original Long Grain White
   Rice

1 can (14½ ounces) whole
   peeled tomatoes,
   undrained, broken up
1½ cups water
2 tablespoons dry white wine
2 chicken bouillon cubes
¾ teaspoon dried leaf oregano,
   crushed
⅛ teaspoon ground black pepper
⅛ teaspoon ground turmeric
½ pound uncooked medium
   shrimp, shelled, deveined
½ cup frozen peas, thawed

Heat oil in large skillet over medium-high heat. Add chicken, onion, bell
pepper, ham and garlic. Cook 5 to 7 minutes or until chicken is no longer
pink. Add rice; stir to coat. Add tomatoes, water, wine, bouillon cubes,
oregano, pepper and turmeric. Bring to a boil. Reduce heat to low. Cover;
simmer 15 minutes. Add shrimp and peas. Cover; cook 10 minutes longer or
until shrimp are opaque and liquid is absorbed. *Makes 4 to 6 servings*

West Indies Curried Drumsticks

# WEST INDIES CURRIED DRUMSTICKS

12 broiler-fryer chicken
    drumsticks
¾ teaspoon salt, divided
½ teaspoon paprika
1 tablespoon cornstarch
1 tablespoon sugar

1 cup orange juice
2 cloves garlic, crushed
1½ teaspoons curry powder
1 teaspoon grated orange peel
½ teaspoon ground ginger
½ cup chopped cashews

Place chicken in large baking dish; sprinkle with ½ teaspoon salt and paprika. Bake in 375°F oven 30 minutes. Mix cornstarch and sugar in small saucepan. Stir in orange juice, garlic, curry powder, orange peel, ginger and remaining ¼ teaspoon salt. Cook and stir over medium heat until mixture boils and thickens. Pour sauce over chicken; bake, basting once with pan juices, about 25 minutes more or until chicken is fork-tender. Sprinkle cashews over chicken.                    *Makes 6 servings*

Favorite recipe from **Delmarva Poultry Industry, Inc.**

## SWEET AND SPICY CHICKEN STIR-FRY

1 can (8 ounces) DEL MONTE®
    Pineapple Chunks in Its
    Own Juice
1 tablespoon vegetable oil
1 boneless skinless chicken
    breast, cubed
    Salt and pepper (optional)

¼ to ½ teaspoon crushed red
    pepper flakes or hot pepper
    sauce
1 can (16 ounces) DEL MONTE®
    Blue Lake Cut Green Beans,
    drained
¾ cup sweet and sour sauce*
    Hot cooked rice (optional)

Drain pineapple, reserving ¼ cup juice. In 10 to 12-inch wok or skillet, heat oil over medium heat. Add chicken; cook and stir 5 minutes. Season with salt and pepper, if desired. Stir in reserved ¼ cup juice and red pepper flakes. Reduce heat; cook, uncovered, 2 minutes. Add green beans, pineapple and sauce. Cover; cook 2 minutes or until heated through. Serve over hot cooked rice, if desired.                    *Makes 4 servings*

**Total time:** 20 minutes

**\*Helpful Hint:** Sweet and sour sauce is available in international section of supermarket. *Or* combine ½ cup water, ¼ cup granulated sugar, 3 tablespoons cider vinegar, 3 tablespoons DEL MONTE® Ketchup and 4 teaspoons cornstarch. Cook, stirring constantly, until thickened and translucent.

## SWEET CHICKEN RISOTTO

1 tablespoon vegetable oil
¾ pound boneless skinless
    chicken breasts, thinly
    sliced
¾ cup onion, chopped
4 cups chicken broth *or* 2 cans
    (14 ounces *each*) chicken
    broth
2 cups uncooked instant brown
    rice

1 tablespoon prepared
    horseradish
4 teaspoons sugar
14 ounces canned black beans,
    rinsed and drained *or*
    2 cups cooked beans
1 medium green bell pepper,
    sliced
1 medium red bell pepper, sliced
¼ cup grated Parmesan cheese

Heat oil in 3 to 4-quart saucepan over medium-high heat. Add chicken and onion; cook 5 minutes, turning to brown both sides. Add chicken broth, rice, horseradish and sugar. Reduce heat to low. Cover and simmer 15 minutes or until rice is tender. (There should be extra liquid.) Add beans and peppers. Simmer 5 minutes. Sprinkle with cheese before serving.
                                   *Makes 4 servings*

Favorite recipe from **The Sugar Association, Inc.**

# CARIBBEAN CHICKEN PAELLA

1 large clove garlic, minced
1 teaspoon dried oregano
    leaves, crushed
6 COOKIN' GOOD® Drumsticks
    and Thighs
2 tablespoons red wine vinegar
1 tablespoon olive oil
½ pound ham, chopped
1 large green pepper, chopped

1 medium onion, chopped
2 large tomatoes, cored and
    chopped
6 cups chicken broth
2 cups uncooked rice
1 cup frozen peas, thawed
¼ cup pimento-stuffed green
    olives
1 tablespoon capers

1. In small bowl, combine garlic and oregano; coat chicken. Place chicken in shallow dish; sprinkle with vinegar. Cover and refrigerate 1 hour.

2. In 5-quart Dutch oven over medium heat, heat oil. Cook chicken about 15 minutes, browning on all sides. Remove chicken to plate.

3. In drippings in Dutch oven over medium heat, cook ham, green pepper and onion 10 minutes or until tender, stirring occasionally. Add tomatoes; cook 5 minutes, stirring frequently. Add broth, rice and chicken. Bring to a boil over high heat.

4. Reduce heat to low. Cover; simmer 25 minutes. Stir in peas, olives and capers; heat through.

*Makes 4 servings*

# TAMALE PIE

1 cup yellow cornmeal
½ cup all-purpose flour
1 teaspoon DAVIS® Baking
    Powder
1 cup water
2 cups shredded Cheddar
    cheese (8 ounces), divided

1 egg, beaten
1 pound chopped cooked
    chicken
1 (12-ounce) jar ORTEGA® Mild,
    Medium or Hot Thick and
    Chunky Salsa
½ cup sliced pitted ripe olives

In medium bowl, blend cornmeal, flour and baking powder; stir in water, 1 cup cheese and egg. Spread half the cornmeal mixture on bottom of greased 9-inch pie plate; set aside.

In medium bowl, combine chicken, salsa and ½ cup cheese; spoon into prepared pie plate. Spoon remaining cornmeal mixture over chicken mixture to within 1 inch of plate edge. Bake at 350°F for 35 minutes or until top is golden brown. Top with remaining cheese and olives; bake 5 minutes more or until cheese melts.

*Makes 6 to 8 servings*

**Prep time:** 20 minutes      **Cook time:** 40 minutes

Caribbean Chicken Paella

# MEXICAN LASAGNA

2 tablespoons vegetable oil
1½ tablespoons chili powder
1½ pounds COOKIN' GOOD®
    Boneless Skinless Chicken
    Breasts *or* COOKIN' GOOD®
    Boneless Skinless Chicken
    Thighs, cut into 1-inch
    pieces
½ teaspoon salt, divided
1 large onion, diced
1 can (4 ounces) chopped green
    chili peppers, drained
2 teaspoons ground cumin

1 can (28 ounces) tomatoes,
    drained and chopped
1 can (15 to 16 ounces) pinto
    beans, drained and rinsed
1 container (15 ounces) light
    ricotta cheese
2 egg whites
2 cups (8 ounces) shredded
    Monterey Jack cheese with
    jalapeño peppers, divided
1 package corn tortillas (12 per
    package)

1. Preheat oven to 375°F. In 10-inch skillet combine oil and chili powder; cook 1 minute over medium heat. Increase heat to medium-high. Add half the chicken pieces and ¼ teaspoon salt. Cook 4 minutes, stirring frequently. Remove chicken to large bowl with slotted spoon. Repeat with remaining chicken and ¼ teaspoon salt. Remove chicken. Cook in drippings remaining in skillet, onion, chili peppers and cumin 5 minutes, stirring frequently. Spoon onion mixture into bowl with chicken. Add tomatoes and beans.

2. Combine ricotta cheese, egg whites and 1 cup Monterey Jack cheese in separate bowl.

3. Line bottom and sides of greased 3-quart round, shallow casserole or baking dish with 8 tortillas. Spoon about ⅔ chicken mixture into casserole. Cover with cheese mixture. Arrange remaining tortillas on top of cheese mixture. Spoon remaining chicken mixture on top. Sprinkle with remaining 1 cup Monterey Jack cheese. Bake 35 minutes or until heated through.

*Makes 6 to 8 servings*

# CHICKEN FAJITAS

¼ cup REGINA® Red Wine
    Vinegar
¼ cup vegetable oil, divided
2 tablespoons A.1.® Steak
    Sauce
2 teaspoons WRIGHT'S®
    Natural Hickory Seasoning
½ teaspoon liquid hot pepper
    seasoning

1 pound boneless skinless
    chicken breasts, cut into
    strips
1 large green pepper, cut into
    strips
1 large onion, cut into wedges
8 flour tortillas, heated
    Sour cream and shredded
    Cheddar cheese, for garnish

Blend vinegar, 2 tablespoons oil, steak sauce, hickory seasoning and hot pepper seasoning. In nonmetal bowl, pour marinade over chicken. Cover; chill for 1 to 2 hours, stirring occasionally. Drain chicken.

In large skillet, over medium-high heat, cook green pepper and onion in remaining 2 tablespoons oil for 5 to 6 minutes or until tender. Remove from skillet with slotted spoon; set aside. In same skillet, cook and stir chicken for 10 to 12 minutes or until no longer pink. Add reserved peppers and onions; cook for 3 to 5 minutes more or until heated through.

Serve hot with tortillas; garnish with sour cream and cheese.

*Makes 4 servings*

# CHICKEN JAMBALAYA

2 cups chicken broth
1 can (14½ ounces) tomatoes, chopped, reserve liquid
1 can (8 ounces) tomato sauce
½ cup finely chopped onions
¼ cup chopped green pepper
½ teaspoon dried basil leaves, crushed
½ teaspoon dried thyme leaves, crushed

1 bay leaf
1 cup uncooked converted rice
1 cup KELLOGG'S® ALL-BRAN® cereal
8 ounces smoked turkey sausage, sliced
3 cups chopped cooked chicken
2 tablespoons chopped parsley

1. In 4-quart saucepan, place chicken broth, tomato liquid, tomato sauce, onions, green pepper and seasonings. Cook over medium heat until mixture boils, stirring occasionally.

2. Stir in tomatoes, rice, Kellogg's® All-Bran® cereal and turkey sausage. Cover pan and cook over medium heat until mixture starts to boil. Stir in chicken. Reduce heat. Cover and simmer 25 minutes or until moisture is absorbed and rice is cooked.

3. Remove bay leaf and stir in parsley. Serve hot.

*Makes 9 cups, 6 servings*

Chicken Rellenos

# CHICKEN RELLENOS

8 small poblano or green bell
    peppers (about 2 ounces
    *each*)
1 can (8½ ounces) whole kernel
    corn, drained
2 cans (4 ounces *each*) chunk
    white chicken, drained
1 can (4 ounces) sliced
    mushrooms, drained
1 cup (4 ounces) shredded
    Monterey Jack cheese
2 tablespoons chopped
    pimiento
1 or 2 canned jalapeño peppers,
    finely chopped
1 clove garlic, minced
1 tablespoon vegetable oil

Remove tops from poblano peppers; scoop out and discard seeds. Mix
corn, chicken, mushrooms, cheese, pimiento, jalapeño peppers and garlic;
spoon mixture into poblano peppers. Heat oil in large skillet over medium-
high heat; cook peppers, browning all sides. Reduce heat to low. Cover;
cook, turning occasionally, until peppers are tender, 5 to 10 minutes.

*Makes 4 servings*

Favorite recipe from **Canned Food Information Council**

# CHICKEN PICADILLO

1 can (16 ounces) whole
   tomatoes, chopped
½ cup golden raisins
1 tablespoon chopped green
   chilies
1 teaspoon sugar
1 teaspoon ground cinnamon
½ teaspoon salt

½ teaspoon ground cumin
⅛ teaspoon ground red pepper
2 tablespoons vegetable oil
8 skinless broiler-fryer chicken
   thighs
½ cup chopped onion
   Hot cooked rice
¼ cup sliced almonds

Mix together tomatoes, raisins, chilies, sugar, cinnamon, salt, cumin and red pepper in small bowl; set aside. Heat oil in large skillet over medium-high heat. Add chicken and cook, turning to brown all sides, about 10 minutes. Cook and stir onion 2 to 3 minutes until soft. Drain off excess fat. Add tomato mixture. Reduce heat to medium. Cover; cook about 15 minutes or until chicken is fork-tender. Uncover; cook 5 minutes longer. Serve chicken and sauce over hot cooked rice. Sprinkle with almonds.

*Makes 4 servings*

Favorite recipe from **Delmarva Poultry Industry, Inc.**

# DREAMY CREAMY CHICKEN LASAGNA

½ of a (1-pound) package
   CREAMETTE® Lasagna,
   uncooked
1 (12-ounce) can evaporated
   milk
2 tablespoons cornstarch
2 cups chicken broth
½ cup grated Parmesan cheese
¼ cup white wine
2 tablespoons Dijon-style
   mustard
2 teaspoons tomato sauce

2 cloves garlic, minced
½ teaspoon dried basil leaves,
   crushed
¼ teaspoon ground nutmeg
⅛ teaspoon ground red pepper
2 cups cooked chicken, torn into
   small pieces
6 cherry tomatoes, sliced into
   thin wedges
1 cup (4 ounces) shredded
   American cheese
   Hungarian sweet paprika

Prepare Creamette® Lasagna according to package directions; drain. In large saucepan, blend together evaporated milk and cornstarch. Whisk in chicken broth, Parmesan cheese, wine, mustard, tomato sauce, garlic, basil, nutmeg and red pepper. Bring to a boil, stirring until thickened and bubbly. Remove from heat. Reserve 1¼ cups. Stir chicken and tomatoes into remaining sauce. Into a 13×9-inch baking dish, spoon ¼ cup reserved sauce. Layer ⅓ the lasagna and half the chicken sauce. Repeat, ending with Lasagna. Spread on remaining 1 cup sauce. Top with cheese and paprika. Bake, covered, in 350°F oven 35 to 40 minutes. Let stand 10 minutes before cutting. Refrigerate leftovers.

*Makes 8 to 10 servings*

Fried Rice

# FRIED RICE

| | |
|---|---|
| 1 cup MJB/FARMHOUSE® Original Long Grain White Rice | ½ cup finely diced boneless skinless chicken breast, uncooked |
| 2 tablespoons vegetable oil, divided | ½ cup finely diced smoked ham |
| 2 eggs, beaten | ¼ cup finely diced carrots |
| | ½ cup frozen peas, thawed |
| | ¼ cup thinly sliced green onions |
| | 3 tablespoons soy sauce |

Prepare rice according to package directions (omitting butter and salt). Meanwhile, heat 1 tablespoon oil in large skillet over medium-high heat. Cook eggs, breaking up with a fork; set aside. Cook chicken, ham and carrots in same skillet in remaining 1 tablespoon oil 5 to 7 minutes or until chicken is cooked. Add cooked rice, peas, green onions and soy sauce. Stir until well blended and heated through. *Makes 6 cups*

# NEW DELHI CHICKEN THIGHS

| | |
|---|---|
| 8 skinless broiler-fryer chicken thighs | 1 tablespoon chopped cilantro |
| 1 cup plain yogurt | 1 teaspoon curry powder |
| ¼ cup mango chutney | 1 teaspoon paprika |
| 2 cloves garlic, halved | 1 teaspoon salt |
| ½-inch piece ginger root | ½ teaspoon ground cumin |
| 1 tablespoon vinegar | ¼ teaspoon ground red pepper |

Arrange chicken in single layer in shallow baking pan. Combine in blender container, yogurt, chutney, garlic, ginger root, vinegar, cilantro, curry powder, paprika, salt, cumin and red pepper; process until smooth. Pour yogurt sauce over chicken, turning pieces to coat all sides. Cover; marinate in refrigerator at least 1 hour, turning chicken occasionally. Bake, basting several times, in 400°F oven 45 to 50 minutes until chicken is brown and fork-tender.

*Makes 4 servings*

Favorite recipe from **Delmarva Poultry Industry, Inc.**

## GREEN CHILE CHICKEN

1 pound boneless skinless
   chicken breasts, cut into
   thin strips
1 medium onion, sliced
1 clove garlic, crushed
2 tablespoons vegetable oil
1 (12-ounce) jar ORTEGA® Mild
   Thick and Chunky Salsa

1 (4-ounce) can ORTEGA® Diced
   Green Chiles
½ teaspoon dried oregano
   leaves, crushed
Hot cooked rice or flour
   tortillas
Dairy sour cream (optional)

In medium skillet, over medium-high heat, cook chicken, onion and garlic in oil until chicken is no longer pink. Add salsa, chiles and oregano. Simmer, uncovered, 10 minutes. Serve over rice with sour cream, if desired.

*Makes 6 servings*

## ROMANCE® CHICKEN MARINARA

1 tablespoon olive oil
¾ pound boneless skinless
   chicken breasts, halved, cut
   into ½-inch strips
1 cup red and/or green bell
   pepper strips

1 medium zucchini, thinly sliced
   (about 1 cup)
1 package (7 ounces)
   ROMANCE® Marinara Sauce
1 package (12 ounces)
   ROMANCE® Linguine

Heat oil in large nonstick skillet over medium heat. Cook chicken, stirring occasionally, until chicken is no longer pink, about 4 minutes. Remove from skillet. Cook peppers and zucchini in same skillet 3 minutes or until crisp-tender. Return chicken to skillet with vegetables; add Marinara Sauce. Reduce heat to low. Cover; simmer 5 minutes. Meanwhile, prepare linguine as directed on package. Serve chicken mixture spooned over linguine.

*Makes 4 servings*

# *Quick & Easy*
# CASSEROLES

# CONTENTS

Durkee®
The Secret to Great Casseroles — 78

Minute-Wise Poultry — 80

No-Fuss Fish & Seafood — 94

Busy-Day Beef — 102

Pronto Pork & Ham — 110

Express Veggies, Pasta & More — 118

Mustard Chicken & Vegetables (*page 86*)

# DURKEE—THE SECRET TO GREAT CASSEROLES

This book was designed with you in mind—the busy cook. Casseroles featuring minimum preparation time, make-ahead convenience and no-watch baking are the perfect answer to today's hectic lifestyles. Whether it's a family meal, a special dinner or a potluck supper, you'll find the perfect time-saving main course or side dish. Most are ready to pop into the oven in 15 minutes or less!

In addition to quick and easy preparation, every casserole in this collection has the "special touch" of Durkee French Fried Onions. The crisp crunch, savory onion flavor and golden eye appeal of French Fried Onions turn ordinary dishes into extraordinary delights!

Just what makes Durkee French Fried Onions such a unique product? For 54 years, Durkee French Fried Onions have been made from select prime quality yellow globe onions grown only in New York State. The onions are sliced, coated with a specially formulated wheat flour batter and fried in vegetable oil. After frying, the onions are dried under controlled conditions and vacuum-packed for maximum freshness.

All the recipes in this book were developed by skilled home economists in the Durkee Famous Foods Test Kitchen, were taste tested by consumers, and were retested again and again to ensure success. The "ready-to-bake" times given for the recipes are based on minutes required to assemble the casseroles. They include such preparations as opening cans, peeling and chopping vegetables, and shredding cheese. The times also take into account that some preparations can be done simultaneously, such as preparing a biscuit topping while a mixture is simmering. Preparations *not* calculated into these times include advance cooking of ingredients, such as pasta, rice and bacon, boning chicken, and the thawing of frozen vegetables.

**Thawing Frozen Vegetables:** Most recipes call for thawed frozen vegetables. It is necessary to thaw the vegetables or baking time and final recipe consistency will be affected. To easily thaw frozen vegetables, place in colander and run under cold water. Or, defrost in microwave oven according to manufacturer's directions. Drain vegetables well. Note: *Do not* thaw frozen potatoes under cold water; thaw according to manufacturer's directions.

**Reheating Pasta and Rice:** Many recipes specify *hot* cooked pasta or rice. If pasta or rice is made in advance, reheat it before adding to recipes or baking time will be affected. To reheat, place in colander; pour boiling water evenly over pasta or rice and let drain.

**Baking Dish Size:** It is important to use the dish size specified in the recipe. A different size could affect the recipe's success.

**Microwave Cooking:** All microwave directions were tested in countertop microwave ovens rated at 600 to 700 watts. Microwave cooking times are approximate due to numerous variables, such as starting temperatures, shape, amount of food, etc. Watch casseroles carefully and adjust cooking times for your specific oven.

## FRENCH FRIED ONION TIPS

- One 2.8-ounce can equals 1⅓ cups.
- One 6-ounce can equals approximately 3 cups.
- To enjoy the total French Fried Onion experience of flavor, crunch and eye appeal, mix ½ can with casserole ingredients and use remaining ½ can for final topping.
- When taking a casserole to a potluck dinner or picnic, reserve final ½ can French Fried Onions and sprinkle on casserole just before serving.
- To toast French Fried Onions for later addition to casseroles or for snacking, bake in 350° oven for 1 to 2 minutes or microwave on HIGH 1 minute.

# MINUTE-WISE POULTRY

## CHICKEN IN FRENCH ONION SAUCE

*Ready to bake in just 7 easy minutes*

1 package (10 ounces) frozen baby carrots, thawed and drained or 4 medium carrots, cut into strips (about 2 cups)
2 cups sliced mushrooms
½ cup thinly sliced celery
1 can (2.8 ounces) Durkee French Fried Onions

4 chicken breast halves, skinned and boned
½ cup white wine
¾ cup prepared chicken bouillon
½ teaspoon garlic salt
½ teaspoon pepper
Paprika

Preheat oven to 375°. In 8×12-inch baking dish, combine vegetables and *½ can* French Fried Onions. Arrange chicken breasts on vegetables. In small bowl, combine wine, bouillon, garlic salt and pepper; pour over chicken and vegetables. Sprinkle chicken with paprika. Bake, covered, at 375° for 35 minutes or until chicken is done. Baste chicken with wine sauce and top with remaining onions; bake, uncovered, 3 minutes or until onions are golden brown.

*Makes 4 servings*

**MICROWAVE DIRECTIONS:** In 8×12-inch microwave-safe dish, combine vegetables and *½ can* onions. Arrange chicken breasts, skinned side down, along sides of dish. Prepare wine mixture as above, except reduce bouillon to ⅓ cup; pour over chicken and vegetables. Cook, covered, on HIGH 6 minutes. Turn chicken breasts over and sprinkle with paprika. Stir vegetables and rotate dish. Cook, covered, 7 to 9 minutes or until chicken is done. Baste chicken with wine sauce and top with remaining onions; cook, uncovered, 1 minute. Let stand 5 minutes.

# CURRIED CHICKEN POT PIE

*Ready to bake in just 10 easy minutes*

2 cups (10 ounces) cubed cooked chicken

1 bag (16 ounces) frozen vegetable combination (cauliflower, carrots, broccoli), thawed and drained

1 can (2.8 ounces) Durkee French Fried Onions

1 cup (4 ounces) shredded Cheddar cheese

1 can (10¾ ounces) condensed cream of chicken soup

⅔ cup milk

½ teaspoon seasoned salt

¼ teaspoon curry powder

1 (9-inch) folded refrigerated unbaked pie crust

Preheat oven to 400°. In 9-inch pie plate, combine chicken, vegetables, *½ can* French Fried Onions and *½ cup* cheese. In small bowl, combine soup, milk and seasonings; pour over chicken mixture and stir to combine. Place pie crust over chicken mixture; seal edges and cut 4 steam vents. Bake, uncovered, at 400° for 40 minutes or until crust is golden brown. Top with remaining cheese and onions; bake, uncovered, 1 to 3 minutes or until onions are golden brown. *Makes 4 to 6 servings*

# LATTICE-TOP CHICKEN

*Ready to bake in just 12 easy minutes*

1 can (10¾ ounces) condensed cream of potato soup

1¼ cups milk

½ teaspoon seasoned salt

1½ cups (7 ounces) cubed cooked chicken

1 bag (16 ounces) frozen vegetable combination (broccoli, carrots, cauliflower), thawed and drained

1 cup (4 ounces) shredded Cheddar cheese

1 can (2.8 ounces) Durkee French Fried Onions

1 cup biscuit baking mix*

¼ cup milk

1 egg, slightly beaten

*1 package (4 ounces) refrigerated crescent rolls may be substituted for baking mix, ¼ cup milk and egg. Separate dough into 2 rectangles; press together perforated cuts. Cut each rectangle lengthwise into 3 strips. Arrange strips on hot chicken mixture to form lattice. Top as directed. Bake, uncovered, at 375° for 15 to 20 minutes or until lattice is golden brown. *(continued)*

**Lattice-Top Chicken**

Preheat oven to 375°. In large bowl, combine soup, 1¼ cups milk, seasoned salt, chicken, vegetables, ½ *cup* cheese and ½ *can* French Fried Onions. Pour into 8×12-inch baking dish. Bake, covered, at 375° for 15 minutes. Meanwhile, in small bowl, combine baking mix, ¼ cup milk and egg to form soft dough. Stir casserole and spoon dough over hot chicken mixture to form lattice design. Bake, uncovered, 20 to 25 minutes or until lattice is golden brown. Top lattice with remaining cheese and onions; bake, uncovered, 3 minutes or until onions are golden brown.

*Makes 4 to 6 servings*

**MICROWAVE DIRECTIONS:** Prepare chicken mixture as above; pour into 8×12-inch microwave-safe dish. Cook, covered, on HIGH 10 minutes or until heated through. Stir chicken mixture halfway through cooking time. Prepare biscuit dough and spoon over casserole as above. Cook, uncovered, 7 to 9 minutes or until lattice is done. Rotate dish halfway through cooking time. Top lattice with remaining cheese and onions; cook, uncovered, 1 minute or until cheese melts. Let stand 5 minutes.

# CHILI-CHICKEN SOMBREROS

*Ready to bake in just 10 easy minutes*

2½ cups (13 ounces) cubed
  cooked chicken
1 can (4 ounces) chopped green
  chilies, drained
1½ cups (6 ounces) shredded
  sharp Cheddar cheese
1 medium tomato, chopped
1 can (10¾ ounces) condensed
  cream of chicken soup
½ cup milk

½ teaspoon Durkee RedHot®
  Cayenne Pepper Sauce
  (optional)
¾ cup biscuit baking mix
⅔ cup cornmeal
⅔ cup milk
1 can (2.8 ounces) Durkee
  French Fried Onions
Chili powder

Preheat oven to 375°. In greased 8×12-inch baking dish, layer chicken, chilies, *1 cup* cheese and the tomato. In small bowl, combine soup, ½ cup milk and cayenne pepper sauce; pour evenly over chicken mixture. Bake, covered, at 375° for 20 minutes. Meanwhile, in medium bowl, combine baking mix, cornmeal, ⅔ cup milk and *½ can* French Fried Onions; beat vigorously 30 seconds. Spoon biscuit dough in 8 mounds over top of casserole. Sprinkle biscuits with chili powder. Bake, uncovered, 20 minutes or until biscuits are light brown. Top biscuits with remaining cheese and onions; bake, uncovered, 3 minutes or until onions are golden brown.

*Makes 6 to 8 servings*

# CREAMY TURKEY & BROCCOLI

*Ready to bake in just 18 easy minutes*

1 package (6 ounces) stuffing
  mix,* plus ingredients to
  prepare mix
1 can (2.8 ounces) Durkee
  French Fried Onions
1 package (10 ounces) frozen
  broccoli spears, thawed and
  drained

1 package (about 1⅛ ounces)
  cheese sauce mix
1¼ cups milk
½ cup sour cream
2 cups (10 ounces) cubed
  cooked turkey or chicken

*3 cups leftover stuffing may be substituted for stuffing mix. If stuffing is dry, stir in water, 1 tablespoon at a time, until moist but not wet.

Preheat oven to 350°. In medium saucepan, prepare stuffing mix according to package directions; stir in *½ can* French Fried Onions. Spread stuffing over bottom of greased 9-inch round baking dish. Arrange broccoli spears over stuffing with flowerets around edge of

*(continued)*

***Creamy Turkey & Broccoli***

dish. In medium saucepan, prepare cheese sauce mix according to package directions using 1¼ cups milk. Remove from heat; stir in sour cream and turkey. Pour turkey mixture over broccoli *stalks*. Bake, covered, at 350° for 30 minutes or until heated through. Sprinkle remaining onions over turkey; bake, uncovered, 5 minutes or until onions are golden brown.   *Makes 4 to 6 servings*

**MICROWAVE DIRECTIONS:** In 9-inch round microwave-safe dish, prepare stuffing mix according to package microwave directions; stir in ½ *can* onions. Arrange stuffing and broccoli spears in dish as above; set aside. In medium microwave-safe bowl, prepare cheese sauce mix according to package microwave directions using 1¼ cups milk. Add turkey and cook, covered, 5 to 6 minutes, stirring turkey halfway through cooking time. Stir in sour cream. Pour turkey mixture over broccoli *stalks*. Cook, covered, 8 to 10 minutes or until heated through. Rotate dish halfway through cooking time. Top turkey with remaining onions; cook, uncovered, 1 minute. Let stand 5 minutes.

# MUSTARD CHICKEN & VEGETABLES

*Ready to bake in just 15 easy minutes* ━━━━━━━━━━

2 cups (8 ounces) fusilli or
   rotini, cooked in unsalted
   water and drained
¼ cup Dijon-style or prepared
   mustard
¼ cup vegetable oil
1 tablespoon red wine vinegar
½ teaspoon dried oregano,
   crumbled
¼ teaspoon pepper
¼ teaspoon salt

2 pounds chicken pieces, fat
   trimmed
1 can (10¾ ounces) condensed
   cream of chicken soup
½ cup milk
1 cup *each* zucchini and yellow
   squash, cut into 1-inch
   chunks
1 can (2.8 ounces) Durkee
   French Fried Onions
1 medium tomato, cut into
   wedges

Preheat oven to 375°. In large bowl, combine mustard, oil, vinegar
and seasonings; mix well. Toss chicken in mustard sauce until
coated. Reserve remaining mustard sauce. Arrange chicken in 9×13-
inch baking dish. Bake, uncovered, at 375° for 30 minutes. Stir soup,
milk, hot pasta, squash and ½ *can* French Fried Onions into
remaining mustard sauce. Spoon pasta mixture into baking dish,
placing it under and around chicken. Bake, uncovered, 15 to 20
minutes or until chicken is done. Top pasta mixture with tomato
wedges and top chicken with remaining onions; bake, uncovered, 3
minutes or until onions are golden brown.    *Makes 4 to 6 servings*

**MICROWAVE DIRECTIONS:** Prepare mustard sauce as above; add
chicken and toss until coated. Reserve remaining mustard sauce. In
8×12-inch microwave-safe dish, arrange chicken with meatiest parts
toward edges of dish. Cook, uncovered, on HIGH 10 minutes.
Rearrange chicken. Prepare pasta mixture and add to chicken as
above. Cook, uncovered, 15 to 17 minutes or until chicken and
vegetables are done. Stir vegetables and pasta and rotate dish
halfway through cooking time. Top with tomato wedges and
remaining onions as above; cook, uncovered, 1 minute. Let stand 5
minutes.

# TURKEY CORDON BLEU

*Ready to bake in just 10 easy minutes* ━━━━━━

1 pound uncooked turkey
    breast slices
1 can (2.8 ounces) Durkee
    French Fried Onions
4 slices (1 ounce *each*) Swiss
    cheese, cut into halves
2 slices (1 ounces *each*) cooked
    turkey ham or ham, cut
    into halves

1 can (10¾ ounces) condensed
    cream of chicken soup
¼ cup milk
1 medium tomato, cut into
    4 slices

Preheat oven to 375°. In 7×11-inch baking dish, arrange turkey slices in 4 equal stacks. Top each stack with ¼ *cup* French Fried Onions, ½ *slice* cheese and ½ *slice* ham. In small bowl, combine soup and milk; pour over turkey stacks. Bake, covered, at 375° for 30 minutes or until turkey is done. Top stacks with remaining cheese slices, the tomato slices and remaining onions. Bake, uncovered, 3 minutes or until onions are golden brown. Serve over rice, noodles or toast.                    *Makes 4 servings*

**MICROWAVE DIRECTIONS:** In 7×11-inch microwave-safe dish, assemble turkey stacks as above. Prepare soup mixture as above; pour over turkey stacks. Cook, covered, on HIGH 10 to 12 minutes or until turkey is done. Rotate dish halfway through cooking time. Top stacks with remaining cheese slices, the tomato slices and remaining onions; cook, uncovered, 1 minute or until cheese melts. Let stand 5 minutes.

# ZESTY CHICKEN & RICE

*Ready to bake in just 7 easy minutes* ━━━━━━

⅔ cup uncooked regular rice
1 can (2.8 ounces) Durkee
    French Fried Onions
½ teaspoon Italian seasoning
1¾ cups prepared chicken
    bouillon
4 chicken breast halves, fat
    trimmed, skinned
    if desired

⅓ cup bottled Italian salad
    dressing
1 bag (16 ounces) frozen
    vegetable combination
    (broccoli, carrots, water
    chestnuts, red pepper)

Preheat oven to 400°. In 9×13-inch baking dish, combine uncooked rice, ½ *can* French Fried Onions and the Italian seasoning. Pour bouillon over rice mixture. Arrange chicken breasts on top; pour

*(continued)*

*Zesty Chicken & Rice*

salad dressing over chicken. Bake, covered, at 400° for 30 minutes. Place vegetables around chicken, covering rice. Bake, uncovered, 20 to 25 minutes or until chicken and rice are done. Top chicken with remaining onions; bake, uncovered, 1 to 3 minutes or until onions are golden brown.                                        *Makes 4 servings*

**MICROWAVE DIRECTIONS:** Reduce bouillon to 1¼ cups. In 8×12-inch microwave-safe dish, combine uncooked rice and bouillon. Cook, covered, on HIGH 5 minutes, stirring rice halfway through cooking time. Stir in vegetables, *½ can* onions and Italian seasoning. Arrange chicken over vegetable mixture with meatiest parts toward edges of dish. Pour salad dressing over chicken. Cook, covered, on MEDIUM (50-60%) 15 to 17 minutes or until chicken and rice are done. Rearrange chicken and rotate dish halfway through cooking time. Top chicken with remaining onions; cook, uncovered, on HIGH 1 minute. Let stand 5 minutes.

# CALIFORNIA-STYLE CHICKEN

*Ready to bake in just 15 easy minutes*

1 can (15 ounces) tomato
   sauce
3 tablespoons red wine vinegar
½ teaspoon dried basil,
   crumbled
¼ teaspoon garlic powder
12 small red potatoes, thinly
   sliced (about 3 cups)

1 can (2.8 ounces) Durkee
   French Fried Onions
2½ pounds chicken pieces, fat
   trimmed, skinned if desired
1 package (10 ounces) frozen
   whole green beans, thawed
   and drained

Preheat oven to 375°. In small bowl, combine tomato sauce, vinegar
and seasonings. Spread *½ cup* tomato mixture in bottom of 9 × 13-
inch baking dish; top with potatoes and *½ can* French Fried Onions.
Arrange chicken over potatoes and onions. Spoon *1 cup* tomato
mixture over chicken and potatoes. Bake, covered, at 375° for 35
minutes. Stir green beans into potatoes. Spoon remaining tomato
mixture over chicken. Bake, covered, 10 to 15 minutes or until
chicken and beans are done. Top chicken with remaining onions;
bake, uncovered, 3 minutes or until onions are golden brown.

*Makes 4 to 6 servings*

# CHICKEN-MAC CASSEROLE

*Ready to bake in just 20 easy minutes*

1½ cups elbow macaroni, cooked
   in unsalted water and
   drained
6 slices bacon, fried crisp and
   crumbled
2 cups (10 ounces) cubed
   cooked chicken
1 can (2.8 ounces) Durkee
   French Fried Onions

1 can (10¾ ounces) condensed
   cream of mushroom soup
1 cup sour cream
1 package (10 ounces) frozen
   chopped spinach, thawed
   and well drained
⅛ teaspoon garlic powder
1½ cups (6 ounces) shredded
   Cheddar cheese

Preheat oven to 375°. Return hot macaroni to saucepan; stir in
bacon, chicken and *½ can* French Fried Onions. In medium bowl,
combine soup, sour cream, spinach, garlic powder and *1 cup*
Cheddar cheese. Spoon *half* the macaroni mixture into greased
8 × 12-inch baking dish; cover with *half* the spinach mixture. Repeat
layers. Bake, covered, at 375° for 30 minutes or until heated
through. Top with remaining cheese and onions. Bake, uncovered,
3 minutes or until onions are golden brown.

*Makes 6 to 8 servings*

# HEARTY CHICKEN BAKE

*Ready to bake in just 12 easy minutes* ────────────

3 cups hot mashed potatoes
1 cup (4 ounces) shredded
   Cheddar cheese
1 can (2.8 ounces) Durkee
   French Fried Onions
1½ cups (7 ounces) cubed cooked
   chicken
1 package (10 ounces) frozen
   mixed vegetables, thawed
   and drained

1 can (10¾ ounces) condensed
   cream of chicken soup
¼ cup milk
½ teaspoon ground mustard
¼ teaspoon garlic powder
¼ teaspoon pepper

Preheat oven to 375°. In medium bowl, combine mashed potatoes, *½ cup* cheese and *½ can* French Fried Onions; mix thoroughly. Spoon potato mixture into greased 1½-quart casserole. Using back of spoon, spread potatoes across bottom and up sides of dish to form a shell. In large bowl, combine chicken, mixed vegetables, soup, milk and seasonings; pour into potato shell. Bake, uncovered, at 375° for 30 minutes or until heated through. Top with remaining cheese and onions; bake, uncovered, 3 minutes or until onions are golden brown. Let stand 5 minutes before serving.

*Makes 4 to 6 servings*

**Hearty Chicken Bake**

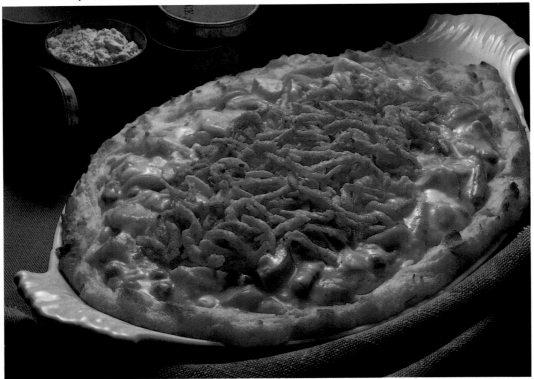

# ITALIAN ANTIPASTO BAKE

*Ready to bake in just 10 easy minutes* ————————

2 cups rotini or elbow
  macaroni, cooked in
  unsalted water and drained
1 bag (16 ounces) frozen
  vegetable combination
  (broccoli, water chestnuts,
  red pepper), thawed and
  drained
2 chicken breast halves,
  skinned, boned and cut
  into strips
⅔ cup bottled Italian salad
  dressing
½ cup drained garbanzo beans
  (optional)
¼ cup sliced pitted ripe olives
  (optional)
¼ cup (1 ounce) grated
  Parmesan cheese
½ teaspoon Italian seasoning
1 cup (4 ounces) shredded
  mozzarella cheese
1 can (2.8 ounces) Durkee
  French Fried Onions

Preheat oven to 350°. In 9×13-inch baking dish, combine hot pasta, vegetables, chicken, salad dressing, garbanzo beans, olives, Parmesan cheese and Italian seasoning. Stir in ½ *cup* mozzarella cheese and ½ *can* French Fried Onions. Bake, covered, at 350° for 35 minutes or until chicken is done. Top with remaining mozzarella cheese and onions; bake, uncovered, 5 minutes or until onions are golden brown.                                    *Makes 4 to 6 servings*

**MICROWAVE DIRECTIONS:** In 8×12-inch microwave-safe dish, combine ingredients, except chicken strips, as above. Arrange uncooked chicken strips around edges of dish. Cook, covered, on HIGH 6 minutes. Stir center of casserole; rearrange chicken and rotate dish. Cook, covered, 5 to 6 minutes or until chicken is done. Stir casserole to combine chicken and pasta mixture. Top with remaining mozzarella cheese and onions; cook, uncovered, 1 minute or until cheese melts. Let stand 5 minutes.

# HOME-STYLE CHICKEN 'N BISCUITS

*Ready to bake in just 15 easy minutes* ————————

5 slices bacon, fried crisp and
  crumbled
1½ cups (7 ounces) cubed cooked
  chicken
1 package (10 ounces) frozen
  mixed vegetables, thawed
  and drained
1½ cups (6 ounces) shredded
  Cheddar cheese
2 medium tomatoes, chopped
  (about 1 cup)
1 can (10¾ ounces) condensed
  cream of chicken soup
¾ cup milk
1½ cups biscuit baking mix
⅔ cup milk
1 can (2.8 ounces) Durkee
  French Fried Onions

*(continued)*

*Home-Style Chicken 'n Biscuits*

Preheat oven to 400°. In large bowl, combine bacon, chicken, mixed vegetables, *1 cup* cheese, the tomatoes, soup and ¾ cup milk. Pour chicken mixture into greased 8×12-inch baking dish. Bake, covered, at 400° for 15 minutes. Meanwhile, in medium bowl, combine baking mix, ⅔ cup milk and ½ *can* French Fried Onions to form soft dough. Spoon biscuit dough in 6 mounds around edges of casserole. Bake, uncovered, 15 to 20 minutes or until biscuits are golden brown. Top biscuits with remaining cheese and onions; bake 1 to 3 minutes or until onions are golden brown. *Makes 6 servings*

**MICROWAVE DIRECTIONS:** Prepare chicken mixture as above, except reduce ¾ cup milk to ½ cup; pour into 8×12-inch microwave-safe dish. Cook, covered, on HIGH 10 minutes or until heated through. Stir chicken mixture halfway through cooking time. Prepare biscuit dough as above. Stir casserole and spoon biscuit dough over hot chicken mixture as above. Cook, uncovered, 7 to 8 minutes or until biscuits are done. Rotate dish halfway through cooking time. Top biscuits with remaining cheese and onions; cook, uncovered, 1 minute or until cheese melts. Let stand 5 minutes.

# NO-FUSS FISH & SEAFOOD

## HERB-BAKED FISH & RICE

*Ready to bake in just 15 easy minutes*

1½ cups hot chicken bouillon
½ cup uncooked regular rice
¼ teaspoon Italian seasoning
¼ teaspoon garlic powder
1 package (10 ounces) frozen chopped broccoli, thawed and drained
1 can (2.8 ounces) Durkee French Fried Onions

1 tablespoon grated Parmesan cheese
1 pound unbreaded fish fillets, thawed if frozen
Paprika (optional)
½ cup (2 ounces) shredded Cheddar cheese

Preheat oven to 375°. In 8×12-inch baking dish, combine hot bouillon, uncooked rice and seasonings. Bake, covered, at 375° for 10 minutes. Top with broccoli, *½ can* French Fried Onions and the Parmesan cheese. Place fish fillets diagonally down center of dish; sprinkle fish lightly with paprika. Bake, covered, at 375° for 20 to 25 minutes or until fish flakes easily with fork. Stir rice. Top fish with Cheddar cheese and remaining onions; bake, uncovered, 3 minutes or until onions are golden brown.          *Makes 3 to 4 servings*

**MICROWAVE DIRECTIONS:** In 8×12-inch microwave-safe dish, prepare rice mixture as above, except reduce bouillon to 1¼ cups. Cook, covered, on HIGH 5 minutes, stirring halfway through cooking time. Stir in broccoli, *½ can* onions and the Parmesan cheese. Arrange fish fillets in single layer on top of rice mixture; sprinkle fish lightly with paprika. Cook, covered, on MEDIUM (50-60%) 18 to 20 minutes or until fish flakes easily with fork and rice is done. Rotate dish halfway through cooking time. Top fish with Cheddar cheese and remaining onions; cook, uncovered, on HIGH 1 minute or until cheese melts. Let stand 5 minutes.

# MEDITERRANEAN FISH & PASTA

*Ready to bake in just 15 easy minutes*

2 cups gnocchi or large shell
    pasta, cooked in unsalted
    water and drained
1 can (14½ ounces) whole
    tomatoes, undrained and
    cut up
1 can (8 ounces) tomato sauce
1 medium zucchini, thinly
    sliced (about 1 cup)
½ cup (2 ounces) grated
    Parmesan cheese

1 can (2.8 ounces) Durkee
    French Fried Onions
⅓ cup sliced pitted ripe olives
½ teaspoon dried basil,
    crumbled
½ teaspoon dried oregano,
    crumbled
1 pound unbreaded fish fillets,
    thawed if frozen

Preheat oven to 375°. Return hot pasta to saucepan; stir in tomatoes, tomato sauce, zucchini, *¼ cup* cheese, *½ can* French Fried Onions, the olives and seasonings. Pour into 8×12-inch baking dish. Place fish fillets, in single layer, over pasta mixture. Bake, covered, at 375° for 25 minutes or until fish flakes easily with fork. Top with remaining cheese and onions; bake, uncovered, 3 minutes or until onions are golden brown. *Makes 3 to 4 servings*

**MICROWAVE DIRECTIONS:** Prepare pasta mixture as above; pour into 8×12-inch microwave-safe dish. Top with fish fillets as above. Cook, covered, on HIGH 10 to 12 minutes or until heated through and fish flakes easily with fork. Rotate dish halfway through cooking time. Top with remaining cheese and onions; cook, uncovered, 1 minute. Let stand 5 minutes.

# TUNA TORTILLA ROLL-UPS

*Ready to bake in just 20 easy minutes*

1 can (10¾ ounces) condensed
    cream of celery soup
1 cup milk
1 can (9¼ ounces) tuna, drained
    and flaked
1 package (10 ounces) frozen
    broccoli spears, thawed,
    drained and cut into 1-inch
    pieces

1 cup (4 ounces) shredded
    Cheddar cheese
1 can (2.8 ounces) Durkee
    French Fried Onions
6 (7-inch) flour or corn tortillas
1 medium tomato, chopped

Preheat oven to 350°. In small bowl, combine soup and milk; set aside. In medium bowl, combine tuna, broccoli, *½ cup* cheese and *½ can* French Fried Onions; stir in *¾ cup* soup mixture. Divide tuna

*(continued)*

*Tuna Tortilla Roll-Ups*

mixture evenly between tortillas; roll up tortillas. Place, seam-side down, in lightly greased 9×13-inch baking dish. Stir tomato into remaining soup mixture; pour down center of roll-ups. Bake, covered, at 350° for 35 minutes or until heated through. Top center of roll-ups with remaining cheese and onions; bake, uncovered, 5 minutes or until onions are golden brown.          *Makes 6 servings*

**MICROWAVE DIRECTIONS:** Use corn tortillas only. Prepare soup mixture and roll-ups as above; place roll-ups, seam-side down, in 8×12-inch microwave-safe dish. Stir tomato into remaining soup mixture; pour down center of roll-ups. Cook, covered, on HIGH 15 to 18 minutes or until heated through. Rotate dish halfway through cooking time. Top center of roll-ups with remaining cheese and onions; cook, uncovered, 1 minute or until cheese melts. Let stand 5 minutes.

# LOUISIANA SEAFOOD BAKE

*Ready to bake in just 15 easy minutes*

⅔ cup uncooked regular rice
1 cup sliced celery
1 cup water
1 can (14½ ounces) whole
  tomatoes, undrained and
  cut up
1 can (8 ounces) tomato
  sauce
1 can (2.8 ounces) Durkee
  French Fried Onions
1 teaspoon Durkee RedHot
  Cayenne Pepper Sauce
½ teaspoon garlic powder

¼ teaspoon dried oregano,
  crumbled
¼ teaspoon dried thyme,
  crumbled
½ pound white fish, thawed if
  frozen and cut into 1-inch
  chunks
1 can (4 ounces) shrimp,
  drained
⅓ cup sliced pitted ripe olives
¼ cup (1 ounce) grated
  Parmesan cheese

Preheat oven to 375°. In 1½-quart casserole, combine uncooked rice, celery, water, tomatoes, tomato sauce, *½ can* French Fried Onions and the seasonings. Bake, covered, at 375° for 20 minutes. Stir in fish, shrimp and olives. Bake, covered, 20 minutes or until heated through. Top with cheese and remaining onions; bake, uncovered, 3 minutes or until onions are golden brown.     *Makes 4 servings*

**MICROWAVE DIRECTIONS:** In 2-quart microwave-safe casserole, prepare rice mixture as above. Cook, covered, on HIGH 15 minutes, stirring rice halfway through cooking time. Add fish, shrimp and olives. Cook, covered, 12 to 14 minutes or until rice is cooked. Stir casserole halfway through cooking time. Top with cheese and remaining onions; cook, uncovered, 1 minute. Let stand 5 minutes.

# SUPERB FILLET OF SOLE & VEGETABLES

*Ready to bake in just 10 easy minutes*

1 can (10¾ ounces) condensed
  cream of celery soup
½ cup milk
1 cup (4 ounces) shredded
  Swiss cheese
½ teaspoon dried basil,
  crumbled
¼ teaspoon seasoned salt
¼ teaspoon pepper

1 package (10 ounces) frozen
  baby carrots, thawed and
  drained
1 package (10 ounces) frozen
  asparagus cuts, thawed and
  drained
1 can (2.8 ounces) Durkee
  French Fried Onions
1 pound unbreaded sole fillets,
  thawed if frozen

Preheat oven to 375°. In small bowl, combine soup, milk, *½ cup* cheese and the seasonings; set aside. In 8×12-inch baking dish,

*(continued)*

*Superb Fillet of Sole & Vegetables*

combine carrots, asparagus and ½ *can* French Fried Onions. Roll up fish fillets. (If fillets are wide, fold in half lengthwise before rolling.) Place fish rolls upright along center of vegetable mixture. Pour soup mixture over fish and vegetables. Bake, covered, at 375° for 30 minutes or until fish flakes easily with fork. Stir vegetables; top fish with remaining cheese and onions. Bake, uncovered, 3 minutes or until onions are golden brown. *Makes 3 to 4 servings*

**MICROWAVE DIRECTIONS:** Prepare soup mixture as above; set aside. In 8×12-inch microwave-safe dish, combine vegetables as above. Roll up fish fillets as above; place upright around edges of dish. Pour soup mixture over fish and vegetables. Cook, covered, on HIGH 14 to 16 minutes or until fish flakes easily with fork. Stir vegetables and rotate dish halfway through cooking time. Top fish with remaining cheese and onions; cook, uncovered, 1 minute or until cheese melts. Let stand 5 minutes.

# FOOLPROOF CLAM FETTUCINE

*Ready to bake in just 15 easy minutes* —————

1 package (6 ounces) fettucine-
    style noodles with creamy
    cheese sauce mix
¾ cup milk
1 can (6½ ounces) chopped
    clams, undrained
¼ cup (1 ounce) grated
    Parmesan cheese

1 teaspoon parsley flakes
1 can (4 ounces) mushroom
    stems and pieces, drained
2 tablespoons diced pimiento
1 can (2.8 ounces) Durkee
    French Fried Onions

Preheat oven to 375°. In large saucepan, cook noodles according to package directions; drain. Return hot noodles to saucepan; stir in sauce mix, milk, undrained clams, Parmesan cheese, parsley flakes, mushrooms, pimiento and ½ *can* French Fried Onions. Heat and stir 3 minutes or until bubbly. Pour into 6×10-inch baking dish. Bake, covered, at 375° for 30 minutes or until thickened. Place remaining onions around edges of casserole; bake, uncovered, 3 minutes or until onions are golden brown. *Makes 4 servings*

**MICROWAVE DIRECTIONS:** Prepare noodle mixture as above; pour into 6×10-inch microwave-safe dish. Cook, covered, on HIGH 4 to 6 minutes or until heated through. Stir noodle mixture halfway through cooking time. Top with remaining onions as above; cook, uncovered, 1 minute. Let stand 5 minutes.

# TUNA LASAGNA BUNDLES

*Ready to bake in just 20 easy minutes* —————

6 lasagna noodles, cooked in
    unsalted water and drained
1 can (10¾ ounces) condensed
    cream of chicken soup
½ cup milk
1 can (6½ ounces) tuna, drained
    and flaked
1 package (10 ounces) frozen
    chopped spinach or
    broccoli, thawed and well
    drained

1 egg, slightly beaten
¼ cup dry seasoned bread
    crumbs
¼ teaspoon garlic salt
1 cup (4 ounces) shredded
    Cheddar cheese
1 can (2.8 ounces) Durkee
    French Fried Onions

Preheat oven to 350°. Place hot noodles under cold running water until cool enough to handle; drain and set aside. In small bowl, blend soup and milk; set aside. In medium bowl, combine tuna, spinach, egg, bread crumbs, garlic salt, ½ *cup* cheese and ½ *can*

*(continued)*

French Fried Onions; stir in ½ cup soup mixture. Cut cooled noodles crosswise into halves. Spoon equal amounts of tuna mixture onto center of each noodle; roll up noodles. Place tuna rolls, seam-side down, in greased 8 × 12-inch baking dish. Top with remaining soup mixture. Bake, covered, at 350° for 35 minutes or until heated through. Top with remaining cheese and onions; bake, uncovered, 5 minutes or until onions are golden brown.        *Makes 6 servings*

**MICROWAVE DIRECTIONS:** Prepare soup mixture and tuna rolls as above. Place rolls, seam-side down, in 8 × 12-inch microwave-safe dish; top with remaining soup mixture. Cook, covered, on HIGH 10 to 12 minutes or until heated through. Rotate dish halfway through cooking time. Top tuna rolls with remaining cheese and onions; cook, uncovered, 1 minute or until cheese melts. Let stand 5 minutes.

# CRUNCHY-TOPPED FISH & VEGETABLES

*Ready to bake in just 10 easy minutes* ━━━━━━━━━━━

1 can (16 ounces) whole
    potatoes, drained
1 bag (16 ounces) frozen
    vegetable combination
    (broccoli, carrots, red
    pepper, water chestnuts),
    thawed and drained
⅓ cup water
2 tablespoons bottled Italian
    salad dressing

1 cup (4 ounces) shredded
    Cheddar cheese
⅓ cup dry bread crumbs
1 can (2.8 ounces) Durkee
    French Fried Onions
2 tablespoons water
½ teaspoon dried dill weed,
    crumbled
1 pound unbreaded fish fillets,
    thawed if frozen

Preheat oven to 375°. Place potatoes and vegetables in 8 × 12-inch baking dish; drizzle with ⅓ cup water and the Italian salad dressing. In small bowl, using fork, combine ½ cup cheese, the bread crumbs, French Fried Onions, 2 tablespoons water and the dill weed; mix thoroughly to crush onions. Sprinkle *half* the onion mixture evenly over vegetables. Arrange fish fillets over vegetables. Top fish with remaining cheese, then sprinkle with remaining onion mixture. Bake, uncovered, at 375° for 20 to 25 minutes or until fish flakes easily with fork.        *Makes 4 servings*

**MICROWAVE DIRECTIONS:** Omit ⅓ cup water. Place potatoes and vegetables in 8 × 12-inch microwave-safe dish; drizzle with Italian salad dressing. Prepare onion mixture and layer with fish and remaining cheese in dish as above. Cook, uncovered, on HIGH 13 to 15 minutes or until fish flakes easily with fork. Rotate dish halfway through cooking time. Let stand 5 minutes.

# BUSY-DAY BEEF

## COUNTDOWN CASSEROLE

*Ready to bake in just 10 easy minutes* ───────────

1 jar (8 ounces) pasteurized
    processed cheese
    spread
¾ cup milk
2 cups (12 ounces) cubed
    cooked roast beef
1 bag (16 ounces) frozen
    vegetable combination
    (broccoli, corn, red pepper),
    thawed and drained

4 cups frozen hash brown
    potatoes, thawed
1 can (2.8 ounces) Durkee
    French Fried Onions
½ teaspoon seasoned salt
¼ teaspoon black pepper
½ cup (2 ounces) shredded
    Cheddar cheese

Preheat oven to 375°. Spoon cheese spread into 8×12-inch baking
dish; place in oven just until cheese melts, about 5 minutes. Using
fork, stir milk into melted cheese until well blended. Stir in beef,
vegetables, potatoes, ½ *can* French Fried Onions and the seasonings.
Bake, covered, at 375° for 30 minutes or until heated through. Top
with Cheddar cheese and sprinkle onions down center. Bake,
uncovered, 3 minutes or until onions are golden brown.

*Makes 4 to 6 servings*

**MICROWAVE DIRECTIONS:** In an 8×12-inch microwave-safe dish,
combine cheese spread and milk. Cook, covered, on HIGH 3
minutes; stir. Add ingredients as above. Cook, covered, 14 minutes
or until heated through. Stir beef mixture halfway through cooking
time. Top with Cheddar cheese and remaining onions as above.
Cook, uncovered, 1 minute or until cheese melts. Let stand 5
minutes.

# CHEESE-STUFFED BEEF ROLLS

*Ready to bake in just 15 easy minutes* ————————

1 jar (15½ ounces) spaghetti
    sauce
1 egg, slightly beaten
¼ teaspoon dried oregano,
    crumbled
¼ teaspoon garlic powder
1 container (15 ounces) ricotta
    cheese
¼ cup (1 ounce) grated
    Parmesan cheese

1 cup (4 ounces) shredded
    mozzarella cheese
1 can (2.8 ounces) Durkee
    French Fried Onions
6 thin slices deli roast beef
    (about ½ pound)
2 medium zucchini, sliced
    (about 3 cups)

Preheat oven to 375°. Spread *½ cup* spaghetti sauce in bottom of
8×12-inch baking dish. In large bowl, thoroughly combine egg,
seasonings, ricotta cheese, Parmesan cheese, *½ cup* mozzarella
cheese and *½ can* French Fried Onions. Spoon equal amounts of
cheese mixture on 1 end of each beef slice. Roll up beef slices jelly-
roll style and arrange, seam-side down, in baking dish. Place
zucchini along both sides of dish. Pour remaining spaghetti sauce
over beef rolls and zucchini. Bake, covered, at 375° for 40 minutes
or until heated through. Top beef rolls with remaining mozzarella
cheese and onions. Bake, uncovered, 3 minutes or until onions are
golden brown.                     *Makes 6 servings*

**MICROWAVE DIRECTIONS:** In large microwave-safe bowl, prepare
cheese mixture as above. Cook, covered, on HIGH 2 to 4 minutes or
until warmed through. Stir cheese mixture halfway through cooking
time. Spread *½ cup* spaghetti sauce in bottom of 8×12-inch
microwave-safe dish. Prepare beef rolls and place in dish as above.
Arrange zucchini along both sides of dish. Pour remaining spaghetti
sauce over beef rolls and zucchini. Cook, loosely covered, 14 to 16
minutes or until heated through. Rotate dish halfway through
cooking time. Top beef rolls with remaining mozzarella cheese and
onions; cook, uncovered, 1 minute or until cheese melts. Let stand 5
minutes.

# TWISTY BEEF BAKE

*Ready to bake in just 10 easy minutes*

2 cups rotini or elbow
    macaroni, cooked in
    unsalted water and
    drained
1 pound ground beef
1 can (2.8 ounces) Durkee
    French Fried Onions
1 cup (4 ounces) shredded
    Cheddar cheese

1 can (10¾ ounces) condensed
    cream of mushroom soup
1 can (14½ ounces) whole
    tomatoes, undrained and
    cut up
¼ cup chopped green pepper
¼ teaspoon seasoned salt

Preheat oven to 375°. In large skillet, brown ground beef; drain. Stir in hot macaroni, *½ can* French Fried Onions, *½ cup* cheese, the soup, tomatoes, green pepper and seasoned salt. Mix well. Pour into 2-quart casserole. Bake, covered, at 375° for 30 minutes or until heated through. Top with remaining cheese and onions; bake, uncovered, 3 minutes or until onions are golden brown.

*Makes 4 to 6 servings*

**MICROWAVE DIRECTIONS:** Crumble ground beef into 2-quart microwave-safe casserole. Cook, covered, on HIGH 4 to 6 minutes or until beef is cooked. Stir beef halfway through cooking time. Drain well. Add remaining ingredients as above. Cook, covered, 10 to 14 minutes or until heated through. Stir beef mixture halfway through cooking time. Top with remaining cheese and onions; cook, uncovered, 1 minute or until cheese melts. Let stand 5 minutes.

# MINI MEAT LOAVES & VEGETABLES

*Ready to bake in just 10 easy minutes*

1½ pounds lean ground beef
1 egg
1 can (8 ounces) tomato sauce
1 can (2.8 ounces) Durkee
    French Fried Onions
½ teaspoon salt
½ teaspoon Italian seasoning

6 small red potatoes, thinly
    sliced (about 1½ cups)
1 bag (16 ounces) frozen
    vegetable combination
    (broccoli, corn, red pepper),
    thawed and drained
Salt
Black pepper

Preheat oven to 375° In medium bowl, combine ground beef, egg, *½ can* tomato sauce, *½ can* French Fried Onions, ½ teaspoon salt and Italian seasoning. Shape into 3 mini loaves and place in 9×13-inch baking dish. Arrange potatoes around loaves. Bake, covered, at 375° for 35 minutes. Spoon vegetables around meat loaves; stir to

*(continued)*

*Mini Meat Loaves & Vegetables*

combine with potatoes. Lightly season vegetables with salt and pepper, if desired. Top meat loaves with remaining tomato sauce. Bake, uncovered, 15 minutes or until meat loaves are done. Top loaves with remaining onions; bake, uncovered, 3 minutes or until onions are golden brown. *Makes 6 servings*

**MICROWAVE DIRECTIONS:** Prepare meat loaves as above. Arrange potatoes on bottom of 8×12-inch microwave-safe dish; place meat loaves on potatoes. Cook, covered, on HIGH 13 minutes. Rotate dish halfway through cooking time. Add vegetables and season as above. Top meat loaves with remaining tomato sauce. Cook, covered, 7 minutes or until meat loaves are done. Rotate dish halfway through cooking time. Top loaves with remaining onions; cook, uncovered, 1 minute. Let stand 5 minutes.

# CHOP SUEY CASSEROLE

*Ready to bake in just 10 easy minutes*

2 cups (12 ounces) cooked roast beef strips
1 can (10¾ ounces) condensed cream of mushroom soup
½ cup milk
1 package (10 ounces) frozen French-style green beans, thawed and drained

1 can (8 ounces) sliced water chestnuts, drained
½ cup diagonally sliced celery
2 tablespoons soy sauce
1 can (2.8 ounces) Durkee French Fried Onions
1 medium tomato, cut into wedges

Preheat oven to 350°. In large bowl, combine beef, soup, milk, beans, water chestnuts, celery, soy sauce and ½ *can* French Fried Onions. Spoon beef mixture into 1½-quart casserole. Bake, covered, at 350° for 30 minutes or until heated through. Arrange tomato wedges around edge of casserole and top with remaining onions. Bake, uncovered, 5 minutes or until onions are golden brown.

*Makes 4 servings*

**MICROWAVE DIRECTIONS:** Prepare beef mixture as above; spoon into 1½-quart microwave-safe casserole. Cook, covered, on HIGH 10 to 12 minutes or until heated through. Stir beef mixture halfway through cooking time. Top with tomato wedges and remaining onions as above; cook, uncovered, 1 minute. Let stand 5 minutes.

# CLASSIC HAMBURGER CASSEROLE

*Ready to bake in just 10 easy minutes*

2 cups hot mashed potatoes
1 pound ground beef
1 package (9 ounces) frozen cut green beans, thawed and drained
1 can (10¾ ounces) condensed tomato soup
¼ cup water

½ teaspoon seasoned salt
⅛ teaspoon pepper
1 can (2.8 ounces) Durkee French Fried Onions
½ cup (2 ounces) shredded Cheddar cheese

Preheat oven to 350°. In medium skillet, brown ground beef; drain. Stir in green beans, soup, water and seasonings; pour into 1½-quart casserole. In medium bowl, combine mashed potatoes and ½ *can* French Fried Onions. Spoon potato mixture in mounds around edge of casserole. Bake, uncovered, at 350° for 25 minutes or until heated through. Top potatoes with cheese and remaining onions; bake, uncovered, 5 minutes or until onions are golden brown.

*Makes 4 to 6 servings*

# TEX-MEX LASAGNA

*Ready to bake in just 20 easy minutes*

1 pound ground beef
1 can (16 ounces) whole tomatoes, undrained and cut up
1 package (about 1⅛ ounces) taco seasoning mix
1 can (2.8 ounces) Durkee French Fried Onions

1½ cups (12 ounces) cream-style cottage cheese
2 cups (8 ounces) shredded Cheddar cheese
2 eggs, slightly beaten
12 (6-inch) flour or corn tortillas
1 medium tomato, chopped
1 cup shredded lettuce

Preheat oven to 350°. In large skillet, brown ground beef; drain. Stir in canned tomatoes and taco seasoning. Reduce heat and simmer, uncovered, 5 minutes. Remove from heat and stir in ½ can French Fried Onions. In medium bowl, combine cottage cheese, *1 cup* Cheddar cheese and the eggs; set aside. Overlap 3 tortillas in bottom of greased 8×12-inch baking dish. Overlap 6 tortillas around sides of dish. Spoon beef mixture evenly over tortillas; top with remaining 3 tortillas. Spoon cheese mixture over beef and tortillas. Bake, covered, at 350° for 45 minutes or until cheese mixture is set. Top with remaining Cheddar cheese. Sprinkle remaining onions down center of casserole. Bake, uncovered, 5 minutes or until onions are golden brown. Just before serving, arrange tomato and lettuce around edges of casserole. Let stand 5 minutes before serving.

*Makes 6 servings*

**Tex-Mex Lasagna**

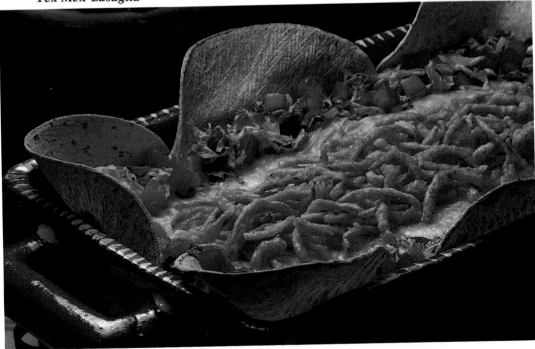

# PRONTO PORK & HAM

## SAUSAGE-CHICKEN CREOLE

*Ready to bake in just 15 easy minutes*

1 can (14½ ounces) whole
   tomatoes, undrained and
   cut up
½ cup uncooked regular
   rice
½ cup hot water
2 teaspoons Durkee RedHot
   Cayenne Pepper Sauce
¼ teaspoon garlic powder
¼ teaspoon dried oregano,
   crumbled

1 bag (16 ounces) frozen
   vegetable combination
   (broccoli, corn, red pepper),
   thawed and drained
1 can (2.8 ounces) Durkee
   French Fried Onions
4 chicken thighs, skinned
½ pound link Italian sausage,
   quartered and cooked*
1 can (8 ounces) tomato sauce

Preheat oven to 375°. In 8×12-inch baking dish, combine tomatoes, uncooked rice, hot water, cayenne pepper sauce and seasonings. Bake, covered, at 375° for 10 minutes. Stir vegetables and ½ can French Fried Onions into rice mixture; top with chicken and cooked sausage. Pour tomato sauce over chicken and sausage. Bake, covered, at 375° for 40 minutes or until chicken is done. Top chicken with remaining onions; bake, uncovered, 3 minutes or until onions are golden brown.

*Makes 4 servings*

*To cook sausage, simmer in water to cover until done. Or, place in microwave-safe dish and cook, covered, on HIGH 3 minutes or until done.

# MAKE-AHEAD BRUNCH BAKE

*Refrigerate overnight; bake next day* ──────────

1 pound bulk pork
   sausage
6 eggs, beaten
2 cups light cream or half-and-
   half
½ teaspoon salt

1 teaspoon ground mustard
1 cup (4 ounces) shredded
   Cheddar cheese
1 can (2.8 ounces) Durkee
   French Fried Onions

Crumble sausage into large skillet. Cook over medium-high heat until browned; drain well. Stir in eggs, cream, salt, mustard, ½ *cup* cheese and ½ *can* French Fried Onions; mix well. Pour into greased 8×12-inch baking dish. Refrigerate, covered, 8 hours or overnight. Bake, uncovered, at 350° for 45 minutes or until knife inserted in center comes out clean. Top with remaining cheese and onions; bake, uncovered, 5 minutes or until onions are golden brown. Let stand 15 minutes before serving.                          *Makes 6 servings*

**MICROWAVE DIRECTIONS:** Crumble sausage into 8×12-inch microwave-safe dish. Cook, covered, on HIGH 4 to 6 minutes or until sausage is cooked. Stir sausage halfway through cooking time. Drain well. Stir in ingredients and refrigerate as above. Cook, covered, 10 to 15 minutes or until center is firm. Stir egg mixture halfway through cooking time. Top with remaining cheese and onions; cook, uncovered, 1 minute or until cheese melts. Let stand 5 minutes.

# PORK CHOPS O'BRIEN

*Ready to bake in just 15 easy minutes* ──────────

1 tablespoon vegetable oil
6 pork chops, ½ to ¾ inch
   thick
   Seasoned salt
1 can (10¾ ounces) condensed
   cream of celery soup
½ cup milk
½ cup sour cream
¼ teaspoon pepper

1 bag (24 ounces) frozen
   O'Brien or hash brown
   potatoes, thawed
1 cup (4 ounces) shredded
   Cheddar cheese
1 can (2.8 ounces) Durkee
   French Fried Onions

Preheat oven to 350°. In large skillet, heat oil. Brown pork chops on both sides; drain. Sprinkle chops with seasoned salt; set aside. In large bowl, combine soup, milk, sour cream, pepper and ½ teaspoon seasoned salt. Stir in potatoes, ½ *cup* cheese and ½ *can* French Fried

*(continued)*

*Pork Chops O'Brien*

Onions. Spoon mixture into 9×13-inch baking dish; arrange pork chops on top. Bake, covered, at 350° for 35 to 40 minutes or until pork chops are done. Top chops with remaining cheese and onions; bake, uncovered, 5 minutes or until onions are golden brown.

*Makes 6 servings*

**MICROWAVE DIRECTIONS:** Omit oil. Prepare soup-potato mixture as above; spoon into 8×12-inch microwave-safe dish. Cook, covered, on HIGH 5 minutes. Stir well. Arrange *unbrowned* pork chops on top with meatiest parts toward edges of dish. Cook, covered, on MEDIUM (50-60%) 15 minutes. Turn chops over; sprinkle with seasoned salt. Stir potatoes and rotate dish. Cook, covered, on MEDIUM 12 to 15 minutes or until pork chops are done. Top chops with remaining cheese and onions; cook, uncovered, on HIGH 1 minute or until cheese melts. Let stand 5 minutes.

# SAUSAGE SUCCOTASH

*Ready to bake in just 15 easy minutes*

1 pound kielbasa, cut into
½-inch slices and cooked*

1 package (10 ounces) frozen
lima beans, thawed and
drained

2 cups frozen hash brown
potatoes, thawed

1 cup (4 ounces) shredded
Cheddar cheese

1 can (2.8 ounces) Durkee
French Fried Onions

1 can (10¾ ounces) condensed
cream of potato soup

¾ cup milk

1 can (8 ounces) creamed corn

¼ teaspoon seasoned salt

Preheat oven to 350°. In large bowl, combine sausage, lima beans, potatoes, ½ cup cheese, ½ can French Fried Onions, the soup, milk, corn and seasoned salt. Pour into 8×12-inch baking dish. Bake, covered, at 350° for 30 minutes or until heated through. Top with remaining cheese and onions; bake, uncovered, 5 minutes or until onions are golden brown. *Makes 4 to 6 servings*

*To cook kielbasa, simmer in water to cover until heated through. Or, place in microwave-safe dish and cook, covered, on HIGH 3 minutes or until heated through.

**MICROWAVE DIRECTIONS:** Prepare sausage mixture as above; pour into 8×12-inch microwave-safe dish. Cook, covered, on HIGH 5 to 8 minutes or until heated through. Stir casserole halfway through cooking time. Top with remaining cheese and onions; cook, uncovered, 1 minute or until cheese melts. Let stand 5 minutes.

# HAM & MACARONI TWISTS

*Ready to bake in just 7 easy minutes*

2 cups rotini or elbow
macaroni, cooked in
unsalted water and drained

1½ cups (8 ounces) cubed cooked
ham

1 can (2.8 ounces) Durkee
French Fried Onions

1 package (10 ounces) frozen
broccoli spears,* thawed
and drained

1 cup milk

1 can (10¾ ounces) condensed
cream of celery soup

1 cup (4 ounces) shredded
Cheddar cheese

¼ teaspoon garlic powder

¼ teaspoon pepper

*1 small head fresh broccoli (about ½ pound) may be substituted for frozen spears. Divide into spears and cook 3 to 4 minutes before using.

*(continued)*

*Ham & Macaroni Twists*

Preheat oven to 350°. In 8×12-inch baking dish, combine hot macaroni, ham and ½ *can* French Fried Onions. Divide broccoli spears into 6 small bunches. Arrange bunches of spears down center of dish, alternating direction of flowerets. In small bowl, combine milk, soup, ½ *cup* cheese and the seasonings; pour over casserole. Bake, covered, at 350° for 30 minutes or until heated through. Top with remaining cheese and sprinkle onions down center; bake, uncovered, 5 minutes or until onions are golden brown.

*Makes 4 to 6 servings*

**MICROWAVE DIRECTIONS:** In 8×12-inch microwave-safe dish, prepare macaroni mixture and arrange broccoli spears as above. Prepare soup mixture as above; pour over casserole. Cook, covered, on HIGH 8 minutes or until broccoli is done. Rotate dish halfway through cooking time. Top with remaining cheese and onions as above; cook, uncovered, 1 minute or until cheese melts. Let stand 5 minutes.

# BAKED HAM & CHEESE MONTE CRISTO

*Ready to bake in just 15 easy minutes* ━━━━━━━━━━━━

6 slices bread
2 cups (8 ounces) shredded
    Cheddar cheese
1 can (2.8 ounces) Durkee
    French Fried Onions
1 package (10 ounces) frozen
    broccoli spears, thawed,
    drained and cut into 1-inch
    pieces

2 cups (10 ounces) cubed
    cooked ham
5 eggs
2 cups milk
½ teaspoon ground mustard
½ teaspoon seasoned salt
¼ teaspoon coarsely ground
    black pepper

Preheat oven to 325°. Cut *3* bread slices into cubes; place in greased
8 × 12-inch baking dish. Top bread with *1 cup* cheese, *½ can* French
Fried Onions, the broccoli and ham. Cut remaining bread slices
diagonally into halves. Arrange bread halves down center of
casserole, overlapping slightly, crusted points all in 1 direction. In
medium bowl, beat eggs, milk and seasonings; pour evenly over
casserole. Bake, uncovered, at 325° for 1 hour or until center is set.
Top with remaining cheese and onions; bake, uncovered, 5 minutes
or until onions are golden brown. Let stand 10 minutes before
serving.                                            *Makes 6 to 8 servings*

# CHEESY PORK CHOPS 'N POTATOES

*Ready to bake in just 15 easy minutes* ━━━━━━━━━━━━

1 jar (8 ounces) pasteurized
    processed cheese spread
1 tablespoon vegetable oil
6 thin pork chops, ¼ to ½ inch
    thick
    Seasoned salt
½ cup milk

4 cups frozen cottage fries
1 can (2.8 ounces) Durkee
    French Fried Onions
1 package (10 ounces) frozen
    broccoli spears,* thawed
    and drained

*1 small head fresh broccoli (about ½ pound) may be substituted for
frozen spears. Divide into spears and cook 3 to 4 minutes before
using.

Preheat oven to 350°. Spoon cheese spread into 8 × 12-inch baking
dish; place in oven just until cheese melts, 5 minutes. Meanwhile,
in large skillet, heat oil. Brown pork chops on both sides; drain.
Sprinkle chops with seasoned salt; set aside. Using fork, stir milk
into melted cheese until well blended. Stir cottage fries and *½ can*
French Fried Onions into cheese mixture. Divide broccoli spears into
*(continued)*

*Cheesy Pork Chops 'n Potatoes*

6 small bunches. Arrange bunches of spears over potato mixture with flowerets around edges of dish. Arrange chops over broccoli *stalks*. Bake, covered, at 350° for 35 to 40 minutes or until pork chops are done. Top chops with remaining onions; bake, uncovered, 5 minutes or until onions are golden brown.

*Makes 4 to 6 servings*

**MICROWAVE DIRECTIONS:** Omit oil. Reduce milk to ¼ cup. In 8 × 12-inch microwave-safe dish, place cheese spread and milk. Cook, covered, on HIGH 3 minutes; stir to blend. Stir in cottage fries and ½ *can* onions. Cook, covered, 5 minutes; stir. Top with broccoli spears as above. Arrange *unbrowned* pork chops over broccoli *stalks* with meatiest parts toward edges of dish. Cook, covered, on MEDIUM (50-60%) 24 to 30 minutes or until pork chops are done. Turn chops over, sprinkle with seasoned salt and rotate dish halfway through cooking time. Top with remaining onions; cook, uncovered, on HIGH 1 minute. Let stand 5 minutes.

# EXPRESS VEGGIES, PASTA & MORE

## CHEESY PASTA SWIRLS

*Ready to bake in just 15 easy minutes*

4 ounces fettucine, cooked in
  unsalted water and drained
1 bag (16 ounces) frozen
  vegetable combination
  (peas, carrots, cauliflower),
  thawed and drained
1 cup (4 ounces) shredded
  mozzarella cheese
½ cup (2 ounces) cubed
  provolone cheese

1 can (2.8 ounces) Durkee
  French Fried Onions
1 can (10¾ ounces) condensed
  cream of mushroom soup
¾ cup milk
½ teaspoon garlic salt
⅓ cup (about 1½ ounces) grated
  Parmesan cheese

Preheat oven to 350°. In 8×12-inch baking dish, combine vegetables,
mozzarella, provolone and ½ *can* French Fried Onions. Twirl a few
strands of hot fettucine around long-tined fork to form a pasta swirl.
Remove pasta swirl from fork; stand upright on top of vegetable
mixture. Repeat process to form 5 more swirls. In medium bowl,
stir together soup, milk and garlic salt; pour over pasta swirls and
vegetable mixture. Bake, loosely covered, at 350° for 30 minutes or
until vegetables are done. Top pasta swirls with Parmesan cheese;
sprinkle remaining onions around swirls. Bake, uncovered, 5
minutes or until onions are golden brown.     *Makes 6 servings*

**MICROWAVE DIRECTIONS:** In 8×12-inch microwave-safe dish,
prepare vegetable mixture as above. Form pasta swirls and place on
vegetables as above. Prepare soup mixture as above; pour over pasta
and vegetables. Cook, loosely covered, on HIGH 14 to 16 minutes or
until vegetables are done. Rotate dish halfway through cooking
time. Top pasta swirls with Parmesan cheese and remaining onions
as above; cook, uncovered, 1 minute. Let stand 5 minutes.

# HOT GERMAN-STYLE POTATO SALAD

*Ready to bake in just 12 easy minutes*

5 slices bacon
1 medium green or red pepper,
    cut into ½-inch chunks
⅓ cup water
3 tablespoons cider vinegar
2 teaspoons sugar
2 teaspoons cornstarch

¼ teaspoon salt
⅛ teaspoon black pepper
2 cans (16 ounces *each*) sliced
    potatoes, drained
1 can (2.8 ounces) Durkee
    French Fried Onions

Preheat oven to 375°. In large skillet, fry bacon until crisp. Remove from skillet; crumble and set aside. Drain all but about 2 tablespoons drippings from skillet; add green pepper and cook until tender-crisp. Stir in water, vinegar, sugar, cornstarch and seasonings. Simmer, uncovered, until thickened. Gently stir in potatoes, crumbled bacon and ½ *can* French Fried Onions; spoon into 1½-quart casserole. Bake, covered, at 375° for 35 minutes or until heated through. Top with remaining onions; bake, uncovered, 3 minutes or until onions are golden brown. *Makes 4 servings*

# MONTEREY SPAGHETTI CASSEROLE

*Ready to bake in just 7 easy minutes*

4 ounces spaghetti, cooked in
    unsalted water and
    drained
1 egg, beaten
1 cup sour cream
¼ cup (1 ounce) grated
    Parmesan cheese
¼ teaspoon garlic powder

2 cups (8 ounces) shredded
    Monterey Jack cheese
1 package (10 ounces) frozen
    chopped spinach, thawed
    and well drained
1 can (2.8 ounces) Durkee
    French Fried Onions

Preheat oven to 350°. In medium bowl, combine egg, sour cream, Parmesan cheese and garlic powder. Stir in Monterey Jack cheese, hot spaghetti, spinach and ½ *can* French Fried Onions. Pour into 8-inch square baking dish. Bake, covered, at 350° for 30 minutes or until heated through. Top with remaining onions; bake, uncovered, 5 minutes or until onions are golden brown.

*Makes 4 main-dish servings*

**MICROWAVE DIRECTIONS:** Prepare spaghetti mixture as above, pour into 8-inch square microwave-safe dish. Cook, covered, on HIGH 8 to 10 minutes or until heated through. Stir spaghetti halfway through cooking time. Top with remaining onions; cook, uncovered, 1 minute. Let stand 5 minutes.

# BUFFET BEAN BAKE

*Ready to bake in just 17 easy minutes*

6 slices bacon
1 cup packed brown sugar
½ cup vinegar
½ teaspoon salt
1 tablespoon prepared mustard
1 can (16 ounces) butter beans, drained
1 can (16 ounces) French-style green beans, drained

1 can (16 ounces) pork and beans, drained
1 can (16 ounces) lima beans, drained
1 can (15½ ounces) yellow wax beans, drained
1 can (15 ounces) kidney beans, drained
1 can (2.8 ounces) Durkee French Fried Onions

Preheat oven to 350°. In medium skillet, fry bacon until crisp. Remove from skillet; crumble and set aside. Drain all but about 2 tablespoons drippings from skillet; add sugar, vinegar, salt and mustard. Simmer, uncovered, 10 minutes. In large bowl, combine drained beans, *½ can* French Fried Onions and hot sugar mixture. Spoon bean mixture into 9×13-inch baking dish. Bake, covered, at 350° for 30 minutes or until heated through. Top with crumbled bacon and remaining onions; bake, uncovered, 5 minutes or until onions are golden brown. *Makes 12 to 14 servings*

# SPINACH-ONION STUFFING BALLS

*Ready to bake in just 7 easy minutes*

1¼ cups water
3 cups seasoned stuffing croutons*
1 package (10 ounces) frozen chopped spinach, thawed and well drained

1 can (2.8 ounces) Durkee French Fried Onions
½ cup (2 ounces) shredded Swiss cheese

Preheat oven to 350°. In large saucepan, heat *1 cup* water to a boil. Add stuffing croutons; stir to moisten. Add spinach and *⅔ can* French Fried Onions; mix until thoroughly combined. Using ½ cup measure, shape stuffing into 6 equal balls; place in 10-inch round baking dish. Add remaining water to dish. Bake, covered, at 350° for 30 minutes or until heated through. Top with cheese and remaining onions; bake, uncovered, 5 minutes or until onions are golden brown. *Makes 6 servings*

*1 package (6 ounces) stuffing mix may be substituted for croutons and 1 cup water. Prepare according to package directions, omitting butter; stir in spinach and onions as above.

# ORIGINAL GREEN BEAN CASSEROLE▶

*Ready to bake in just 5 easy minutes*

2 cans (16 ounces *each)* cut
   green beans, drained or
   2 packages (9 ounces *each*)
   frozen cut green beans,
   cooked and drained
¾ cup milk

1 can (10¾ ounces) condensed
   cream of mushroom soup
⅛ teaspoon pepper
1 can (2.8 ounces) Durkee
   French Fried Onions

Preheat oven to 350°. In medium bowl, combine beans, milk, soup, pepper and *½ can* French Fried Onions; pour into 1½-quart casserole. Bake, uncovered, at 350° for 30 minutes or until heated through. Top with remaining onions; bake, uncovered, 5 minutes or until onions are golden brown.      *Makes 6 servings*

**MICROWAVE DIRECTIONS:** Prepare green bean mixture as above; pour into 1½-quart microwave-safe casserole. Cook, covered, on HIGH 8 to 10 minutes or until heated through. Stir beans halfway through cooking time. Top with remaining onions; cook, uncovered, 1 minute. Let stand 5 minutes.


# SWISS VEGETABLE MEDLEY▶

*Ready to bake in just 5 easy minutes*

1 bag (16 ounces) frozen
   vegetable combination
   (broccoli, carrots,
   cauliflower), thawed and
   drained
1 can (10¾ ounces) condensed
   cream of mushroom soup
1 cup (4 ounces) shredded
   Swiss cheese

⅓ cup sour cream
¼ teaspoon pepper
1 jar (4 ounces) diced pimiento,
   drained (optional)
1 can (2.8 ounces) Durkee
   French Fried Onions

Preheat oven to 350°. In large bowl, combine vegetables, soup, *½ cup* cheese, the sour cream, pepper, pimiento and *½ can* French Fried Onions. Pour into shallow 1-quart casserole. Bake, covered, at 350° for 30 minutes or until vegetables are done. Sprinkle remaining cheese and onions in diagonal rows across top; bake, uncovered, 5 minutes or until onions are golden brown.     *Makes 6 servings*

**MICROWAVE DIRECTIONS:** Prepare vegetable mixture as above; pour into shallow 1-quart microwave-safe casserole. Cook, covered, on HIGH 8 to 10 minutes or until vegetables are done. Stir vegetables halfway through cooking time. Top with remaining cheese and onions as above; cook, uncovered, 1 minute or until cheese melts. Let stand 5 minutes.

# SIMPLY SPECIAL VEGETABLE PIE

*Ready to bake in just 10 easy minutes*

1 package (10 ounces) frozen
   chopped spinach, thawed
   and well drained
1 can (2.8 ounces) Durkee
   French Fried Onions
1 egg
½ teaspoon garlic salt
1 package (about 1⅛ ounces)
   cheese sauce mix

1 cup milk
1 bag (16 ounces) frozen
   vegetable combination
   (broccoli, carrots, red
   pepper, water chestnuts),
   thawed and drained

Preheat oven to 350°. In small bowl, combine spinach, ½ can French Fried Onions, the egg and garlic salt; stir until well mixed. Using back of spoon, spread spinach mixture across bottom and up side of greased 9-inch pie plate to form a shell. In medium saucepan, prepare cheese sauce mix according to package directions using milk; stir in vegetables. Pour vegetable mixture into spinach shell. Bake, covered, at 350° for 30 minutes or until heated through. Top with remaining onions; bake, uncovered, 5 minutes or until onions are golden brown. *Makes 6 servings*

**MICROWAVE DIRECTIONS:** In medium microwave-safe bowl, prepare cheese sauce mix according to package microwave directions using milk; stir vegetables into sauce. Prepare spinach mixture as above; spread in 9-inch microwave-safe pie plate as above. Pour vegetable mixture into spinach shell. Cook, loosely covered, 6 to 8 minutes or until vegetables are done. Rotate dish halfway through cooking time. Top with remaining onions; cook, uncovered, 1 minute. Let stand 5 minutes.

# SAUCY GARDEN PATCH VEGETABLES

*Ready to bake in just 7 easy minutes*

1 can (11 ounces) condensed
   Cheddar cheese soup
½ cup sour cream
¼ cup milk
½ teaspoon seasoned salt
1 bag (16 ounces) frozen
   vegetable combination
   (broccoli, corn, red pepper),
   thawed and drained

1 bag (16 ounces) frozen
   vegetable combination
   (brussels sprouts, carrots,
   cauliflower), thawed and
   drained
1 cup (4 ounces) shredded
   Cheddar cheese
1 can (2.8 ounces) Durkee
   French Fried Onions

*(continued)*

**Saucy Garden Patch Vegetables**

Preheat oven to 375°. In large bowl, combine soup, sour cream, milk, seasoned salt, vegetables, ½ cup cheese and ½ *can* French Fried Onions. Spoon into 8×12-inch baking dish. Bake, covered, at 375° for 40 minutes or until vegetables are done. Top with remaining cheese and onions; bake, uncovered, 3 minutes or until onions are golden brown.          *Makes 8 to 10 servings*

**MICROWAVE DIRECTIONS:** Prepare vegetable mixture as above; spoon into 8×12-inch microwave-safe dish. Cook, covered, on HIGH 10 to 12 minutes or until vegetables are done. Stir vegetables halfway through cooking time. Top with remaining cheese and onions; cook, uncovered, 1 minute or until cheese melts. Let stand 5 minutes.

# CONTENTS

Classics Revisited   **128**

Single Serving   **138**

Light 'n' Easy Suppers   **146**

Entertaining Ideas   **154**

Ethnic Specialties   **164**

Microwave Marvels   **174**

West Coast Bouillabaisse (*page 134*)

# *Classics* REVISITED

## Wisconsin Tuna Cake with Lemon-Dill Sauce

*For light frying, choose a nonstick skillet to make these tuna cakes.*

1 can (12½ ounces) StarKist
    Tuna, drained and finely
    flaked
¾ cup seasoned bread crumbs
¼ cup minced green onions
2 tablespoons chopped drained
    pimiento

1 egg
½ cup low-fat milk
½ teaspoon grated lemon peel
2 tablespoons butter or
    margarine

### Lemon-Dill Sauce

¼ cup chicken broth
1 tablespoon lemon juice

¼ teaspoon dill weed

• • •

Hot steamed shredded zucchini
    and carrots

Lemon slices

In a large bowl toss together tuna, bread crumbs, onions and pimiento. In a small bowl beat together egg and milk; stir in lemon peel. Stir into tuna mixture; toss until moistened. With lightly floured hands, shape mixture into eight 4-inch patties.

In a large nonstick skillet melt butter. Fry patties, a few at a time, until golden brown on both sides, about 3 minutes per side. Place on an ovenproof platter in a 300°F. oven until ready to serve.

For sauce, in a small saucepan heat broth, lemon juice and dill. For each serving, spoon shredded carrots and zucchini onto each plate; top with 2 tuna cakes. Top each cake with a half-slice lemon; spoon sauce over. Makes 4 servings.

**Preparation time:** 25 minutes
**Calorie count:** 278 calories, including 1 tablespoon sauce, per serving.

Wisconsin Tuna Cake with Lemon-Dill Sauce

# Easy Niçoise Salad

Lettuce leaves
2 medium tomatoes, thinly sliced
1½ cups sliced cooked potatoes
1¼ cups cooked green beans
1 can (12½ ounces) StarKist Tuna, drained and broken into chunks

4 slices red or white onion, separated into rings
½ cup sliced pitted ripe olives
1 hard-cooked egg, sliced
4 whole anchovies (optional)

### Vinegar 'n' Oil Dressing

½ cup white vinegar
⅓ cup vegetable oil
1 tablespoon chopped parsley

½ teaspoon salt
¼ teaspoon pepper

On a large platter or 4 individual salad plates, arrange lettuce leaves. Arrange tomatoes, potatoes, beans, tuna, onion rings, olives and egg in a decorative design. Garnish with anchovies if desired.

For dressing, in a shaker jar combine remaining ingredients. Cover and shake until well blended. Drizzle some of the dressing over salad; serve remaining dressing. Makes 4 servings.

**Preparation time:** 20 minutes
**Calorie count:** 411 calories, including about ¼ cup dressing, per serving.

# Veal Tonnato

*Veal with tuna sauce is an old classic; you can serve this piquant cold sauce over almost any leftover meat.*

1 can (3¼ ounces) StarKist Tuna, drained and flaked
2 tablespoons olive oil
2 tablespoons dry white wine
1 tablespoon reduced-calorie mayonnaise or salad dressing
1 clove garlic, minced

1 teaspoon dried basil, crushed
½ teaspoon dry mustard
¼ teaspoon white or black pepper
1 tablespoon chopped parsley
½ teaspoon drained capers
Sliced cold veal, roast beef or turkey

In blender container or food processor bowl place tuna, oil, wine, mayonnaise, garlic, basil, mustard and pepper. Cover and process until nearly smooth. Stir in parsley and capers. Ladle about 3 tablespoons sauce over each serving of cold sliced meat. Makes 4 servings.

**Preparation time:** 10 minutes
**Calorie count:** 125 calories per serving of sauce.

# Tuna Veronique

*Besides toast, you can also serve this fruited tuna sauce over rice or pasta.*

2 leeks or green onions
½ cup carrot cut into thin strips
1 stalk celery, cut diagonally into slices
1 tablespoon vegetable oil
1¾ cups or 1 can (14½ ounces) chicken broth
2 tablespoons cornstarch
⅓ cup dry white wine

1¼ cups seedless red and green grapes, cut into halves
1 can (12½ ounces) StarKist Tuna, drained and broken into chunks
1 tablespoon chopped chives
¼ teaspoon white or black pepper
4 to 5 slices bread, toasted and cut into quarters or 8 to 10 slices toasted French bread

If using leeks, wash thoroughly between leaves. Cut off white portion; trim and slice ¼ inch thick. Discard green portion. For green onions, trim and slice ¼ inch thick. In a large nonstick skillet sauté leeks, carrot and celery in oil for 3 minutes. In a small bowl stir together chicken broth and cornstarch until smooth; stir into vegetables. Cook and stir until mixture thickens and bubbles. Stir in wine; simmer for 2 minutes. Stir in grapes, tuna, chives and pepper. Cook for 2 minutes more to heat through. To serve, ladle sauce over toast points. Makes 4 to 5 servings.

**Preparation time:** 20 minutes
**Calorie count:** 273 calories per serving. (Based on 4 servings.)

# Elaine's Tuna Tetrazzini

*You can also use a combination of tuna and shrimp in this hearty pasta sauce.*

8 ounces fresh mushrooms, sliced
1 cup chopped onion
2 tablespoons vegetable oil
3 tablespoons all-purpose flour
1 cup chicken broth
½ cup low-fat milk
½ teaspoon paprika
½ teaspoon salt
¼ teaspoon pepper

1 can (6⅛ ounces) StarKist Tuna, drained and broken into chunks
¼ cup grated Parmesan or Romano cheese
2 tablespoons minced parsley
8 ounces thin spaghetti or linguine, broken into halves, hot cooked

In a large skillet sauté mushrooms and onion in oil for 3 minutes, or until limp. Sprinkle flour over vegetables; stir until blended. Add chicken broth and milk all at once; cook and stir until mixture thickens and bubbles. Stir in paprika, salt and pepper; cook for 2 minutes more. Stir in tuna, cheese and parsley; cook for 1 to 2 minutes, or until heated through. Spoon over pasta. Makes 4 servings.

**Preparation time:** 20 minutes
**Calorie count:** 447 calories per serving.

**Tuna Veronique**

# West Coast Bouillabaisse

*This easy adaptation of the classic is faster and less expensive to make.*

1 cup sliced onion
2 stalks celery, cut diagonally into slices
2 cloves garlic, minced
1 tablespoon vegetable oil
4 cups chicken broth
1 can (28 ounces) tomatoes with juice, cut up
1 can (6½ ounces) minced clams with juice
½ cup dry white wine
1 teaspoon Worcestershire sauce

½ teaspoon dried thyme, crushed
¼ teaspoon bottled hot pepper sauce
1 bay leaf
1 cup frozen cooked bay shrimp, thawed
1 can (6⅛ ounces) StarKist Tuna, drained and broken into chunks
Salt and pepper to taste
6 slices lemon
6 slices French bread

In a Dutch oven sauté onion, celery and garlic in oil for 3 minutes. Stir in broth, tomatoes with juice, clams with juice, wine, Worcestershire, thyme, hot pepper sauce and bay leaf. Bring to a boil; reduce heat. Simmer for 15 minutes. Stir in shrimp and tuna; cook for 2 minutes to heat. Remove bay leaf. Season with salt and pepper. Garnish with lemon slices and serve with bread. Makes 6 servings.

**Preparation time:** 15 minutes
**Calorie count:** 212 calories per serving with bread.

# Tuna-Waldorf Salad Mold

*Here's a cool summer salad to keep on hand for easy lunches and dinners.*

1 package (6 ounces) lemon-flavored gelatin
2½ cups boiling water
1 cup apple juice
1 can (6⅛ ounces) StarKist Tuna, drained and flaked

1 cup finely chopped unpeeled apple
⅓ cup chopped pecans or walnuts
⅓ cup finely chopped celery
⅓ cup reduced-calorie mayonnaise or salad dressing
3 tablespoons low-fat milk

In a large, shallow bowl dissolve gelatin in boiling water. Stir in apple juice until blended. Cover; chill mixture about 30 minutes, or until the consistency of unbeaten egg whites. Fold in tuna, apple, pecans and celery. Spray a 4- or 5-cup mold (or 5 individual 1-cup molds) with aerosol shortening; pour in mixture. Cover; chill several hours until set. For dressing, in a small bowl stir together mayonnaise and milk; serve with salad. Makes 4 main-dish or 8 side-dish servings.

**Preparation time:** 15 minutes
**Calorie count:** 374 calories, including about 2 tablespoons dressing, per main-dish serving; 187 calories, including about 1 tablespoon dressing, per side-dish serving.

# No Fuss Tuna Quiche

*Frozen or refrigerated rolled pastry works well for this recipe.*

1 unbaked 9-inch deep dish
  pastry shell
1½ cups low-fat milk
3 extra-large eggs
⅓ cup chopped green onions
1 tablespoon chopped drained
  pimiento

1 teaspoon dried basil, crushed
½ teaspoon salt
1 can (6⅛ ounces) StarKist Tuna,
  drained and flaked
½ cup shredded low-fat Cheddar
  cheese
8 spears (4 inches each) broccoli

Preheat oven to 450°F. Bake pastry shell for 5 minutes; remove to rack to cool. Reduce oven temperature to 325°F.

For filling, in a bowl whisk together milk and eggs. Stir in onions, pimiento, basil and salt. Fold in tuna and cheese. Pour into prebaked pastry shell. Bake at 325°F. for 30 minutes. Meanwhile, in a saucepan steam broccoli spears over simmering water for 5 minutes. Drain; set aside. After 30 minutes, arrange broccoli spears, spoke-fashion, over quiche. Bake for 25 to 35 minutes, or until a knife inserted 2 inches from center comes out clean. Let stand for 5 minutes. Cut into 8 wedges, centering a broccoli spear in each wedge. Makes 8 servings.

Note: If desired, 1 cup chopped broccoli may be added to the filling before baking.

**Preparation time:** 20 minutes
**Calorie count:** 226 calories per serving.

# Tuna & Mushroom Stroganoff

3 cups sliced fresh mushrooms
½ cup chopped green onions
2 cloves garlic, minced
2 tablespoons vegetable oil
2 tablespoons all-purpose flour
1½ cups low-fat milk
½ teaspoon dried tarragon,
  crushed

½ teaspoon Worcestershire sauce
¼ teaspoon pepper
1 can (12½ ounces) StarKist
  Tuna, drained and broken
  into chunks
⅓ cup reduced-calorie sour cream
⅓ cup plain low-fat yogurt
  Hot cooked pasta or rice

In a large skillet sauté mushrooms, onions and garlic in oil for 3 minutes, stirring frequently. Sprinkle flour over vegetables; stir until blended. Add milk all at once; cook and stir until mixture thickens and bubbles. Stir in tarragon, Worcestershire and pepper. Add tuna, sour cream and yogurt. Cook over low heat for 2 minutes, or until heated. (Do not boil.) Serve over pasta. Makes 4 to 6 servings.

**Preparation time:** 20 minutes
**Calorie count:** 400 calories, including 1 cup cooked pasta, per serving. (Based on 4 servings.)

# Puffy Tuna Omelet

*A puffy omelet is simple to make and it's a bit more special for a single serving.*

2 eggs, separated
¼ teaspoon pepper
1 tablespoon water
1 tablespoon butter or margarine
2 tablespoons chicken broth
½ small red or green bell pepper, cut into strips
1 cup chopped spinach leaves

1 can (3¼ ounces) StarKist Tuna, drained and broken into chunks
¼ teaspoon dried oregano, crushed
Salt and pepper to taste
2 teaspoons grated Parmesan cheese

In a small bowl beat egg yolks and pepper on high speed of electric mixer about 5 minutes, or until thick and lemon-colored. In a medium bowl beat egg whites and water until stiff peaks form. Pour yolks over whites and gently fold in.

Preheat oven to 325°F. In a 7-inch nonstick skillet with ovenproof handle melt butter over low heat. Lift and tilt skillet to coat sides. Pour egg mixture into hot skillet, mounding it slightly higher around edges. Cook over low heat about 6 minutes, or until eggs are puffed and set and bottom is golden brown. Bake for 6 to 8 minutes, or until a knife inserted near center comes out clean.

Meanwhile, in a small skillet heat chicken broth. Cook and stir bell pepper and spinach in broth for 2 minutes. Stir in tuna and oregano; season to taste with salt and pepper. Drain; keep warm. Loosen sides of omelet with spatula. Make a shallow cut across omelet, cutting slightly off center; fill with tuna mixture. Fold smaller portion of omelet over larger portion. Sprinkle with cheese. Serve immediately. Makes 1 serving.

**Preparation time:** 10 minutes
**Calorie count:** 422 calories per serving.

**Puffy Tuna Omelet**

# Tuna-Lettuce Bundles

*This salad makes one hearty serving; smaller appetites may want to save a portion of this salad for the next day's lunch.*

2 large leaves leaf lettuce
1 can (3¼ ounces) StarKist Tuna, drained and broken into small chunks
½ cup shredded red cabbage
¼ cup shredded zucchini

¼ cup alfalfa sprouts
1 tablespoon reduced-calorie Thousand Island or blue cheese dressing
Pepper to taste
2 red or green bell pepper rings

Trim stalks from lettuce leaves. In a small bowl toss together tuna, cabbage, zucchini and sprouts. Stir in dressing; season to taste with pepper. Spoon ½ of the salad mixture in center of each leaf. Roll up leaves, enclosing filling. Secure lettuce bundles by slipping a bell pepper ring over each. Place bundles seam side down on plate. Makes 1 serving.

**Preparation time:** 10 minutes
**Calorie count:** 190 calories per serving.

# Tuna-Citrus Salad with Honey Dressing

1 orange, tangerine or ½ large pink grapefruit, peeled, seeded and sectioned
1 can (3¼ ounces) StarKist Tuna, drained and broken into chunks

¼ cup sliced fresh mushrooms
Lettuce leaves
2 tablespoons chopped green onion

## Honey Dressing

2 tablespoons vegetable oil
2 tablespoons white wine vinegar

1 to 2 teaspoons honey
⅛ teaspoon pepper

Arrange citrus, tuna and mushrooms on lettuce-lined plate. Sprinkle with onion. In a shaker jar combine remaining ingredients. Cover and shake until well blended. Pour over salad. Makes 1 serving.

**Preparation time:** 15 minutes
**Calorie count:** 484 calories per serving.

# Fettucine à la Tuna

½ cup broccoli florets
½ cup chopped red bell pepper
1 tablespoon sliced green onion
1 clove garlic, minced
1 tablespoon butter or margarine
¼ cup low-fat milk
¼ cup low-fat ricotta cheese
    Salt and pepper to taste

1 can (3¼ ounces) StarKist Tuna, drained and broken into small chunks
2 ounces fettucine or linguine, cooked and drained
1 tablespoon grated Parmesan or Romano cheese (optional)

In a saucepan steam broccoli and bell pepper over simmering water for 5 minutes. Drain liquid from vegetables and remove steamer. In same pan sauté onion and garlic in butter for 2 minutes. Add milk and ricotta cheese, stirring well with wire whisk. Season to taste with salt and pepper. Add tuna and vegetables; cook over low heat for 2 minutes more. Toss fettucine with tuna mixture. Spoon onto plate; sprinkle with Parmesan cheese if desired. Makes 1 serving.

**Preparation time:** 15 minutes
**Calorie count:** 415 calories per serving.

# Gazpacho Tuna Salad

*If you like gazpacho, that tomato-based soup filled with crisp, cold vegetables, you'll enjoy this salad takeoff.*

1 cup shredded lettuce
1 can (3¼ ounces) StarKist Tuna, drained and flaked
⅓ cup chopped carrot
⅓ cup chopped celery
⅓ cup chopped cucumber or zucchini

⅓ cup tomato-vegetable juice
1 tablespoon vegetable oil
    Bottled hot pepper sauce to taste
2 tablespoons croutons

Line a dinner plate with shredded lettuce. In a large shaker jar combine tuna, chopped vegetables, vegetable juice, oil and hot pepper sauce to taste. Cover and shake until well blended. Use a slotted spoon to arrange mixture over lettuce-lined plate; sprinkle croutons over salad. Makes 1 serving.

**Preparation time:** 15 minutes
**Calorie count:** 371 calories per serving.

# Individual Pizza

*Flour tortillas make handy, low-calorie pizza "crusts" for individual pizzas.*

1 (8-inch) flour tortilla
¼ cup spaghetti sauce or pizza sauce
1 can (3¼ ounces) StarKist Tuna, drained and broken into small chunks

¼ cup sliced mushrooms
¼ cup tomato slices
2 green or red bell pepper rings, cut into halves
¼ cup shredded low-fat Cheddar or mozzarella cheese

Preheat oven to 375°F. Place tortilla on a small baking sheet. Bake for 5 minutes, or until tortilla begins to crisp. Spread spaghetti sauce to within ½ inch of edge. Sprinkle tuna, mushrooms and tomato over tortilla. Arrange bell pepper half-rings on top. Sprinkle cheese over pizza. Bake for 8 to 10 minutes more, or until heated through. Makes 1 serving.

**Preparation time:** 10 minutes
**Calorie count:** 366 calories per serving.

# Tuna Poor-Boy

*If you've never thought about making a submarine sandwich with tuna, this easy interpretation is worth sampling.*

1 individual French or poor-boy sandwich roll, split
1 can (3¼ ounces) StarKist Tuna, drained and flaked
2 tablespoons reduced-calorie mayonnaise or salad dressing
1 tablespoon chopped pickle relish
Lettuce leaves

1 slice red onion, separated into rings
2 rings red or green bell pepper
2 large slices tomato
1 slice (1 ounce) reduced-calorie American cheese, cut diagonally into halves
Pickled chili peppers (optional)

Toast roll if desired. In a small bowl stir together tuna, mayonnaise and pickle relish. Arrange lettuce over bottom half of roll; spoon tuna mixture over lettuce. Top with onion rings, bell pepper rings, tomato slices and cheese. Replace top half of roll; cut sandwich in half crosswise. Serve with pickled chili peppers if desired. Makes 1 large sandwich.

**Preparation time:** 15 minutes
**Calorie count:** 475 calories per serving.

# *Light 'n' Easy* SUPPERS

## Tuna & Vegetables à la Grecque

*This makes a terrific cold salad for any meal, and it's superb for picnics.*

1½ cups French-cut green beans, cooked
1 cup cherry tomatoes, cut into halves or tomato wedges
1 cup sliced cooked carrots
1 cup sliced yellow squash or zucchini

½ cup slivered green bell pepper
1 can (12½ ounces) StarKist Tuna, drained and broken into chunks

### Red Vinaigrette

⅓ cup red wine vinegar
¼ cup olive or vegetable oil
2 tablespoons chopped parsley
1 teaspoon sugar

1 teaspoon dried rosemary, crushed
1 clove garlic, crushed
Salt and pepper to taste

In a large nonmetallic bowl stir together beans, tomatoes, carrots, squash, bell pepper and tuna. For Red Vinaigrette dressing, in a large shaker jar combine remaining ingredients. Cover and shake until well blended. Pour over salad. Toss salad to coat. Cover and chill 2 to 24 hours before serving. Serve salad with a slotted spoon. Makes 4 to 5 servings.

**Preparation time:** 15 minutes
**Calorie count:** 273 calories per serving. (Based on 4 servings.)

**Tuna & Vegetables à la Grecque**

# Tuna & Fresh Fruit Salad

*Use in-season fruits to enjoy this salad at any time of year.*

Lettuce leaves (optional)
1 can (12½ ounces) StarKist Tuna, drained and broken into chunks

4 cups slices or wedges fresh fruit*
¼ cup slivered almonds (optional)

## Fruit Dressing

1 container (8 ounces) lemon, mandarin orange or vanilla low-fat yogurt

2 tablespoons orange juice
¼ teaspoon ground cinnamon

Line a large platter or 4 individual plates with lettuce leaves if desired. Arrange tuna and desired fruit in a decorative design over lettuce. Sprinkle almonds over salad if desired.

For Fruit Dressing, in a small bowl stir together yogurt, orange juice and cinnamon until well blended. Serve dressing with salad. Makes 4 servings.

*Suggested fruits are: pineapple, melon, apples, pears, peaches, kiwifruit, bananas, berries, papaya or citrus fruit.

**Preparation time:** 15 minutes
**Calorie count:** 233 calories, including about ¼ cup dressing, per serving.

# Tuna-Vegetable Chowder

1½ cups chopped vegetables*
2 tablespoons butter or margarine
¼ cup all-purpose flour
2⅔ cups low-fat milk or buttermilk
1 cup chicken broth

1 can (6⅛ ounces) StarKist Tuna, drained and flaked
1½ teaspoons dried chervil, basil or Italian seasoning, crushed
¼ teaspoon pepper
2 tablespoons sherry (optional)

In a saucepan steam vegetables over simmering water for 5 to 8 minutes, or until almost tender. Set aside.

In a large saucepan melt butter; stir in flour. Add milk and broth all at once. Cook and stir until mixture thickens and bubbles. Cook and stir for 2 minutes more. Stir in cooked vegetables, tuna, herb and pepper. Cook for 2 minutes to heat through. Stir in sherry. Makes 4 to 5 servings.

*Suggested vegetables are: broccoli, cauliflower, carrot, zucchini, mushrooms or a combination.

**Preparation time:** 15 minutes
**Calorie count:** 245 calories per serving. (Based on 4 servings.)

# Tuna in Red Pepper Sauce

*Puréed red bell peppers are the base for a rich red wine sauce.*

2 cups chopped red bell peppers
  (about 2 peppers)
½ cup chopped onion
1 clove garlic, minced
2 tablespoons vegetable oil

¼ cup dry red or white wine
¼ cup chicken broth
2 teaspoons sugar
¼ teaspoon pepper

• • •

1 red bell pepper, slivered and cut
  into ½-inch pieces
1 yellow or green bell pepper,
  slivered and cut into ½-inch
  pieces

½ cup julienne-strip carrots
1 can (9¼ ounces) StarKist Tuna,
  drained and broken into
  chunks
Hot cooked pasta or rice

In a skillet sauté chopped bell peppers, onion and garlic in oil for 5 minutes, or until vegetables are very tender. In a blender container or food processor bowl place vegetable mixture; cover and process until puréed. Return to pan; stir in wine, chicken broth, sugar and pepper. Keep warm. In a 2-quart saucepan steam bell pepper pieces and carrot over simmering water for 5 minutes. Stir steamed vegetables into sauce with tuna; cook for 2 minutes, or until heated through. Serve tuna mixture over pasta. Makes 4 to 5 servings.

**Preparation time:** 20 minutes
**Calorie count:** 284 calories, including 2 ounces cooked pasta, per serving. (Based on 4 servings.)

# Tuna Frittata

*"Frittata" is simply a fancy name for an open-faced omelet.*

1 cup thinly sliced zucchini
½ cup thinly sliced onion
2 tablespoons vegetable oil
5 extra-large eggs
¼ cup low-fat milk

1 can (3¼ ounces) StarKist Tuna,
  drained and flaked
½ teaspoon salt
¼ teaspoon pepper
½ cup shredded Swiss or Monterey
  Jack cheese

In a large ovenproof skillet sauté zucchini and onion in oil for 3 minutes, or until vegetables are limp. In a medium bowl beat eggs lightly with milk. Stir in tuna, salt and pepper. Preheat broiler. Pour egg mixture over sautéed vegetables, reduce heat to medium. Cook, covered, for 5 to 8 minutes, or until set. Uncover frittata; sprinkle cheese over top. Place frittata under broiler until cheese is melted. Cut into quarters to serve. Makes 4 servings.

**Preparation time:** 15 minutes
**Calorie count:** 282 calories per serving.

Tuna in Red Pepper Sauce

# "Grilled" Tuna with Vegetables in Herb Butter

*Serve with a fruit salad and warm bread.*

4 pieces heavy-duty aluminum foil, each 12×18 inches
1 can (12½ ounces) StarKist Tuna, drained and broken into chunks
1 cup slivered red or green bell pepper
1 cup slivered yellow squash or zucchini
1 cup pea pods, cut crosswise into halves
1 cup slivered carrots
4 green onions, cut into 2-inch slices
¼ cup butter or margarine, melted
1 tablespoon lemon or lime juice
1 clove garlic, minced
2 teaspoons dried tarragon, crushed
1 teaspoon dill weed
Salt and pepper to taste

On each piece of foil mound tuna, bell pepper, squash, pea pods, carrots and onions. For herb butter, in a small bowl stir together butter, lemon juice, garlic, tarragon and dill weed. Drizzle over tuna and vegetables. Sprinkle with salt and pepper. Fold edges of each foil square together to make packets.

To grill: Place foil packets about 4 inches above hot coals. Grill for 10 to 12 minutes, or until heated through, turning packet over halfway through grill time.

To bake: Place foil packets on a baking sheet. Bake in preheated 450°F. oven for 15 to 20 minutes, or until heated through.

To serve, cut an "X" on top of each packet; peel back the foil. Makes 4 servings.

**Preparation time: 25 minutes**
**Calorie count: 235 calories per serving.**

# Scrambled Eggs with Tuna & Onions

6 extra-large eggs
½ cup low-fat milk
1 can (3¼ ounces) StarKist Tuna, drained and flaked
1 tablespoon chopped green chilies (optional)
¼ teaspoon bottled hot pepper sauce
½ cup chopped green onions
1 tablespoon butter or margarine

In a bowl whisk together eggs and milk. Add tuna, chilies and hot pepper sauce; stir. In a nonstick skillet sauté onions in butter for 2 minutes. Add egg mixture. Cook, stirring frequently, over medium heat until mixture begins to set. Continue lifting and folding partially cooked eggs to allow uncooked portion to flow underneath. Cook until eggs are cooked but still moist. Makes 4 servings.

**Preparation time: 10 minutes**
**Calorie count: 212 calories per serving.**

"Grilled" Tuna with Vegetables in Herb Butter

# *Entertaining* IDEAS

## Tuna-Stuffed Artichokes

*Fresh artichokes should have tightly closed leaves and a compact shape.*

4 medium artichokes
Lemon juice
1½ cups sliced fresh mushrooms
1 cup diced yellow squash or
   zucchini
⅓ cup chopped green onions
1 clove garlic, minced
2 tablespoons vegetable oil

1 can (12½ ounces) StarKist
   Tuna, drained and flaked
½ cup shredded low-fat Cheddar,
   mozzarella or Monterey Jack
   cheese
¼ cup seasoned bread crumbs
2 tablespoons diced drained
   pimiento

With a kitchen shear trim sharp points from artichoke leaves. Trim stems; remove loose outer leaves. Cut 1 inch from the tops. Brush cut edges with lemon juice. In a large covered saucepan or Dutch oven bring artichokes and salted water to a boil; reduce heat. Simmer until a leaf pulls out easily, 20 to 30 minutes. Drain upside down.

Preheat oven to 450°F. When cool enough to handle, cut artichokes lengthwise into halves. Remove fuzzy chokes and hearts. Finely chop hearts; discard chokes. In a medium skillet sauté mushrooms, artichoke hearts, squash, onions and garlic in oil for 3 minutes, stirring frequently. Stir in tuna. Place artichoke halves, cut side up, in a lightly oiled baking dish. Mound tuna mixture in center of artichokes. In a small bowl stir together cheese, bread crumbs and pimiento; sprinkle over filling. Bake for 5 to 8 minutes, or until cheese is melted and topping is golden. Makes 4 main-dish or 8 appetizer servings.

**Preparation time:** 35 minutes
**Calorie count:** 272 calories per main-dish serving; 136 calories per appetizer serving.

**Tuna-Stuffed Artichokes**

# Spiral Pasta Salad

*Pasta bow ties or shells are ideal for this salad too!*

8 ounces tri-color spiral pasta, cooked according to package directions
1 can (12½ ounces) StarKist Tuna, drained and broken into chunks
1 cup slivered pea pods

1 cup chopped yellow squash or zucchini
1 cup asparagus, cut into 2-inch pieces
½ cup slivered red onion
½ cup sliced pitted ripe olives

## Dijon Vinaigrette

⅓ cup white wine vinegar
¼ cup olive or vegetable oil
2 tablespoons water

2 teaspoons Dijon mustard
1 teaspoon dried basil, crushed
¼ teaspoon pepper

• • •

Lettuce leaves

For salad, rinse pasta in cool water; drain well. In a large bowl toss together pasta, tuna, pea pods, squash, asparagus, onion and olives. For dressing, in a shaker jar combine remaining ingredients except lettuce. Cover and shake until well blended. Pour over salad; toss well. Serve on lettuce-lined plates. Makes 5 servings.

**Preparation time:** 15 minutes
**Calorie count:** 390 calories per serving.

# Easy Seafood Salad

1 can (6⅛ ounces) StarKist Tuna, drained and flaked
1 can (6 ounces) salmon, drained, flaked and skin and bones removed
1½ cups cooked diced potatoes
½ cup frozen peas, thawed
½ cup frozen niblet corn, thawed
⅓ cup chopped onion

¼ cup reduced-calorie mayonnaise or salad dressing
¼ cup reduced-calorie cream cheese
1 tablespoon low-fat milk
1 tablespoon tartar sauce
Salt and pepper to taste
Lettuce leaves

In a large bowl toss together tuna, salmon, potatoes, peas, corn and onion. For dressing, in a small blender container or food processor bowl combine mayonnaise, cream cheese, milk and tartar sauce. Cover and blend until smooth. Stir dressing into salad; toss well. Serve salad on lettuce-lined plates. Makes 4 to 6 servings.

**Preparation time:** 15 minutes
**Calorie count:** 348 calories per serving. (Based on 4 servings.)

Spiral Pasta Salad

# Scandinavian Smörgåsbord

*Use the ingredients listed below to get your imagination started; you may have other interesting tidbits or vegetables on hand to use as attractive garnishes.*

36 slices party bread, crackers or flat bread
    Reduced-calorie mayonnaise or salad dressing
    Mustard
36 small lettuce leaves or Belgian endive leaves
1 can (6⅛ ounces) StarKist Tuna, drained and flaked or broken into chunks

2 hard-cooked eggs, sliced
¼ pound frozen cooked bay shrimp, thawed
½ medium cucumber, thinly sliced
36 pieces steamed asparagus tips or pea pods
    Capers, plain yogurt, dill sprigs, pimiento strips, red or black caviar, sliced green onion for garnish

Arrange party bread on a tray; spread each with 1 teaspoon mayonnaise and/or mustard. Top with a small lettuce leaf. Top with tuna, egg slices, shrimp, cucumber or steamed vegetables. Garnish as desired. Makes 36 appetizers.

**Preparation time:** 20 minutes
**Calorie count:** 47 calories per appetizer. Garnishes are extra.

# Tuna & Wild Rice Amandine

*Purchase "instant" wild rice that's been presoaked, so you can cook it whenever you need it—such as for this molded pilaf.*

1 package (4 ounces) presoaked wild rice
    Beef broth
2 cups sliced fresh mushrooms
1 cup slivered carrots
½ cup minced onion
2 tablespoons butter or margarine

2 tablespoons all-purpose flour
1⅓ cups low-fat milk
1 can (9¼ ounces) StarKist Tuna, drained and flaked
1 cup cooked white rice
1 to 2 tablespoons dry sherry
2 tablespoons toasted slivered almonds

In a 2-quart saucepan cook wild rice according to package directions, except use beef broth in place of the water. In a large skillet sauté mushrooms, carrots and onion in butter for 3 to 5 minutes, or until vegetables are crisp-tender. Sprinkle flour over mixture, stirring until blended. Add milk all at once. Cook and stir until mixture thickens and bubbles. Reduce heat; stir in cooked wild rice (drained if necessary), tuna, white rice and sherry to taste. Cook for 2 to 3 minutes to heat. Pour into a 5-cup lightly greased mold; let stand for 5 minutes. Unmold onto a serving platter; sprinkle with toasted almonds. Makes 4 to 5 servings.

**Preparation time:** 25 minutes
**Calorie count:** 405 calories per serving. (Based on 4 servings.)

# Tuna & Zucchini-Stuffed Manicotti

*Use a cookie press or pastry bag fitted with a large round tip to fill the manicotti shells easily. An iced tea spoon with a long, slender handle also works well.*

1 cup diced zucchini
½ cup chopped onion
1 clove garlic, minced
1 tablespoon vegetable oil
1 can (6⅛ ounces) StarKist Tuna, drained and flaked
1 cup low-fat ricotta cheese

½ cup shredded mozzarella cheese
¼ cup grated Parmesan or Romano cheese
1 extra-large egg, lightly beaten
2 teaspoons dried basil, crushed
8 manicotti shells, cooked and drained

## Marinara Sauce

1½ cups chopped fresh tomatoes
1¼ cups tomato sauce
2 tablespoons minced parsley
1 teaspoon dried basil, crushed

1 teaspoon dried oregano or marjoram, crushed
Salt and pepper to taste

In a medium skillet sauté zucchini, onion and garlic in oil for 3 minutes; remove from heat. Stir in tuna. In a medium bowl stir together ricotta, mozzarella, Parmesan, egg and basil until blended. Stir cheese mixture into tuna mixture; set aside.

Preheat oven to 350°F. Place drained manicotti shells in a bowl of cold water. Set aside. For Marinara Sauce, in a medium saucepan stir together tomatoes, tomato sauce and herbs. Heat to a boil; remove from heat. Season to taste with salt and pepper. Transfer mixture to blender container or food processor bowl. Cover and process in 2 batches until nearly smooth. Spray a 13×9×2-inch baking dish with aerosol shortening.

Spread ½ cup of the Marinara Sauce over bottom of baking dish. Blot manicotti shells carefully with paper towels. Generously pipe filling into shells. In baking dish arrange manicotti in a row. Pour remaining sauce over manicotti; cover with foil. Bake for 30 minutes; uncover and bake for 5 to 10 minutes more, or until sauce is bubbly. Let stand for 5 minutes before serving. Makes 4 servings.

**Preparation time:** 30 minutes
**Calorie count:** 333 calories per serving.

# Tuna Salad Elegante

*A round bread loaf serves as an attractive container for an asparagus-olive tuna salad.*

1 round bread loaf (about 1½ pounds)

1 can (12½ ounces) StarKist Tuna, drained and flaked

6 spears cooked asparagus, trimmed and cut into 2-inch pieces

2 hard-cooked eggs, chopped

½ cup sliced pitted ripe and stuffed green olives

⅓ cup chopped green onions

## Dressing

⅓ cup reduced-calorie mayonnaise or salad dressing

¼ cup plain low-fat yogurt

2 tablespoons red wine vinegar

1 teaspoon dried tarragon, crushed

1 teaspoon dried basil, crushed

• • •

Lettuce leaves

With a sharp knife, cut a 1-inch-thick slice from top of bread loaf. Reserve to use later for the lid. Then, hollow out loaf, making a 1-inch shell. If preparing ahead, wrap hollow loaf and bread top in plastic wrap. Save bread for another use.

To make salad, in a large bowl toss together tuna, asparagus, eggs, olives and onions. In a small bowl stir together mayonnaise, yogurt, vinegar, tarragon and basil. Spoon over salad; toss well to coat. If preparing ahead, cover and chill.

To serve salad, line bread shell with lettuce leaves. Spoon tuna mixture into shell. Add bread top if desired. Serve with flat crackers or party bread. Makes 3½ cups salad; about 5 to 6 main-dish or about 30 appetizer servings.

**Preparation time:** 30 minutes

**Calorie count:** 212 calories per main-dish serving (based on 5 servings); 36 calories per appetizer serving.

# *Ethnic* SPECIALTIES

## Tuna & Shrimp Fajitas

1 large red onion, cut in half and thinly sliced

1 red bell pepper, cut into bite-sized strips

1 large green bell pepper, cut into bite-sized strips

2 tablespoons vegetable oil

1 jar (12 ounces) salsa

1 can (6⅛ ounces) StarKist Tuna, drained and broken into chunks

½ pound frozen cooked bay shrimp, thawed

8 (8-inch) flour tortillas, warmed if desired

Diced avocado, shredded low-fat Cheddar or Monterey Jack cheese, sliced pitted ripe olives and bottled salsa for toppings

In a large skillet or wok stir-fry onion and bell peppers in oil for 3 minutes over high heat. Add ¼ cup of the salsa, the tuna and shrimp; stir-fry for 2 minutes more, or until heated through.

To assemble fajitas, spoon some of the tuna mixture in center of each tortilla, then add desired toppings and serve immediately. Makes 4 servings.

**Preparation time:** 10 minutes
**Calorie count:** 375 calories per serving. Toppings are extra.

**Tuna & Shrimp Fajitas**

# Tortellini with Three-Cheese Tuna Sauce

1 pound cheese-filled tortellini,
    spinach and egg
2 green onions, thinly sliced
1 clove garlic, minced
1 tablespoon butter or margarine
1 cup low-fat ricotta cheese
½ cup low-fat milk
1 can (6⅛ ounces) StarKist Tuna,
    drained and broken into
    chunks

½ cup shredded low-fat mozzarella
    cheese
¼ cup grated Parmesan or
    Romano cheese
2 tablespoons chopped fresh basil
    or 2 teaspoons dried basil,
    crushed
1 teaspoon grated lemon peel
    Fresh tomato wedges for
    garnish (optional)

Cook tortellini in boiling salted water according to package directions. When tortellini is nearly done, in another saucepan sauté onions and garlic in butter for 2 minutes. Whisk in ricotta cheese and milk. Add tuna, cheeses, basil and lemon peel. Cook over medium-low heat until mixture is heated and cheeses are melted.

Drain pasta; add to sauce. Toss well to coat; garnish with tomato wedges if desired. Serve immediately. Makes 4 to 5 servings.

**Preparation time:** 25 minutes
**Calorie count:** 550 calories per serving. (Based on 4 servings.)

# Tuna Chilies Rellenos

*Stuffed chilies are traditionally deep-fried, but in this recipe, the chilies are baked to keep the fat content low.*

8 Anaheim or large mild green
    chilies
1 can (6⅛ ounces) StarKist Tuna,
    drained and flaked
1 cup shredded Monterey Jack
    cheese or pepper cheese

½ cup low-fat ricotta cheese
½ cup niblet corn, drained
1 extra-large egg
    Fresh cilantro or parsley sprigs
    (optional)

Preheat oven to 425°F. Wash and dry chilies.* Cut stems from chilies; cut lengthwise into halves. Remove seeds and ribs. In a small bowl stir together tuna, cheeses, corn and egg until well mixed. Stuff each chili with about ¼ cup of the mixture. Spray a baking sheet with aerosol shortening; place stuffed chilies on baking sheet. Cover with foil. Bake for 20 to 25 minutes, or until chilies are soft and filling is heated through. Makes 4 servings; 2 chilies per serving.

*Do not touch face or eyes while handling chilies; wash hands thoroughly in soapy water after handling.

**Preparation time:** 10 minutes
**Calorie count:** 287 calories per serving.

**Tortellini with Three-Cheese Tuna Sauce**

# Baha Roll

*This Mexican takeoff on sushi features tuna in a colorful filling. Serve this as an appetizer or entrée.*

1 cup uncooked quick-cooking rice

1½ cups chicken broth

¼ cup reduced-calorie mayonnaise or salad dressing

1 tablespoon rice vinegar or white wine vinegar

1 tablespoon minced green onion

2 teaspoons grated gingerroot or ¼ teaspoon ground ginger

4 (8-inch) flour tortillas

½ pound fresh spinach (1 bunch), stems removed

1 can (6⅛ ounces) StarKist Tuna, drained and flaked

¾ cup thin julienne-strip, peeled cucumber

¼ medium-ripe avocado, pitted, peeled and thinly sliced

1 egg white, beaten

Pickled ginger strips, thin julienne-strip carrot and fresh cilantro or parsley for garnish (optional)

Cook rice according to package directions, using chicken broth in place of water. Fluff rice; cool or cover and chill if preparing ahead. In a small bowl stir together mayonnaise, vinegar, onion and gingerroot; stir mixture into cooked rice until well combined. To assemble rolls, place tortillas on flat surface. Spread ¼ of the rice mixture evenly over each tortilla to within ½ inch of edge. Arrange spinach leaves, overlapping slightly, over rice layer. Sprinkle tuna and cucumber evenly over spinach. On each tortilla, place 2 slices of avocado crosswise over center of filling. Starting at bottom edge of each tortilla, roll up tightly, enclosing filling and avocado in center. Moisten opposite edge of tortilla with egg white; press edges together to seal. Wrap in waxed paper and twist ends; chill at least 2 hours before serving.

To serve, unwrap rolls; slice each roll crosswise into eight 1-inch slices. Garnish as desired. Makes 4 main-dish or about 32 appetizer servings.

**Preparation time:** 35 minutes
**Calorie count:** 381 calories per main-dish serving; 48 calories per appetizer.

# Easy Paella

*Paella is a delicious Spanish recipe that has seafood, rice and tomatoes.*

1 medium onion, cut into halves and chopped
1 large red or green bell pepper, sliced
1 clove garlic, minced
2 tablespoons vegetable oil
1 can (16 ounces) tomatoes with juice, cut up
1 package (10 ounces) frozen artichoke hearts, cut into quarters

½ cup dry white wine
½ teaspoon dried thyme, crushed
¼ teaspoon salt
⅛ teaspoon saffron or turmeric
2 cups cooked rice
1 cup frozen peas
1 can (6⅛ ounces) StarKist Tuna, drained and broken into chunks
½ pound large shrimp, peeled and deveined

In a large skillet sauté onion, bell pepper and garlic in oil for 3 minutes. Stir in tomatoes with juice, artichoke hearts, wine and seasonings. Bring to a boil; reduce heat. Simmer for 10 minutes. Stir in rice, peas, tuna and shrimp. Cook for 3 to 5 minutes more, or until shrimp turn pink and mixture is heated. Makes 4 servings.

**Preparation time:** 30 minutes
**Calorie count:** 382 calories per serving.

# Santa Fe Tuna Salad with Chili-Lime Dressing

*Cilantro, chilies and lime juice lend this salad a southwestern flavor.*

6 cups torn spinach or romaine lettuce leaves
1 cup half-slices red onion
½ cantaloupe melon or 1 ripe papaya, peeled, seeded and cut into thin half-slices

1 can (12½ ounces) StarKist Tuna, drained and broken into chunks
½ cup chopped fresh cilantro

## Chili-Lime Dressing

¼ cup lime juice
¼ cup vegetable oil
2 teaspoons minced jalapeños or mild green chilies

1 clove garlic, minced
½ teaspoon salt
¼ teaspoon pepper

For salad, in a large bowl toss together spinach, onion, fruit, tuna and cilantro. For Chili-Lime Dressing, in a shaker jar combine remaining ingredients. Cover and shake until well blended. Pour over salad; toss well . Makes 4 servings.

**Preparation time:** 15 minutes
**Calorie count:** 298 calories per serving.

**Easy Paella**

# Jade Salad with Sesame Vinaigrette

5 cups fresh spinach or romaine
  leaves, torn
1 can (9¼ ounces) StarKist Tuna,
  drained and broken into
  chunks

1 cup frozen cooked bay shrimp,
  thawed
¾ cup shredded cucumber
½ cup shredded red radishes

## Sesame Vinaigrette

3 tablespoons rice vinegar or
  cider vinegar
2 tablespoons sesame oil
2 tablespoons vegetable oil

2 teaspoons soy sauce
2 teaspoons sesame seed
1 teaspoon sugar
  Salt and pepper to taste

In a large salad bowl toss together spinach, tuna, shrimp, cucumber and radishes. For dressing, in a shaker jar combine Sesame Vinaigrette ingredients. Cover and shake until well blended. Drizzle over salad; toss well. Makes 4 servings.

**Preparation time:** 15 minutes
**Calorie count:** 339 calories per serving.

# Seafood Wontons

*You'll find wonton skins in the refrigerated produce section or freezer case of large supermarkets. You may freeze any unused wontons for future use.*

1 cup finely chopped bok choy or
  cabbage
1 can (3¼ ounces) StarKist Tuna,
  drained and finely flaked
⅓ cup shredded carrot
¼ cup minced green onions
1 egg, beaten
2 tablespoons soy sauce

1 tablespoon minced fresh
  gingerroot or 1 teaspoon
  ground ginger
28 to 30 wonton skins
  Vegetable oil for deep frying
  Plum sauce or soy sauce for
  dipping

In a medium bowl combine bok choy, tuna, carrot, onions, egg, soy sauce and gingerroot until mixed. Position wonton skin with 1 point facing you. Spoon 1½ teaspoons of the tuna mixture in center of skin (use a slotted spoon if filling is wet); moisten edges of skins with water. Fold bottom corner over filling; fold side corners over first fold. Roll remaining corner over to seal. Repeat with remaining ingredients.

In a wok or deep saucepan heat 3 inches of oil to 365°F. Fry wontons, a few at a time, for 2 to 3 minutes, or until deep golden brown. Drain well on paper towels. Serve hot with plum sauce. Makes 28 to 30 appetizers.

**Preparation time:** 30 minutes
**Calorie count:** 50 calories per wonton. Plum Sauce is extra.

Jade Salad with Sesame Vinaigrette

# *Microwave* MARVELS

## Tuna-Stuffed Sole with Lime Sauce

½ cup carrot cut into thin strips
½ cup zucchini or yellow squash, cut into thin strips
2 green onions, cut into thin strips
1 can (6⅛ ounces) StarKist Tuna, drained and flaked

2 tablespoons lemon juice
1 teaspoon dried basil, crushed
½ teaspoon dill weed
8 thin sole or other white fish fillets (about 1½ pounds)
16 large fresh spinach leaves, washed

### Lime Sauce

½ cup chicken broth
2 tablespoons butter or margarine
2 tablespoons lime juice

1 tablespoon cornstarch
¼ teaspoon pepper
Lemon or lime peel for garnish (optional)

In a 1-quart microwavable bowl combine carrot, zucchini and onions. Cover with waxed paper; micro-cook on High power for 2 to 3 minutes, or until nearly tender, stirring once during cooking. Stir in tuna, lemon juice, basil and dill. Arrange 1 sole fillet on a microwavable roasting rack or plate. Top with 2 spinach leaves, overlapping if necessary. Spoon ⅛ of the vegetable mixture onto spinach; roll up fillet from the short side, enclosing filling. Secure with wooden picks; transfer to a shallow microwavable dish, filling side up. Repeat with remaining fillets and filling.

Cover dish with vented plastic wrap. Micro-cook on High power for 8 to 11 minutes, or until fish flakes easily and center is hot, rotating dish once during cooking. Let stand while making Lime Sauce.

For Lime Sauce, in a medium microwavable bowl combine all sauce ingredients until well blended. Micro-cook on High power for 1 to 3 minutes, or until thickened, stirring once. Serve fish with sauce. Makes 4 servings; 2 fillets per serving.

**Preparation time:** 15 minutes
**Calorie count:** 222 calories, including 3 tablespoons sauce, per serving.

Tuna-Stuffed Sole with Lime Sauce

# Sweet 'n' Sour Tuna with Pineapple

1½ cups red and green bell pepper chunks
2 green onions, cut into 2-inch pieces
2 teaspoons grated gingerroot
1 clove garlic, minced
1 can (12½ ounces) StarKist Tuna, drained and broken into chunks
1 can (11 ounces) mandarin oranges, drained
1 can (8¼ ounces) pineapple chunks in juice, drained; reserve juice
1 cup orange juice
2 tablespoons cornstarch
3 tablespoons catsup
2 tablespoons wine vinegar
1 tablespoon soy sauce
1 tablespoon brown sugar
Hot cooked saffron-flavored rice

In a 2-quart microwavable casserole combine bell pepper, onions, ginger and garlic. Cover loosely; micro-cook on High power for 2½ to 4 minutes, or until vegetables are tender; stir once. Stir in tuna, oranges and pineapple. Set aside.

In a microwavable bowl combine orange juice, pineapple juice and cornstarch. Stir in catsup, vinegar, soy sauce and brown sugar. Cover loosely; micro-cook on High power for 4 to 6 minutes, or until sauce thickens and bubbles; stir twice. Stir into tuna mixture. Cover loosely; micro-cook on High power for 2 to 3 minutes, or until heated; stir once. Serve over hot cooked rice. Makes 4 servings.

**Preparation time:** 15 minutes
**Calorie count:** 389 calories, including ¾ cup cooked rice, per serving.

# Southern-Style Fish Cassoulet

*Serve this stew with hot cooked noodles, rice or corn bread.*

¼ cup chicken broth
1½ cups sliced fresh okra
1 cup sliced onion
1 can (16 ounces) whole tomatoes with juice, cut up
1 can (8 ounces) niblet corn, drained
1 can (6⅛ ounces) StarKist Tuna, drained and broken into chunks
1 can (6 ounces) minced clams, drained
1 can (6 ounces) tomato paste
1 cup water
½ cup dry white wine
1 teaspoon curry powder
1 teaspoon dried basil, crushed
¼ teaspoon pepper

In a 3-quart microwavable casserole combine broth, okra and onion. Cover; micro-cook on High power for 1½ minutes. Stir in remaining ingredients. Cover; micro-cook on High for 12 to 14 minutes; stir twice. Makes 4 servings.

**Preparation time:** 10 minutes
**Calorie count:** 204 calories per serving.

Sweet 'n' Sour Tuna with Pineapple

# Tuna & Asparagus au Gratin

1 pound fresh asparagus
¼ cup water
¼ cup butter or margarine
3 tablespoons all-purpose flour
¼ teaspoon salt
⅛ teaspoon pepper
¾ cup low-fat milk

¼ cup dry white wine
1 can (12½ ounces) StarKist
   Tuna, drained and broken
   into chunks
3 tablespoons seasoned bread
   crumbs
3 tablespoons grated Parmesan

Trim asparagus; place in microwavable dish with tips toward center. Add water. Cover; micro-cook on High power 5 minutes, or until tender; rotate dish once.

In a 1-quart microwavable bowl micro-cook ½ of the butter on High power for 30 seconds, or until melted. Stir in flour, salt and pepper. Blend in milk and wine. Micro-cook on High power for 4 to 6 minutes, or until mixture thickens; stir every 2 minutes. Stir in tuna. Pour into 4 microwavable ramekins. Drain asparagus; arrange over tuna mixture. Melt remaining butter in microwavable dish on High power for 30 seconds. Drizzle over tops. Sprinkle with bread crumbs and cheese. Micro-cook on High power for 3 to 5 minutes, or until heated; rotate once. Makes 4 servings.

**Preparation time:** 10 minutes
**Calorie count:** 329 calories per serving.

# Tuna Provençale on French Bread

*Toasted bread or English muffins can be substituted for the French bread.*

1 tablespoon butter or margarine
½ cup sliced onion
1 clove garlic, minced
1 can (16 ounces) Italian-style
   tomatoes with juice, cut up
1 can (9¼ ounces) StarKist Tuna,
   drained and broken into
   chunks
1 tablespoon chopped parsley

1 tablespoon lime or lemon juice
½ teaspoon dried thyme, crushed
½ teaspoon dried basil, crushed
½ cup dry white or red wine
1 tablespoon cornstarch
4 pieces (5 inches each) French
   bread, cut lengthwise into
   halves
⅓ cup sliced pitted ripe olives

In 3-quart microwavable casserole melt butter on High power for 40 seconds. Add onion and garlic. Cover; micro-cook on High power for 2 to 3 minutes, until tender. Stir in tomatoes with juice, tuna, parsley, lime juice and herbs. Combine wine and cornstarch until smooth; stir into tuna mixture. Cover; micro-cook on High power for 5 to 8 minutes, or until heated; turn dish ¼ turn twice. Let stand for 2 minutes. Serve over bread; sprinkle with olives. Makes 4 servings.

**Preparation time:** 10 minutes
**Calorie count:** 233 calories per serving.

# Tuna-Stuffed Bakers

*Use your favorite in-season vegetables for the filling.*

4 large baking potatoes or sweet
   potatoes, scrubbed
2 cups chopped or sliced fresh or
   frozen vegetables*
¼ cup chopped green onions
1 can (12½ ounces) StarKist
   Tuna, drained and flaked
⅓ cup low-fat ricotta cheese
2 tablespoons drained pimiento
   strips

1 tablespoon chopped parsley
   (optional)
¼ teaspoon dry mustard
⅛ teaspoon pepper
4 slices (1 ounce each) reduced-
   calorie American cheese, cut
   into ¼-inch strips

Pierce potatoes twice with fork. Arrange potatoes 1 inch apart on paper towel in microwave oven. Micro-cook on High power for 10½ to 12½ minutes, turning and rearranging potatoes halfway through cooking time. Wrap potatoes in foil; let stand for 5 minutes to finish cooking while preparing filling.

For filling, in a 2-quart microwavable casserole place desired vegetables and onions. Cover with waxed paper; micro-cook on High power for 3 to 5 minutes, or until vegetables are crisp-tender, stirring twice. Drain. Stir in tuna, ricotta cheese, pimiento, parsley, mustard and pepper until well combined. Cover; micro-cook on High power for 2 minutes, or until mixture is heated through, stirring once.

Unwrap potatoes; cut lengthwise into halves. Flake interior with fork. Spoon vegetable filling mixture over potatoes, mounding filling on top. Place potatoes in a shallow microwavable dish. Place strips of cheese diagonally over filling. Micro-cook on High power for 1 to 2 minutes, or until cheese is melted. Makes 4 servings; 2 halves per serving.

*Suggested vegetables are: broccoli or cauliflower florets, mushrooms, carrots, pea pods, peas, asparagus or corn.

**Preparation time:** 20 minutes
**Calorie count:** 358 calories per serving.

# CONTENTS

Barbecue Basics                       184

Hot Off the Grill Meats               188

Tempting Poultry                      204

Quick & Fabulous Seafood              218

Spectacular Side Dishes               228

Lemon Herbed Chicken (*page 207*) and
Skewered Vegetables (*page 234*)

# BARBECUE BASICS

## A DASH OF HISTORY

Henry Ford deserves credit for more than the Model T. His ingenuity helped create America's passion for outdoor cooking. In the early 1900s, Ford operated a northern Michigan sawmill that made wooden framing for his Model Ts. As piles of wood scraps grew, he searched for a way to make them useful. He soon learned how to chip the wood and convert it into the now familiar pillow-shaped briquets. These convenient briquets were originally sold through Ford automobile agencies and marked the beginning of the all-American tradition of barbecuing.

Ford Charcoal, later named **Kingsford®** charcoal briquets, is the original and still the number one brand sold in the nation today.

## WHAT TYPE OF CHARCOAL?

Successful barbecuing starts with a good fire. Premium quality briquets, such as **Kingsford®** charcoal, help deliver a perfect fire in three ways. They light quicker so the coals are ready sooner. They burn longer to provide more cooking time. They perform consistently, bag after bag. The renewed interest in authentic charcoal cooking has spawned extra convenience and improved flavor in the types of charcoal available.

**Ready to Light Charcoal Briquets:** These coals are an especially good choice for midweek barbecues when time is at a premium. Products such as **Match Light®** ready to light briquets already contain just the right amount of lighter fluid to produce a quick-starting fire. Simply stack the briquets into a pyramid and light several briquets with a match. The coals will be ready in about 20 minutes. Be sure to close the bag tightly after each use.

A single-use lightable bag of charcoal, such as **BBQ Bag®,** is the convenient choice for tailgate parties or anytime grilling. Just light the bag, which is filled with enough ready to light briquets for one barbecue.

**Charcoal Briquets with Mesquite Wood Chips:** This is the perfect selection for cooks who enjoy the wonderful flavor of mesquite but feel uncomfortable grilling over pure mesquite charcoal, which burns hotter and less evenly than regular charcoal. For example, **Kingsford® with Mesquite** charcoal briquets are a blend of compressed charcoal briquets and mesquite chips. These briquets produce real mesquite smoke to enhance the flavor of outdoor fare.

It is important to remember that charcoal is porous and will absorb moisture. Always store briquets in a dry area, and keep the bag in a tightly closed or covered container. Charcoal that has been exposed to humidity or moisture can be more difficult to light.

## SAFETY FIRST

Make sure the grill is on a solid surface and is set away from shrubbery, grass and overhangs. Also, make sure grill vents are not clogged with ashes before starting a fire. NEVER use gasoline or kerosene as a lighter fluid starter. Either one can cause an explosion. To get a sluggish fire going, do not add lighter fluid directly to hot coals. Instead, place 2 to 3 additional briquets in a small metal can, add lighter fluid, stack them on the pyramid of briquets with tongs, then light with a match. These briquets will restart the fire.

Remember that coals are hot (up to 1000°F) and that the heat transfers to the barbecue grill, grid, tools and food. Always wear heavy-duty mitts when cooking and handling grill and tools.

# BUILDING PERFECT FIRES

**How Much Charcoal?** A 5-pound bag of **Kingsford®** charcoal contains 75 to 90 briquets; a 10-pound bag between 150 and 180; and a 20-pound bag 300 to 360 briquets. The number of briquets required for barbecuing depends on the size and type of grill and the amount of food to be prepared. Weather conditions also have an effect; strong winds, very cold temperatures or highly humid conditions increase the number of briquets needed for a good fire. As a rule, it takes about 30 briquets to grill 1 pound of meat. For example, you'll need 45 briquets to grill six 4-ounce hamburgers.

For **direct cooking,** food is placed directly over the coals. Make sure there is enough charcoal in a single layer to extend 1 to 2 inches beyond the area of the food on the grill. Pour briquets into the grill to determine the quantity needed, then stack them into a pyramid.

For **indirect cooking,** food is placed over a drip pan and the coals are banked either to one side or on both sides of the pan. This method is recommended for large cuts of meat, such as roasts, and fatty meats to eliminate flame flare-ups. Here's how to determine the number of briquets needed:

### BRIQUETS NEEDED FOR INDIRECT COOKING, COVERED GRILL

| | Diameter of Grill (inches) | | | |
| --- | --- | --- | --- | --- |
| | 26¾ | 22½ | 18½ | 14 |
| Briquets needed on each side of drip pan for cooking 45 to 50 minutes | 30 | 25 | 16 | 15 |
| Briquets needed to be added on each side of drip pan every 45 minutes – use only regular briquets | 9 | 8 | 5 | 4 |

**Using Lighter Fluid: Kingsford™** Odorless charcoal lighter is formulated to meet strict air quality standards. Stack briquets into a pyramid. Use 2½ ounces of fluid per pound of briquets, then light with a match. Coals will be ready in 20 to 30 minutes, when they are about 80% ashed over. At night, they will have a noticeable reddish glow.

**Using a Chimney Starter:** This method is essentially failure-proof and no lighter fluid is required. First, remove the grid from the grill and set the chimney starter in the base of the grill. Then crumble a couple of sheets of newspaper and place them in the bottom portion of the chimney starter. Fill the top portion with charcoal briquets. Light the newspaper. Do not disturb the starter; coals will be ready in 20 to 30 minutes. Be sure to wear fireproof mitts when moving coals from the chimney starter into the base of the grill.

**Using an Electric Starter:** Nestle the electric starter in the coals. Plug the starter into a heavy-duty extension cord, then plug the cord into an outlet. After 8 to 10 minutes, when ash begins to form on the briquets, unplug the starter, remove it, and carefully set it aside. Arrange the briquets in a single layer, close together.

**How Hot is the Grill?** If you don't have a grill thermometer, here is a quick, easy way to estimate the temperature on the grill surface. Hold your hand, palm-side-down, just above the grid. Count "one thousand one, one thousand two," etc., until the heat is uncomfortable. If you can keep your hand in place before pulling away:

2 seconds - it's a hot fire, 375°F or more.
3 seconds - it's a medium-hot fire, 350° to 375°F.
4 seconds - it's a medium fire, 300° to 350°F.
5 seconds - it's a low fire, 200° to 300°F.

# FLAVORED SMOKE

Flavored smoke, a combination of heady aromas from hardwoods and fresh or dried herbs, imparts a special flavor in barbecued foods. Outdoor cooks find it's both easy and fun to experiment with different meats and flavor combinations. Here are some suggestions for getting started:

As a general rule, a little goes a long way. Added flavorings should complement, not overpower, food's natural taste. Always soak flavorings, such as wood chunks, wood chips or herbs, in water at least 30 minutes before adding to the coals. The flavorings should smolder and smoke, not burn.

Hickory and mesquite chips or wood chunks are the most readily available flavorings. Other good choices are oak (good with heartier meats), cherry or apple wood (flavorful companions to poultry) and alder wood from the Northwest (marvelous with fish). Look for **Kingsford®** Heart-O-Hickory smoke chips in your store's barbecue section.

Grapevine cuttings and even shells from nuts, such as almonds, pecans or walnuts can add interesting flavor. You can also try water-soaked garlic cloves and orange or lemon peels.

Small bunches of fresh or dried herbs soaked in water can add fragrant flavor as well. Rosemary, bay leaves, oregano and tarragon, for example, can be teamed with wood chips or simply used by themselves for a new taste twist.

## BARBECUE TOOLS AND ACCESSORIES

These tools will help make your barbecue cooking safer and more convenient.

**Long-Handled Tongs, Basting Brush and Spatula:** Moving hot coals and food around the grill, as well as basting and turning foods, can be dangerous. Select tools with long handles and hang them where you are working. You may want to purchase two pairs of tongs, one for coals and one for food.

**Meat Thermometer:** There is no better way to judge the doneness of meat than with a high quality meat thermometer. Always remember to insert the thermometer into the center of the largest muscle of the meat, with the point away from bone, fat or rotisserie rod.

**Heavy-Duty Mitts:** You will prevent many burns by safeguarding your hands with big, thick mitts. Keep them close to the barbecue so they are always handy.

**Aluminum Foil Drip Pans:** A drip pan placed beneath grilling meats will prevent flare-ups. The pan should be 1½ inches deep and extend about 3 inches beyond either end of the meat. The juices that collect in the drip pan may be used for a sauce or gravy. Bring drippings to a boil before using.

**Water Spritzer:** To quench flare-ups, keep a water-filled spray bottle near the barbecue.

**Other Tools and Accessories:** A charcoal chimney or electric charcoal starter is useful for starting the fire without lighter fluid. Hinged wire baskets facilitate the turning of some foods, such as fish fillets. Long skewers made of metal or bamboo are indispensable for kabobs. Bamboo skewers should be soaked in water at least 20 minutes before grilling to prevent the bamboo from burning.

## DRY RUBS AND MARINADES

Dry rubs are combinations of seasonings and spices rubbed onto meat before grilling. Basic rubs often include coarsely ground black or white pepper, paprika and garlic powder. Some include mustard, brown sugar and even ground red pepper. Crushed herbs, such as sage, basil, thyme and oregano are other good choices.

Marinades, such as dry rubs, add flavor, but they also help tenderize less tender cuts of meat. Basic marinades include an acidic ingredient responsible for tenderizing—generally from wine, vinegar, soy sauce or lemon juice—combined with herbs, seasonings and oil. Fish and vegetables don't usually need tenderizing and should be marinated for only short periods of time (15 to 30 minutes). Beef, pork, lamb and chicken all benefit from being marinated for a few hours to overnight. Turn marinating foods occasionally to let the flavor infuse evenly. For safety, marinate all meats in the refrigerator. Resealable plastic bags are great to hold foods as they marinate.

Reserve some of the marinade before adding the meat. Use this reserved marinade as a baste while the meat is cooking. You can also serve marinade that has been drained from the meat as a dipping sauce. However, follow food safety practices; place marinade in a small saucepan and bring to a full boil. These precautions are necessary to prevent the cooked food from becoming contaminated with bacteria from the raw meat that may be present in the marinade.

## A WORD ABOUT SAUCES

Sauces—rich and thick, savory or sweet—add delicious flavors to almost any grilled fare. Premium sauces, such as K.C. Masterpiece® Barbecue Sauce, capture real homemade taste and are a barbecue staple worth using often. Serve warmed sauce on the side for added zest. Here's how to protect the rich, deep color and spicy flavor of barbecue sauce, especially tomato- and molasses-based ones that can burn if applied too early:

**For grilled steaks and chops:** Baste with sauce after meat has been turned for the last time, about the last 3 minutes of grilling.

**For grilled chicken:** Baste with sauce the last 10 minutes; turn once.

**For hot dogs and sausage:** Baste with sauce the last 5 to 6 minutes.

**For barbecued meats (cooked by indirect heat):** Baste with sauce the last hour of cooking.

**For smoked meats:** Baste with sauce the last 30 to 45 minutes.

Basting sauces made from seasoned oils and butters may be brushed on throughout grilling.

## BARBECUE TIPS

To keep food from sticking to the grid and make it easy to turn, brush the hot grid with vegetable oil before cooking.

To "line" your food with appetizing grill marks, allow the grid to heat thoroughly before adding the food.

To avoid flare-ups and charred food when grilling, remove visible fat from meat or cook indirectly.

Watch foods carefully during grilling. Total cooking time will vary with the type of food, position on the grill, weather, temperature of the coals and degree of doneness you desire.

Use a meat thermometer to accurately determine the doneness of large cuts of meat or poultry cooked on the rotisserie or covered grill.

Foods wrapped in foil and cooked on the grill should be turned often to prevent burning and ensure even cooking.

If you partially cook foods in a microwave or on a range, immediately finish cooking the food on the grill. Do not refrigerate partially cooked foods or let them sit at room temperature before grilling is completed.

In hot weather, food should never sit out for over 1 hour. Remember, keep hot foods hot and cold foods cold.

Always serve cooked food from the grill on a clean plate, not one that held raw food.

Always use tongs or a spatula when handling meat. Piercing meat with a fork allows delicious juices to escape and makes meat less moist.

The secret to evenly cooked vegetable kabobs is to parboil solid or starchy vegetables before they are threaded onto skewers for grilling. For best results, grill vegetables on skewers separate from meat.

If you use wooden or bamboo skewers when making kabobs, be sure to soak them in cold water at least 20 minutes before grilling.

Herb brushes lightly season barbecued foods. To make, fasten a bunch of freshly picked herb sprigs to the tip of a wooden spoon handle with kitchen twine or cotton string. Dip herb brushes in olive oil and baste whatever you're grilling. Then untie and throw the sprigs into the fire.

When barbecuing food for more than an hour, add 10 to 12 **Kingsford®** charcoal briquets around the outer edge of the fire as cooking starts. When these briquets are ready, add them to the center of the fire as needed to maintain constant temperature. Use only regular briquets (not instant lighting briquets).

# Hot Off the Grill
# MEATS

## BEEF WITH DRY SPICE RUB

*You can grill mushrooms and new potatoes on skewers over medium coals while you wait for the briquets to burn down to medium-low to cook the beef.*

> **3 tablespoons firmly packed brown sugar**
> **1 tablespoon black peppercorns**
> **1 tablespoon yellow mustard seeds**
> **1 tablespoon whole coriander seeds**
> **4 cloves garlic**
> **1½ to 2 pounds beef top round steak or London Broil**
> **(about 1½ inches thick)**
> **Vegetable or olive oil**
> **Salt**

Place brown sugar, peppercorns, mustard seeds, coriander seeds and garlic in a blender or food processor; process until seeds and garlic are crushed. Rub beef with oil, then pat on spice mixture. Season generously with salt.

Oil hot grid to help prevent sticking. Grill beef, on a covered grill, over medium-low Kingsford briquets, 16 to 20 minutes for medium doneness, turning once. Let stand 5 minutes before slicing. Cut across the grain into thin, diagonal slices.                    *Makes 6 servings*

**Grilled Mushrooms:** Thread mushrooms, 1½ to 2 inches in diameter, on metal or bamboo skewers. Brush lightly with oil; season with salt and pepper. Grill 7 to 12 minutes, turning occasionally.

**Grilled New Potatoes:** Cook or microwave small new potatoes until barely tender. Thread on metal or bamboo skewers. Brush lightly with oil; season with salt and pepper. Grill 10 to 15 minutes, turning occasionally.

**Note:** Bamboo skewers should be soaked in water for at least 20 minutes to keep them from burning.

*Beef with Dry Spice Rub*

# MEAT GRILLING POINTERS

- Turn small cuts, such as patties, chops, steaks and kabobs, halfway through grilling time.

- Turn large cuts, such as roasts, every 20 to 30 minutes.

- Check final temperature of large cuts with a meat thermometer inserted in the thickest portion of the meat. The thermometer should not touch bone or fat. Let meat stand 10 minutes on cutting board before slicing.

## Meat Grilling Chart

| Cut of Meat | Method/Grill | Temperature of Briquets | Grilling Time in Minutes/Doneness |
|---|---|---|---|
| **Ground Beef Patties** | | | |
| ¾ inch | Direct/Uncovered | Medium | 10 to 11/Medium |
| ½ inch | Direct/Uncovered | Medium | 7 to 10/Medium |
| **Beef Top Round Steak** | | | |
| ¾ to 1 inch | Direct/Uncovered | Medium | 12 to 14/Medium |
| 1½ inches | Direct/Uncovered | Medium-Low | 23 to 25/Medium |
| **Beef Eye Round Steak** | | | |
| ¾ to 1 inch | Direct/Uncovered | Medium | 12 to 16/Medium |
| **Beef Rib Eye Steak or Top Loin Steak** | | | |
| ¾ inch | Direct/Uncovered | Medium | 7 to 9/Medium |
| 1 inch | Direct/Uncovered | Medium-Low | 9 to 12/Medium |
| 1½ inches | Direct/Uncovered | Medium-Low | 21 to 24/Medium |
| **Beef Porterhouse or T-Bone Steak** | | | |
| 1 inch | Direct/Uncovered | Medium | 10 to 14/Medium |
| 1½ inches | Direct/Uncovered | Medium-Low | 26 to 30/Medium |
| **Beef Tenderloin Steak** | | | |
| 1 inch | Direct/Uncovered | Medium | 11 to 13/Medium |
| 1½ inches | Direct/Uncovered | Medium | 15 to 17/Medium |
| **Beef Boneless Sirloin Steak** | | | |
| ¾ inch | Direct/Uncovered | Medium | 8 to 11/Medium |
| 2 inches | Direct/Uncovered | Medium-Low | 34 to 40/Medium |
| **Beef Flank Steak** | | | |
| 1½ pounds | Direct/Uncovered | Medium | 12 to 15/Medium |
| **Beef Sirloin Kabobs** | | | |
| 1 to 1½ inch cubes | Direct/Uncovered | Medium | 8 to 11/Medium |

| Cut of Meat | Method/Grill | Temperature of Briquets | Grilling Time in Minutes/Doneness |
|---|---|---|---|
| **Beef Bottom Round Roast**<br>3 to 3½ pounds | Indirect/Covered | Medium-Low | 21 to 25/Rare |
| **Beef Eye Round Roast Butterflied**<br>2 to 4 pounds | Direct/Covered | Medium | 16 to 20/Medium |
| **Beef Top Round Roast**<br>3 to 3½ pounds | Indirect/Covered | Medium-Low | 23 to 27/Rare to Medium-Rare |
| **Beef Boneless Chuck Roast**<br>3 to 4 pounds | Indirect/Covered | Medium-Low | 25 to 30/Medium |
| **Beef Tri-Tip Roast**<br>1¾ to 2 pounds | Direct/Covered | Medium | 21 to 25/Medium |
| **Beef Round Tip Roast**<br>5 to 8 pounds | Indirect/Covered | Medium-Low | 20 to 25/Medium |
| **Beef Tenderloin Roast**<br>1½ to 2 pounds | Direct/Covered | Medium | 16 to 24/Medium |
| **Pork Loin Chops**<br>Bone-In ¾ inch | Indirect/Covered | Medium | 8 to 11/Well |
| Bone-In 1½ inches | Indirect/Covered | Medium | 19 to 22/Well |
| Boneless ¾ inch | Indirect/Covered | Medium | 16 to 18/Well |
| Boneless 1½ inches | Indirect/Covered | Medium | 16 to 18/Well |
| **Pork Kabobs**<br>1 inch pieces | Indirect/Covered | Medium | 9 to 13/Well |
| **Pork Tenderloin Roast**<br>½ to 1½ pounds | Indirect/Covered | Medium | 16 to 21/Well |
| **Lamb Loin or Rib Chops**<br>Bone-In 1 inch | Direct/Uncovered | Medium | 9 to 10/Medium |
| **Lamb Sirloin Steaks**<br>1 inch | Direct/Uncovered | Medium | 9 to 10/Medium |
| **Lamb Kabobs**<br>1-inch pieces | Direct/Uncovered | Medium | 7 to 8/Medium |
| **Lamb Butterflied Leg**<br>4 to 7 pounds | Direct/Uncovered | Medium | 40 to 50/Medium |

Cooking times are courtesy of National Live Stock and Meat Board, National Pork Producers Council and American Lamb Council.

# PORK TENDERLOIN WITH ORANGE GLAZE

1 cup orange juice
¼ cup cider vinegar
1 tablespoon finely grated fresh ginger
1 teaspoon finely grated orange peel
1 pork tenderloin (about 1 pound)
    Salt and black pepper
    Orange Glaze (recipe follows)

Combine orange juice, vinegar, ginger and orange peel in a shallow glass dish or large heavy plastic bag. Add pork tenderloin; cover dish or close bag. Marinate in refrigerator at least 4 hours, turning several times.

Meanwhile, prepare Orange Glaze. Reserve about ¼ cup for brushing on meat. Remove pork from marinade; discard marinade. Season pork with salt and pepper.

Oil hot grid to help prevent sticking. Grill pork, on a covered grill, over medium Kingsford briquets, 18 to 25 minutes until a meat thermometer inserted in the thickest part registers 155°F. Brush with reserved Orange Glaze the last 5 to 10 minutes of cooking. Let pork stand 5 to 10 minutes to allow the internal temperature to rise to 160°F before slicing. Slice and serve with remaining Orange Glaze. Garnish, if desired.          *Makes 4 servings*

## ORANGE GLAZE

1 cup orange marmalade
1 tablespoon finely grated ginger
2 tablespoons soy sauce
2 tablespoons cider vinegar
1 tablespoon Dijon mustard
¼ teaspoon salt
¼ teaspoon black pepper

Melt orange marmalade in a small saucepan. Stir in remaining ingredients; reduce heat to low. Cook about 10 minutes. Reserve ¼ cup of glaze for brushing pork; place remaining glaze in a small bowl to serve as accompaniment. Makes about 1 cup.

*Pork Tenderloin with Orange Glaze*

# WINE & ROSEMARY LAMB SKEWERS

1 cup dry red wine
¼ cup olive oil
3 cloves garlic, cut into slivers
1 tablespoon chopped fresh thyme *or* 1 teaspoon
    dried thyme leaves, crumbled
1 tablespoon chopped fresh rosemary *or* 1 teaspoon
    dried rosemary leaves, crumbled
2 pounds boneless lamb, cut into 1-inch cubes
    Salt and black pepper
4 or 5 sprigs fresh rosemary (optional)
    Grilled Bread (recipe follows)

Combine wine, oil, garlic, thyme and rosemary in a shallow glass dish or large heavy plastic bag. Add lamb; cover dish or close bag. Marinate lamb in the refrigerator up to 12 hours, turning several times. Remove lamb from marinade; discard marinade. Thread lamb onto 6 long metal skewers. Season to taste with salt and pepper.

Oil hot grid to help prevent sticking. Grill lamb, on a covered grill, over medium Kingsford briquets, 8 to 12 minutes, turning once or twice. Remove grill cover and throw rosemary onto coals the last 4 to 5 minutes of cooking, if desired. Move skewers to side of grid to keep warm while bread is toasting. Garnish, if desired. *Makes 6 servings*

## GRILLED BREAD

¼ cup olive oil
2 tablespoons red wine vinegar
1 baguette (about 12 inches long), sliced
    lengthwise, then cut into pieces
    Salt and freshly ground black pepper

Mix oil and vinegar in cup; brush over cut surfaces of bread. Season lightly with salt and pepper. Grill bread cut side down, on an uncovered grill, over medium Kingsford briquets until lightly toasted. Makes 6 servings.

*Wine & Rosemary Lamb Skewers*
*and Grilled Bread*

# NUTTY BURGERS

1½ pounds ground beef
1 medium onion, finely chopped
1 clove garlic, minced
1 cup dry bread crumbs
⅓ cup grated Parmesan cheese
⅔ cup pine nuts
⅓ cup chopped parsley
2 eggs
1½ teaspoons salt
1 teaspoon black pepper
12 slices French bread (each ¼ inch thick) *or*
    6 hamburger buns
Green onions for garnish

Combine beef, onion, garlic, bread crumbs, cheese, pine nuts, parsley, eggs, salt and pepper in a medium bowl. Shape meat mixture into 6 thick patties.

Oil hot grid to help prevent sticking. Grill patties, on a covered grill, over medium-hot Kingsford briquets, 10 minutes for medium doneness, turning once. Serve on French bread. Garnish with chopped green onion, if desired.

*Makes 6 servings*

# BBQ BABY BACK RIBS

1 cup seasoned rice vinegar
1 cup freshly squeezed orange juice
½ cup maple syrup
½ cup water
2 tablespoons finely grated fresh ginger
2 tablespoons finely chopped fresh cilantro
4 cloves garlic, coarsely chopped
2 teaspoons Oriental sesame oil
   Black pepper
1 teaspoon crushed red pepper flakes
3 to 5 pounds pork loin back ribs
1 tablespoon cornstarch
   Salt

Combine vinegar, orange juice, maple syrup, water, ginger, cilantro, garlic, sesame oil, 1 teaspoon black pepper and red pepper flakes in a medium bowl. Reserve 1 cup of marinade. Place ribs in a shallow glass dish or large heavy plastic bag. Pour remaining marinade over ribs; cover dish or close bag. Marinate in refrigerator 4 to 24 hours.

To make glaze, place reserved 1 cup marinade in a small saucepan; whisk in cornstarch. Bring to a boil, stirring frequently. Boil about 30 seconds until mixture thickens, stirring constantly; set aside. Remove ribs from marinade; discard marinade.

Oil hot grid to help prevent sticking. Grill ribs, on a covered grill, over medium Kingsford briquets, 8 to 12 minutes, turning and rearranging the ribs frequently. Brush ribs with glaze the last few minutes of cooking. Remove ribs from grill; baste with glaze.

*Makes 4 to 6 servings*

# PORK TENDERLOIN WITH FRESH PLUM SAUCE

**Fresh Plum Sauce (recipe follows)**
**Toasted Oriental sesame oil**
**1 pork tenderloin (about 1 pound)**
**Salt and black pepper**

Prepare Fresh Plum Sauce. Rub sesame oil into pork. Season generously with salt and pepper.

Oil hot grid to help prevent sticking. Grill pork, on a covered grill, over medium Kingsford briquets, 18 to 25 minutes until a meat thermometer inserted in the thickest part registers 155°F. Let stand 5 to 10 minutes to allow the internal temperature to rise to 160°F before slicing. Slice and serve with sauce. *Makes 4 servings*

## FRESH PLUM SAUCE

**1 tablespoon vegetable oil**
**1 tablespoon minced garlic**
**1 tablespoon grated or minced fresh ginger**
**1½ teaspoons minced jalapeño chili pepper**
**1 pound plums, cut into halves, pitted, chopped**
**½ cup sliced green onions, with tops**
**¼ cup firmly packed dark brown sugar or to taste**
**2 tablespoons soy sauce**
**2 tablespoons seasoned rice vinegar or apple cider vinegar**
**¼ cup chopped fresh cilantro**

Heat oil in a medium saucepan. Add garlic, ginger and chili peppers; sauté, stirring, about 1 minute. Add all remaining ingredients except cilantro. Simmer 15 minutes, stirring frequently, until mixture has a chunky, saucelike texture. Adjust flavors to taste. Remove from heat and cool to room temperature. Stir in cilantro. Makes about 2 cups.

# GRILLED SMOKED SAUSAGE

**1 cup apricot or pineapple preserves**
**1 tablespoon lemon juice**
**1½ pounds smoked sausage**

Heat preserves in small saucepan until melted. Strain; reserve fruit pieces. Combine strained preserve liquid with lemon juice in a small bowl.

Oil hot grid to help prevent sticking. Grill whole sausage on an uncovered grill, over low Kingsford briquets, 10 minutes. Halfway through cooking, baste with glaze, then turn and continue grilling until heated through. Remove sausage from grill; baste with glaze. Garnish with fruit pieces.
*Makes 6 servings*

# PORK CHOPS WITH ORANGE–RADISH RELISH

2 cups orange juice
⅓ cup lime juice
⅓ cup firmly packed brown sugar
3 medium oranges, peeled, seeded and cut into ¼-inch pieces
¼ cup chopped red onion
¼ cup diced radishes
2 tablespoons finely chopped fresh cilantro
6 pork chops (about ¾ inch thick)
Salt and black pepper
Orange curls and radishes for garnish

Combine both juices and brown sugar in a saucepan. Cook mixture at a low boil about 20 minutes until reduced to about ½ cup and it has a syruplike consistency, stirring often. Set aside ¼ cup of sauce for basting.

Meanwhile, prepare Orange-Radish Relish by combining oranges, onion, and diced radishes in a colander or strainer and drain well; transfer to a bowl. Add cilantro and gently stir in remaining orange syrup. Season pork with salt and pepper.

Oil hot grid to help prevent sticking. Grill pork, on a covered grill, over medium Kingsford briquets, 7 to 10 minutes. (Pork is done at 160°F; it should be juicy and still slightly pink in the center.) Halfway through cooking, brush with reserved ¼ cup orange syrup and turn once. Serve with Orange-Radish Relish. Garnish with orange curls and radishes.

*Makes 6 servings*

# WINE COUNTRY STEAK

½ cup olive oil
Juice of 1 lime or lemon
1 cup Cabernet, Merlot or other dry red wine
¼ cup soy sauce
3 cloves garlic, minced or pressed
1½ tablespoon Dijon mustard
1 teaspoon black pepper
1 beef flank steak (about 2 pounds), pounded to about ½ inch thick

Whisk together oil, lime juice, wine, soy sauce, garlic, mustard and pepper in a medium bowl. Place beef in a shallow glass dish or large heavy plastic bag; pour marinade over beef. Cover dish or close bag. Marinate in refrigerator 12 to 24 hours, turning once or twice. Remove beef from marinade; discard marinade.

Oil grid to help prevent sticking. Grill beef, on a covered grill, over medium Kingsford briquets, 6 to 8 minutes for rare doneness; 9 to 12 minutes for medium-rare doneness, turning once or twice. Cut across grain into thin, diagonal slices.

*Makes 6 servings*

*Pork Chops with Orange-Radish Relish*

# TERIYAKI GLAZED BEEF KABOBS

1¼ to 1½ pounds beef top or bottom sirloin, cut into
    1-inch cubes
½ cup bottled teriyaki baste & glaze
1 teaspoon Oriental sesame oil (optional)
1 clove garlic, minced
8 to 12 green onions
1 or 2 plum tomatoes, cut into slices (optional)

Thread beef cubes on metal or bamboo skewers. (Soak bamboo skewers in water for at least 20 minutes to keep them from burning.) Combine teriyaki glaze, sesame oil and garlic in a small bowl. Brush beef and onions with part of the glaze, saving some for grilling; let stand 15 to 30 minutes.

Oil hot grid to help prevent sticking. Grill beef, on a covered grill, over medium Kingsford briquets, 6 to 9 minutes for medium doneness, turning several times and brushing with glaze. Add onions and tomatoes, if desired, to the grid 3 or 4 minutes after the beef; grill until onions and tomatoes are tender. Remove from grill; brush skewers, onions and tomatoes with remaining glaze.

*Makes 4 servings*

# PORK KABOBS WITH MUSTARD–BOURBON GLAZE

1 boneless pork loin roast (1 to 1¼ pounds)
    Salt and black pepper
3 tablespoons Dijon mustard
3 tablespoons bourbon or water
¼ cup soy sauce
¼ cup firmly packed brown sugar
1 tablespoon Worcestershire sauce

Cut pork into 1-inch cubes; season with salt and pepper. Combine mustard, bourbon, soy sauce, brown sugar and Worcestershire sauce in a shallow glass dish or large heavy plastic bag. Add pork; cover dish or close bag. Marinate in refrigerator up to 4 hours. Remove pork from marinade; discard marinade. Thread pork onto metal or bamboo skewers. (Soak bamboo skewers in water for at least 20 minutes to prevent burning.)

Oil hot grid to help prevent sticking. Grill pork, on a covered grill, over medium Kingsford briquets, 8 to 12 minutes until pork is cooked through, turning once. Pork should be juicy and slightly pink in the center.

*Makes 4 servings*

*Teriyaki Glazed Beef Kabobs*

# BEEF TENDERLOIN WITH DIJON−CREAM SAUCE

*Beef tenderloin roasts can be purchased in different weights, depending on how they are cut out of the tenderloin. The tenderloin is elongated with a rounded large end, gradually tapering to a thin, flat end. Purchase a center-cut piece or a piece cut from the thicker end if you can, as they will grill more evenly. Allow 4 to 5 ounces of meat per serving. Test doneness with a thermometer and remove beef from the grill just before it reaches the desired temperature since the internal temperature can rise 5°F as the roast stands.*

2 tablespoons olive oil
3 tablespoons balsamic vinegar*
1 beef tenderloin roast (about 1½ to 2 pounds)
  Salt
1½ tablespoons white peppercorns
1½ tablespoons black peppercorns
3 tablespoons mustard seeds
  Dijon-Cream Sauce (recipe follows)

Combine oil and vinegar in a cup; rub onto beef. Season generously with salt. Let stand 15 minutes.

Meanwhile, coarsely crush peppercorns and mustard seeds in a blender or food processor or by hand with a mortar and pestle. Roll beef in crushed mixture, pressing it into the surface to coat.

Oil hot grid to help prevent sticking. Grill beef, on a covered grill, over medium Kingsford briquets, 16 to 24 minutes (depending on size and thickness) until a meat thermometer inserted in the center almost registers 150°F for medium-rare. (Cook until 160°F for medium or 170°F well-done; add another 5 minutes for every 10°F.) Turn halfway through cooking. Let stand 5 to 10 minutes before slicing. Slice and serve with a few spoonfuls of sauce.

*Makes 6 servings*

*Substitute 2 tablespoons red wine vinegar *plus* 1½ teaspoons sugar for the balsamic vinegar.

## DIJON−CREAM SAUCE

1 can (14½ ounces) beef broth
1 cup whipping cream
2 tablespoons butter, softened
1½ to 2 tablespoons Dijon mustard
1 to 1½ tablespoons balsamic vinegar*
  Coarsely crushed black peppercorns and mustard
    seeds for garnish

Bring beef broth and whipping cream to a boil in a saucepan. Boil gently until reduced to about 1 cup; sauce will be thick enough to coat a spoon. Remove from heat; stir in butter, a little at a time, until all the butter is melted. Stir in mustard and vinegar, adjusting amounts to taste. Sprinkle with peppercorns and mustard seeds. Makes about 1 cup.

*Substitute 2 teaspoons red wine vinegar *plus* 1 teaspoon sugar for the balsamic vinegar.

*Beef Tenderloin with Dijon-Cream Sauce*

# *Tempting* POULTRY

## CHICKEN RIBBONS SATAY

½ cup creamy peanut butter
½ cup water
¼ cup soy sauce
4 cloves garlic, pressed
3 tablespoons lemon juice
2 tablespoons firmly packed brown sugar
¾ teaspoon ground ginger
½ teaspoon crushed red pepper flakes
4 boneless skinless chicken breast halves
Sliced green onion tops for garnish

Combine peanut butter, water, soy sauce, garlic, lemon juice, brown sugar, ginger and red pepper flakes in small saucepan. Cook over medium heat 1 minute or until smooth; cool. Remove garlic from sauce; discard. Reserve half of sauce for dipping. Cut chicken lengthwise into 1-inch-wide strips. Thread onto 8 metal or bamboo skewers. (Soak bamboo skewers in water at least 20 minutes to keep them from burning.)

Oil hot grid to help prevent sticking. Grill chicken, on a covered grill, over medium-hot Kingsford briquets, 6 to 8 minutes until chicken is cooked through, turning once. Baste with sauce once or twice during cooking. Serve with reserved sauce garnished with sliced green onion tops.

*Makes 4 servings*

*Chicken Ribbons Satay*

# TURKEY GRILLING POINTERS

- Some larger turkey cuts have an automatic cooking device that pops up when the turkey is done. To determine doneness, rely on the automatic cooking device and a meat thermometer inserted in the thickest portion of turkey meat. Breast meat is done at 170°F; dark meat is done at 180°F.

- When turkey is done, the meat just under the skin may look pink. This is not a sign of undercooked meat; this is caused by the smoke from the coals.

## Turkey Grilled with K.C. Masterpiece Barbecue Sauce

| Turkey Product | Method | Approximate Grilling Time on Covered Grill | Brush Barbecue Sauce on During the Last Minutes of Cooking |
|---|---|---|---|
| Bone-in Turkey Breast Half 2 to 3 pounds | Indirect Heat | 1 to 1½ hours | 20 minutes |
| Bone-in Turkey Breast 4 to 6 pounds | Indirect Heat | 2 to 2½ hours | 20 minutes |
| Boneless Turkey Roast 3 pounds | Indirect Heat | 1 to 1½ hours | 20 minutes |
| Turkey Drumsticks ½ pound each | Indirect Heat | 50 to 60 minutes | 15 minutes |
| Bone-in Turkey Thighs ¾ to 1 pound each | Indirect Heat | 50 minutes to 1¼ hours | 15 minutes |
| Turkey Wings ¾ pounds each | Indirect Heat | 50 to 60 minutes | 15 minutes |
| Ground Turkey Burger ½ inch thick, ¼ pound | Direct Heat | 5 to 8 minutes | 3 to 4 minutes |
| Turkey Franks up to 2 ounces each | Direct Heat | 4 to 5 minutes | 2 to 3 minutes |

- Warm extra K.C. Masterpiece Barbecue Sauce to serve on the side with grilled turkey.

# LEMON HERBED CHICKEN

          ½ cup butter or margarine
          ½ cup vegetable oil
          ⅓ cup lemon juice
           2 tablespoons finely chopped parsley
           2 tablespoons garlic salt
           1 teaspoon dried rosemary, crushed
           1 teaspoon dried summer savory, crushed
          ½ teaspoon dried thyme, crushed
          ¼ teaspoon coarsely cracked black pepper
           6 chicken quarters (breast-wing or thigh-drumstick
              combinations)

Combine butter, oil, lemon juice, parsley, garlic salt, rosemary, summer savory, thyme and pepper in a small saucepan. Heat until butter melts. Place chicken in a shallow glass dish. Brush with some of the sauce. Let stand 10 to 15 minutes.

Oil hot grid to help prevent sticking. Place dark meat pieces on grill 10 minutes before white meat pieces (dark meat takes longer to cook). Grill chicken, on an uncovered grill, over medium-hot Kingsford briquets, 30 to 45 minutes for breast quarters or 50 to 60 minutes for leg quarters. Chicken is done when meat is no longer pink by bone. Turn quarters over and baste with sauce every 10 minutes. *Makes 6 servings*

# BARBECUED TURKEY WITH HERBS

           1 turkey (9 to 13 pounds), thawed if frozen
          ¾ cup vegetable oil
          ½ cup chopped fresh parsley
           2 tablespoons chopped fresh sage *or* 2 teaspoons
              dried sage, crushed
           2 tablespoons chopped fresh rosemary *or*
              2 teaspoons dried rosemary, crushed
           1 tablespoon chopped fresh thyme *or* 1 teaspoon
              dried thyme, crushed
          Salt and cracked black pepper

Remove neck and giblets from turkey. Rinse turkey; pat dry with paper towels. Combine oil, parsley, sage, rosemary, thyme, salt and pepper in a small bowl. Brush cavities and outer surface of turkey generously with herb mixture. Pull skin over neck and secure with skewer. Tuck wings under back and tie legs together with cotton string. Insert a meat thermometer into center of thickest part of thigh, not touching bone.

Arrange medium-hot Kingsford briquets on each side of a large rectangular metal or foil drip pan. Pour in hot tap water to fill pan half full. Place turkey breast side up on grid, directly above the drip pan. Grill turkey, on a covered grill, 9 to 13 minutes per pound or until a meat thermometer inserted in the thickest part registers 185°F. Baste occasionally with herb mixture. Add a few briquets to both sides of the fire every hour, or as necessary, to maintain a constant temperature. Garnish with additional fresh herbs, if desired. *Makes 8 to 10 servings*

# CITRUS MARINATED CHICKEN

1 cup orange juice
¼ cup lemon juice
¼ cup lime juice
2 cloves garlic, pressed or minced
4 boneless skinless chicken breast halves
Salt and black pepper
Citrus Tarragon Butter (recipe follows)
Hot cooked couscous with green onion slices and
  slivered almonds (optional)
Lemon and lime slices and Italian parsley for
  garnish

Combine orange, lemon and lime juices and garlic in a shallow glass dish or large heavy plastic bag. Add chicken; cover dish or close bag. Marinate in refrigerator no more than 2 hours. (Lemon and lime juice will "cook" the chicken if it's left in too long.) Remove chicken from marinade; discard marinade. Season chicken with salt and pepper.

Oil hot grid to help prevent sticking. Grill chicken, on a covered grill, over medium Kingsford briquets, 6 to 8 minutes until chicken is cooked through, turning once. Serve topped with a dollop of Citrus Tarragon Butter. Serve over couscous. Garnish, if desired. *Makes 4 servings*

## CITRUS TARRAGON BUTTER

½ cup butter, softened
1 teaspoon finely grated orange peel
1 teaspoon finely grated lemon peel
1 tablespoon lemon juice
1 tablespoon orange juice
1 tablespoons finely chopped fresh tarragon

Beat butter in a small bowl until soft and light. Stir in remaining ingredients. Cover and refrigerate until ready to serve. Makes about ½ cup.

# GRILLED GAME HENS

½ cup K.C. Masterpiece Barbecue Sauce
¼ cup dry sherry
3 tablespoons frozen orange juice concentrate, thawed
4 Cornish game hens (each about 1 to 1½ pounds)

Combine barbecue sauce, sherry and orange juice concentrate in a small saucepan. Bring to a boil. Simmer 10 minutes; cool. Rinse hens; pat dry with paper towels. Brush sauce onto hens. Oil hot grid to help prevent sticking. Grill hens, on a covered grill, over medium-hot Kingsford briquets, 40 to 50 minutes or until thigh moves easily and juices run clear, turning once. Baste with sauce during last 10 minutes of grilling. Remove hens from grill; baste with sauce. *Makes 4 to 6 servings*

*Citrus Marinated Chicken topped with*
*Citrus Tarragon Butter*

# TURKEY PICATTA ON GRILLED ROLLS

¼ cup lemon juice
¼ cup olive oil
2 tablespoons capers in liquid, chopped
2 cloves garlic, crushed
Black pepper to taste
1 pound turkey breast slices
4 soft French rolls, cut lengthwise into halves
4 thin slices mozzarella or Swiss cheese (optional)
Lettuce (optional)
Red pepper slivers (optional)
Additional capers (optional)

Combine lemon juice, oil, 2 tablespoons capers with liquid, garlic and pepper in a shallow glass dish or large heavy plastic bag. Add turkey; cover dish or close bag. Marinate in refrigerator several hours or overnight. Remove turkey from marinade; discard marinade.

Oil hot grid to help prevent sticking. Grill turkey, on an uncovered grill, over medium-hot Kingsford briquets, 2 minutes until turkey is cooked through, turning once. Move cooked turkey slices to edge of grill to keep warm. Grill rolls, cut side down, until toasted. Fill rolls with hot turkey slices, dividing equally. Add mozzarella to sandwiches, if desired. Serve with lettuce, red pepper and additional capers, if desired.

*Makes 4 servings*

# ORANGE–DIJON CHICKEN

*Many supermarkets now carry boneless skinless chicken thighs, and they cook in even less time than boneless breasts. If you prefer dark meat, this recipe is for you.*

⅓ cup vegetable oil
⅓ cup soy sauce
⅓ cup firmly packed brown sugar
⅓ cup frozen orange juice concentrate, thawed
⅓ cup Dijon mustard
8 boneless skinless chicken thighs or 8 bone-in skinless thighs
Salt and black pepper

Whisk together oil, soy sauce, brown sugar, orange juice concentrate and mustard in medium bowl. Place chicken in a shallow glass dish or large heavy plastic bag. Pour marinade over chicken; cover dish or close bag. Marinate in refrigerator at least 2 hours, turning several times. Remove chicken from marinade; discard marinade. Season chicken with salt and pepper.

Oil hot grid to help prevent sticking. Grill chicken, on a covered grill, over medium Kingsford briquets, 4 to 7 minutes for boneless thighs and 15 minutes for bone-in thighs, turning once or twice. Chicken is done when meat is no longer pink in center.

*Makes 4 servings*

# HOT, SPICY, TANGY, STICKY CHICKEN

1 chicken (3½ to 4 pounds), cut up
1 cup cider vinegar
1 tablespoon Worcestershire sauce
1 tablespoon chili powder
1 teaspoon salt
1 teaspoon black pepper
1 teaspoon hot pepper sauce
¾ cup K.C. Masterpiece Barbecue Sauce (about)

Place chicken in a shallow glass dish or large heavy plastic bag. Combine vinegar, Worcestershire sauce, chili powder, salt, pepper and hot pepper sauce in small bowl; pour over chicken pieces. Cover dish or close bag. Marinate in refrigerator at least 4 hours, turning several times.

Oil hot grid to help prevent sticking. Place dark meat pieces on grill 10 minutes before white meat pieces (dark meat takes longer to cook). Grill chicken, on a covered grill, over medium Kingsford briquets, 30 to 45 minutes, turning once or twice. Turn and baste with K.C. Masterpiece Barbecue Sauce the last 10 minutes of cooking. Remove chicken from grill; baste with sauce. Chicken is done when meat is no longer pink by bone.

*Makes 4 servings*

# BARBECUED TURKEY BREAST

1 bone-in turkey breast (about 5 pounds)
¼ cup firmly packed dark brown sugar
2 tablespoons paprika
1 tablespoon minced garlic
1 teaspoon salt
1 teaspoon black pepper
½ teaspoon ground red pepper
1½ cups K.C. Masterpiece Barbecue Sauce (about)

Rinse turkey; pat dry with paper towels. Combine brown sugar, paprika, garlic, salt and peppers in small bowl; rub sugar mixture on inside and outside of turkey breast.

Arrange medium Kingsford briquets on each side of a rectangular metal or foil drip pan. Pour in hot tap water to fill pan half full. Oil hot grid to help prevent sticking. Place turkey breast on grid directly above drip pan. Grill turkey, on a covered grill, 20 to 24 minutes per pound until a meat thermometer inserted in the thickest part registers 170°F. If your grill has a thermometer, maintain a cooking temperature of about 300°F. Add a few more briquets to both sides of the fire after 45 minutes to 1 hour, or as necessary, to maintain a constant temperature. Warm about 1 cup barbecue sauce in a small saucepan to serve with turkey. Brush remaining ½ cup sauce on turkey during the last 20 to 30 minutes of cooking. Let turkey stand 10 minutes before slicing.

*Makes 6 to 8 servings*

# CHICKEN WITH MEDITERRANEAN SALSA

¼ cup olive oil
3 tablespoons lemon juice
4 to 6 boneless skinless chicken breast halves
Salt and black pepper
Rosemary sprigs (optional)
Mediterranean Salsa (recipe follows)
Additional rosemary sprigs for garnish

Combine olive oil and lemon juice in a shallow glass dish; add chicken. Turn breasts to lightly coat with mixture; let stand 10 to 15 minutes. Remove chicken from dish and wipe off excess oil; season with salt and pepper.

Oil hot grid to help prevent sticking. Place chicken on grid and place a sprig of rosemary on each breast. Grill chicken, on a covered grill, over medium Kingsford briquets, 10 to 15 minutes until chicken is cooked through, turning once or twice. Serve with Mediterranean Salsa. Garnish, if desired.

*Makes 4 to 6 servings*

## MEDITERRANEAN SALSA

2 tablespoons olive oil
2 tablespoons white wine vinegar
1 clove garlic, minced
2 tablespoons finely chopped fresh basil *or*
    1 teaspoon dried basil leaves, crushed
1 tablespoon finely chopped fresh rosemary *or*
    1 teaspoon dried rosemary, crushed
1 teaspoon sugar
¼ teaspoon black pepper
10 to 15 kalamata olives*, seeded and coarsely
    chopped *or* ⅓ cup coarsely chopped whole
    pitted ripe olives
½ cup chopped seeded cucumber
¼ cup finely chopped red onion
1 cup chopped seeded tomatoes (about ½ pound)
⅓ cup crumbled feta cheese

Combine oil, vinegar, garlic, basil, rosemary, sugar and pepper in a medium bowl. Add olives, cucumber and onion; toss to coat. Cover and refrigerate until ready to serve. Just before serving, gently stir in tomatoes and feta cheese. Makes about 2 cups.

*Kalamata olives are brine-cured Greek-style olives. They are available in large supermarkets.

*Chicken with Mediterranean Salsa*

# LEMON−GARLIC ROASTED CHICKEN

*The chicken is delicious served simply with its own juices, but this garlic sauce is so good you may want to double the recipe.*

    1 chicken (3½ to 4 pounds)
      Salt and black pepper
    2 tablespoons butter or margarine, softened
    2 lemons, cut into halves
    4 to 6 cloves garlic, peeled, left whole
    5 to 6 sprigs fresh rosemary
      Garlic Sauce (recipe follows)
      Additional rosemary sprigs and lemon wedges for
        garnish

Rinse chicken; pat dry with paper towels. Season with salt and pepper, then rub the skin with butter. Place lemons, garlic and rosemary in cavity of chicken. Tuck wings under back and tie legs together with cotton string.

Arrange medium-low Kingsford briquets on each side of a rectangular metal or foil drip pan. Pour in hot tap water to fill pan half full. Place chicken breast side up on grid, directly above the drip pan. Grill chicken, on a covered grill, about 1 hour until a meat thermometer inserted in the thigh registers 175° to 180°F or until the joints move easily and juices run clear when chicken is pierced. Add a few briquets to both sides of the fire, if necessary, to maintain a constant temperature.

While the chicken is cooking, prepare Garlic Sauce. When chicken is done, carefully lift it from the grill to a wide shallow bowl so that all the juices from the cavity run into the bowl. Transfer juices to a small bowl or gravy boat. Carve chicken; serve with Garlic Sauce and cooking juices. Garnish with additional rosemary sprigs and lemon wedges. *Makes 4 servings*

## GARLIC SAUCE

    2 tablespoons olive oil
    1 large head of garlic, cloves separated and peeled
    2 (1-inch-wide) strips lemon peel
    1 can (14½ ounces) low-salt chicken broth
    ½ cup water
    1 sprig *each* sage and oregano *or* 2 to 3 sprigs
        parsley
    ¼ cup butter, softened

Heat oil in a saucepan; add garlic cloves and lemon peel; sauté over medium-low heat, stirring frequently, until garlic just starts to brown in a few spots. Add broth, water and herbs, simmer to reduce mixture by about half. Discard herb sprigs and lemon peel. Transfer broth mixture to blender or food processor; process until smooth. Return garlic purée to the saucepan and whisk in butter over very low heat until smooth. Sauce can be rewarmed before serving. Makes about 1 cup.

*Lemon-Garlic Roasted Chicken*

# TURKEY BURRITOS

*This recipe is great for casual get-togethers. Just prepare the fixings and let the guests make their own burritos.*

> 1 tablespoon ground cumin
> 1 tablespoon chili powder
> 1½ teaspoons salt
> 1½ to 2 pounds turkey tenderloin, cut into ½-inch cubes
> Lime wedges
> Flour tortillas
> Sour cream (optional)
> Tomato slices for garnish

Combine cumin, chili powder and salt in cup. Place turkey cubes in a shallow glass dish or large heavy plastic bag; pour dry rub over turkey and thoroughly coat. Let turkey stand while preparing Avocado-Corn Salsa. Thread turkey on metal or bamboo skewers. (Soak bamboo skewers in water at least 20 minutes to prevent them from burning).

Oil hot grid to help prevent sticking. Grill turkey, on a covered grill, over medium Kingsford briquets, about 6 minutes until turkey is cooked through, turning once. Remove skewers from grill; squeeze lime wedges on skewers. Warm flour tortillas in the microwave oven, or brush each tortilla very lightly with water and grill 10 to 15 seconds per side. Top with Avocado-Corn Salsa and sour cream, if desired. Garnish with tomato slices.

*Makes 6 servings*

# AVOCADO-CORN SALSA

> 2 small to medium, ripe avocados, finely diced
> 1 cup cooked fresh corn or thawed frozen corn
> 2 medium tomatoes, seeded, finely diced
> 2 to 3 tablespoons lime juice
> 2 to 3 tablespoons chopped fresh cilantro
> ½ to 1 teaspoon minced hot green chili pepper
> ½ teaspoon salt

Gently stir together all ingredients in a medium bowl; adjust flavors to taste. Cover and refrigerate until ready to serve. Makes about 1½ cups.

*Turkey Burritos and Avocado-Corn Salsa*

# Quick & Fabulous
# SEAFOOD

## SNAPPER WITH PESTO BUTTER

½ cup butter or margarine, softened
1 cup packed fresh basil leaves, coarsely chopped *or*
   ½ cup chopped fresh parsley *plus* 2
   tablespoons dried basil leaves, chopped
3 tablespoons finely grated fresh Parmesan cheese
1 clove garlic, minced
   Olive oil
2 to 3 teaspoons lemon juice
4 to 6 red snapper, rock cod, salmon or other
   medium-firm fish fillets (at least ½ inch thick)
   Salt and black pepper
   Lemon wedges
   Fresh basil or parsley sprigs and lemon strips for
   garnish

To make Pesto Butter, place butter, basil, cheese, garlic and 1 tablespoon oil in blender or food processor; process until blended. Add lemon juice to taste. Rinse fish; pat dry with paper towels. Brush one side of fish lightly with oil; season with salt and pepper.

Oil hot grid to help prevent sticking. Grill fillets oil side down, on a covered grill, over medium Kingsford briquets, 5 to 9 minutes. Halfway through cooking time, brush top with oil and season with salt and pepper, then turn and continue grilling until fish turns from translucent to opaque throughout. (Grilling time depends on the thickness of fish; allow 3 to 5 minutes for each ½ inch of thickness.) Serve each fillet with a spoonful of Pesto Butter and a wedge of lemon. Garnish with basil sprigs and lemon strips.
*Makes 4 to 6 servings*

*Snapper with Pesto Butter*

# POINTERS FOR GRILLING FISH

- Firm-textured fish, such as swordfish, shark, tuna, New Zealand hoki and monkfish, are excellent choices for grilling because they don't fall apart easily when grilled.

- Medium-firm fish, such as salmon, mahi-mahi, grouper, orange roughy, halibut and cod, are well suited for grilling, too. These fish are easiest to handle as steaks, fillets with the skin on or fillets at least ¾ inch thick.

- Fish high in oil, such as salmon, bluefish and mackerel, are good for the grill because they retain their moisture in the high, dry heat of grilling and because their flavors are enhanced by smoke.

- Delicate fish, such as sole, flounder, sand dabs or sable fish, are generally less suitable for grilling. They tend to fall through the grid and their delicate flavor is overwhelmed by the smoke.

- Purchase steaks and fillets that are at least ½ inch thick; anything thinner will quickly overcook and fall apart easily on the grid.

- To prevent sticking, the grid should be very clean. Heat the grid 2 or 3 minutes over hot coals, then brush lightly with oil. Baste fish prior to turning to keep it from sticking to the grid.

- Allow 3 to 5 minutes cooking time for each ½ inch of thickness. Fish continues to cook off the grill and you can always return it to cook a bit longer if necessary.

- To test for doneness, separate the fish with a fork or tip of a knife. The flesh will be just slightly translucent in the center, and it will look very moist. As you remove it from the grill, the fish will turn from translucent to opaque throughout.

- Using a grill cover will intensify the smoky flavor and help keep fish moist and tender.

- If you marinate fish, 15 to 30 minutes is all the time you'll need. Long immersion in high-acid marinades (lemon juice, wine, vinegar) causes fish to "cook" like seviche. It actually turns opaque and firm.

- To thread shrimp on a skewer, pierce both the "shoulder" and tail so shrimp forms a U on the skewer.

# COMPOUND BUTTERS FOR GRILLED FISH OR CHICKEN

• *Keep these on hand for mid-week grilling!*

• *Compound butters are a quick and easy way to flavor grilled fish and poultry. They can be made ahead, shaped in a roll and refrigerated or frozen. Slice off what you need and place it on the hot food immediately after removing from the grill. The Honey-Lime Butter can also be melted and used for basting.*

• *Once blended, shape butter into a roll about 1 inch in diameter. Wrap in plastic wrap. Refrigerate up to 1 week; freeze up to 6 weeks.*

## MELON BUTTER

1 cup coarsely chopped cantaloupe, papaya or
    peaches
½ cup butter or margarine, softened
2 tablespoons lime juice
1 teaspoon finely grated lime peel
¼ teaspoon black pepper

In a small saucepan, simmer fruit until softened or microwave fruit in a small microwave-safe dish on HIGH (100% power) 3 minutes.* Cool to room temperature. Place all ingredients in a blender or food processor; process until smooth. Makes about ⅔ cup.

*This recipe was tested in a 700-watt microwave oven. If your oven's wattage is different, the cooking time will need to be adjusted.

## HONEY–LIME BUTTER

½ cup butter or margarine, softened
3 to 4 tablespoons lime juice
1 tablespoon honey
1 clove garlic, pressed or minced
1 teaspoon finely grated lime peel
¼ to ½ teaspoon crushed red pepper flakes

Beat all ingredients in a small bowl until well blended. Makes about ¾ cup.

**Variation:** Add minced or grated ginger.

## NIÇOISE BUTTER

½ cup butter or margarine, softened
¼ cup niçoise olives, pitted, finely chopped
2 tablespoons finely chopped fresh basil

Beat all ingredients in a small bowl until well blended. Makes about ⅔ cup.

# SHRIMP SKEWERS WITH
# TROPICAL FRUIT SALSA

½ cup soy sauce
¼ cup lime juice
2 cloves garlic, minced
1½ pounds large shrimp, shelled and deveined
 Tropical Fruit Salsa (recipe follows)
 Vegetable oil
 Salt and black pepper

Combine soy sauce, lime juice and garlic in a shallow glass dish or large heavy plastic bag. Add shrimp; cover dish or close bag. Marinate in refrigerator no longer than 30 minutes.

Meanwhile, prepare Tropical Fruit Salsa. (Salsa should not be made more than two hours before serving.)

Remove shrimp from marinade; discard marinade. Thread shrimp on metal or bamboo skewers. (Soak bamboo skewers in water at least 20 minutes to keep them from burning.) Brush one side of shrimp lightly with oil; season with salt and pepper.

Oil hot grid to help prevent sticking. Grill shrimp oil side down, on a covered grill, over medium-hot Kingsford briquets, 6 to 8 minutes. Halfway through cooking time, brush top with oil, season with salt and pepper, then turn and continue grilling until shrimp firm up and turn opaque throughout. Serve with Tropical Fruit Salsa.             *Makes 4 servings*

## TROPICAL FRUIT SALSA

2 mangos*
2 kiwifruit
3 tablespoons finely chopped or finely slivered red
 onion
3 tablespoons lime juice
¼ teaspoon salt
⅓ teaspoon crushed red pepper flakes
1 teaspoon sugar
1 tablespoon finely chopped fresh mint leaves
1 tablespoon finely chopped fresh cilantro

Peel fruit. Cut mango into ¼-inch pieces; cut kiwifruit into wedges. Combine with remaining ingredients in medium bowl; adjust flavors to taste. Cover and refrigerate at least 2 hours. Makes about 1 cup.

*Substitute 1 papaya or 2 large or 3 medium peaches for the mangos.

**Tip:** Mangos are available most of the year in many large supermarkets. They are ripe when they yield to gentle pressure; the color of the skin does not indicate ripeness. Unripe mangos will ripen in a few days when stored at room temperature. The mango has a long, flat seed in the center of the fruit that adheres to the flesh. To dice the fruit, first peel the skin, then cut it lengthwise away from the seed, then cut crosswise into ¼-inch pieces.

*Shrimp Skewers with Tropical Fruit Salsa*

# GRILLED FISH STEAKS WITH TOMATO BASIL BUTTER SAUCE

Tomato Basil Butter Sauce (recipe follows)
4 fish steaks, such as halibut, swordfish, tuna or
    salmon (at least ¾ inch thick)
Olive oil
Salt and black pepper
Fresh basil leaves and summer squash slices for
    garnish
Hot cooked seasoned noodles (optional)

Prepare Tomato Basil Butter Sauce; set aside. Rinse fish; pat dry with paper towels. Brush one side of fish lightly with oil; season with salt and pepper.

Oil hot grid to help prevent sticking. Grill fish oil side down, on a covered grill, over medium Kingsford briquets, 6 to 10 minutes. Halfway through cooking time, brush top with oil and season with salt and pepper, then turn and continue grilling until fish turns from translucent to opaque throughout. (Grilling time depends on the thickness of fish; allow 3 to 5 minutes for each ½ inch of thickness.) Serve with Tomato Basil Butter Sauce. Garnish with basil leaves and squash slices. Serve with noodles, if desired. *Makes 4 servings*

## TOMATO BASIL BUTTER SAUCE

4 tablespoons butter or margarine, softened, divided
1½ cups chopped seeded peeled tomatoes (about
    1 pound)
½ teaspoon sugar
1 clove garlic, minced
    Salt and black pepper
1½ tablespoons very finely chopped fresh basil

Melt 1 tablespoon butter in a small skillet. Add tomato, sugar and garlic. Cook over medium-low heat, stirring frequently, until liquid evaporates and mixture thickens. Remove pan from heat; stir in remaining butter until mixture has a saucelike consistency. Season to taste with salt and pepper, then stir in basil. Makes about 1 cup.

*Grilled Fish Steaks with*
*Tomato Basil Butter Sauce*

# SEAFOOD KABOBS

24 large sea scallops
12 medium shrimp, shelled and deveined
 1 can (8½ ounces) whole small artichoke hearts,
    drained and cut into halves
 2 red or yellow peppers, cut into 2-inch pieces
¼ cup olive or vegetable oil
¼ cup lime juice
    Lime slices and sage sprigs for garnish

Thread scallops, shrimp, artichoke hearts and peppers alternately on metal or bamboo skewers. (Soak bamboo skewers in water at least 20 minutes to keep them from burning.) Combine oil and lime juice in a small bowl; brush kabobs with lime mixture.

Oil hot grid to help prevent sticking. Grill kabobs, on an uncovered grill, over low Kingsford briquets, 6 to 8 minutes. Halfway through cooking time, baste top with lime mixture, then turn kabobs and continue grilling until scallops and shrimp firm up and turn opaque throughout. Remove kabobs from grill; baste with lime mixture. Garnish with lime slices and sage sprigs.

*Makes 6 servings*

# SWORDFISH WITH HONEY–LIME GLAZE

½ cup lime juice
3½ tablespoons honey
 2 cloves garlic, minced
½ to 1 serrano or jalapeño chili pepper, fresh or
    canned, seeded and minced
1½ teaspoons cornstarch
    Salt
 2 tablespoons finely chopped fresh cilantro
    (optional)
 6 swordfish steaks (at least ¾ inch thick)
    Black pepper
 2 cups diced seeded tomatoes (about 1½ pounds)
    Cilantro sprigs for garnish

To make Honey-Lime Glaze, combine lime juice, honey, garlic, chili pepper, cornstarch and ½ teaspoon salt in a small saucepan. Boil about 1 minute until slightly thickened, stirring constantly. Stir in cilantro, if desired. Reserve half of Honey-Lime Glaze in a small bowl; cool. Rinse steaks; pat dry with paper towels. Season fish with salt and pepper. Brush fish with some of the remaining glaze.

Oil hot grid to help prevent sticking. Grill fish, on a covered grill, over medium Kingsford briquets, 6 to 10 minutes. Halfway through cooking time, brush top with glaze, then turn and continue grilling until fish turns from transparent to opaque throughout. (Grilling time depends on the thickness of fish; allow 3 to 5 minutes for each ½ inch of thickness.) Stir tomatoes into reserved, cooled glaze and serve as a topping for fish. Garnish with cilantro sprigs.

*Makes 6 servings*

# *Spectacular* SIDE DISHES

## GRILLED VEGETABLES WITH BALSAMIC VINAIGRETTE

*Vegetables cut lengthwise, rather than crosswise, won't slip through the grid.*

     1 medium eggplant (about 1¼ pounds)
     2 medium zucchini
     2 to 3 medium yellow squash
     2 medium red bell peppers
     ¾ cup olive oil
     ¼ cup balsamic vinegar
     1 teaspoon salt
     ¼ teaspoon black pepper
     1 clove garlic, minced
     2 to 3 tablespoons finely chopped mixed fresh herbs
       Herb sprigs for garnish

Trim, then slice eggplant, zucchini and yellow squash lengthwise into
¼- to ½-inch-thick slices. Core, seed and cut red peppers into 1-inch-wide
strips. Place vegetables in a deep serving platter or wide shallow casserole.
Combine oil, vinegar, salt, black pepper, garlic and chopped herbs in small
bowl. Pour vinaigrette over vegetables; turn to coat. Let stand 30 minutes or
longer. Lift vegetables from vinaigrette, leaving vinaigrette that doesn't cling
to the vegetables in the dish.

Oil hot grid to help prevent sticking. Grill vegetables, on a covered grill,
over medium Kingsford briquets, 8 to 16 minutes until fork-tender, turning
once or twice. (Time will depend on the vegetable; eggplant takes the
longest.) As vegetables are done, return them to the platter, then turn to coat
with vinaigrette. (Or, cut eggplant, zucchini and yellow squash into cubes,
then toss with red peppers and vinaigrette.) Garnish with herb sprigs. Serve
warm or at room temperature. *Makes 6 servings*

*Grilled Vegetables with
Balsamic Vinaigrette*

# GRILLED ANTIPASTO PLATTER

16 medium scallops
16 medium shrimp, shelled and deveined
12 mushrooms (about 1 inch diameter)
 3 ounces thinly sliced prosciutto or deli-style ham
16 slender asparagus spears
 1 jar (6½ ounces) marinated artichoke hearts,
     drained
 2 medium zucchini, cut lengthwise into slices
 1 large *or* 2 small red bell peppers, cored, seeded
     and cut into 1-inch-wide strips
 1 head radicchio, cut lengthwise into quarters
     (optional)
    Lemon Baste (recipe follows)
    Lemon wedges

Soak 12 long bamboo skewers in water for at least 20 minutes to keep them from burning. Thread 4 scallops on each of 4 skewers and 4 shrimp on each of another 4 skewers. Thread 6 mushrooms on each of 2 more skewers. Cut prosciutto into 2×1-inch strips. Wrap 2 asparagus spears together with 2 strips of prosciutto; secure with a toothpick. Repeat with remaining asparagus spears. Wrap each artichoke heart in 1 strip of prosciutto; thread on 2 remaining skewers. Place ingredients except radicchio and lemon wedges on a baking sheet. Reserve ¼ cup Lemon Baste. Brush remaining Lemon Baste liberally over ingredients on baking sheet.

Spread medium Kingsford briquets in a wide single layer over the bed of the grill. Oil hot grid to help prevent sticking. Grill skewers, asparagus bundles, zucchini and red peppers, on an uncovered grill, 7 to 12 minutes until vegetables are tender, seafood firms up and turns opaque and prosciutto around wrapped vegetables is crisp, turning once or twice. Remove each item from grill to a large serving platter as it is done. Pour remaining baste over all. Serve hot or at room temperature. Garnish with radicchio and lemon wedges.        *Makes 4 main-dish servings or 8 appetizer servings*

## LEMON BASTE

½ cup olive oil
¼ cup lemon juice
½ teaspoon salt
¼ teaspoon black pepper

Whisk together all ingredients in small bowl until well blended. Makes about ¾ cup.

*Grilled Antipasto Platter*

# GRILLED PIZZA

*A fun idea for parties, these pizzas are assembled on the grill. Because they're individual size, guests can make their own. Create your own combinations or follow the ideas given below.*

**2 loaves (1 pound each) frozen bread dough, thawed\***
**Olive oil**
**K.C. Masterpiece Barbecue Sauce or pizza sauce**
**Seasonings: finely chopped garlic and fresh or dried herbs**
**Toppings: any combination of slivered ham, leftover shredded barbecued chicken and grilled vegetables, such as thinly sliced mushrooms, zucchini, yellow squash, bell peppers, eggplant, pitted olives, pineapple chunks, sliced tomatoes**
**Salt and black pepper**
**Cheese: any combination of shredded mozzarella, Provolone, Monterey Jack, grated Parmesan or crumbled feta**

Divide each loaf of dough into 4 balls. Roll on cornmeal or lightly floured surface and pat out dough to ¼-inch thickness to make small circles. Brush each circle with oil.

Arrange hot Kingsford briquets on one side of the grill. Oil hot grid to help prevent sticking. Vegetables, such as mushrooms, zucchini, yellow squash, bell peppers and eggplant need to be grilled until tender before using them as toppings. (See tip below.)

Place 4 circles directly above medium Kingsford briquets. (The dough will not fall through the grid.) Grill circles, on an uncovered grill, until dough starts to bubble in spots on the top and the bottom gets lightly browned. Turn over using tongs. Continue to grill until the other side is lightly browned, then move the crusts to the cool part of the grill.

Brush each crust lightly with barbecue sauce, top with garlic and herbs, then meat or vegetables. Season with salt and pepper, then top with cheese. Cover pizzas and grill, about 5 minutes until cheese melts, bottom of crust is crisp and pizza looks done. Repeat with remaining dough.

*Makes 8 individual pizzas*

**Note:** Vegetables such as mushrooms, zucchini, yellow squash, bell peppers and eggplant should be grilled before adding to pizza. If used raw, they will not have enough time to cook through. To grill, thread cut-up vegetables on skewers. Brush lightly with oil. Grill vegetables, on an uncovered grill, over hot Kingsford briquets, until tender, turning frequently. Or place a piece of wire mesh on the grid, such as the type used for screen doors, to keep the vegetables from slipping through the grid.

*continued on page 234*

*Grilled Pizzas*

## Pizza Combos

**Ham & Pineapple Pizza:** Brush crust lightly with K.C. Masterpiece Barbecue Sauce and top with minced garlic, slivered ham, grilled bell peppers, pineapple chunks and shredded mozzarella or Monterey Jack cheese.

**Veggie-Herb Pizza:** Brush crust lightly with pizza sauce and top with finely chopped basil, minced garlic and grilled mushrooms, zucchini and green bell pepper. Sprinkle with grated Parmesan cheese.

**Tomato-Feta Pizza:** Top crust with minced garlic and crumbled dried herbs or minced fresh herbs, such as oregano, rosemary and basil. Top with chopped fresh tomato, slivered red onion and coarsely chopped olives. Sprinkle with grated Parmesan cheese and crumbled feta cheese.

*Substitute your favorite pizza crust recipe. Dough for 1 large pizza will make 4 individual ones.

# SKEWERED VEGETABLES

> 2 medium zucchini, cut lengthwise into halves, then
>   cut into 1-inch slices
> 8 pearl onions, cut into halves
> ½ red bell pepper, cut into 1-inch pieces
> 8 fresh medium mushrooms (optional)
> 16 lemon slices
> 2 tablespoons butter or margarine, melted
>   Salt and black pepper

Place zucchini, onions and red pepper in a medium saucepan with enough water to cover. Bring to a boil; cover and continue boiling for 1 minute. Remove with slotted spoon and drain. Alternately thread zucchini, onions, red pepper, mushrooms and lemon slices onto 8 metal or bamboo skewers. (Soak bamboo skewers in water at least 20 minutes to keep them from burning.)

Oil hot grid to help prevent sticking. Grill vegetables, on a covered grill, over medium-hot Kingsford briquets, 6 minutes or until tender, carefully turning skewers once. Season to taste with salt and pepper. Serve immediately.

*Makes 8 servings*

# FIESTA RANCH BEAN DIP

1 envelope (1.0 ounce) Hidden Valley Ranch Fiesta
    Ranch Dip Mix
1 can (16 ounces) refried beans
½ pint (8 ounces) sour cream
1 can (7 ounces) diced green chilies, drained
Shredded cheese, optional

Combine ingredients in a medium saucepan until well blended. Warm over medium heat until heated through, stirring occasionally. Pour into serving bowl; top with cheese. Serve with tortilla chips. *Makes 3½ cups*

# SOUTHWESTERN GUACAMOLE

1 cup mashed avocados (about 2 small)
¼ cup prepared Hidden Valley Ranch Southwestern
    Ranch Creamy Dressing

Combine avocado and dressing in a small bowl until blended. Serve with tortilla chips. *Makes 1 cup*

# CUCUMBER DILL DIP

2 cups prepared Hidden Valley Reduced Calorie
    Party Dip
1 cup chopped seeded peeled cucumber
1 tablespoon grated Parmesan cheese
¼ teaspoon dried dill weed

Combine all ingredients in a small bowl until well blended. Cover and refrigerate 1 to 2 hours to allow flavors to blend. *Makes about 2½ cups*

# MEXICAN–STYLE CORN SALAD

1 can (11 ounces) Mexican-style corn
¼ cup sliced radishes
½ cup prepared Hidden Valley Ranch Southwestern
    Ranch Creamy Dressing

Combine all ingredients in a small bowl until blended. Cover and refrigerate until chilled. *Makes 4 servings*

# NEW TASTE OF
# Mexico

# CONTENTS

Appetizers      **238**

Entrées
     Beef & Pork      **248**

     Poultry      **258**

     Fish & Seafood      **270**

Salads & Side Dishes      **278**

Deluxe Fajita Nachos (*page 242*)

# Appetizers

*Snacking is everyone's favorite pastime. This section is filled with tasty tidbits to satisfy that incredible urge to munch. Many of these festive foods can be enjoyed as main dishes as well.*

## MARIACHI DRUMSTICKS

*A crispy chicken appetizer with Mexican flair.*

1¼ cups crushed tortilla chips
1 package (1.25 ounces) Lawry's
Taco Spices & Seasonings

2 dozen chicken drummettes

In large resealable plastic bag, combine chips and Taco Spices & Seasonings. Dampen chicken with water and shake off excess. Place a few pieces at a time in plastic bag; shake thoroughly to coat with chips. Arrange in greased shallow baking pan. Bake, uncovered, in 350°F oven 30 to 45 minutes or until crispy.

*Makes 2 dozen appetizers*

**PRESENTATION:** Serve with salsa and sour cream for dipping.

**MICROWAVE DIRECTIONS:** Prepare and coat chicken as above. Arrange on 10-inch greased glass pie plate in "spoke" pattern with thick ends of chicken toward outside edge of plate. Cover with waxed paper. Microwave on MEDIUM-HIGH (70% power) 10 minutes, turning plate after 5 minutes.

# CHILE CON QUESO SPREAD

*A great appetizer for parties or to keep in the refrigerator for snacks.*

1 pound mild Cheddar cheese, grated
1 package (3 ounces) cream cheese, softened
½ cup chopped red bell pepper
2 teaspoons Worcestershire sauce
1 can (4 ounces) diced green chiles

3 tablespoons chopped green onion
½ teaspoon hot pepper sauce
½ teaspoon Lawry's Garlic Powder with Parsley
½ teaspoon Lawry's Lemon Pepper Seasoning

In food processor, combine Cheddar cheese, cream cheese, bell pepper and Worcestershire sauce. Pulse until blended. Add remaining ingredients and pulse until blended. Line 2-cup bowl or mold with plastic wrap and fill with cheese mixture. Refrigerate 30 minutes to blend flavors. *Makes 2 cups*

**PRESENTATION:** Unmold cheese spread onto serving plate. Serve with assorted crackers or tortilla chips.

# CRISPY TORTELLINI BITES

*A great addition to your party tray.*

⅓ cup grated Parmesan cheese
1 teaspoon dried basil, crushed
½ teaspoon Lawry's Seasoned Pepper
⅛ teaspoon cayenne pepper
1 package (8 or 9 ounces) cheese tortellini

⅓ cup vegetable oil
1 cup dairy sour cream
¾ to 1 teaspoon Lawry's Garlic Powder with Parsley

In medium bowl, combine cheese, basil, Seasoned Pepper and cayenne; set aside. Cook tortellini according to package directions, omitting salt. Run cold water over tortellini; drain. In large skillet, heat oil. Fry cooled tortellini in oil until golden-crisp; drain. Toss cooked tortellini with cheese-spice mixture. In small bowl, blend sour cream and Garlic Powder with Parsley. Serve tortellini with sour cream mixture for dipping. *Makes 6 servings*

**PRESENTATION:** Serve with frill toothpicks or mini-skewers.

**HINT:** Can also be served with prepared Lawry's Extra Rich & Thick Spaghetti Sauce.

# MOLLETES
## Mexican Toasts

*A quick and easy snack for any time.*

Imperial margarine
8 to 10 French rolls, cut
    lengthwise into halves or
    quarters
Lawry's Garlic Powder with
    Parsley

1 can (16 ounces) refried beans
    Salsa
2 cups (8 ounces) grated Cheddar
    or Monterey Jack cheese

Spread margarine on rolls; lightly sprinkle on Garlic Powder with Parsley. Toast under broiler until just golden. Spread each with refried beans and salsa. Top with cheese. Place under broiler to melt cheese.

*Makes 16 to 20 appetizers*

**PRESENTATION:** Serve with guacamole.

# LAWRY'S FIESTA DIP

*Easy as 1-2-3. A crowd-pleasing favorite.*

1 package (1.25 ounces) Lawry's
    Taco Spices & Seasonings

1 pint (16 ounces) dairy sour
    cream

In medium bowl, combine ingredients. Blend well. Refrigerate until ready to serve.

*Makes 2 cups*

**PRESENTATION:** Serve in medium-size bowls with tortilla chips and fresh cut vegetables such as carrots, broccoli, cauliflower or zucchini sticks.

# SOUTH-OF-THE-BORDER MEATBALLS

*A spicy appetizer ideal for a Mexican fiesta buffet.*

1¼ pounds ground beef
1 package (1.25 ounces) Lawry's
    Taco Spices & Seasonings
¼ cup unseasoned dry bread
    crumbs

¼ cup finely chopped onion
¼ cup finely chopped green bell
    pepper
1 egg, beaten
1½ cups chunky salsa

In large bowl, combine all ingredients except salsa; blend well. Form into 1-inch balls. In large skillet, brown meatballs on all sides; drain fat. Add salsa to skillet. Bring to a boil; reduce heat and simmer, uncovered, 10 minutes.

*Makes 6 servings*

**PRESENTATION:** Serve with your favorite Mexican beer or sangria.

# DELUXE FAJITA NACHOS ▶

*A new twist on everyone's favorite dish.*

2½ cups shredded, cooked chicken
1 package (1.27 ounces) Lawry's
 Spices & Seasonings for
 Fajitas
⅓ cup water
8 ounces tortilla chips
1¼ cups (5 ounces) grated Cheddar
 cheese

1 cup (4 ounces) grated Monterey
 Jack cheese
1 large tomato, chopped
1 can (2¼ ounces) sliced ripe
 olives, drained
¼ cup sliced green onions
 Salsa

In medium skillet, combine chicken, Spices & Seasonings for Fajitas and water; blend well. Bring to a boil; reduce heat and simmer 3 minutes. In large shallow ovenproof platter, arrange chips. Top with chicken and cheeses. Place under broiler to melt cheese. Top with tomato, olives, green onions and desired amount of salsa. *Makes 4 appetizer or 2 main-dish servings*

**PRESENTATION:** Serve with guacamole and sour cream.

**SUBSTITUTION:** 1¼ pounds cooked ground beef can be used in place of shredded chicken.

**HINT:** For a spicier version, add sliced jalapeños.


# EMPANDILLAS

*These are delectable little turnovers.*

½ pound ground beef
1 cup chopped ripe olives
¾ cup chopped fresh mushrooms
¼ cup water
1 package (1.25 ounces) Lawry's
 Taco Spices & Seasonings

1 package (17¼ ounces) frozen
 puff pastry sheets, thawed
1 egg white, beaten

In medium bowl, combine ground beef, olives, mushrooms, water and Taco Spices & Seasonings; blend well. Roll each pastry sheet into a 12-inch square. Cut each sheet into 9 squares. Place approximately 2 teaspoons meat mixture in center of each square; moisten edges with water. Fold one corner over to form triangle and pinch edges together to seal. Brush with egg white. Place on ungreased baking sheet. Bake in 375°F oven 15 to 20 minutes or until golden brown. *Makes 18 appetizers*

**PRESENTATION:** Serve with guacamole and sour cream.

**HINTS:** Two cans (9 ounces) refrigerated crescent roll dough can be used in place of puff pastry sheets. Roll out dough into 12-inch squares. Follow directions above. Stir 3 tablespoons grated cheese into the filling for extra flavor.

# SOUTHWESTERN POTATO SKINS

*Just like the ones you love at restaurants.*

6 large russet potatoes
¾ pound ground beef
1 package (1.25 ounces) Lawry's
   Taco Spices & Seasonings
¾ cup water
¾ cup sliced green onions
1 medium tomato, chopped

1 can (2¼ ounces) sliced ripe
   olives, drained
1 cup (4 ounces) grated Cheddar
   cheese
2 cups Lawry's Fiesta Dip
   (page 241)

Pierce potatoes with fork. Microwave on HIGH 30 minutes, turning over after 15 minutes; let cool. Cut in half and scoop out potatoes leaving ¼-inch shell. In medium skillet, brown ground beef until crumbly; drain fat. Stir in Taco Spices & Seasonings and water. Bring to a boil; reduce heat and simmer, uncovered, 15 minutes. Stir in green onions. Spoon meat mixture into potato shells. Top with tomato, olives and cheese. Place on baking sheet and heat under broiler to melt cheese. Spoon dollops of Lawry's Fiesta Dip on each shell.
*Makes 1 dozen appetizers*

**PRESENTATION:** Sprinkle with additional green onions. Serve with salsa.

# POLENTA STRIPS WITH CREAMY ▶ SALSA SPREAD

*A new way to replace ordinary crackers and chips.*

1 package (8 ounces) cream
   cheese, softened
2 tablespoons chili sauce
2 tablespoons dairy sour cream
1 tablespoon diced green chiles
½ teaspoon Lawry's Seasoned
   Pepper

3 cups water
1 teaspoon Lawry's Seasoned Salt
¾ cup instant polenta, uncooked
¼ cup chopped fresh cilantro
¼ cup grated Parmesan cheese
½ cup vegetable oil

For Creamy Salsa Spread, in small bowl, blend together cream cheese, chili sauce, sour cream, green chiles and Seasoned Pepper; chill. In medium saucepan, bring water and Seasoned Salt to a boil. Add polenta in a slow stream, stirring constantly. Reduce heat; simmer, uncovered, 20 minutes or until mixture pulls away from side of pan. Stir in cilantro. Pour mixture into lightly greased 8×4×3-inch loaf pan. Let cool at least 30 minutes to set. Remove from pan. Cut loaf into very thin slices; sprinkle both sides with cheese. Broil 3 inches from heat 5 minutes or until slightly golden brown. In large skillet, heat oil and fry slices until brown and crisp. Place on paper towels to drain. Serve with Creamy Salsa Spread.
*Makes 3 dozen strips*

**PRESENTATION:** Great with grilled beef, pork or chicken entrées.

**HINT:** To prepare in advance, prepare recipe up to loaf stage, then refrigerate (up to 2 weeks) until ready to fry.

# EIGHT LAYER FIESTA DIP ▶

*This Southwestern favorite is the life of the party.*

1 package (1.25 ounces) Lawry's
  Taco Spices & Seasonings
1 pound ground beef
¾ cup water
1 can (16 ounces) refried beans
½ cup (2 ounces) grated Cheddar
  cheese
1 can (2¼ ounces) sliced ripe
  olives, drained

1 medium tomato, chopped
1 large avocado, mashed
½ cup dairy sour cream
¾ cup salsa
¼ cup thinly sliced green onions
  Tortilla chips

In medium skillet, prepare Taco Spices & Seasonings with ground beef and water according to package directions. Add refried beans and heat 5 minutes. In 1-quart bowl, spread beef and bean mixture. Layer remaining ingredients except tortilla chips in order given above. Serve with tortilla chips for dipping.

*Makes 8 servings*

**PRESENTATION:** Fruit juice coolers make for a refreshing accompaniment.

**MICROWAVE DIRECTIONS:** In 2-quart microwave-safe bowl, place ground beef and microwave on HIGH 5 to 6 minutes, stirring after 3 minutes. Drain fat and crumble beef. Add Taco Spices & Seasonings and ½ cup water; blend well. Cover with waxed paper and microwave on HIGH 6 minutes, stirring after 4 minutes. Add refried beans; blend well. Cover and microwave on HIGH 1½ minutes. Layer as directed above.

# TACOS BOTANAS
## Snacks

*A new way to serve the flavor of tacos.*

2 packages (8 ounces each)
  refrigerated pizza dough
2 cups (3 medium) grated
  zucchini
1 can (16 ounces) refried beans
1 package (1.25 ounces) Lawry's
  Taco Spices & Seasonings

½ cup dairy sour cream
  Salsa
1 cup (4 ounces) grated Cheddar
  cheese
½ cup sliced green onions
1 can (2¼ ounces) sliced ripe
  olives, drained

Roll dough to fit into a 15½×10½×1-inch jelly-roll pan. Bake in 425°F oven 15 minutes or until crisp around edges. Let cool. In small bowl, combine zucchini, refried beans and Taco Spices & Seasonings. Spread bean mixture and sour cream on baked crust. Drizzle on salsa; top with cheese, green onions and olives. Return to oven to melt cheese. Cut into squares. Serve immediately or cover and refrigerate.

*Makes 1 dozen appetizers*

**PRESENTATION:** Serve as an appetizer or as an afternoon snack.

# Entrées

Mexican food means more than tacos and enchiladas. With Lawry's spice and seasoning blends the possibilities for fresh, delicious Mexican ideas are endless. Here we offer a kaleidoscope of entrées to satisfy even the most insatiable appetites.

▼ ▼ ▼

## ━━Beef & Pork ━━

### CARNE ASADA

*An authentic favorite.*

1 (1¼-pound) top sirloin steak
2 tablespoons vegetable oil
½ cup Lawry's Fajitas Skillet
  Sauce

¼ cup orange juice
½ teaspoon dried oregano,
  crushed
Salsa

Pierce steak with fork on both sides and coat with oil; place in large resealable plastic bag. In measuring cup, combine Fajitas Skillet Sauce, orange juice and oregano; pour over steak. Marinate in refrigerator 1 to 2 hours, turning steak occasionally. Remove steak; reserve marinade. Broil steak 4 to 5 minutes on each side until cooked to desired doneness, basting often with reserved marinade. Serve with salsa. *Makes 4 servings*

**PRESENTATION:** Thinly slice steak for taco or burrito filling, or serve with refried beans and Mexican rice for a hearty meal.

## MU SHU-STYLE FAJITAS ▶

*Combining ethnic cuisines creates a flavorful, unique recipe.*

1 tablespoon Imperial margarine
2 eggs, beaten
¼ teaspoon Lawry's Garlic
　　Powder with Parsley
1 medium carrot, diagonally cut
　　into thin slices
2 tablespoons vegetable oil
1 pound boneless pork, cut into
　　thin strips
1 cup Lawry's Fajitas Skillet
　　Sauce

2 cups shredded cabbage
1 cup sliced fresh mushrooms
1 can (8 ounces) sliced bamboo
　　shoots, drained
6 medium green onions,
　　diagonally cut into 1-inch
　　pieces
1 teaspoon lemon juice
8 medium flour tortillas, warmed

In large skillet, melt margarine and scramble eggs with Garlic Powder with Parsley; remove and set aside. In same skillet, sauté carrot in 1 tablespoon oil until crisp-tender; remove and set aside. In same skillet, brown pork in remaining 1 tablespoon oil; drain fat. Add Fajitas Skillet Sauce; blend well. Bring to a boil; reduce heat and simmer, uncovered, 3 to 5 minutes. Add eggs, carrot and remaining ingredients except tortillas; heat 2 minutes until vegetables are crisp-tender. Serve piping hot mixture wrapped in warm flour tortillas.

*Makes 8 servings*

**PRESENTATION:** Serve with plum sauce, if desired.

**HINT:** Also works well with boneless, skinless chicken breast.

## SPICY BURRITO BONANZA

*Spicy pork adds a slight kick to this traditional burrito filling.*

½ pound ground beef
½ pound spicy pork sausage
1 medium tomato, chopped
¼ cup thinly sliced green onions
1½ teaspoons chili powder
½ teaspoon Lawry's Garlic
　　Powder with Parsley

1 can (8¼ ounces) refried beans
6 large flour tortillas, warmed
1½ cups (6 ounces) grated
　　Monterey Jack cheese
Shredded lettuce

In large skillet, brown ground beef and sausage; drain fat. Add tomato, green onions, chili powder and Garlic Powder with Parsley; blend well. Bring to a boil; reduce heat and simmer, uncovered, 10 minutes. Add refried beans; heat 5 minutes. Spread ½ cup meat mixture on each warm tortilla. Top with a sprinkling of cheese and lettuce. Fold in sides and roll to enclose filling.

*Makes 6 servings*

**PRESENTATION:** Serve topped with sour cream and avocado slices.

# ALBONDIGAS SOUP ▶

*An authentic meatball soup.*

1 pound ground beef
¼ cup long-grain rice
1 egg
1 tablespoon chopped fresh
  cilantro
1 teaspoon Lawry's Seasoned Salt
¼ cup ice water
2 cans (14½ ounces each) chicken
  broth

1 can (14½ ounces) whole peeled
  tomatoes, undrained and
  cut up
¼ cup chopped onion
1 stalk celery, diced
1 large carrot, diced
1 medium potato, diced
¼ teaspoon Lawry's Garlic
  Powder with Parsley

In medium bowl, combine ground beef, rice, egg, cilantro, Seasoned Salt and ice water; form into small meatballs. In large saucepan, combine broth with vegetables and Garlic Powder with Parsley. Bring to a boil; add meatballs. Reduce heat, cover and simmer 30 to 40 minutes, stirring occasionally.

*Makes 6 to 8 servings*

**PRESENTATION:** Serve with lemon wedges and warm tortillas.

**HINT:** For a lower salt version, use homemade chicken broth or low-sodium chicken broth.

# FRUITED BEEF KABOBS

*Fruit gives a cool flavor to these spiced kabobs.*

1 small green bell pepper, cut
  into 1-inch pieces
1 can (8 ounces) pineapple
  chunks in juice
¾ pound sirloin steak, cut into
  1-inch cubes
1 can (10½ ounces) mandarin
  oranges, drained

1 onion, cut into wedges
1 package (1.27 ounces) Lawry's
  Spices & Seasonings for
  Fajitas
½ cup undiluted orange juice
  concentrate
½ teaspoon freshly grated orange
  peel

In medium microwave-safe bowl, place bell pepper. Cover and microwave on HIGH 3 minutes. Let cool. Drain pineapple; reserve juice. Alternately thread bell pepper, beef cubes, orange segments, pineapple and onion on wooden skewers. Place kabobs in 13×9×2-inch glass baking dish. Combine Spices & Seasonings for Fajitas, orange juice concentrate, reserved pineapple juice and orange peel; pour over kabobs. Cover and marinate in refrigerator 2 hours or overnight. Bake, covered, in 350°F oven 15 to 20 minutes or until beef is to desired doneness. Uncover, baste with marinade and place under broiler. Broil 1 to 2 minutes to brown.

*Makes 6 servings*

**PRESENTATION:** Serve with crisp green salad and a rice side dish.

**HINT:** If desired, you may omit cooking bell pepper in microwave oven.

# SPICY-SWEET PINEAPPLE PORK ▶

*For those who like their food with extra spice.*

1 pound pork loin, cut into
½-inch strips or cubes
¾ cup Lawry's Fajitas Skillet
Sauce
1 tablespoon finely chopped fresh
ginger
2 tablespoons vegetable oil
1 green bell pepper, cut into
chunks

3 green onions, diagonally sliced
into 1-inch pieces
1 cup hot salsa
3 tablespoons brown sugar
2 tablespoons cornstarch
2 cans (8 ounces each) pineapple
chunks in juice
½ cup whole cashews

Place pork in large resealable plastic bag. Combine Fajitas Skillet Sauce and ginger; add to pork and marinate in refrigerator 1 hour. In large skillet or wok, heat 1 tablespoon oil. Add bell pepper and green onions and stir-fry 3 minutes; remove and set aside. Add pork and remaining 1 tablespoon oil to skillet; stir-fry 5 minutes or until just browned. Return bell pepper and green onions to skillet. In small bowl, combine salsa, brown sugar, cornstarch and juice from one can pineapple. Add to skillet; cook until thickened, stirring constantly. Drain remaining can pineapple. Add all pineapple chunks and cashews; simmer 5 minutes. *Makes 6 servings*

**PRESENTATION:** Serve over hot fluffy rice.

# CANCUN STEAK SANDWICHES

*A surprisingly delicious sandwich.*

1 (¾-pound) flank steak or
London broil
¾ cup Lawry's Fajitas Skillet
Sauce
1 small onion, thinly sliced
1 tablespoon vegetable oil
⅓ cup reduced calorie mayonnaise

2 tablespoons Lawry's Fajitas
Skillet Sauce
8 slices sourdough bread
4 slices Muenster or Monterey
Jack cheese
4 slices pineapple
Vegetable cooking spray

Pierce steak several times with fork; place in large resealable plastic bag. Pour in ¾ cup Fajitas Skillet Sauce. Marinate in refrigerator at least 1 hour. Remove steak; reserve marinade. Broil steak 5 to 7 minutes on each side or until cooked to desired doneness, basting often with marinade. Slice very thinly or shred. In large skillet, sauté onion in oil; set aside. In small bowl, combine mayonnaise and 2 tablespoons Fajitas Skillet Sauce; spread on 4 bread slices. Top each with steak, cheese, pineapple and onion. Top with remaining bread slices. Generously spray skillet with vegetable cooking spray; heat. Place sandwiches in skillet; brown on both sides until golden. *Makes 4 sandwiches*

**PRESENTATION:** Cut in half and serve with fresh fruit and coleslaw.

**HINT:** Using shredded meat makes the sandwich easier to eat.

# GOURMET OLÉ BURGERS ▶

*A spicy version of America's favorite dish.*

1½ pounds ground beef
1 package (1.25 ounces) Lawry's
 Taco Spices & Seasonings

¼ cup ketchup
Monterey Jack cheese slices
Salsa

In medium bowl, combine ground beef, Taco Spices & Seasonings and ketchup; blend well. Shape into patties. Grill or broil burgers 5 to 7 minutes on each side or to desired doneness. Top each burger with a slice of cheese. Return to grill or broiler until cheese melts. Top with a dollop of salsa.

*Makes 6 to 8 servings*

**PRESENTATION:** Serve on lettuce-lined hamburger buns. Garnish with avocado slices, if desired.

**HINT:** Cut cheese with cookie cutters for interesting shapes.

# MEXICALI PIZZA

*A unique combination of Mexican and Italian cuisines.*

Vegetable oil
2 large flour tortillas *or* 4 small
 flour tortillas
1 pound ground beef
1 package (1.25 ounces) Lawry's
 Taco Spices & Seasonings
¾ cup water
1½ cups (6 ounces) grated
 Monterey Jack or Cheddar
 cheese

3 tablespoons diced green chiles
2 medium tomatoes, sliced
1 can (2¼ ounces) sliced ripe
 olives, drained
½ cup salsa

In large skillet, pour in oil to ¼ inch depth; heat. (For small tortillas, use small skillet.) Fry each tortilla about 5 seconds. While still pliable, turn tortilla over. Fry until golden brown. (Edges of tortilla should turn up about ½ inch.) Drain well on paper towels. In medium skillet, brown ground beef until crumbly; drain fat. Add Taco Spices & Seasonings and water; blend well. Bring to a boil; reduce heat and simmer, uncovered, 5 minutes. Place fried tortillas on pizza pan. Layer taco meat, ½ of cheese, chiles, tomatoes, remaining ½ of cheese, olives and salsa. Bake, uncovered, in 425°F oven 15 minutes for large pizzas or 7 to 8 minutes for small pizzas.

*Makes 4 servings*

**PRESENTATION:** For large pizza, cut in wedges for serving. Small pizzas may be cut in half or left whole.

**HINT:** One pound ground turkey or 1½ cups shredded, cooked chicken can be used in place of beef.

# Poultry

## ARROZ CON POLLO BURRITOS ▶
### Chicken with Rice Burritos

*A hearty burrito filling, but still mild enough to be enjoyed
by the entire family.*

2½ cups shredded, cooked chicken
1 package (1.25 ounces) Lawry's
  Taco Spices & Seasonings
3¼ cups water
2 tablespoons vegetable oil
1 cup long-grain rice
1 can (8 ounces) tomato sauce

1 teaspoon Lawry's Lemon
  Pepper Seasoning
1 large tomato, chopped
¼ cup chopped green onions
8 medium flour tortillas, warmed
Grated Cheddar cheese

In large deep skillet, combine chicken, Taco Spices & Seasonings and ¾ cup
water. Bring to a boil; reduce heat and simmer, uncovered, 10 minutes. Remove
and set aside. In same skillet, heat oil. Add rice; sauté until golden. Add remaining 2½ cups water, tomato sauce and Lemon Pepper Seasoning. Bring to a
boil; reduce heat, cover and simmer 20 minutes. Stir in chicken mixture, tomato
and green onions; blend well. Heat 5 minutes. Place a heaping ½ cup filling on
each tortilla. Fold in sides and roll to enclose filling. Place filled burritos seam-
side down on baking sheet. Sprinkle with cheese. Heat in 350°F oven 5 minutes
to melt cheese. *Makes 8 servings*

**PRESENTATION:** Garnish with salsa and guacamole.

## TAMALE SAUCE

*This sauce is thick! For a thinner consistency, add more chicken broth.*

1 small onion, finely chopped
1½ tablespoons vegetable oil
1 can (14½ ounces) stewed
  tomatoes, undrained and
  cut up

1 package (1.62 ounces) Lawry's
  Spices & Seasonings for Chili
1¾ cups chicken broth
¼ cup creamy-style peanut butter

In medium skillet, sauté onion in oil until tender. Stir in tomatoes and Spices &
Seasonings for Chili; blend well. Add chicken broth and peanut butter; blend
well. Bring to a boil; reduce heat and simmer, uncovered, 15 minutes, stirring
occasionally. *Makes about 3 cups*

**PRESENTATION:** Serve over grilled chicken breasts or pork chops. Or, use as
a topping for tamales or in a filling mixture. Garnish with sliced green onions,
if desired.

# AMIGO PITA POCKET SANDWICHES ▶

*A similar flavor to Sloppy Joes—a favorite of kids.*

1 pound ground turkey
1 package (1.25 ounces) Lawry's
    Taco Spices & Seasonings
1 can (6 ounces) tomato paste
½ cup water
½ cup chopped green bell pepper

1 can (7 ounces) whole kernel
    corn, drained
8 pita breads
    Curly lettuce leaves
    Grated Cheddar cheese

In large skillet, brown turkey; drain fat. Add remaining ingredients except pita bread, lettuce and cheese; blend well. Bring to a boil; reduce heat and simmer, uncovered, 15 minutes. Cut off top ¼ of pita breads. Open pita breads to form pockets. Line each with lettuce leaves. Spoon ½ cup filling into each pita bread and top with cheese.               *Makes 8 servings*

**PRESENTATION:** Serve with vegetable sticks and fresh fruit.

# TORTILLA STACK TAMPICO

*A satisfying easy-to-prepare tortilla dish.*

1¼ cups shredded, cooked chicken
1 package (1.25 ounces) Lawry's
    Taco Spices & Seasonings
1 cup water
1 can (8 ounces) tomato sauce
8 medium corn tortillas
2 cups (8 ounces) grated
    Monterey Jack or Cheddar
    cheese

1 can (4 ounces) whole green
    chiles, rinsed and seeds
    removed
1 can (4¼ ounces) chopped ripe
    olives
½ cup salsa
    Sliced green onions

In large skillet, combine chicken, Taco Spices & Seasonings, water and tomato sauce. Bring to a boil; reduce heat and simmer, uncovered, 10 minutes. Lightly grease 12×8×2-inch baking dish. Dip tortillas in chicken mixture. Place 2 tortillas in bottom of baking dish. Top with ½ of chicken mixture. Sprinkle with ⅔ cup cheese and top with 2 more tortillas. Layer whole chiles on top of tortillas. Sprinkle with ½ of olives, reserving 2 tablespoons for garnish. Sprinkle ⅔ cup cheese over olives. Top with 2 more tortillas and remaining chicken mixture. Top with remaining 2 tortillas. Pour salsa over tortillas. Garnish with remaining ⅔ cup cheese, reserved 2 tablespoons olives and green onions. Bake, uncovered, in 350°F oven 15 to 20 minutes or until heated through and cheese melts. Cut each stack into quarters to serve.               *Makes 8 servings*

**PRESENTATION:** Serve with dollops of sour cream and wedges of fresh pineapple and watermelon, if desired.

**HINTS:** If made in advance, cover tightly with foil or plastic wrap to prevent tortillas from drying out. One can (4 ounces) diced green chiles can be used in place of whole chiles.

# ONE SKILLET SPICY CHICKEN 'N RICE ▶

*A one-dish meal with a delightful taco flavor.*

¼ cup all-purpose flour
1 teaspoon Lawry's Seasoned Salt
6 to 8 chicken pieces, skinned
2 tablespoons vegetable oil
2 cans (14½ ounces each) whole
    peeled tomatoes, undrained
    and cut up

1 package (1.25 ounces) Lawry's
    Taco Spices & Seasonings
1 cup thinly sliced celery
1 cup long-grain rice
½ cup chopped onion

In plastic bag, combine flour and Seasoned Salt. Add chicken; shake to coat well. In large skillet, brown chicken in oil; continue cooking, uncovered, over low heat 15 minutes. Add remaining ingredients; blend well. Bring to a boil; reduce heat, cover and simmer 20 minutes or until liquid is absorbed and chicken is cooked through. *Makes 4 to 6 servings*

**PRESENTATION:** Sprinkle with chopped parsley.

# MOLÉ SAUCE FOR CHICKEN OR TURKEY

*This traditional dish is an intriguing harmony of flavors.*

1 small onion, finely chopped
2 tablespoons vegetable oil
1 package (1.62 ounces) Lawry's
    Spices & Seasonings for Chili
3¼ cups chicken broth
1 can (14½ ounces) whole peeled
    tomatoes, undrained and
    cut up

Dash ground cinnamon
Dash ground cloves
¼ cup chunky-style peanut butter
1 square (1 to 2 ounces) Mexican
    chocolate, grated
2 teaspoons sesame seeds
3 pounds chicken or turkey
    pieces, cooked

In Dutch oven, sauté onion in oil until tender. Add Spices & Seasonings for Chili, chicken broth, tomatoes, cinnamon and cloves. Bring to a boil; stir in peanut butter, chocolate and sesame seeds. Reduce heat, cover and simmer 15 minutes, stirring occasionally. Add chicken and heat through.

*Makes 8 servings*

**PRESENTATION:** Sprinkle with additional sesame seeds, if desired. Serve with hot fluffy rice or warm corn tortillas.

**HINT:** If Mexican chocolate is not readily available, use 1 square (1 ounce) semi-sweet chocolate, 1 tablespoon sugar and 2 dashes of cinnamon.

# TOLUCA TATERS ▶

*A hearty meal, sure to please a hungry crowd.*

1 package (1.62 ounces) Lawry's
  Spices & Seasonings for Chili
1 pound ground turkey
1 can (15¼ ounces) kidney beans,
  undrained
1 can (14½ ounces) whole peeled
  tomatoes, undrained and
  cut up

½ cup water
8 medium russet potatoes,
  washed and pierced with fork
1 cup (4 ounces) grated Cheddar
  cheese
½ cup thinly sliced green onions

In large glass bowl, prepare Spices & Seasonings for Chili with ground turkey, kidney beans, tomatoes and water according to package microwave directions; keep warm. Microwave potatoes on HIGH 25 minutes, turning over after 12 minutes. Slit potatoes lengthwise and pull back skin. Fluff with fork. Top each potato with ½ to ¾ cup prepared chili, 2 tablespoons cheese and 1 tablespoon green onions. *Makes 8 servings*

**PRESENTATION:** Top with sour cream, if desired. Serve with a mixed green salad and fresh fruit.

**HINT:** This recipe is a great way to use leftover chili.

# COLACHE CON POLLO
## Mexican Succotash

*Give your pasta dish a new twist and a bite of spice.*

1 pound boneless, skinless
  chicken, beef or pork, cut
  into strips
⅔ cup Lawry's Fajitas Skillet
  Sauce
2 tablespoons Dijon-style mustard
2 teaspoons lime juice
2 tablespoons vegetable oil
1 cup slivered red bell pepper

1 can (7 ounces) whole kernel
  corn, drained
½ cup sliced okra or zucchini
¼ cup sliced green onions
1½ tablespoons chopped fresh
  cilantro
8 ounces linguine, cooked and
  drained

In large resealable plastic bag, place chicken. In small bowl, combine Fajitas Skillet Sauce, mustard and lime juice; pour over chicken. Marinate in refrigerator 2 hours. Remove chicken; reserve marinade. In large skillet, heat oil. Stir-fry chicken 3 minutes or until browned. Add bell pepper, corn, okra and green onions; cook until tender. Add reserved marinade; boil 1 minute longer. Add cilantro. Serve over hot linguine. *Makes 6 servings*

**PRESENTATION:** Top with sour cream, if desired. Serve with fresh bread.

## RIO GRANDE QUESADILLAS ▶

*Quick and easy to prepare—just right for a light main course or snack.*

2 cups shredded, cooked chicken
1 package (1.25 ounces) Lawry's
    Taco Spices & Seasonings
¾ cup water
1 can (16 ounces) refried beans
6 large flour tortillas

1½ cups (6 ounces) grated Monterey
    Jack cheese
¼ cup chopped pimiento
¼ cup chopped green onions
¼ cup chopped fresh cilantro
    Vegetable oil

In medium skillet, combine chicken, Taco Spices & Seasonings and water. Bring to a boil; reduce heat and simmer, uncovered, 15 minutes. Stir in refried beans. On ½ side of each tortilla, spread approximately ⅓ cup of chicken-bean mixture. Layer ¼ each of cheese, pimiento, green onions and cilantro on top. Fold each tortilla in half. In large skillet, heat a small amount of oil and quickly fry folded tortilla on each side until slightly crisp. Repeat with each folded tortilla. *Makes 6 servings*

**PRESENTATION:** Cut each quesadilla in quarters and serve with chunky salsa and guacamole.

## CHICKEN ENCHILADA CASSEROLE

*For a crowd pleasing entrée, simply double the recipe.*

1 medium onion, chopped
2 tablespoons vegetable oil
4 cups shredded, cooked chicken
    or turkey
1 can (15 ounces) tomato sauce
1 can (14½ ounces) whole peeled
    tomatoes, undrained and
    cut up
1 package (1.25 ounces) Lawry's
    Taco Spices & Seasonings

½ teaspoon Lawry's Garlic Powder
    with Parsley
1 dozen medium corn tortillas
2 cans (2¼ ounces each) sliced
    ripe olives, drained
3 cups (12 ounces) grated
    Monterey Jack cheese

In large skillet, sauté onion in oil. Add chicken, tomato sauce, tomatoes, Taco Spices & Seasonings and Garlic Powder with Parsley; blend well. Bring to a boil; reduce heat and simmer, uncovered, 15 minutes. In 13×9×2-inch glass baking dish, place 4 corn tortillas. Pour ⅓ of chicken mixture on tortillas, spreading evenly. Layer with ⅓ of olives and ⅓ of cheese. Repeat layers 2 times, ending with cheese. Bake, uncovered, in 350°F oven 30 to 40 minutes or until heated through and cheese melts. *Makes 8 to 10 servings*

**PRESENTATION:** Serve with prepared Mexican rice and a green salad.

# SIERRA CHICKEN BUNDLES ▶

*Cut into a surprise filling!*

2 cups prepared Mexican or
  Spanish-style rice mix
¼ cup thinly sliced green onions
½ teaspoon Lawry's Seasoned
  Pepper
4 whole boneless, skinless chicken
  breasts

½ cup unseasoned dry bread
  crumbs
¼ cup grated Parmesan cheese
½ teaspoon chili powder
½ teaspoon Lawry's Garlic Salt
¼ teaspoon ground cumin
¼ cup Imperial margarine, melted

In medium bowl, combine prepared rice, green onions and Seasoned Pepper. Pound chicken breasts between 2 sheets of waxed paper to ¼-inch thickness. Place about ⅓ cup rice mixture in center of each chicken breast; roll and tuck ends under and secure with wooden skewers. In pie plate, combine remaining ingredients except margarine; blend well. Roll chicken bundles in margarine, then in crumb mixture. Place seam-side down in 12×8×2-inch baking dish. Bake, uncovered, in 400°F oven 15 to 20 minutes or until chicken is cooked through. Remove skewers before serving. *Makes 4 servings*

**PRESENTATION:** Serve with assorted sautéed vegetables and corn bread.

# LEMON CHICKEN BROIL

*Marinating gives these chicken breasts an extraordinary flavor.*

¼ cup fresh lemon juice
1 can (4 ounces) chopped green
  chiles
3 tablespoons olive or
  vegetable oil
¾ teaspoon Lawry's Lemon
  Pepper Seasoning

½ teaspoon Lawry's Garlic Powder
  with Parsley
½ teaspoon Lawry's Seasoned Salt
1½ pounds chicken breasts
  Lawry's Seasoned Salt

In blender or food processor, combine lemon juice, green chiles, oil, Lemon Pepper Seasoning, Garlic Powder with Parsley and ½ teaspoon Seasoned Salt. Blend until smooth. Place chicken in glass dish; cover with marinade. Refrigerate, covered, at least 1 hour. Remove chicken; reserve marinade. Broil or grill chicken 20 to 25 minutes, turning and basting often with marinade, until chicken is cooked through. Season with additional Seasoned Salt, if desired. *Makes 4 servings*

**PRESENTATION:** Serve with coleslaw and warm flour tortillas.

**HINT:** Do not baste chicken with marinade during last 5 minutes of cooking.

# Fish & Seafood

## TEX-MEX STIR-FRY

*A wonderful blend of Oriental and Mexican flavors.*

2 tablespoons vegetable oil
1½ cups broccoli flowerettes
2 carrots, thinly sliced diagonally
1 red or green bell pepper, thinly sliced
½ cup thinly sliced celery
1 pound medium shrimp, peeled and deveined

⅓ cup Lawry's Fajitas Skillet Sauce
2 tablespoons brown sugar
1 teaspoon ground ginger
1 teaspoon dry mustard
3 cups chilled, cooked rice
Sliced almonds, lightly toasted (optional)

In large skillet or wok, heat 1 tablespoon oil; add broccoli, carrots, bell pepper and celery. Stir-fry 3 minutes. Remove; set aside. Add remaining 1 tablespoon oil and shrimp to same *hot* skillet; stir-fry 3 minutes. Return vegetables to skillet. Pour in Fajitas Skillet Sauce, brown sugar, ginger and mustard. Cook 2 minutes longer, tossing gently to blend. Cover and set aside. In *hot* medium skillet, place chilled rice. Stir-fry over high heat 3 to 5 minutes or until slightly crisp and browned. Serve shrimp and vegetables over rice. Sprinkle with almonds, if desired.

*Makes 6 servings*

**PRESENTATION:** Accompany with almond or fortune cookies.

**HINTS:** One pound thinly sliced boneless chicken or pork can be used in place of shrimp. Add 2 teaspoons chopped cilantro for extra flavor.

# BAJA FRUITED SALMON ▶

*Oranges and grapefruit give an interesting twist to salsa.*

1 large navel orange, peeled and
 diced
1 small grapefruit, peeled and
 diced
1 medium tomato, seeded and
 diced
¼ cup diced red onion
1 small jalapeño, seeded and
 finely chopped

2 tablespoons snipped fresh
 cilantro
2 tablespoons red wine vinegar
1 tablespoon vegetable oil
½ teaspoon Lawry's Seasoned Salt
¼ teaspoon Lawry's Garlic
 Powder with Parsley
4 (5-ounce) salmon steaks
Lemon juice

In medium bowl, combine all ingredients except salmon and lemon juice; re-frigerate. Brush salmon steaks with lemon juice. Grill or broil 5 inches from heat source 5 to 7 minutes on each side or until fish flakes easily with fork. Spoon chilled fruit salsa over salmon. *Makes 4 servings*

**PRESENTATION:** Serve with pan-fried potatoes. Garnish with lemon slices and parsley.

# SEVICHE

*A tropical favorite with the added zest of lemon and herbs.*

½ pound sea scallops, halved
½ pound fresh firm white fish,
 cubed
¼ cup lime juice
¼ cup lemon juice
1 large tomato, seeded and
 chopped
2 tablespoons chopped red onion
2 tablespoons olive or
 vegetable oil

1 tablespoon diced green chiles
1 tablespoon chopped fresh
 cilantro
1 teaspoon Lawry's Seasoned Salt
¼ teaspoon Lawry's Garlic
 Powder with Parsley
¼ teaspoon dried oregano,
 crushed

In large glass bowl, combine scallops and fish with lime and lemon juice. Cover and refrigerate 4 hours or overnight, stirring occasionally. Drain; stir in remaining ingredients. *Makes 4 main-dish or 8 appetizer servings*

**PRESENTATION:** Serve on lettuce leaves with lemon or lime wedges.

**HINT:** Be sure to use the freshest possible scallops and fish.

# SONORA SHRIMP ▶

*A quick and easy recipe to prepare for entertaining on a busy schedule.*

2 tablespoons Imperial margarine
1 medium green bell pepper,
  coarsely chopped
½ cup chopped onion
½ cup chopped celery
1 can (14½ ounces) whole peeled
  tomatoes, undrained and
  cut up
½ cup dry white wine
½ teaspoon Lawry's Seasoned Salt

½ teaspoon Lawry's Seasoned
  Pepper
¼ teaspoon Lawry's Garlic
  Powder with Parsley
¼ teaspoon dried thyme, crushed
1 pound medium shrimp, peeled
  and deveined
1 can (2¼ ounces) sliced ripe
  olives, drained

In large skillet, melt margarine and sauté bell pepper, onion and celery. Add remaining ingredients except shrimp and olives; blend well. Bring to a boil; reduce heat and simmer, uncovered, 15 minutes, stirring occasionally. Add shrimp and olives; cook 10 minutes or until shrimp turn pink.

*Makes 4 to 6 servings*

**PRESENTATION:** Serve over hot fluffy rice.

# PESCADO BORRACHO
## Drunken Fish

*Red wine gives this dish its flavor, as well as its appropriate name.*

1½ pounds red snapper fillets
  All-purpose flour
4 tablespoons vegetable oil
1 small onion, chopped
1 can (14½ ounces) whole peeled
  tomatoes, undrained and
  cut up

1 package (1.25 ounces) Lawry's
  Taco Spices & Seasonings
2 tablespoons diced green chiles
½ cup dry red wine

Dip fish in flour to coat. In large skillet, brown fish in 2 tablespoons oil. In 2-quart oblong baking dish, place browned fish; set aside. Add remaining 2 tablespoons oil and onion to skillet; sauté onion about 5 minutes or until soft. Add remaining ingredients except wine. Bring to a boil, stirring constantly; add wine and blend well. Pour tomato mixture over fish. Bake, uncovered, in 400°F oven 15 to 20 minutes or until fish flakes easily with fork.

*Makes 4 to 6 servings*

**PRESENTATION:** Serve each fillet with sauce; garnish with parsley.

# PESCADO VIEJO ▶
## Fish Stew

*Catch it while it's hot!*

2 medium onions, chopped
1 green bell pepper, diced
1 tablespoon vegetable oil
2 cans (14½ ounces each) whole
   peeled tomatoes, undrained
   and cut up
1 large red potato
1 can (14½ ounces) beef broth
⅓ cup red wine
1 bay leaf

1 package (1.5 ounces) Lawry's
   Original Style Spaghetti Sauce
   Spices & Seasonings
¾ teaspoon Lawry's Garlic
   Powder with Parsley
½ teaspoon Lawry's Seasoned Salt
½ teaspoon celery seed
1 pound halibut or swordfish
   steaks, rinsed and cubed

In Dutch oven, sauté onions and bell pepper in oil until tender. Stir in remaining ingredients except fish. Bring to a boil; reduce heat, cover and simmer 20 minutes. Add fish. Simmer 10 to 15 minutes longer or until fish flakes easily with fork. Remove bay leaf before serving.          *Makes 10 servings*

**PRESENTATION:** Serve with thick, crusty bread sticks.

# SPANISH-STYLE BAKED CATFISH

*Enjoy the full flavors of Spain with this colorful dish.*

1½ pounds catfish fillets
½ cup yellow cornmeal
   Paprika
1 medium onion, chopped
1 tablespoon olive or vegetable oil
1 cup chunky salsa

¼ cup sliced ripe olives
1 teaspoon Lawry's Garlic Salt
1 teaspoon freshly grated lemon
   peel
Chopped fresh parsley

Rinse and cut catfish into serving pieces; dip in cornmeal to coat. Place in lightly greased 12×8×2-inch baking dish. Sprinkle with paprika. Bake in 425°F oven 20 to 25 minutes or until fish flakes easily with fork. In medium skillet, sauté onion in oil 3 minutes or until tender. Stir in salsa, olives, Garlic Salt and lemon peel; heat through. Serve over baked fish. Sprinkle with parsley.
*Makes 6 servings*

**PRESENTATION:** Serve with lemon wedges.

**HINT:** Seasoned dry bread crumbs can be used in place of cornmeal.

# Salads & Side Dishes

*Lawry's seasonings used with everyday staples team up to create savory side dishes that are sure to please. Plus, you'll find a superb selection of sensational salads— many of them meals in themselves.*

## AZTEC CHILI SALAD

*A wonderful way to serve everyone's favorite chili.*

1 pound ground beef
1 package (1.62 ounces) Lawry's
   Spices & Seasonings for Chili
½ cup water
1 can (15¼ ounces) kidney beans,
   undrained
1 can (14½ ounces) whole peeled
   tomatoes, undrained and
   cut up
½ cup dairy sour cream
3 tablespoons mayonnaise

1 fresh medium tomato, diced
¼ cup chopped fresh cilantro
½ teaspoon Lawry's Seasoned
   Pepper
1 head lettuce
1 red bell pepper, sliced
¼ cup sliced green onions
1½ cups (6 ounces) grated Cheddar
   cheese
¼ cup sliced ripe olives

In large skillet, brown ground beef until crumbly; drain fat. Stir in Spices & Seasonings for Chili, water, beans and canned tomatoes; blend well. Bring to a boil; reduce heat and simmer, uncovered, 10 minutes. For dressing, in blender or food processor, blend sour cream, mayonnaise, fresh tomato, cilantro and Seasoned Pepper. Refrigerate until chilled. On 6 individual plates, layer lettuce, chili meat, bell pepper, green onions, cheese and olives. Drizzle with chilled dressing.
*Makes 6 servings*

**PRESENTATION:** Serve with jicama wedges arranged around salad plates.

**HINT:** Ground turkey or shredded chicken can be used in place of ground beef in chili mixture.

## TOMATO-BREAD CASSEROLE ▶

*A perfect side dish for those last minute meals.*

½ pound loaf French bread, sliced
3 tablespoons Imperial
   margarine, softened
1 can (14½ ounces) whole peeled
   tomatoes, cut up
1½ pounds fresh tomatoes, thinly
   sliced
1 cup lowfat cottage or ricotta
   cheese

¼ cup olive or vegetable oil
¾ teaspoon Lawry's Seasoned Salt
½ teaspoon dried oregano,
   crushed
½ teaspoon Lawry's Garlic
   Powder with Parsley
½ cup Parmesan cheese

Spread bread slices with margarine; cut into large cubes. Arrange on jelly-roll pan. Toast in 350°F oven about 7 minutes. Place ½ of cubes in greased 13×9×2-inch baking dish. Drain canned tomatoes, reserving liquid. Top bread cubes with ½ of fresh tomato slices, ½ reserved tomato liquid, ½ of cottage cheese, ½ of oil, ½ of canned tomatoes, ½ of Seasoned Salt, ½ of oregano and ½ of Garlic Powder with Parsley. Repeat layers. Sprinkle with Parmesan cheese. Bake, covered, in 350°F oven 40 minutes. Uncover and bake 5 minutes longer to brown top. *Makes 8 to 10 servings*

**PRESENTATION:** Sprinkle with parsley. Serve with any grilled or baked meat, fish or poultry entrée.

## MONTEREY POTATOES

*Easy and tasty—prepared in the microwave.*

4 cups peeled and sliced russet
   potatoes
¾ cup sliced red bell pepper
¼ cup chopped shallots
1 tablespoon all-purpose flour
1 teaspoon Lawry's Garlic Salt

½ teaspoon dried basil, crushed
¼ teaspoon dry mustard
½ cup milk
1 cup (4 ounces) grated Monterey
   Jack cheese

In lightly greased 8-inch square microwave-safe baking dish, combine potatoes, bell pepper and shallots. Cover with plastic wrap, venting one corner. Microwave on HIGH 10 to 12 minutes, stirring every 4 minutes. Set aside and keep covered. In 2-cup glass measure, combine flour, Garlic Salt, basil and mustard; blend well. Gradually stir in milk. Microwave on HIGH 3 minutes, stirring after 1½ minutes. Add cheese; stir until cheese melts. Pour over potato mixture and toss to coat. *Makes 4 servings*

**PRESENTATION:** Serve as a side dish for most entrées.

# AVOCADO RASPBERRY SPICE SALAD ▶

*This salad is easy to prepare and elegant enough for entertaining.*

¼ cup seedless raspberry jam
3 tablespoons vegetable oil
2½ tablespoons white wine vinegar
¾ teaspoon Lawry's Lemon
    Pepper Seasoning
¾ teaspoon Lawry's Seasoned Salt
2½ cups shredded napa cabbage

1½ cups shredded red cabbage
2 medium tomatoes, cut into
    wedges
1 avocado, cubed
½ medium cucumber, thinly sliced
2 tablespoons chopped green
    onion

In container with stopper or lid, combine raspberry jam, oil, vinegar, Lemon Pepper Seasoning and Seasoned Salt; blend well. On 4 individual serving plates, arrange napa and red cabbage. Decoratively arrange tomatoes, avocado and cucumber on top. Sprinkle with green onion. Drizzle dressing over each serving.                                                                    *Makes 4 servings*

**PRESENTATION:** Serve with a light French bread or croissants.

# SIMPLY GREEN BEANS

*Classic fresh green beans are the star of this dish.*

1 pound fresh green beans, ends
    removed and cut in half
    crosswise
1 tablespoon Imperial margarine,
    melted
3 tablespoons coarsely grated
    Romano cheese

¼ to ½ teaspoon Lawry's Seasoned
    Pepper
¼ teaspoon Lawry's Garlic
    Powder with Parsley

In large saucepan, bring 2 quarts of water to a boil; add beans. After water has returned to a boil, cook beans 4 minutes. Drain; rinse under cold water. In medium skillet, melt margarine; sauté green beans 3 minutes or until tender. Add remaining ingredients; toss well. Serve hot.                    *Makes 4 servings*

**PRESENTATION:** Great accompaniment to roast chicken or fresh fish fillets.

**MICROWAVE DIRECTIONS:** In microwave-safe shallow dish, place green beans and ¼ cup water. Cover with plastic wrap, venting one corner. Microwave on HIGH 14 to 16 minutes, stirring after 7 minutes; drain. Add margarine, Seasoned Pepper and Garlic Powder with Parsley. Stir; let stand covered 1 minute. Sprinkle with cheese.

# SPICY RAVIOLI AND CHEESE ▶

*This spicy pasta dish is perfect for those who like their sauce with a little heat.*

1 medium red bell pepper, thinly
  sliced
1 medium green bell pepper,
  thinly sliced
1 medium yellow bell pepper,
  thinly sliced
1 tablespoon olive or vegetable oil
½ teaspoon Lawry's Seasoned Salt
¼ teaspoon Lawry's Garlic
  Powder with Parsley

¼ teaspoon sugar
1 package (8 or 9 ounces) fresh or
  frozen ravioli
1½ cups chunky salsa
4 ounces mozzarella cheese,
  thinly sliced
2 green onions, sliced

Place bell peppers in baking dish; sprinkle with oil, Seasoned Salt, Garlic Powder with Parsley and sugar. Broil 15 minutes or until tender and browned, turning once. Prepare ravioli according to package directions. Pour ½ of salsa in bottom of 8-inch square baking dish. Alternate layers of bell peppers, ravioli, cheese and green onions. Pour remaining salsa over layers. Cover with foil; bake in 350°F oven 15 to 20 minutes or until heated through and cheese melts.

*Makes 4 to 6 servings*

**PRESENTATION:** Serve as either a side dish or as a main dish.

**HINT:** You may also prepare this recipe in individual casseroles.

# ZUCCHINI MEXICANA

*Lightly seasoned zucchini with a hint of Mexican seasonings.*

1 medium onion, thinly sliced
1 tablespoon vegetable oil
1½ pounds zucchini, thinly sliced
1 can (14½ ounces) whole peeled
  tomatoes, drained and cut up
2 tablespoons diced green chiles
1 teaspoon Lawry's Seasoned Salt

¾ teaspoon Lawry's Garlic Powder
  with Parsley
½ teaspoon Lawry's Seasoned
  Pepper
1 cup (4 ounces) grated Monterey
  Jack cheese

In medium skillet, sauté onion in oil; add remaining ingredients except cheese. Bring to a boil; reduce heat and simmer, uncovered, 5 to 10 minutes. Place zucchini mixture in 8-inch square baking dish and top with cheese. Bake, uncovered, in 375°F oven 10 minutes or until cheese melts.

*Makes 6 to 8 servings*

**PRESENTATION:** Serve as a side dish with other Mexican specialties.

# ACAPULCO SALAD ▶

*Cool, refreshing vegetables dressed with a mild splash of cilantro.*

2 medium navel oranges, peeled,
    sectioned and chopped
2 cups peeled and diced jicama
1 red bell pepper, diced
1 medium cucumber, diced
½ cup thinly sliced radishes
1 large tomato, diced
⅓ cup olive or vegetable oil

3 tablespoons red wine vinegar
2 tablespoons lime juice
1 tablespoon chopped fresh
    cilantro
¾ teaspoon Lawry's Lemon
    Pepper Seasoning
½ teaspoon Lawry's Seasoned Salt

In large bowl, combine oranges and vegetables. In container with stopper or lid, combine remaining ingredients; blend well. Pour over vegetable mixture and toss to coat. Marinate in refrigerator 1 hour before serving.

*Makes 4 servings*

**PRESENTATION:** Serve this salad alongside your favorite Mexican dishes.

# SPAGHETTI SQUASH MEDLEY

*Spaghetti squash is fun to prepare and has a unique texture.*

1 (4-pound) spaghetti squash
1 tablespoon Imperial margarine
½ cup finely chopped onion
¼ cup diced green bell pepper
2 tablespoons chopped pimiento
1½ cups (6 ounces) grated
    Monterey Jack cheese

1 can (2¼ ounces) sliced ripe
    olives, drained
2 tablespoons unseasoned dry
    bread crumbs
¾ teaspoon Lawry's Garlic Salt
½ teaspoon Lawry's Seasoned
    Pepper

Cut squash lengthwise; remove seeds. Bake, cut-side down, in 350°F oven 45 minutes. Turn squash over and bake about 15 minutes or until skin is tender. In small skillet, melt margarine. Sauté onion and bell pepper until tender. Add pimiento; set aside. Remove strands of "spaghetti" squash with fork. Drain squash strands on paper towels 5 minutes. In 1½-quart baking dish, combine squash strands, onion mixture and remaining ingredients. Return to oven 5 to 10 minutes or until cheese melts.

*Makes 6 servings*

**PRESENTATION:** Serve with any meat, poultry or fish entrée.

**MICROWAVE DIRECTIONS:** With fork, deeply pierce squash in several places. Microwave on HIGH 20 minutes, turning squash over after 10 minutes. In small microwave-safe dish, combine margarine, onion and bell pepper; microwave on HIGH 3 minutes or until tender. Add pimiento; set aside. Cut squash in half lengthwise. Remove seeds, then remove strands of "spaghetti" squash with fork. Drain squash strands on paper towels 5 minutes. In 1½-quart glass baking dish, combine squash strands, onion mixture and remaining ingredients. Microwave on HIGH 3 minutes or until cheese melts.

# EL DORADO RICE CASSEROLE ▶

*A creamy, rich casserole with mild seasoning.*

1 can (14½ ounces) whole peeled
   tomatoes, cut up
1½ cups chicken broth
1 medium onion, chopped
1 tablespoon vegetable oil
1 cup long-grain rice

1 teaspoon Lawry's Garlic Salt
1 cup dairy sour cream
1 can (4 ounces) diced green
   chiles
1½ cups (6 ounces) grated
   Monterey Jack cheese

Drain tomatoes, reserving juice. Add reserved juice to broth to make 2½ cups liquid; set aside. In medium saucepan, sauté onion in oil until tender. Add tomato-broth mixture, tomatoes, rice and Garlic Salt. Bring to a boil; reduce heat, cover and simmer 25 minutes or until liquid is absorbed. In small bowl, combine sour cream and chiles. In 1½-quart casserole, layer ½ of prepared rice, ½ of sour cream mixture and ½ of cheese. Repeat layers. Bake, uncovered, in 350°F oven 20 minutes or until bubbly. *Makes 6 servings*

**PRESENTATION:** Top casserole with avocado and pimiento slices.

# TOSTADA SALAD

*This recipe has become a classic for every household.*

1 pound ground beef
1 package (1.25 ounces) Lawry's
   Taco Spices & Seasonings
¾ cup water
1 can (15¼ ounces) kidney beans,
   drained
4 medium tomatoes, cut into
   wedges

1 avocado, thinly sliced
8 ounces tortilla chips
1 head iceberg lettuce, torn into
   bite-size pieces
1 cup (4 ounces) grated Cheddar
   cheese
1 cup chopped onion

In large skillet, brown ground beef until crumbly; drain fat. Add Taco Spices & Seasonings, water and beans; blend well. Bring to a boil; reduce heat, cover and simmer 10 minutes. Reserve some tomato wedges, avocado slices and tortilla chips for garnish. In large salad bowl, combine all remaining ingredients; add ground beef mixture and toss lightly. *Makes 6 to 8 servings*

**PRESENTATION:** Garnish with reserved tomatoes, avocado and tortilla chips. Serve with sour cream and salsa or Thousand Island dressing.

**HINT:** Omit tortilla chips and layer remaining ingredients on heated Lawry's Tostada Shells.

# ENSALADA SIMPLESE ▶

*An easy salad made with everyday ingredients.*

5 cups torn lettuce (combination
    of romaine and iceberg)
½ cup chopped zucchini
1 can (7 ounces) whole kernel
    corn, drained
½ cup diced red bell pepper
¼ cup sliced green onions

⅓ cup dairy sour cream
2 tablespoons mayonnaise
1 teaspoon lemon juice
¾ teaspoon dry mustard
½ teaspoon Lawry's Seasoned Salt
½ teaspoon Lawry's Garlic
    Powder with Parsley

In large bowl, combine lettuce, zucchini, corn, bell pepper and green onions. Refrigerate. In separate small bowl, combine remaining ingredients. Refrigerate. To serve, gently toss greens and dressing.      *Makes 4 to 6 servings*

**PRESENTATION:** Serve on individual salad plates.

**HINT:** Adding shredded, cooked chicken or cooked shrimp turns this salad into a main dish.

# SOUR CREAM TORTILLA CASSEROLE

*A favorite side dish at the Garden Restaurant, Lawry's California Center.*

½ cup chopped onion
2 tablespoons vegetable oil
1 can (28 ounces) whole peeled
    tomatoes, drained and cut up
¼ cup chunky salsa
1 package (1.25 ounces) Lawry's
    Taco Spices & Seasonings

12 corn tortillas
    Vegetable oil
¾ cup chopped onion
1 pound Monterey Jack cheese,
    grated
1½ cups dairy sour cream
    Lawry's Seasoned Pepper

In medium skillet, sauté ½ cup onion in 2 tablespoons oil until tender. Add tomatoes, salsa and Taco Spices & Seasonings. Bring to a boil; reduce heat and simmer, uncovered, 15 minutes. In small skillet, fry tortillas lightly, one at a time, in small amount of oil, 10 to 15 seconds on each side. In bottom of 13×9×2-inch baking dish, pour ½ cup sauce. Arrange layer of 4 tortillas over sauce; top with ⅓ of remaining sauce, ⅓ of onion and ⅓ of cheese. Repeat layers 2 times. Spread sour cream over cheese. Sprinkle lightly with Seasoned Pepper. Bake in 325°F oven 25 to 30 minutes or until heated through and cheese melts.      *Makes 10 to 12 servings*

**PRESENTATION:** Cut into squares.

**HINTS:** One package (1.62 ounces) Lawry's Spices & Seasonings for Chili can be used in place of Lawry's Taco Spices & Seasonings. For convenience, do not fry tortillas.

## SALSA SHRIMP IN PAPAYA ▶

*Salsa adds zesty flavor to shrimp.*

Lemon juice
12 ounces cooked bay shrimp,
   rinsed and drained
¾ cup chunky salsa
½ teaspoon Lawry's Lemon
   Pepper Seasoning

¼ teaspoon Lawry's Garlic Powder
   with Parsley
3 ripe papayas, halved, peeled
   and seeds removed

In medium bowl, sprinkle lemon juice over shrimp. Add salsa, Lemon Pepper Seasoning and Garlic Powder with Parsley; cover and marinate in refrigerator 1 hour or overnight. Fill each papaya half with marinated shrimp.

*Makes 6 servings*

**PRESENTATION:** Arrange papaya halves on lettuce leaves. Garnish each with chopped parsley and lemon slices.

## CELERY SAUTÉ

*This crisp-tender side dish adds variety to almost any meal.*

2 tablespoons Imperial margarine
2 cups diagonally sliced celery
½ cup diagonally sliced green
   onions, including tops
1 can (4 ounces) sliced
   mushrooms, drained

1 can (5 ounces) water chestnuts,
   drained and sliced
1½ teaspoons Lawry's Seasoned
   Salt
½ teaspoon Lawry's Seasoned
   Pepper

In large skillet or wok, melt margarine. Add remaining ingredients and sauté 2 minutes or until crisp-tender, stirring constantly. *Makes 4 servings*

**PRESENTATION:** Serve with any chicken or fish entrée.

## SQUASH OLÉ

*A hearty side dish spiced with the flavors of the Southwest.*

6 medium zucchini
1 can (12 ounces) whole kernel
   corn, drained
2 eggs, beaten
¼ cup chopped chives

2 teaspoons Lawry's Seasoned
   Salt
½ cup (2 ounces) grated sharp
   Cheddar cheese
Paprika

In large saucepan, cook zucchini in boiling water to cover 5 minutes. Cut in half lengthwise; remove pulp. Chop pulp into small pieces, then combine with corn, eggs, chives and Seasoned Salt. Pour mixture into zucchini shells. Place in 2-quart oblong baking dish. Sprinkle with cheese and paprika. Bake, uncovered, in 350°F oven 30 minutes or until cheese melts. *Makes 6 servings*

**PRESENTATION:** Serve with grilled chicken or fish entrées.

# SANTA FE POTATO SALAD ▶

*Enough for a hungry crowd.*

6 medium white potatoes
½ cup vegetable oil
½ cup red wine vinegar
1 package (1.25 ounces) Lawry's
    Taco Spices & Seasonings
1 can (7 ounces) whole kernel
    corn, drained
⅔ cup sliced celery

⅔ cup shredded carrot
⅔ cup chopped red or green bell
    pepper
2 cans (2¼ ounces each) sliced
    ripe olives, drained
½ cup chopped red onion
2 tomatoes, wedged and halved

In large saucepan, cook potatoes in boiling water to cover until tender, about 40 minutes; drain. Cool slightly; cut into cubes. In small bowl, combine oil, vinegar and Taco Spices & Seasonings. Add to warm potatoes and toss gently to coat. Cover; refrigerate at least 1 hour. Gently fold in remaining ingredients. Refrigerate until thoroughly chilled.    *Makes 10 servings*

**PRESENTATION:** Serve in lettuce-lined bowl with hamburgers or deli sandwiches.

**CREAMIER VERSION:** Prepare potatoes as above. Replace the vinegar and oil with ½ cup *each* mayonnaise, dairy sour cream and salsa. Mix with Taco Spices & Seasonings and continue as above.

# SHOESTRING JICAMA SAUTÉ

*Jicama is delicious either raw or cooked.*

½ pound jicama, peeled and
    julienne-cut into 1-inch pieces
½ red bell pepper, julienne-cut
    into 1-inch pieces
½ green bell pepper, julienne-cut
    into 1-inch pieces

1 tablespoon vegetable oil
½ teaspoon Lawry's Lemon
    Pepper Seasoning
½ teaspoon Lawry's Garlic Salt

In medium skillet, sauté jicama and bell peppers in oil. Stir in Lemon Pepper Seasoning and Garlic Salt. Cook until jicama turns golden and vegetables are crisp-tender.    *Makes 4 servings*

**PRESENTATION:** Serve over parsley egg noodles, if desired. A colorful side dish for meat, poultry or fish entrées.

# KIKKOMAN

# Oriental
## Cooking

# CONTENTS

Appetizers     298

Beef     312

Pork     320

Poultry     328

Seafood     338

Side Dishes     344

Spring Rolls (*page 303*),
Classic Chinese Pepper Steak (*page 312*) and
New Year Fried Rice (*page 346*)

# APPETIZERS

## MEAT-FILLED ORIENTAL PANCAKES

*Makes 2 dozen appetizers*

6 Oriental Pancakes (recipe follows)
1 tablespoon cornstarch
3 tablespoons Kikkoman Soy Sauce
1 tablespoon dry sherry
3/4 pound ground beef
1/2 pound ground pork
2/3 cup chopped green onions and tops
1 teaspoon minced fresh ginger root
1 clove garlic, pressed

Prepare Oriental Pancakes on page 300. Combine cornstarch, soy sauce and sherry in large bowl. Add beef, pork, green onions, ginger and garlic; mix until thoroughly combined. Spread 1/2 cup meat mixture evenly over each pancake, leaving about a 1/2-inch border on 1 side. Starting with opposite side, roll up pancake jelly-roll fashion. Place rolls, seam side down, in single layer, on heatproof plate; place plate on steamer rack. Set rack in large pot or wok of boiling water. Cover and steam 15 minutes. (For best results, steam all rolls at the same time.) Just before serving, cut rolls diagonally into quarters. Arrange on serving platter and serve hot.

## ORIENTAL PANCAKES:

Beat *4 eggs* in large bowl with wire whisk. Combine *½ cup water, 3 tablespoons cornstarch, 2 teaspoons Kikkoman Soy Sauce* and *½ teaspoon sugar*; pour into eggs and beat well. Heat an 8-inch omelet or crepe pan over medium heat. Brush bottom of pan with *½ teaspoon vegetable oil*; reduce heat to low. Beat egg mixture; pour ¼ cupful into skillet, lifting and tipping pan from side to side to form a thin round pancake. Cook about 1 to 1½ minutes, or until firm. Carefully lift with spatula and transfer to a sheet of waxed paper. Continue procedure, adding *½ teaspoon oil* to pan for each pancake. Makes 6 pancakes.

# SHRIMP WITH SWEET & SOUR SAUCE

*Makes 10 appetizer servings*

- 2 pounds medium-size raw shrimp
- ⅔ cup vinegar
- ⅔ cup brown sugar, packed
- 2 teaspoons cornstarch
- 2 tablespoons Kikkoman Soy Sauce
- 1 cup water
- ½ teaspoon Tabasco pepper sauce

Peel shrimp, leaving tails on; devein. Simmer in large pot of boiling salted water 5 minutes; drain and cool. Wrap and refrigerate. Combine vinegar, brown sugar, cornstarch, soy sauce and water in small saucepan. Simmer, stirring constantly, until thickened, about 1 minute; stir in pepper sauce. Pour into chafing dish; serve with cold shrimp.

# CRISPY WONTONS

*Makes 10 appetizer servings*

- ¾ pound ground pork
- 8 water chestnuts, finely chopped
- ¼ cup finely chopped green onions and tops
- 1 tablespoon Kikkoman Soy Sauce
- ½ teaspoon salt
- 1 teaspoon cornstarch
- ½ teaspoon grated fresh ginger root
- 1 package (1 lb.) wonton skins
  Vegetable oil for frying
  Tomato catsup and hot mustard *or* Kikkoman Sweet & Sour Sauce

Combine pork, water chestnuts, green onions, soy sauce, salt, cornstarch and ginger in medium bowl; mix well. Place ½ teaspoonful pork mixture in center of each wonton skin. Fold wonton skin over filling to form a triangle. Turn top of triangle down to meet fold. Turn over; moisten 1 corner with water. Overlap opposite corner over moistened corner; press firmly. Heat oil in wok or large saucepan over medium-high heat to 375°F. Deep fry wontons, a few at a time, 2 to 3 minutes, or until brown and crispy. Drain on paper towels. Serve warm with catsup and mustard or sweet & sour sauce, as desired.

# EGG DROP SOUP

*Makes about 12 cups*

- 3 quarts water
- 9 chicken bouillon cubes
- ⅓ cup Kikkoman Soy Sauce
- 6 eggs, well beaten
- 1½ cups finely chopped green onions and tops

Bring water to boil in large saucepan; add bouillon cubes and stir until dissolved. Stir in soy sauce; return to boil. Remove from heat; add eggs all at once, stirring rapidly in 1 direction with spoon. (Eggs will separate to form fine threads.) Stir in green onions. Serve immediately.

*Crispy Wontons*

# EMPRESS CHICKEN WINGS

*Makes 4 to 6 appetizer servings*

1 1/2 pounds chicken wings (about 8 wings)
3 tablespoons Kikkoman Soy Sauce
1 tablespoon dry sherry
1 tablespoon minced fresh ginger root
1 clove garlic, minced
2 tablespoons vegetable oil
1/4 to 1/3 cup cornstarch
2/3 cup water
2 green onions and tops, cut diagonally into thin slices
1 teaspoon slivered fresh ginger root

Disjoint chicken wings; discard tips (or save for stock). Combine soy sauce, sherry, minced ginger and garlic in large bowl; stir in chicken. Cover and refrigerate 1 hour, stirring occasionally. Remove chicken; reserve marinade. Heat oil in large skillet over medium heat. Lightly coat chicken pieces with cornstarch; add to skillet and brown slowly on all sides. Remove chicken; drain off fat. Stir water and reserved marinade into same skillet. Add chicken; sprinkle green onions and slivered ginger evenly over chicken. Cover and simmer 5 minutes, or until chicken is tender.

*Empress Chicken Wings*

# SPRING ROLLS

*Makes 8 appetizer servings*

- 1/2 pound ground pork
- 1 teaspoon Kikkoman Soy Sauce
- 1 teaspoon dry sherry
- 1/2 teaspoon garlic salt
- 2 tablespoons vegetable oil
- 3 cups fresh bean sprouts
- 1/2 cup sliced onion
- 1 tablespoon Kikkoman Soy Sauce
- 1 tablespoon cornstarch
- 3/4 cup water, divided
- 8 sheets egg roll skins
- 1/2 cup prepared biscuit mix
- 1 egg, beaten
  Vegetable oil for frying
  Hot mustard, tomato catsup and
    Kikkoman Soy Sauce

Combine pork, 1 teaspoon soy sauce, sherry and garlic salt; mix well. Let stand 15 minutes. Heat 2 tablespoons oil in hot wok or large skillet over medium-high heat; brown pork mixture in hot oil. Add bean sprouts, onion and 1 tablespoon soy sauce. Stir-fry until vegetables are tender-crisp; drain and cool. Dissolve cornstarch in 1/4 cup water. Place about 1/3 cupful pork mixture on lower half of egg roll skin. Moisten left and right edges with cornstarch mixture. Fold bottom edge up to just cover filling. Fold left and right edges 1/2 inch over; roll up jelly-roll fashion. Moisten top edge with cornstarch mixture and seal. Complete all rolls. Combine biscuit mix, egg and remaining 1/2 cup water in small bowl; dip each roll in batter. Heat oil for frying in wok or large saucepan over medium-high heat to 370°F. Deep fry rolls, a few at a time, in hot oil 5 to 7 minutes, or until golden brown, turning often. Drain on paper towels. Slice each roll in half. Serve with mustard, catsup and soy sauce as desired.

# SHRIMP TERIYAKI

*Makes 10 appetizer servings*

- 1/2 cup Kikkoman Soy Sauce
- 2 tablespoons sugar
- 1 tablespoon vegetable oil
- 1 1/2 teaspoons cornstarch
- 1 clove garlic, crushed
- 1 teaspoon minced fresh ginger root
- 2 tablespoons water
- 2 pounds medium-size raw shrimp, peeled and deveined

Blend soy sauce, sugar, oil, cornstarch, garlic, ginger and water in small saucepan. Simmer, stirring constantly, until thickened, about 1 minute; cool. Coat shrimp with sauce; drain off excess. Place on rack of broiler pan. Broil 5 inches from heat source 3 to 4 minutes on each side, or until shrimp are opaque and cooked. Serve immediately with wooden picks.

# FRESH PINEAPPLE WITH SESAME DIP

*Makes about 6 appetizer servings*

- 2 tablespoons sesame seed, toasted
- 1 package (8 oz.) cream cheese, softened
- 1 tablespoon Kikkoman Soy Sauce
- 1/4 teaspoon Tabasco pepper sauce
- 6 tablespoons water
- 1 fresh pineapple

Crush sesame seed in blender at high speed. Add cream cheese, soy sauce, pepper sauce and water; blend well. Turn into serving bowl; set aside. Cut a thick slice from both top and bottom of pineapple; discard. Peel and remove "eyes." Cut lengthwise into 8 strips; remove core. Cut each strip crosswise into thirds; cut each third lengthwise into 3 bite-size pieces. Serve with sesame dip.

# PRAWNS-IN-SHELL

*Makes 8 appetizer servings*

1 pound large raw prawns
2 tablespoons dry white wine, divided
1/2 teaspoon grated fresh ginger root
1/4 cup vegetable oil
2 tablespoons coarsely chopped green
    onions and tops
1 teaspoon coarsely chopped fresh ginger
    root
1 clove garlic, chopped
2 small red chili peppers,* coarsely
    chopped
1 tablespoon sugar
3 tablespoons tomato catsup
2 tablespoons Kikkoman Soy Sauce
1/2 teaspoon cornstarch

Wash and devein prawns; do not peel. Cut prawns diagonally into halves; place in medium bowl. Sprinkle 1 tablespoon wine and grated ginger over prawns. Heat oil in hot wok or large skillet over high heat. Add prawns; stir-fry until completely pink or red. Add green onions, chopped ginger, garlic and chili peppers; stir-fry only until onions are tender. Combine sugar, catsup, soy sauce, remaining 1 tablespoon wine and cornstarch; pour into pan. Cook and stir until sauce boils and thickens. Serve immediately. Garnish as desired.

*Wear rubber gloves when working with chilis and wash hands in warm soapy water. Avoid touching face or eyes.

# TERIYAKI LAMB RIBLETS

*Makes 8 appetizer servings*

3 pounds lamb breast riblets, cut into
    serving-size pieces
1/3 cup Kikkoman Teriyaki Sauce

Place riblets in large saucepan; add enough water to cover and bring to boil. Reduce heat; simmer, covered, 20 minutes. Remove riblets from saucepan; cool. Pat dry with paper towel to remove excess water. Place riblets on rack of broiler pan; brush thoroughly with teriyaki sauce. Broil riblets about 4 inches from heat source 4 minutes on each side, brushing frequently with teriyaki sauce.

# SESAME PORK TIDBITS WITH SWEET & SOUR SAUCE

*Makes about 3 dozen appetizers*

1 1/2 pounds boneless pork loin
1/2 cup cornstarch
1/4 cup Kikkoman Teriyaki Sauce
3 tablespoons sesame seed, lightly
    toasted
    Sweet & Sour Sauce (recipe follows)
3 cups vegetable oil

Trim excess fat from pork; cut into 1-inch cubes and set aside. Thoroughly combine cornstarch, teriyaki sauce and sesame seed in medium bowl (mixture will be very stiff). Stir in pork cubes; let stand 30 minutes. Meanwhile, prepare Sweet & Sour Sauce; keep warm. Heat oil in medium saucepan over medium-high heat to 300°F. Add 1/3 of the pork cubes and cook, stirring constantly, until golden brown, about 2 minutes. Remove and drain thoroughly on paper towels. Repeat with remaining pork. Serve immediately with warm Sweet & Sour Sauce.

### SWEET & SOUR SAUCE:

Combine *1/4 cup sugar, 1/4 cup vinegar, 1/4 cup catsup, 1/4 cup water, 1 tablespoon Kikkoman Teriyaki Sauce and 1 1/2 teaspoons cornstarch* in small saucepan. Cook over high heat, stirring constantly, until thickened.

*Prawns-in-Shell*

# HOT & SOUR SOUP

*Makes about 5 cups*

- 1 can (10 1/2 oz.) condensed chicken broth
- 2 soup cans water
- 1 can (4 oz.) sliced mushrooms
- 2 tablespoons cornstarch
- 2 tablespoons Kikkoman Soy Sauce
- 2 tablespoons distilled white vinegar
- 1/2 teaspoon Tabasco pepper sauce
- 1 egg, beaten
- 2 green onions and tops, chopped

Combine chicken broth, water, mushrooms, cornstarch, soy sauce, vinegar and pepper sauce in medium saucepan. Bring to boil over high heat, stirring constantly, until slightly thickened. Gradually pour egg into boiling soup, stirring constantly in 1 direction. Remove from heat; stir in green onions. Garnish with additional chopped green onions or cilantro, as desired. Serve immediately.

# BITS O' TERIYAKI CHICKEN

*Makes 6 appetizer servings*

- 1/2 cup Kikkoman Teriyaki Sauce
- 1 teaspoon sugar
- 2 whole chicken breasts, skinned and boned
- 1 teaspoon cornstarch
- 1 tablespoon water
- 1 tablespoon vegetable oil
- 2 tablespoons sesame seed, toasted

Combine teriyaki sauce and sugar in small bowl. Cut chicken into 1-inch pieces; stir into teriyaki sauce mixture. Marinate 30 minutes, stirring occasionally. Remove chicken; reserve 2 tablespoons marinade. Combine reserved marinade, cornstarch and water in small bowl; set aside. Heat oil in hot wok or large skillet over medium-high heat. Add chicken and sesame seed; stir-fry 2 minutes. Stir in cornstarch mixture. Cook and stir until mixture boils and thickens and chicken is tender, about 1 minute. Turn into chafing dish or onto serving platter. Serve warm with wooden picks.

*Hot & Sour Soup*

# POLYNESIAN KABOBS

*Makes 25 appetizers*

1 can (20 oz.) pineapple chunks in syrup
6 tablespoons Kikkoman Soy Sauce
3 tablespoons honey
1 tablespoon dry sherry
1 teaspoon grated orange peel
1/8 teaspoon garlic powder
2 pounds cooked ham, cut into 25 cubes
    (1 inch)
1 pound thickly sliced bacon
25 large stuffed olives
25 cherry tomatoes

Drain pineapple; reserve syrup. Blend syrup, soy sauce, honey, sherry, orange peel and garlic powder in large bowl; stir in ham cubes. Cover; refrigerate 1 hour, stirring occasionally. Cut each bacon slice crosswise in half; wrap pineapple chunks with halved bacon slices. Thread bamboo or metal skewers with a wrapped pineapple chunk, an olive, another wrapped pineapple, a marinated ham cube and a cherry tomato. Place skewers on rack of broiler pan; brush with marinade. Broil 3 to 4 inches from heat source 2 to 3 minutes on each side, or until bacon is crisp.

# BEEF AND FRUIT SKEWERS

*Makes 2 dozen appetizers*

1 can (20 oz.) pineapple chunks in syrup
1/2 cup Kikkoman Soy Sauce
1 tablespoon cornstarch
2 cloves garlic, pressed
2 teaspoons minced crystallized ginger
1 1/2 pounds boneless beef sirloin, about
    1/2 inch thick
1 package (12 oz.) pitted prunes
1 bunch green onions, cut into 1-inch
    lengths
2 dozen drained maraschino cherries
    (optional)

Drain pineapple; reserve syrup. Blend syrup, soy sauce, cornstarch, garlic and ginger in small saucepan. Cook and stir until sauce thickens; cool. Meanwhile, cut beef into 1-inch pieces. Thread beef onto bamboo or metal skewers alternately with pineapple chunks, prunes and green onions (spear through side), ending with cherries. Dip into sauce, brushing to thoroughly coat meat and fruit; drain slightly. Place skewers on rack of broiler pan. Broil to desired degree of doneness, turning once and brushing with sauce.

# GARLIC CHICKEN BUNDLES

*Makes 8 to 10 appetizer servings*

2¼ pounds chicken breasts, skinned and boned

4 tablespoons Kikkoman Soy Sauce, divided

5½ teaspoons cornstarch, divided

4 teaspoons minced garlic, divided

¾ teaspoon sugar

⅓ cup water

2 tablespoons vegetable oil, divided

1 cup diced carrot

½ cup chopped green onions and tops

¼ cup chopped toasted almonds

1 tablespoon minced fresh cilantro or parsley

8 to 10 butter or iceberg lettuce leaves

Cut chicken into ½-inch pieces. Combine 3 tablespoons soy sauce, 4½ teaspoons cornstarch, 3 teaspoons garlic and sugar in small bowl; stir in chicken. Let stand 15 minutes. Meanwhile, combine water, remaining 1 tablespoon soy sauce and 1 teaspoon cornstarch; set aside. Heat 1 tablespoon oil in hot wok or large skillet over high heat. Add chicken and stir-fry 4 minutes; remove. Heat remaining 1 tablespoon oil in same pan. Add carrot and remaining 1 teaspoon garlic; stir-fry 1 minute. Add green onions; stir-fry 1 minute longer. Stir in chicken and soy sauce mixture. Cook and stir until mixture boils and thickens. Remove from heat and stir in almonds and cilantro. To serve, fill each lettuce leaf with about ¼ cup chicken mixture. If desired, fold lettuce around filling to enclose.

*Garlic Chicken Bundles*

*Glazed Ginger Chicken*

# GLAZED GINGER CHICKEN

*Makes 8 appetizer servings*

1 tablespoon sesame seed, toasted
1 tablespoon cornstarch
5 tablespoons Kikkoman Soy Sauce
3 tablespoons plum jam
1 tablespoon minced fresh ginger root
1 clove garlic, pressed
8 small chicken thighs (about 2 pounds)

Cut eight 8-inch squares of aluminum foil; set aside. Combine sesame seed, cornstarch, soy sauce, plum jam, ginger and garlic in small saucepan. Bring to boil over medium heat, stirring constantly. Remove from heat and cool slightly. Stir in thighs, a few at a time, to coat each piece well. Place 1 thigh, skin side up, on each foil square. Divide and spoon remaining sauce evenly over thighs. Fold ends of foil to form a package; crease and fold down to secure well. Place foil bundles, seam side up, in single layer, on steamer rack. Set rack in large pot or wok of boiling water. (Do not allow water level to reach bundles.) Cover and steam 30 minutes, or until chicken is tender. Garnish as desired. Serve immediately.

## SPICY PORK STRIPS

*Makes 6 to 8 appetizer servings*

1 pound boneless pork chops, 1/2 inch thick
1/3 cup Kikkoman Soy Sauce
1/4 cup minced green onions and tops
1 tablespoon sugar
1 tablespoon sesame seed, toasted
3 tablespoons water
1 1/2 teaspoons minced fresh ginger root
1 teaspoon Tabasco pepper sauce
1 clove garlic, minced

Slice pork into 1/4-inch-thick strips, about 4 inches long. Thread onto metal or bamboo skewers, keeping meat as flat as possible. Arrange skewers in large shallow pan. Blend soy sauce, green onions, sugar, sesame seed, water, ginger, pepper sauce and garlic, stirring until sugar dissolves. Pour mixture evenly over skewers; turn over to coat all sides. Let stand 30 minutes, turning skewers over occasionally. Reserving marinade, remove skewers and place on rack of broiler pan; brush with reserved marinade. Broil 3 minutes, or until pork is tender, turning once and basting with additional marinade.

## SAUCY SHRIMP

*Makes 6 appetizer servings*

1/2 pound medium-size raw shrimp
1/4 cup Kikkoman Teriyaki Baste & Glaze
2 tablespoons dry sherry
1 tablespoon lime juice
1 tablespoon sliced green onions and tops
3 to 4 drops Tabasco pepper sauce

Peel, devein and butterfly shrimp. Combine teriyaki baste & glaze, sherry, lime juice, green onions and pepper sauce in medium bowl; stir in shrimp. Cover; refrigerate at least 1 hour, stirring occasionally. Remove shrimp and place on rack of broiler pan. Broil 2 to 3 minutes on each side, or until shrimp are opaque and cooked. Serve immediately with wooden picks.

## BEEF KUSHISASHI

*Makes 10 to 12 appetizer servings*

1/2 cup Kikkoman Soy Sauce
1/4 cup chopped green onions and tops
2 tablespoons sugar
1 tablespoon vegetable oil
1 1/2 teaspoons cornstarch
1 clove garlic, pressed
1 teaspoon grated fresh ginger root
2 1/2 pounds boneless beef sirloin steak

Blend soy sauce, green onions, sugar, oil, cornstarch, garlic and ginger in small saucepan. Simmer, stirring constantly, until thickened, about 1 minute; cool. Cover and set aside. Slice beef into 1/8-inch-thick strips about 4 inches long and 1 inch wide. Thread onto bamboo or metal skewers keeping meat as flat as possible; brush both sides of beef with sauce. Place skewers on rack of broiler pan; broil to desired degree of doneness.

## MARINATED MUSHROOMS

*Makes 4 appetizer servings*

1/4 cup distilled white vinegar
1 tablespoon sugar
2 teaspoons Kikkoman Soy Sauce
1 tablespoon water
1 can (4 oz.) whole mushrooms, drained
Toasted sesame seed (optional)

Thoroughly combine vinegar, sugar, soy sauce and water in small bowl. Add mushrooms and toss to coat; sprinkle with sesame seed. Marinate 45 to 60 minutes, stirring occasionally. Drain off marinade; serve mushrooms with wooden picks.

*Top: Spicy Pork Strips*
*Bottom: Beef Kushisashi*

# BEEF

## CLASSIC CHINESE
## PEPPER STEAK

*Makes 4 servings*

1 pound boneless beef sirloin steak
1 tablespoon Kikkoman Stir-Fry Sauce
2 tablespoons vegetable oil, divided
2 medium-size green, red or yellow bell peppers,
   cut into 1-inch squares
2 medium onions, cut into 1-inch squares
1/4 cup Kikkoman Stir-Fry Sauce
   Hot cooked rice (optional)

Cut beef across grain into thin strips, then into 1-inch
squares; coat with 1 tablespoon stir-fry sauce. Heat 1
tablespoon oil in hot wok or large skillet over high
heat. Add beef and stir-fry 1 minute; remove. Heat
remaining 1 tablespoon oil in same pan. Add peppers
and onions; stir-fry 5 minutes. Stir in beef and 1/4 cup
stir-fry sauce; cook and stir just until beef and
vegetables are coated with sauce. Serve immediately
with rice.

# DRAGON BEEF KABOBS

*Makes 4 servings*

1¼ pounds boneless beef sirloin steak,
  1½ inches thick
¼ cup Kikkoman Teriyaki Sauce
 1 tablespoon peanut butter
 1 teaspoon brown sugar
 1 teaspoon garlic powder
½ teaspoon Tabasco pepper sauce
 1 can (8¼ oz.) pineapple chunks,
  drained

**MICROWAVE DIRECTIONS:**
Cut beef into 1½-inch cubes; place in medium bowl. Blend teriyaki sauce, peanut butter, brown sugar, garlic powder and pepper sauce. Pour mixture over beef, turning pieces over to coat thoroughly. Marinate 1 hour, turning pieces over occasionally. Reserving marinade, remove beef and thread alternately with pineapple chunks on 4 wooden or bamboo skewers. Arrange skewers in single layer on 12-inch round microwave-safe platter. Brush with reserved marinade. Microwave on High 2 minutes. Turn skewers over and rotate positions on platter, moving center skewers to edge. Brush with marinade. Microwave on High 2 minutes longer, or to desired degree of doneness.

# YANGTZE STIR-FRY

*Makes 2 to 3 servings*

½ pound boneless tender beef steak
  (sirloin, rib eye or top loin)
 4 tablespoons Kikkoman Stir-Fry Sauce,
  divided
 1 pound Swiss chard or romaine lettuce
 2 tablespoons vegetable oil, divided
 1 medium onion, cut into ½-inch strips
⅛ to ¼ teaspoon crushed red pepper
⅛ teaspoon salt
½ cup unsalted roasted peanuts

Cut beef across grain into thin slices. Coat with 1 tablespoon stir-fry sauce; let stand 10 minutes. Separate and rinse chard; pat dry. Cut leaves crosswise into 1-inch strips, separating stems from leaves. Heat 1 tablespoon oil in hot wok or large skillet over high heat. Add beef and stir-fry 1 minute; remove. Heat remaining 1 tablespoon oil in same pan. Add chard stems, onion and red pepper. Sprinkle with salt and stir-fry 4 minutes. Add chard leaves; stir-fry 2 minutes. Add beef and remaining 3 tablespoons stir-fry sauce; cook and stir until vegetables are coated with sauce. Remove from heat; stir in peanuts.

# SICHUAN BEEF & SNOW PEAS

*Makes 2 to 3 servings*

½ pound boneless tender beef steak
  (sirloin, rib eye or top loin)
 2 tablespoons cornstarch, divided
 3 tablespoons Kikkoman Soy Sauce,
  divided
 1 tablespoon dry sherry
 1 clove garlic, minced
¾ cup water
¼ to ½ teaspoon crushed red pepper
 2 tablespoons vegetable oil, divided
 6 ounces fresh snow peas, trimmed
 1 medium onion, chunked
  Salt
 1 medium tomato, chunked
  Hot cooked rice

Slice beef across grain into thin strips. Combine 1 tablespoon *each* cornstarch and soy sauce with sherry and garlic in small bowl; stir in beef. Let stand 15 minutes. Meanwhile, combine water, remaining 1 tablespoon cornstarch, 2 tablespoons soy sauce and red pepper; set aside. Heat 1 tablespoon oil in hot wok or large skillet over high heat. Add beef and stir-fry 1 minute; remove. Heat remaining 1 tablespoon oil in same pan. Add snow peas and onion; lightly sprinkle with salt and stir-fry 3 minutes. Add beef, soy sauce mixture and tomato. Cook and stir until sauce boils and thickens and tomato is heated through. Serve immediately with rice.

*Sichuan Beef & Snow Peas*

# KOREAN BEEF &
VEGETABLE SALAD

*Makes 4 servings*

3/4 pound boneless beef sirloin steak
1 tablespoon cornstarch
2 tablespoons Kikkoman Lite Soy Sauce
2 cloves garlic, minced
1 teaspoon sesame seed, toasted
1/4 teaspoon crushed red pepper
   Korean Dressing (recipe follows)
3/4 pound bok choy cabbage
   Boiling water
1/4 pound fresh snow peas, trimmed
1 small cucumber
1/4 pound fresh bean sprouts
1 carrot, cut into julienne strips
1 tablespoon vegetable oil

Cut beef across grain into thin slices, then into strips. Combine cornstarch, lite soy sauce, garlic, sesame seed and pepper in small bowl; stir in beef. Let stand 15 minutes. Meanwhile, prepare Korean Dressing. Separate and rinse bok choy; pat dry. Slice bok choy stems and leaves crosswise into thin strips. Pour boiling water over snow peas in bowl; let stand 30 seconds. Drain; cool under cold water and drain thoroughly. Cut cucumber in half lengthwise; remove seeds. Cut halves crosswise into thin slices. Arrange vegetables on large platter or in shallow bowl; cover and refrigerate until chilled. Heat oil in hot wok or large skillet over high heat. Add beef; stir-fry 2 minutes. Remove from heat and cool slightly; spoon onto platter with vegetables. To serve, pour desired amount of Korean Dressing over meat and vegetables; toss to combine. Garnish as desired.

## KOREAN DRESSING:

Whisk together *2/3 cup mayonnaise, 4 teaspoons lemon juice, 1 tablespoon Kikkoman Lite Soy Sauce, 1 tablespoon minced green onion, 1 tablespoon water* and *2 teaspoons sesame seed, toasted.* Cover and refrigerate until ready to serve.

*Korean Beef & Vegetable Salad*

# BROCCOLI & BEEF
STIR-FRY

*Makes 2 to 3 servings*

1/2 pound boneless tender beef steak
   (sirloin, rib eye or top loin)
1 tablespoon cornstarch
4 tablespoons Kikkoman Soy Sauce,
   divided
1 teaspoon sugar
1 teaspoon minced fresh ginger root
1 clove garlic, minced
1 pound fresh broccoli
1 1/4 cups water
4 teaspoons cornstarch
3 tablespoons vegetable oil, divided
1 onion, chunked
   Hot cooked rice

Cut beef across grain into thin slices. Combine 1 tablespoon *each* cornstarch and soy sauce with sugar, ginger and garlic in small bowl; stir in beef. Let stand 15 minutes. Meanwhile, remove flowerets from broccoli; cut in half lengthwise. Peel stalks; cut crosswise into 1/8-inch slices. Combine water, 4 teaspoons cornstarch and remaining 3 tablespoons soy sauce; set aside. Heat 1 tablespoon oil in hot wok or large skillet over high heat. Add beef and stir-fry 1 minute; remove. Heat remaining 2 tablespoons oil in same pan. Add broccoli and onion; stir-fry 4 minutes. Stir in beef and soy sauce mixture. Cook and stir until mixture boils and thickens. Serve immediately over rice.

# MONGOLIAN BEEF

*Makes 4 servings*

- 3/4 pound boneless tender beef steak (sirloin, rib eye or top loin)
- 3 tablespoons cornstarch, divided
- 4 tablespoons Kikkoman Teriyaki Sauce, divided
- 1 tablespoon dry sherry
- 1 clove garlic, minced
- 1 cup water
- 1 teaspoon distilled white vinegar
- 1/4 to 1/2 teaspoon crushed red pepper
- 2 tablespoons vegetable oil, divided
- 2 carrots, cut diagonally into thin slices
- 1 onion, chunked and separated
- 1 green pepper, chunked

Cut beef across grain into strips, then into 1½-inch squares. Combine 2 tablespoons cornstarch, 1 tablespoon teriyaki sauce, sherry and garlic in medium bowl; stir in beef. Let stand 30 minutes. Meanwhile, combine water, remaining 1 tablespoon cornstarch, 3 tablespoons teriyaki sauce, vinegar and red pepper; set aside. Heat 1 tablespoon oil in hot wok or large skillet over high heat. Add beef and stir-fry 1 minute; remove. Heat remaining 1 tablespoon oil in same pan. Add carrots, onion and green pepper; stir-fry 4 minutes. Add beef and teriyaki sauce mixture; cook and stir until sauce boils and thickens.

*Mongolian Beef*

*Thai Beef Salad*

# THAI BEEF SALAD

*Makes 4 servings*

1 boneless beef sirloin steak, about
   3/4 inch thick (about 1 pound)
3 tablespoons Kikkoman Lite Soy Sauce
3 tablespoons lime juice
2 teaspoons brown sugar
2 large cloves garlic, pressed
2 tablespoons vegetable oil
2 heads butter lettuce, washed and
   drained
2 tablespoons chopped fresh mint
2 tablespoons chopped fresh cilantro
2 tablespoons chopped unsalted roasted
   peanuts

Place steak in large plastic bag. Blend lite soy sauce, lime juice, brown sugar and garlic, stirring until sugar dissolves. Remove 1/4 cup mixture; pour over steak. Press air out of bag; tie top securely. Turn over several times to coat both sides. Marinate 30 minutes, turning bag over occasionally. Meanwhile, combine remaining soy sauce mixture and oil in jar with screw-top lid. Tear lettuce into bite-size pieces and toss with mint and cilantro in large bowl; cover and refrigerate until chilled. Remove steak from marinade and place on rack of broiler pan. Broil 4 minutes on each side (for rare), or to desired degree of doneness. Cut steak across grain into thin slices. Shake dressing and pour over greens; toss to combine. Turn out onto large serving platter; arrange beef slices over greens. Sprinkle peanuts over greens and beef. Serve immediately.

# PORK

## ORIENTAL PORK BUNDLES

*Makes 4 to 6 servings*

Plum Sauce (recipe follows)
1/3 cup Kikkoman Stir-Fry Sauce
 1 clove garlic, pressed
1/2 pound boneless lean pork, diced
1/2 teaspoon vegetable oil
 2 eggs, beaten
 2 tablespoons vegetable oil, divided
 2 stalks celery, diced
 1 medium carrot, diced
 1 small onion, diced
 2 ounces fresh mushrooms, coarsely chopped
 6 (8-inch) flour tortillas, warmed
 3 cups finely shredded iceberg lettuce

Prepare Plum Sauce; cool while preparing filling. Combine stir-fry sauce and garlic. Coat pork with 1 tablespoon stir-fry sauce mixture; let stand 10 minutes. Meanwhile, heat 1/2 teaspoon oil in hot wok or large skillet over medium-high heat. Pour in eggs and scramble; remove. Heat 1 tablespoon oil in same pan. Add pork and stir-fry 3 minutes; remove. Heat remaining 1 tablespoon oil in same pan. Add celery, carrot, onion and mushrooms; stir-fry 4 minutes. Stir in eggs, pork and remaining stir-fry sauce mixture. Cook and stir just until pork and vegetables are coated with sauce. Spread 1 tablespoon Plum Sauce on each tortilla; top with desired amount of shredded lettuce and pork mixture. Wrap or fold over to enclose filling.

### PLUM SAUCE:
Combine *1/4 cup plum jam, 2 tablespoons Kikkoman Stir-Fry Sauce* and *1/2 teaspoon distilled white vinegar* in small saucepan. Cook, stirring constantly, over medium-high heat until mixture comes to a boil and is smooth.

*Tofu & Vegetable Stir-Fry*

# TOFU & VEGETABLE STIR-FRY

*Makes 4 servings*

1/2 block tofu
1 pound napa (Chinese cabbage) or romaine lettuce*
1/2 cup water
2 tablespoons cornstarch, divided
4 tablespoons Kikkoman Soy Sauce, divided
1/4 pound boneless lean pork
2 teaspoons minced fresh ginger root
1 clove garlic, minced
1/2 teaspoon sugar
2 tablespoons vegetable oil, divided
1 medium onion, chunked
2 medium tomatoes, chunked

Cut tofu into 1/2-inch cubes; drain well on several layers of paper towels. Separate and rinse cabbage; pat dry. Cut leaves crosswise into 1-inch strips; set aside. Blend water, 1 tablespoon cornstarch and 3 tablespoons soy sauce; set aside. Cut pork into thin slices, then into thin strips. Combine remaining 1 tablespoon cornstarch and 1 tablespoon soy sauce, ginger, garlic and sugar in small bowl; stir in pork. Heat 1 tablespoon oil in hot wok or large skillet over high heat. Add pork and stir-fry 2 minutes; remove. Heat remaining 1 tablespoon oil in same pan. Add onion; stir-fry 2 minutes. Add cabbage; stir-fry 1 minute. Add tomatoes, pork and soy sauce mixture. Cook and stir gently until sauce boils and thickens. Gently fold in tofu; heat through.

*If using romaine, increase water to 2/3 cup.

# CELEBRATION PORK & RICE

*Makes 4 servings*

- ³/₄ pound boneless lean pork
- 6 tablespoons Kikkoman Stir-Fry Sauce, divided
- ¹/₈ to ¹/₄ teaspoon pepper
- 2 tablespoons vegetable oil, divided
- 1¹/₂ cups frozen peas & carrots, thawed
- ¹/₂ cup chopped onion
- ¹/₈ teaspoon salt
- 3¹/₂ cups cold cooked rice

Cut pork across grain into thin slices, then into slivers; combine with 2 tablespoons stir-fry sauce. Stir pepper into remaining 4 tablespoons stir-fry sauce; set aside. Heat 1 tablespoon oil in hot wok or large skillet over high heat. Add pork and stir-fry 3 minutes; remove. Heat remaining 1 tablespoon oil in same pan. Add peas & carrots, onion and salt; stir-fry 2 minutes. Remove from heat and gently stir in rice to combine. Return to medium-high heat; stir in pork and stir-fry sauce mixture. Cook and stir until rice is thoroughly heated and coated with sauce.

# BAKE & GLAZE TERI RIBS

*Makes 4 servings*

- 3 pounds pork spareribs
- ¹/₂ teaspoon garlic powder
- ¹/₂ teaspoon pepper
- ²/₃ cup Kikkoman Teriyaki Baste & Glaze
- ¹/₂ teaspoon grated lemon peel

Cut ribs into serving pieces; place, meaty side up, in shallow foil-lined baking pan. Sprinkle garlic powder and pepper evenly over ribs; cover pan loosely with foil. Bake in 350°F. oven 45 minutes. Meanwhile, combine teriyaki baste & glaze and lemon peel. Remove foil and brush both sides of ribs with baste & glaze mixture. Cover and bake 40 minutes longer, or until ribs are tender, brushing with baste & glaze mixture occasionally.

*Celebration Pork & Rice*

# PORK CHOPS TERIYAKI

*Makes 4 to 6 servings*

1 can (8 oz.) pineapple chunks in juice
1 tablespoon vegetable oil
6 boneless pork chops, ³/₄ inch thick
¹/₂ cup Kikkoman Teriyaki Sauce
¹/₄ cup water
1 clove garlic, minced
1 tablespoon sesame seed, toasted
2 teaspoons grated fresh ginger root
1 tablespoon cornstarch
1 tablespoon water
¹/₂ cup finely chopped green onions and tops

Drain pineapple; reserve juice. Heat oil in Dutch oven over medium-high heat. Brown pork chops on both sides in hot oil. Combine reserved juice, teriyaki sauce, ¹/₄ cup water, garlic, sesame seed and ginger; pour over chops and simmer, covered, 30 minutes. Turn chops over and continue cooking, covered, 30 minutes longer, or until chops are tender; remove. Dissolve cornstarch in 1 tablespoon water and stir into pan juices. Cook and stir until sauce boils and thickens. Stir in pineapple chunks and green onions, cooking until pineapple is heated through. Return chops to pan and coat both sides with sauce.

# SICHUAN PORK SALAD

*Makes 2 to 3 servings*

¹/₂ pound boneless lean pork
4 tablespoons Kikkoman Teriyaki Sauce, divided
¹/₈ to ¹/₄ teaspoon crushed red pepper
1 cup water
2 tablespoons cornstarch
1 tablespoon distilled white vinegar
2 tablespoons vegetable oil, divided
1 onion, chunked and separated
12 radishes, thinly sliced
2 medium zucchini, cut into julienne strips
Salt
4 cups shredded lettuce

Cut pork across grain into thin slices, then into narrow strips. Combine pork, 1 tablespoon teriyaki sauce and red pepper in small bowl; set aside. Combine water, cornstarch, remaining 3 tablespoons teriyaki sauce and vinegar; set aside. Heat 1 tablespoon oil in hot wok or large skillet over high heat. Add pork and stir-fry 2 minutes; remove. Heat remaining 1 tablespoon oil in same pan. Add onion; stir-fry 2 minutes. Add radishes and zucchini; lightly sprinkle with salt and stir-fry 1 minute longer. Stir in pork and teriyaki sauce mixture. Cook and stir until mixture boils and thickens. Spoon over bed of lettuce on serving platter; serve immediately.

# SPICY SICHUAN PORK STEW

*Makes 6 servings*

2 pounds boneless pork shoulder (Boston butt)
¹/₄ cup all-purpose flour
2 tablespoons vegetable oil
1³/₄ cups water, divided
¹/₄ cup Kikkoman Soy Sauce
3 tablespoons dry sherry
2 cloves garlic, pressed
1 teaspoon minced fresh ginger root
¹/₂ teaspoon crushed red pepper
¹/₄ teaspoon fennel seed, crushed
8 green onions and tops, cut into 1-inch lengths, separating whites from tops
2 large carrots, chunked
Hot cooked rice

Cut pork into 1-inch cubes. Coat in flour; reserve 2 tablespoons flour. Heat oil in Dutch oven or large pan over medium-high heat; brown pork on all sides in hot oil. Add 1¹/₂ cups water, soy sauce, sherry, garlic, ginger, red pepper, fennel and white parts of green onions. Cover pan; bring to boil. Reduce heat and simmer 30 minutes. Add carrots; simmer, covered, 30 minutes longer, or until pork and carrots are tender. Meanwhile, combine reserved flour and remaining ¹/₄ cup water; set aside. Stir green onion tops into pork mixture; simmer 1 minute. Add flour mixture; bring to boil. Cook and stir until mixture is slightly thickened. Serve over rice.

*Spicy Sichuan Pork Stew*

# CRISPY LITE SPARERIBS

*Makes 4 to 6 servings*

**4 pounds pork spareribs, sawed into thirds across bones**
**¼ cup Kikkoman Lite Soy Sauce**
**2 tablespoons dry sherry**
**1 clove garlic, pressed**
**Mandarin Peach Sauce (recipe follows)**

Cut ribs into 1-rib pieces. Place in steamer basket or on steamer rack. Set basket in large pot or wok of boiling water. (Do not allow water level to reach ribs.) Cover and steam 30 minutes. Meanwhile, combine lite soy sauce, sherry and garlic in large bowl; add ribs and stir to coat each piece well. Marinate 1 hour, stirring frequently. Remove ribs and place, meaty side up, on rack of broiler pan. Bake in 425°F. oven 15 minutes, or until crispy. Serve with warm Mandarin Peach Sauce.

### MANDARIN PEACH SAUCE:

Drain *1 can (16 oz.) cling peach slices in juice or extra light syrup;* reserve liquid for another use. Place peaches in blender container. Process on high speed until smooth; pour into small saucepan. Combine *3 tablespoons Kikkoman Teriyaki Sauce* and *1 tablespoon cornstarch;* stir into peaches with *1 tablespoon sugar, ¼ teaspoon fennel seed, crushed, ¼ teaspoon pepper* and *⅛ teaspoon ground cloves.* Bring mixture to boil over medium heat. Simmer until sauce thickens, about 2 minutes, stirring constantly. Remove from heat and stir in *⅛ teaspoon garlic powder.* Makes 1 cup.

# HAWAIIAN PORK STEW

*Makes 6 servings*

**2 pounds boneless pork shoulder (Boston butt)**
**¼ cup all-purpose flour**
**1 teaspoon ground ginger**
**2 tablespoons vegetable oil**
**1 can (8 oz.) pineapple chunks in juice**
**1¾ cups water, divided**
**⅓ cup Kikkoman Teriyaki Sauce**
**1 pound fresh yams or sweet potatoes, peeled and cut into 2-inch chunks**
**1 large onion, cut into eighths**
**Hot cooked rice**

Cut pork into 1½-inch cubes. Coat in mixture of flour and ginger; reserve 2 tablespoons flour mixture. Heat oil in Dutch oven or large pan; brown pork on all sides in hot oil. Drain pineapple; reserve juice. Add juice, 1 cup water and teriyaki sauce to pork. Cover pan; bring to boil. Reduce heat and simmer 1 hour, stirring occasionally. Add yams to pork; simmer, covered, 10 minutes. Stir in onion; simmer, covered, 20 minutes longer, or until pork and yams are tender. Meanwhile, combine reserved flour mixture and remaining ¾ cup water; stir into pork mixture and cook until slightly thickened. Stir in pineapple; cook only until heated through. Serve with rice.

# GLAZED PORK ROAST

*Makes 6 servings*

**1 (3-pound) boneless pork shoulder roast (Boston butt)**
**1 cup Kikkoman Teriyaki Sauce**
**3 tablespoons brown sugar, packed**
**3 tablespoons dry sherry**
**1 teaspoon minced fresh ginger root**
**1 clove garlic, minced**
**¼ cup water**
**2 tablespoons sugar**
**1 tablespoon cornstarch**

### MICROWAVE DIRECTIONS:

Pierce meaty parts of roast with fork; place in large plastic bag. Combine teriyaki sauce, brown sugar, sherry, ginger and garlic; pour over roast. Press air out of bag; tie top securely. Refrigerate 8 hours or overnight, turning bag over occasionally. Reserving marinade, remove roast and place, fat side down, in 8×8-inch shallow microwave-safe dish. Brush thoroughly with reserved marinade. Cover roast loosely with waxed paper. Microwave on Medium-high (70%) 30 minutes, or until meat thermometer inserted into thickest part registers 165°F., rotating dish once and brushing with marinade. Remove roast; let stand 10 minutes before slicing. Meanwhile, combine reserved marinade, water, sugar and cornstarch in 2-cup microwave-safe measuring cup. Microwave on High 3 minutes, until mixture boils and thickens, stirring occasionally. Serve teriyaki glaze with roast.

# HUNAN STIR-FRY WITH TOFU

*Makes 4 servings*

1 block tofu
1/2 pound ground pork
1 tablespoon dry sherry
1 teaspoon minced fresh ginger root
1 clove garlic, minced
1/2 cup regular-strength chicken broth
1 tablespoon cornstarch
3 tablespoons Kikkoman Soy Sauce
1 tablespoon vinegar
1/2 teaspoon crushed red pepper
1 tablespoon vegetable oil
1 onion, cut into 3/4-inch pieces
1 green pepper, cut into 3/4-inch pieces
Hot cooked rice

Cut tofu into 1/2-inch cubes; drain well on several layers of paper towels. Meanwhile, combine pork, sherry, ginger and garlic in small bowl; let stand 10 minutes. Blend broth, cornstarch, soy sauce, vinegar and red pepper; set aside. Heat wok or large skillet over medium-high heat; add pork. Cook, stirring to separate pork, about 3 minutes, or until lightly browned; remove. Heat oil in same pan. Add onion and green pepper; stir-fry 4 minutes. Add pork and soy sauce mixture. Cook and stir until mixture boils and thickens. Gently fold in tofu; heat through. Serve immediately over rice.

*Hunan Stir-Fry with Tofu*

## SPICY CHICKEN

*Makes 4 servings*

3/4 pound boneless chicken
3 tablespoons Kikkoman Soy Sauce, divided
1 tablespoon cornstarch
1 tablespoon dry sherry
4 teaspoons water
2 tablespoons vegetable oil
1 teaspoon minced fresh ginger root
3/4 teaspoon crushed red pepper
1 small onion, chunked
1 small red or green bell pepper, cut into matchsticks
1 small zucchini, cut into matchsticks
1/2 cup water

Cut chicken into thin slices. Combine chicken and 1 tablespoon soy sauce in small bowl; let stand 30 minutes. Meanwhile, combine remaining 2 tablespoons soy sauce, cornstarch, sherry and 4 teaspoons water. Heat oil in hot wok or large skillet over high heat. Add ginger and crushed red pepper; cook until fragrant. Add chicken and stir-fry 3 minutes. Add onion, bell pepper, zucchini and 1/2 cup water; mix well. Cover and cook 1 minute, or until vegetables are tender-crisp. Add soy sauce mixture; cook and stir until sauce boils and thickens.

*Cantonese Chicken Salad*

# CANTONESE CHICKEN SALAD

*Makes 6 servings*

- 3 chicken breast halves
- 2 cups water
- 5 tablespoons Kikkoman Soy Sauce, divided
- 4 cups shredded iceberg lettuce
- 1 medium carrot, peeled and shredded
- 1/2 cup finely chopped green onions and tops
- 1/3 cup distilled white vinegar
- 2 tablespoons sesame seed, toasted
- 2 teaspoons sugar
- 1/2 teaspoon ground ginger
- 2 tablespoons minced fresh cilantro or parsley

Simmer chicken in mixture of water and 1 tablespoon soy sauce in covered saucepan 15 minutes, or until chicken is tender. Remove chicken and cool. (Refrigerate stock for another use, if desired.) Skin and bone chicken; shred meat with fingers into large mixing bowl. Add lettuce, carrot and green onions. Combine vinegar, remaining 4 tablespoons soy sauce, sesame seed, sugar and ginger; stir until sugar dissolves. Pour over chicken and vegetables; toss to coat all ingredients. Cover and refrigerate 1 hour. Just before serving, add cilantro and toss to combine. Garnish as desired.

# SHANTUNG CHICKEN

*Makes 4 servings*

- 1 whole chicken breast, skinned and boned
- 2 tablespoons cornstarch, divided
- 3 tablespoons Kikkoman Soy Sauce, divided
- 1 tablespoon dry sherry
- 1 clove garlic, minced
- 1 cup water
- 3 tablespoons vegetable oil, divided
- 1/2 pound fresh bean sprouts
- 1/4 pound green onions and tops, cut into 1 1/2-inch lengths, separating whites from tops
- 1 tablespoon slivered fresh ginger root
- 1 tablespoon sesame seed, toasted
  Hot cooked noodles

Cut chicken into narrow strips. Combine 1 tablespoon *each* cornstarch and soy sauce with sherry and garlic in small bowl; stir in chicken. Let stand 5 minutes. Meanwhile, blend water, remaining 1 tablespoon cornstarch and 2 tablespoons soy sauce; set aside. Heat 1 tablespoon oil in hot wok or large skillet over high heat. Add chicken and stir-fry 2 minutes; remove. Heat remaining 2 tablespoons oil in same pan; add bean sprouts, white parts of green onions and ginger; stir-fry 3 minutes. Stir in chicken, soy sauce mixture, green onion tops and sesame seed. Cook and stir until mixture boils and thickens. Serve immediately over noodles.

*Shantung Chicken*

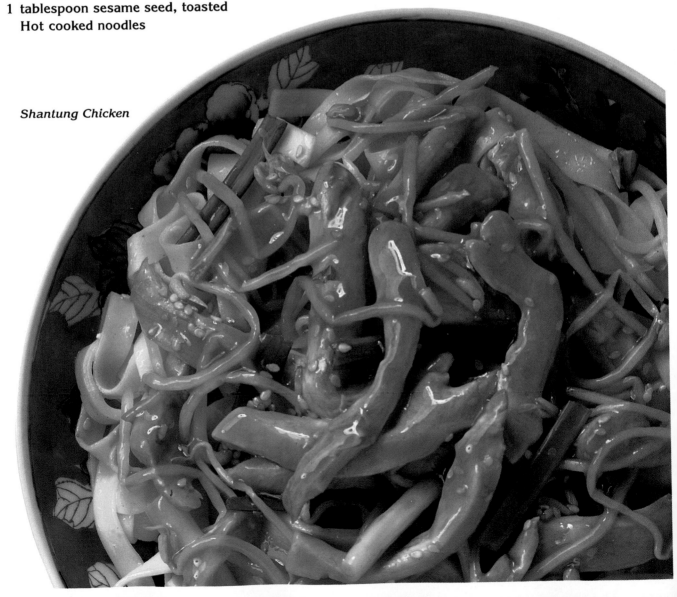

# CHINESE-STYLE POT ROAST CHICKEN

*Makes 4 servings*

- 3 pounds frying chicken pieces
- 1/4 cup Kikkoman Soy Sauce
- 2 tablespoons vegetable oil
- 1 tablespoon dry sherry
- 1 clove garlic, minced
- 2 stalks celery, cut diagonally into 1/4-inch slices
- 2 green onions and tops, cut into 1-inch lengths
- 3/4 cup water
- 1 tablespoon cornstarch
- 2 tablespoons Kikkoman Soy Sauce
- 1 teaspoon sugar

Rinse chicken pieces and pat dry with paper towels. Rub chicken thoroughly with 1/4 cup soy sauce; let stand 15 minutes. Heat oil in Dutch oven or large skillet over medium heat; add chicken and brown slowly in hot oil. Add sherry and garlic; cover and simmer 30 minutes, or until tender. Remove chicken from pan; keep warm. Add celery and green onions to pan; cook 1 to 2 minutes. Combine water, cornstarch, 2 tablespoons soy sauce and sugar; stir into pan and cook until thickened. Serve sauce and vegetables over chicken.

# BRAISED CHINESE DUCKLING

*Makes 4 servings*

- 1 (4- to 5-pound) frozen duckling, thawed and quartered
- 3 tablespoons Kikkoman Lite Soy Sauce, divided
- 1 tablespoon vegetable oil
- 2 tablespoons dry sherry
- 1 clove garlic, minced
- 1 teaspoon ginger juice*
- 4 green onions and tops, cut into 2-inch lengths
- 1/3 cup water
- 2 teaspoons cornstarch

Wash duckling quarters; dry thoroughly with paper towels. Rub thoroughly with 2 tablespoons lite soy sauce. Let stand 30 minutes. Heat oil in Dutch oven or large skillet over medium heat. Brown duckling slowly in hot oil; drain off fat. Add sherry and garlic. Cover and cook over low heat 45 minutes, or until tender, turning quarters over once. Remove duckling to serving platter; keep warm. Spoon off and discard excess fat from pan juices; return 1/3 cup juices to pan. Add remaining 1 tablespoon lite soy sauce, ginger juice and green onions; cook 1 minute. Combine water with cornstarch; stir into pan. Cook and stir until sauce boils and thickens. To serve, spoon sauce over duckling quarters.

*Peel fresh ginger root, then squeeze through garlic press.

*Chinese-Style Pot Roast Chicken*

# KUNG PAO STIR-FRY

*Makes 4 servings*

1 whole chicken breast, skinned and boned
2 tablespoons cornstarch, divided
3 tablespoons Kikkoman Teriyaki Sauce, divided
1/4 teaspoon ground red pepper (cayenne)
3/4 cup water
4 teaspoons distilled white vinegar
3/4 pound romaine lettuce
2 tablespoons vegetable oil, divided
1/3 cup roasted peanuts

Cut chicken into thin strips. Combine 1 tablespoon *each* cornstarch and teriyaki sauce with red pepper in small bowl; stir in chicken. Let stand 15 minutes. Meanwhile, combine water, remaining 1 tablespoon cornstarch and 2 tablespoons teriyaki sauce with vinegar; set aside. Separate and rinse lettuce; pat dry. Cut leaves crosswise into 2-inch strips. Heat 1 tablespoon oil in hot wok or large skillet over high heat. Add chicken and stir-fry 2 minutes; remove. Heat remaining 1 tablespoon oil in same pan. Add lettuce; stir-fry 1 minute. Stir in chicken and teriyaki sauce mixture. Cook and stir until mixture boils and thickens. Remove from heat; stir in peanuts. Serve immediately.

# ORANGE-CASHEW CHICKEN

*Makes 4 servings*

1 pound boneless chicken breasts
1/2 cup Kikkoman Teriyaki Baste & Glaze
2 tablespoons orange juice
2 tablespoons dry white wine
2 tablespoons vegetable oil
1 green pepper, cut into thin strips
1/2 cup diagonally sliced celery
1 can (11 oz.) mandarin orange segments, drained
1/2 cup roasted cashews

Cut chicken into thin slices. Combine teriyaki baste & glaze, orange juice and wine; set aside. Heat oil in hot wok or large skillet over medium heat. Add chicken, green pepper and celery; stir-fry 3 to 4 minutes. Pour in baste & glaze mixture; cook and stir until chicken and vegetables are coated with sauce. Remove from heat; stir in orange segments and cashews. Serve immediately.

# LOTUS CHICKEN CHOP SUEY

*Makes 2 to 3 servings*

1/2 chicken breast, skinned and boned
4 tablespoons Kikkoman Teriyaki Sauce, divided
1 cup water
2 tablespoons cornstarch
1 tablespoon dry sherry
1 large carrot, cut diagonally into 1/8-inch slices
1 onion, chunked and separated
1/8 teaspoon salt
1/4 pound fresh bean sprouts
1 package (6 oz.) frozen Chinese pea pods, thawed and drained

**MICROWAVE DIRECTIONS:**

Cut chicken into narrow strips; place in small bowl. Stir in 2 tablespoons teriyaki sauce; let stand 20 minutes. Meanwhile, blend water, cornstarch, sherry and remaining 2 tablespoons teriyaki sauce in 2-cup microwave-safe measuring cup. Microwave on High 4 minutes, until mixture boils and thickens, stirring occasionally to prevent lumping; set aside. Combine carrot, onion and salt in 2-quart microwave-safe casserole. Microwave, covered, on High 4 minutes, stirring after 2 minutes. Stir in bean sprouts; cover and microwave on High 1 minute. Stir in chicken; microwave, covered, on High 3 minutes, stirring once. Combine cornstarch mixture with chicken and vegetables. Microwave, uncovered, on High 1 minute. Stir in pea pods. Microwave, uncovered, on High 2 minutes, or until mixture is heated through, stirring once.

# BRAISED DUCKLING AND PEARS

*Makes 3 to 4 servings*

1 (4- to 5-pound) frozen duckling, thawed and quartered
1 can (16 oz.) pear halves in heavy syrup
1/3 cup Kikkoman Stir-Fry Sauce
1 cinnamon stick, about 3 inches long

Wash duckling quarters; dry thoroughly with paper towels. Heat large skillet or Dutch oven over medium heat. Add duckling; brown slowly on both sides about 15 minutes, or until golden. Meanwhile, drain pears; reserve all syrup. Remove 1/4 cup pear syrup and combine with stir-fry sauce; set aside. Drain off fat from pan. Pour syrup mixture over duckling; add cinnamon stick. Cover and simmer 40 minutes, or until tender, turning quarters over once. Remove duckling to serving platter; keep warm. Remove and discard cinnamon stick. Pour drippings into measuring cup; skim off fat. Combine 1/2 cup drippings with 2 tablespoons reserved pear syrup; return to pan with pears. Gently bring to boil and cook until pears are heated through, stirring occasionally. Serve duckling with pears and sauce.

# ANGEL HAIR STIR-FRY

*Makes 4 servings*

1 whole chicken breast, skinned and boned
1 tablespoon Kikkoman Stir-Fry Sauce
4 ounces angel hair pasta (capellini)
1/3 cup Kikkoman Stir-Fry Sauce
3 tablespoons water
2 tablespoons vegetable oil, divided
1/4 pound fresh snow peas, cut into julienne strips
1 large carrot, cut into julienne strips
1/8 teaspoon salt
2 teaspoons sesame seed, toasted

Cut chicken into thin strips; coat with 1 tablespoon stir-fry sauce. Let stand 30 minutes. Meanwhile, cook pasta according to package directions, omitting salt. Drain; rinse under cold water and drain thoroughly. Combine 1/3 cup stir-fry sauce and water; set aside. Heat 1 tablespoon oil in hot wok or large skillet over high heat. Add chicken and stir-fry 2 minutes; remove. Heat remaining 1 tablespoon oil in same pan; add peas and carrot. Sprinkle vegetables with salt; stir-fry 4 minutes. Add stir-fry sauce mixture, chicken, pasta and sesame seed. Cook and stir until all ingredients are coated with sauce and pasta is heated through.

# CHICKEN ADOBO

*Makes 4 servings*

3 pounds frying chicken pieces
1/2 cup Kikkoman Soy Sauce
1/2 cup distilled white vinegar
2 tablespoons sugar
1 teaspoon pepper
6 large cloves garlic, pressed

**MICROWAVE DIRECTIONS:**
Rinse chicken pieces and pat dry with paper towels. Combine soy sauce, vinegar, sugar, pepper and garlic in large microwave-safe casserole with lid; add chicken pieces, skin side down. Cover and microwave on High 10 minutes. Turn chicken pieces over; rearrange in dish. Cover and microwave on High 13 minutes longer, or until chicken is tender, rearranging pieces once. Serve immediately.

*Braised Duckling and Pears*

*Hearty Chicken Stir-Fry with Noodles*

# HEARTY CHICKEN STIR-FRY WITH NOODLES

*Makes 4 servings*

1 whole chicken breast, skinned and boned
1 tablespoon cornstarch
5 tablespoons Kikkoman Teriyaki Sauce, divided
1 clove garlic, minced
1 cup water
4 teaspoons cornstarch
2 teaspoons tomato catsup
2 medium zucchini
2 cups uncooked fine egg noodles
2 tablespoons vegetable oil, divided
1 medium onion, chunked
10 cherry tomatoes, halved

Cut chicken into ½-inch square pieces. Combine 1 tablespoon *each* cornstarch and teriyaki sauce with garlic in small bowl; stir in chicken. Let stand 30 minutes. Meanwhile, combine water, remaining 4 tablespoons teriyaki sauce, 4 teaspoons cornstarch and catsup; set aside. Cut zucchini in half lengthwise, then diagonally into 1-inch pieces. Cook noodles according to package directions; drain and keep warm on serving plate. Heat 1 tablespoon oil in hot wok or large skillet over high heat. Add chicken and stir-fry 2 minutes; remove. Heat remaining 1 tablespoon oil in same pan. Add zucchini and onion; stir-fry 4 minutes. Add chicken, teriyaki sauce mixture and tomatoes. Cook and stir until sauce boils and thickens. Pour over noodles; toss to combine before serving.

# CLASSIC SWEET & SOUR CHICKEN

*Makes 4 servings*

- 1 whole chicken breast, skinned and boned
- 1 tablespoon cornstarch
- 1 tablespoon Kikkoman Soy Sauce
- 1 teaspoon minced fresh ginger root
- 1 can (11 oz.) mandarin orange segments
- 2/3 cup Kikkoman Sweet & Sour Sauce
- 2 tablespoons vegetable oil, divided
- 1/2 pound fresh snow peas, trimmed
- 5 green onions and tops, cut diagonally into thin slices
- 1/2 cup unsalted roasted peanuts
  Hot cooked rice

Cut chicken into 1-inch pieces. Combine cornstarch, soy sauce and ginger in small bowl; stir in chicken. Let stand 15 minutes. Meanwhile, drain mandarin oranges; reserve 1/4 cup syrup. Blend reserved syrup with sweet & sour sauce; set aside. Heat 1 tablespoon oil in hot wok or large skillet over medium-high heat. Add chicken and stir-fry 2 minutes; remove. Heat remaining 1 tablespoon oil in same pan. Add snow peas; stir-fry 1 minute. Add green onions; stir-fry 30 seconds longer. Add chicken, peanuts and sweet & sour sauce mixture; cook and stir until chicken, vegetables and peanuts are coated with sauce. Gently stir in mandarin oranges; heat through. Serve with rice.

*Classic Sweet & Sour Chicken*

# SEAFOOD

## SAUCY SHRIMP OVER CHINESE NOODLE CAKES

*Makes 4 servings*

Chinese Noodle Cakes (recipe follows)
1¼ cups water
2 tablespoons cornstarch, divided
4 tablespoons Kikkoman Soy Sauce, divided
1 teaspoon tomato catsup
½ pound medium-size raw shrimp, peeled and deveined
2 tablespoons vegetable oil, divided
1 clove garlic, minced
½ teaspoon minced fresh ginger root
1 green pepper, chunked
1 medium onion, chunked
2 stalks celery, cut diagonally into thin slices
2 tomatoes, chunked

Prepare Chinese Noodle Cakes on page 340. Combine water, 1 tablespoon cornstarch and 3 tablespoons soy sauce with catsup; set aside. Blend remaining 1 tablespoon cornstarch and 1 tablespoon soy sauce in small bowl; stir in shrimp until coated. Heat 1 tablespoon oil in hot wok or large skillet over high heat. Add shrimp and stir-fry 1 minute; remove. Heat remaining 1 tablespoon oil in same pan. Add garlic and ginger; stir-fry until fragrant. Add green pepper, onion and celery, stir-fry 4 minutes. Stir in soy sauce mixture, shrimp and tomatoes. Cook and stir until sauce boils and thickens. Cut Chinese Noodle Cakes into squares and serve with shrimp mixture.

## CHINESE NOODLE CAKES:

Cook *8 ounces capellini (angel hair pasta)* according to package directions. Drain; rinse under cold water and drain thoroughly. Heat *1 tablespoon vegetable oil* in large, nonstick skillet over medium-high heat. Add half the capellini; slightly spread to fill bottom of skillet to form noodle cake. Without stirring, cook 5 minutes, or until golden on bottom. Lift cake with wide spatula; add *1 tablespoon oil* to skillet and turn cake over. Cook 5 minutes longer, or until golden brown, shaking skillet occasionally to brown evenly; remove to rack and keep warm in 200°F. oven. Repeat with remaining capellini.

# CHINESE PORCUPINE MEATBALLS

*Makes 4 servings*

- 1/2 cup uncooked rice
- 6 ounces medium-size raw shrimp
- 1 pound ground pork
- 2/3 cup chopped green onions and tops
- 3 tablespoons Kikkoman Soy Sauce
- 1 tablespoon dry sherry
- 2 cloves garlic, pressed
  Mandarin Peach Sauce (see page 326)

Cover rice with warm water and let stand 20 minutes; drain. Meanwhile, peel, devein and mince shrimp. Combine shrimp with pork, green onions, soy sauce, sherry, garlic and rice; mix well. Divide into 8 equal portions; shape portions into meatballs. Arrange meatballs on steamer rack. Set rack in large saucepan or wok of boiling water. (Do not allow water level to reach meatballs.) Cover and steam 45 minutes, or until meatballs are cooked. Serve with warm Mandarin Peach Sauce.

# SHANGHAI SWEET & SOUR FISH

*Makes 4 servings*

- 1 cup water
- 1/4 cup brown sugar, packed
- 1/4 cup orange juice
- 2 1/2 tablespoons cornstarch
- 3 tablespoons Kikkoman Lite Soy Sauce
- 3 tablespoons vinegar
- 1 tablespoon tomato catsup
- 2 teaspoons minced fresh ginger root
- 1 large onion, chunked and separated
- 1 large green pepper, chunked
- 1 large carrot, sliced diagonally into very thin slices
- 1 pound firm fish fillets (swordfish, halibut, mahi-mahi, shark), 3/4 inch thick

## MICROWAVE DIRECTIONS:

Combine water, brown sugar, orange juice, cornstarch, lite soy sauce, vinegar, catsup and ginger; set aside. Combine onion, green pepper and carrot in large microwave-safe casserole. Cover and microwave on High 4 minutes. Stir in soy sauce mixture; cover and microwave on High 4 minutes. Remove from oven and let stand, covered, about 5 minutes. Meanwhile, cut fish into 1-inch pieces and place in single layer in separate small microwave-safe casserole. Cover and microwave on Medium-high (70%) 4 to 5 minutes, or until fish flakes easily when tested with fork, rotating dish once. Remove fish and add to vegetable mixture, stirring gently to combine. Serve immediately.

*Chinese Porcupine Meatballs*

*Grilled Oriental Fish Steaks*

## GINGER FISH FILLETS

*Makes 4 servings*

1 pound fresh or thawed fish fillets
1/4 cup Kikkoman Teriyaki Sauce
1 tablespoon vegetable oil
1 teaspoon sugar
1 tablespoon slivered fresh ginger root
1 large green onion and top, cut into
    1-inch lengths and slivered
1/3 cup water
1 1/2 teaspoons cornstarch

Place fillets in single layer in shallow baking pan. Combine teriyaki sauce, oil and sugar; pour over fish. Turn fillets over to coat well. Marinate 20 minutes, turning fish over occasionally. (If fillets are very thin, marinate for only 10 minutes.) Sprinkle ginger and green onion evenly over each fillet. Bake in marinade at 350°F. 6 to 10 minutes, or until fish flakes easily when tested with fork. Remove to serving platter and keep warm; reserve 1/4 cup pan juices. Blend water and cornstarch in small saucepan. Stir in reserved pan juices. Cook and stir until mixture boils and thickens. To serve, spoon sauce over fish.

## GRILLED ORIENTAL FISH STEAKS

*Makes 4 servings*

4 fish steaks (halibut, salmon or
    swordfish), about 3/4 inch thick
1/4 cup Kikkoman Lite Soy Sauce
3 tablespoons minced onion
1 tablespoon chopped fresh ginger root
1 tablespoon sesame seed, toasted
1/2 teaspoon sugar

Place fish in single layer in shallow baking pan. Measure lite soy sauce, onion, ginger, sesame seed and sugar into blender container; process on low speed 30 seconds, scraping sides down once. Pour sauce over fish; turn over to coat both sides. Marinate 30 minutes, turning fish over occasionally. Remove fish and broil or grill 4 inches from heat source or moderately hot coals 5 minutes on each side, or until fish flakes easily when tested with fork. Garnish as desired.

# SHANGHAI SHRIMP STIR-FRY

*Makes 4 servings*

2 tablespoons cornstarch, divided
3 tablespoons Kikkoman Soy Sauce, divided
1 tablespoon minced fresh ginger root
1/2 teaspoon sugar
1/2 pound medium-size raw shrimp, peeled and deveined
1 1/4 cups water
1/4 teaspoon fennel seed, crushed
1/8 teaspoon ground cloves
1/8 teaspoon pepper
1 pound fresh broccoli
3 tablespoons vegetable oil, divided
1 onion, chunked and separated

Combine 1 tablespoon *each* cornstarch and soy sauce with ginger and sugar in small bowl; stir in shrimp. Let stand 10 minutes. Meanwhile, combine water, remaining 1 tablespoon cornstarch and 2 tablespoons soy sauce, fennel, cloves and pepper; set aside. Remove flowerets from broccoli; cut into bite-size pieces. Peel stalks; cut into thin slices. Heat 1 tablespoon oil in hot wok or large skillet over high heat. Add shrimp and stir-fry 1 minute; remove. Heat remaining 2 tablespoons oil in same pan. Add broccoli; stir-fry 2 minutes. Add onion; stir-fry 3 minutes longer. Stir in shrimp and soy sauce mixture; cook and stir until sauce boils and thickens.

# SEA BREEZE FISH SALAD

*Makes 4 servings*

1 pound firm white fish fillets (red snapper, sea bass or orange roughy), about 1 inch thick
1 3/4 cups water
1 tablespoon grated lemon peel
6 tablespoons lemon juice, divided
3 tablespoons Kikkoman Lite Soy Sauce, divided
6 ounces fresh snow peas, trimmed and cut diagonally into 1-inch pieces
2 tablespoons vegetable oil
1 tablespoon minced onion
1/2 teaspoon thyme, crumbled
1/4 teaspoon sugar
1/2 medium cantaloupe, chunked
1 tablespoon minced fresh cilantro or parsley

Cut fish into 1-inch cubes. Combine water, lemon peel, 4 tablespoons lemon juice and 1 tablespoon lite soy sauce in large skillet. Heat only until mixture starts to simmer. Add fish; simmer, uncovered, 3 minutes, or until fish flakes easily when tested with fork. Remove fish with slotted spoon to plate. Cool slightly; cover and refrigerate 1 hour, or until thoroughly chilled. Meanwhile, cook snow peas in boiling water 2 minutes, or until tender-crisp; cool under cold water and drain thoroughly. Chill. Measure remaining 2 tablespoons lemon juice and 2 tablespoons lite soy sauce, oil, onion, thyme and sugar into jar with screw-top lid; cover and shake well. Combine peas, cantaloupe and cilantro in large bowl; add dressing and toss to coat all ingredients. Add fish and gently stir to combine. Serve immediately.

*Sea Breeze Fish Salad*

# SIDE DISHES

## JAPANESE RICE SALAD

*Makes 6 servings*

2 cups water
3 tablespoons Kikkoman Lite Soy Sauce, divided
1 cup uncooked long-grain rice, washed and
   drained
½ pound cooked baby shrimp
1 carrot, peeled and shredded
½ cup frozen green peas, thawed and drained
½ cup chopped green onions and tops
1 tablespoon minced fresh ginger root
¼ cup distilled white vinegar
2 tablespoons sugar
2 teaspoons sesame seed, toasted
2 teaspoons water
   Lettuce leaves

Combine 2 cups water and 2 tablespoons lite soy sauce
in medium saucepan. Bring to boil; stir in rice. Reduce
heat and simmer, covered, 20 minutes, or until water is
absorbed. Remove from heat and cool in pan. Rinse
shrimp; drain thoroughly. Remove and reserve ½ cup.
Combine remaining shrimp, carrot, peas, green onions
and ginger in large bowl. Fluff rice with fork; fold into
shrimp mixture. Cover and refrigerate until chilled.
Meanwhile, measure vinegar, sugar, remaining 1
tablespoon lite soy sauce, sesame seed and 2
teaspoons water into jar with screw-top lid. Cover and
shake until blended and sugar dissolves. Pour over rice
mixture; toss to coat all ingredients well. Spoon over
lettuce leaves on serving plates; sprinkle with reserved
shrimp. Garnish as desired.

*Sunomono Salad*

# SUNOMONO SALAD

*Makes 4 servings*

- 2 medium cucumbers, peeled
- 1 teaspoon salt
- 1/4 cup shredded carrot
- 1/4 cup distilled white vinegar
- 1 tablespoon sugar
- 2 tablespoons water
- 1 teaspoon sesame seed, toasted
- 1 1/2 teaspoons Kikkoman Soy Sauce
- 1/4 teaspoon grated fresh ginger root

Cut cucumbers in half lengthwise; remove seeds. Cut halves crosswise into thin slices. Place in medium bowl; sprinkle with salt and toss lightly. Let stand 45 minutes, or until no longer crisp, tossing occasionally. Drain and squeeze out excess liquid. Return cucumbers to same bowl and toss with carrot. Combine vinegar, sugar, water, sesame seed, soy sauce and ginger. Pour over cucumber mixture; toss to mix well. Cover and refrigerate until chilled. To serve, remove cucumber mixture with slotted spoon to small individual serving bowls.

# NEW YEAR FRIED RICE

*Makes 6 to 8 servings*

- 3 strips bacon, diced
- 3/4 cup chopped green onions and tops
- 1/3 cup diced red bell pepper
- 1/4 cup frozen green peas, thawed
- 1 egg, beaten
- 4 cups cold, cooked rice
- 2 tablespoons Kikkoman Soy Sauce

Cook bacon in wok or large skillet over medium heat until crisp. Add green onions, red pepper and peas; stir-fry 1 minute. Add egg and scramble. Stir in rice and cook until heated, gently separating grains. Add soy sauce; cook and stir until heated through. Serve immediately.

# BEAN SPROUT & SPINACH SALAD

*Makes 4 servings*

- Boiling water
- 1 pound fresh spinach, washed
- 1/2 pound fresh bean sprouts
- 1 tablespoon sugar
- 4 teaspoons distilled white vinegar
- 1 tablespoon Kikkoman Soy Sauce
- 1 teaspoon sesame seed, toasted

Pour boiling water over spinach in colander; rinse immediately with cold water. Drain thoroughly and place in medium serving bowl. Repeat procedure with bean sprouts and place in same bowl. Combine sugar, vinegar, soy sauce and sesame seed; pour over vegetables and toss to combine. Cover and refrigerate at least 1 hour before serving.

# STEAMED CHINESE BUNS

*Makes 10 buns*

- ½ pound fresh bean sprouts, chopped
- ¼ pound medium-size raw shrimp, peeled, deveined and chopped
- 2 green onions and tops, chopped
- 1 clove garlic, minced
- 2 tablespoons cornstarch
- 2 tablespoons Kikkoman Soy Sauce
- ½ teaspoon ground ginger
- 1 can (7.5 oz.) refrigerated biscuits

**MICROWAVE DIRECTIONS:**

Combine bean sprouts, shrimp, green onions, garlic, cornstarch, soy sauce and ginger in 1½-quart microwave-safe square dish. Microwave on High 6 minutes, until vegetables are tender-crisp, stirring once. Divide biscuit dough into 10 pieces. Flatten each piece into 3½-inch round, flouring hands if dough is sticky. Place about 2 tablespoonfuls shrimp mixture in center of each round. Bring edges together to enclose filling, pinching edges to seal securely. Place half the filled buns on 6- to 7-inch microwave-safe plate. Set plate in 1½-quart microwave-safe dish. Add ¼ cup hot water to bottom of dish. Microwave on High 5 minutes, or until buns are cooked. Repeat with remaining buns. Serve hot.

# CHAWAN MUSHI

*Makes 4 servings*

- ½ chicken breast, skinned and boned
- 1 tablespoon Kikkoman Soy Sauce
- ½ teaspoon sugar
- 3 medium-size fresh mushrooms, sliced
- 4 eggs
- 1 bottle (8 oz.) clam juice
- ¼ cup water
- ½ teaspoon Kikkoman Soy Sauce
- ¼ cup fresh or frozen green peas

Cut chicken into 1-inch square pieces. Combine 1 tablespoon soy sauce and sugar in small bowl. Stir in chicken and mushrooms, turning pieces over to coat well. Let stand 15 minutes. Beat eggs in medium bowl. Gently stir in clam juice, water and ½ teaspoon soy sauce. Divide chicken, mushrooms and peas equally among 4 chawan mushi cups or four 10-ounce custard cups. Pour about ½ cup egg mixture into each cup. Cover with chawan mushi lids or cover tops tightly with foil or plastic wrap. Carefully place filled cups on steamer rack. Pour water into large heavy pan or Dutch oven to a depth of ¾ inch; set rack in pan. Bring water to boil; cover and steam 12 to 15 minutes, or until knife inserted into center comes out clean.

*Chawan Mushi*

## ORIENTAL TOSS

*Makes 6 servings*

Boiling water
1/4 pound fresh snow peas, trimmed
1/4 pound fresh bean sprouts
1 head curly leaf lettuce, washed and drained
1/4 pound fresh mushrooms, sliced
1/4 cup distilled white vinegar
2 tablespoons sugar
2 tablespoons Kikkoman Soy Sauce
2 tablespoons water
1/2 teaspoon ground ginger

Pour enough boiling water over snow peas in small bowl to cover; let stand 10 minutes. Drain; cool under cold water and drain thoroughly. Pour boiling water over bean sprouts in colander; cool immediately under cold water and drain thoroughly. Tear lettuce into bite-size pieces; combine with snow peas, bean sprouts and mushrooms in large serving bowl. Cover and refrigerate until chilled. Meanwhile, combine vinegar, sugar, soy sauce, water and ginger until sugar dissolves. Pour desired amount of dressing over salad mixture; toss well to coat all ingredients.

## HOT & SPICY GLAZED CARROTS

*Makes 4 servings*

2 tablespoons vegetable oil
2 dried red chili peppers
1 pound carrots, peeled and cut diagonally into 1/8-inch slices
1/4 cup Kikkoman Teriyaki Baste & Glaze

Heat oil in hot wok or large skillet over high heat. Add peppers and stir-fry until darkened; remove and discard. Add carrots; reduce heat to medium. Stir-fry 4 minutes, or until tender-crisp. Stir in teriyaki baste & glaze and cook until carrots are glazed. Serve immediately.

## CUCUMBER FAN SALAD

*Makes 6 servings*

2 large cucumbers
1 teaspoon salt
1 teaspoon sesame seed
2 tablespoons vegetable oil
1/8 teaspoon ground red pepper (cayenne)
1/4 cup distilled white vinegar
2 tablespoons sugar
1 tablespoon Kikkoman Soy Sauce

Trim off and discard ends of cucumbers, then peel lengthwise with vegetable peeler to form stripes. Cut each cucumber in half lengthwise; remove seeds. Slice each half crosswise into 1-inch pieces. Score each piece crosswise, making cuts close together to within 1/4 inch of edges. Place cucumbers in large bowl and sprinkle evenly with salt; let stand 30 minutes, tossing occasionally. Meanwhile, toast sesame seed in small dry skillet over medium-high heat. Remove from heat and stir in oil and red pepper; cool. Blend vinegar, sugar and soy sauce; stir into sesame seed mixture. Rinse cucumbers. Drain and pat dry; return to bowl. Pour dressing over cucumbers and toss to coat well. Cover and refrigerate 1 hour, stirring occasionally. Remove cucumbers from dressing. Gently spread each piece to form a fan and arrange on serving dish.

## EAST MEETS WEST SALAD

*Makes 6 to 8 servings*

6 cups shredded iceberg lettuce
1 large carrot, peeled and shredded
1 tablespoon minced fresh cilantro or parsley
2 tablespoons distilled white vinegar
4 teaspoons Kikkoman Soy Sauce
1 tablespoon sesame seed, toasted
1 tablespoon water
2 teaspoons sugar

Toss lettuce with carrot and cilantro. Measure vinegar, soy sauce, sesame seed, water and sugar into jar with screw-top lid; cover and shake well until sugar dissolves. Pour over lettuce mixture and toss lightly to combine. Serve immediately.

*East Meets West Salad*

## PAGODA FRIED RICE

*Makes 6 servings*

2 strips bacon, cut crosswise into ¹/₄-inch-wide pieces
6 green onions and tops, thinly sliced
1 egg, beaten
4 cups cold, cooked rice
2 tablespoons Kikkoman Soy Sauce

Cook bacon in hot wok or large skillet over medium heat until crisp. Add green onions and stir-fry 1 minute. Add egg and scramble. Stir in rice and cook until heated through, gently separating grains. Add soy sauce and stir until mixture is well blended.

## HOT ORIENTAL SALAD

*Makes 6 to 8 servings*

1 small head napa (Chinese cabbage)
³/₄ pound fresh spinach
1 tablespoon vegetable oil
2 cloves garlic, minced
¹/₂ teaspoon ground ginger
2 stalks celery, cut into julienne strips
¹/₂ pound fresh mushrooms, sliced
2 tablespoons Kikkoman Soy Sauce

Separate and rinse napa; pat dry. Slice enough leaves crosswise into 1-inch pieces to measure 8 cups. Wash and drain spinach; tear into pieces. Heat oil in Dutch oven over medium-high heat; add garlic and ginger. Stir-fry until garlic is lightly browned. Add celery; stir-fry 2 minutes. Add cabbage and mushrooms; stir-fry 2 minutes. Add spinach; stir-fry 2 minutes longer. Stir in soy sauce; serve immediately.

## SHRIMP FRIED RICE

*Makes 6 servings*

2 eggs
2 tablespoons water
2 tablespoons vegetable oil
3 green onions and tops, chopped
3 cups cold, cooked rice
¹/₄ pound cooked baby shrimp, chopped
3 tablespoons Kikkoman Soy Sauce

Beat eggs with water just to blend; set aside. Heat oil in hot wok or large skillet over medium heat. Add green onions; stir-fry 30 seconds. Add eggs and scramble. Stir in rice and cook until heated, gently separating grains. Add shrimp and soy sauce; cook and stir until heated through. Serve immediately.

*Firecracker Salad*

# FIRECRACKER SALAD

*Makes 6 servings*

- 1 tablespoon sesame seed, toasted
- 2 tablespoons distilled white vinegar
- 2 teaspoons sugar
- 1 teaspoon minced fresh ginger root
- 4 teaspoons Kikkoman Soy Sauce
- 1 cup julienne-stripped radishes
- 1 cup julienne-stripped cucumber
- 4 cups finely shredded iceberg lettuce
- 1½ teaspoons minced fresh cilantro or parsley

Measure sesame seed, vinegar, sugar, ginger and soy sauce into jar with screw-top lid; cover and shake well until sugar dissolves. Combine radishes, cucumber and 3 tablespoons dressing; cover and refrigerate 30 minutes, stirring occasionally. Toss lettuce with cilantro in large bowl. Pour radish mixture and remaining dressing over lettuce. Toss lightly to combine.

# HALEAKALA RICE

*Makes 6 servings*

- 1 can (20 oz.) crushed pineapple in syrup
- 2 tablespoons butter or margarine
- 1 cup uncooked white rice
- 2 tablespoons chopped parsley
- 2 tablespoons Kikkoman Soy Sauce
- 1 teaspoon dried mint
- 2 tablespoons freeze-dried chopped chives

Drain pineapple well; reserve syrup. Melt butter in 2-quart saucepan; stir in rice until well coated. Add enough water to reserved pineapple syrup to measure 2 cups; stir into rice. Add parsley, soy sauce and mint; bring to boil. Cover; reduce heat and simmer 35 to 40 minutes, or until liquid is absorbed. Remove from heat; stir in pineapple and chives.

# ORIENTAL TEA EGGS

*Makes 8 eggs*

- 8 tea bags or 3 tablespoons loose black tea leaves
- 3 cups water
- ½ cup Kikkoman Teriyaki Sauce
- 8 eggs, room temperature

Combine tea bags, water and teriyaki sauce in medium saucepan; add eggs. Bring to full boil over high heat. Remove from heat; cover tightly and let stand 10 minutes. Remove eggs; reserve liquid. Place eggs under cold running water until cool enough to handle. Gently tap each eggshell with back of metal spoon until eggs are covered with fine cracks *(do not peel eggs)*. Return eggs to reserved liquid. Bring to boil; reduce heat, cover and simmer 25 minutes. Drain off liquid and refrigerate eggs until chilled, about 1 hour. Peel carefully before serving.

# SAVORY LUAU RICE

*Makes 8 to 10 servings*

- ¼ cup butter or margarine
- 2 cups uncooked white rice
- 3½ cups water
- ½ cup Kikkoman Soy Sauce
- ½ cup chopped green onions and tops

Melt butter in 2-quart saucepan; stir in rice until well coated. Add water and soy sauce; bring to boil. Cover; reduce heat and simmer 30 minutes, or until liquid is absorbed. Remove from heat and let stand, covered, 20 minutes. Before serving, stir in green onions.

# CHICKEN FRIED RICE

*Makes 6 to 8 servings*

- ½ pound boneless, skinless chicken breast
- 2 tablespoons vegetable oil
- 3 green onions and tops, chopped
- 1 carrot, cut into julienne strips
- 1 egg, beaten
- 4 cups cold, cooked rice
- 3 tablespoons Kikkoman Soy Sauce

Cut chicken into thin strips. Heat oil in hot wok or large skillet over high heat. Add chicken, green onions and carrot. Stir-fry 3 minutes, or until chicken is browned and carrot is tender-crisp. Add egg; cook, stirring gently, until firm. Stir in rice and cook until heated through, gently separating grains. Add soy sauce and stir until mixture is well blended.

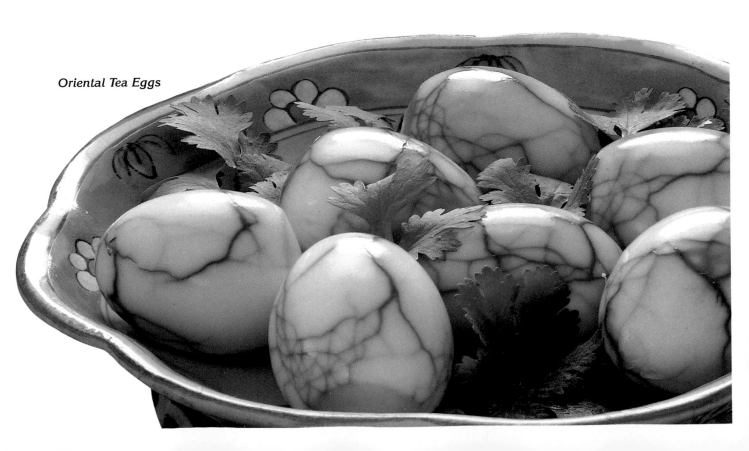

*Oriental Tea Eggs*

# JELL-O®
BRAND

# KIDS' COOKING FUN

# CONTENTS

Rules of the Kitchen     **354**

Cooking Tips     **355**

Equipment     **356**

Cooking Words to Know     **358**

The Real Easy Stuff     **359**

JIGGLERS Mania     **369**

Rainy Day Fun     **377**

Family Dinners     **387**

Left to right: Funny Face Desserts (*page 362*);
Ice Cream Shop Pies—Pistachio Chocolate Bar Pie and
Rocky Road Pie (*page 386*); Gelatin Pizza (*page 380*)

# RULES OF THE KITCHEN

1. Wash your hands with soap and water before you begin.

2. Read the **whole** recipe carefully before starting. If you don't understand any part, ask an adult to help you. Read "Cooking Tips," "Equipment" and "Cooking Words To Know" (pages 355-358) so you will know the meanings of all the words in the recipe.

3. Collect all the ingredients and equipment you need for the recipe before you start to cook.

4. Do one step of the recipe at a time. Do not skip steps.

5. Watch for symbols. Read and learn what the symbols mean (see below). When you see one of these symbols in the recipe, ask an adult to help you.

6. Measure carefully, using the correct equipment.

7. Use the size of pan called for in the recipe.

8. Follow the times given in the recipe. If a recipe says shake for 45 seconds, be sure you shake for at least 45 seconds.

9. Clean up when you are finished!

10. Share your tasty creations with family and friends.

# SYMBOLS

Boiling water is used in the recipe. **Always have an adult help you** when you are using boiling water.

A microwave is used in the recipe. **Have an adult help you** select a microwavable bowl. Be careful when taking the bowl out of the microwave. Use pot holders because the bowl could be hot.

An oven is used in the recipe. **Have an adult help you** remove hot pans from the oven. **Always use pot holders.** Be sure to turn the oven off when you are finished.

A stove is used in the recipe. **Have an adult help you** set the right temperature. Use pot holders to handle hot pans. Be sure to turn the stove off when you are finished.

A sharp knife is used in the recipe. **Have an adult help you** cut and chop. Put the knife in a safe place when you are finished using it. Be sure to carry the knife point down!

The recipe may be a little difficult. **Have an adult help you** to make sure you understand how to make the recipe.

# COOKING TIPS

## *Have an adult help you!*

## BOILING WATER

**Boiling water on the stove**

Boil water in a tea kettle. Pour the boiling water **carefully** into a measuring cup. Always put the tea kettle back on the stove.

**Boiling water in the microwave**

Pour water into a **microwavable** measuring cup. Microwave until water boils. Remove cup by handle **very carefully!** The cup could be very hot!

Remember, when you make JELL-O Gelatin, pour the boiling water **over** the gelatin. (Do **not** pour the gelatin **into** the boiling water.)

## HOW TO MEASURE

When using a measuring cup, hold it at eye level to be sure that you have measured correctly.

Use a set of metal or plastic measuring spoons. Choose the right size spoon. When the recipe calls for a teaspoon or tablespoon, be sure to use measuring spoons, not the spoons you use for eating.

## USING A SHAKER

1. Any 1-quart plastic container with a tight lid can be a shaker. After putting the ingredients into the shaker, put the lid on the shaker **very tightly.**

2. Put one hand on the top of the shaker and the other hand on the bottom of the shaker. Hold on very tightly. Shake hard for the amount of time given in the recipe.

# EQUIPMENT

*Be sure to use the right equipment if you want to be a good cook.*

*Yeah, yeah, yeah, yeah!*

"Read your JELL-O boxes carefully."

"Check package size."

"Make sure you use *Instant*."

## MEASURING EQUIPMENT

measuring spoons          measuring cups

## BOWLS

small mixing bowl    medium mixing bowl    large mixing bowl

## CONTAINERS

**1-quart shaker with a tight lid (any plastic container with a tight lid will do) (4 cups = 1 quart)**

# PANS, ETC.

**tea kettle**

**5-cup mold
(any shape will do)**

**muffin pan**

**8- or 9-inch
square pan**

**8 × 4-inch loaf pan**

**9-inch glass pie plate**

**12-inch pizza pan**

**13 × 9-inch pan**

**cookie sheet**

# UTENSILS AND TOOLS

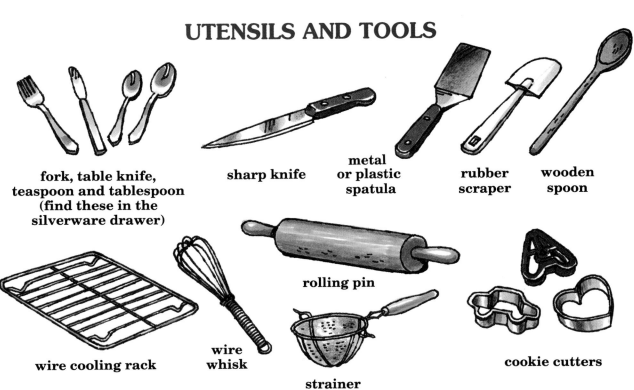

**fork, table knife,
teaspoon and tablespoon
(find these in the
silverware drawer)**

**sharp knife**

**metal
or plastic
spatula**

**rubber
scraper**

**wooden
spoon**

**rolling pin**

**wire cooling rack**

**wire
whisk**

**strainer**

**cookie cutters**

# COOKING WORDS TO KNOW

**BEAT** – to stir hard

**BLEND** – to mix thoroughly

**BOILING** – when bubbles are popping in hot water

**CHILL** – to put into the refrigerator to cool

**CHILL UNTIL SLIGHTLY THICKENED** – when the mixture is thick like catsup

**CHILL UNTIL THICKENED** – when you pull a spoon through the mixture, it leaves a track

**CHILL UNTIL SET** – when you touch the mixture, it sticks to your finger

**CHILL UNTIL FIRM** – when you touch the mixture, it will wiggle

**CHOP** – to cut into small pieces

**CRUMBLE** – to break into crumbs

**CRUSH** – to break into very small bits using a tool such as a rolling pin

**DISSOLVE GELATIN** – to stir boiling water and gelatin until all the crystals disappear

**STIR** – to mix together with a large spoon or rubber scraper

**THAW** – to become unfrozen and soft

**WEDGE** – a piece shaped like a triangle

# The Real Easy Stuff

*Start here! Learn how to make easy, delicious "Plain Gelatin." After you've made it, you'll be enough of a JELL-O chef to make great treats like "Funny Face Desserts!"*

**FUNNY FACE DESSERTS**
*(recipe on page 362)*

# PLAIN GELATIN

| INGREDIENTS | EQUIPMENT |
|---|---|
| 1 package (4-serving size) JELL-O Gelatin, any flavor<br>1 cup boiling water<br>1 cup cold water | Medium mixing bowl<br>Measuring cups<br>Rubber scraper or large spoon<br>4 dessert dishes |

**1** **POUR** gelatin into bowl.

**2** **ADD** 1 cup boiling water to gelatin.

**3** **STIR** with rubber scraper until gelatin is completely dissolved, about 2 minutes.

**4** **ADD** 1 cup cold water. Stir. Using measuring cup, scoop gelatin into dessert dishes.

**5** **PUT** dishes into refrigerator to chill until firm, about 3 hours.

Makes 4 servings

# FUNNY FACE DESSERTS

<table>
<tr><td>

## INGREDIENTS

2  cups cold milk

1  package (4-serving size)
   JELL-O Instant Pudding,
   any flavor

   Decorations, such as: fruit,
   candies, nuts, chocolate
   chips, peanut butter chips,
   miniature marshmallows,
   coconut

</td><td>

## EQUIPMENT

Measuring cup
1-quart shaker with a tight lid
4  dessert dishes

</td></tr>
</table>

**1** **POUR** 2 cups of cold milk into
shaker. Add pudding mix. Put lid
on shaker very tightly. Shake very
hard for at least 45 seconds. (Be sure
to hold top and bottom of shaker
tightly.)

**2** **OPEN** shaker. Pour pudding into
dessert dishes. Let pudding stand
for 5 minutes. Make faces on the
pudding with decorations. Eat
immediately, if you wish, or put dishes
into refrigerator to chill until serving
time.

**OR**

**MAKE** faces on JELL-O Gelatin.
Make Plain Gelatin (see page 360).
Pour gelatin into 4 dessert dishes.
After gelatin is firm, make the faces.

Makes 4 servings

# BREAKFAST MAGIC

<table>
<tr><td>

## INGREDIENTS

1 package (4-serving size)
   JELL-O Gelatin, any flavor
Cold cereal with milk
   OR
Any sliced fruit
   OR
Ready-to-eat waffles
Butter

</td><td>

## EQUIPMENT

Spoon or sprinkler (empty, clean salt shaker will do)
Table knife

</td></tr>
</table>

Sprinkle some dry gelatin over cereal and watch the magic color appear!

**OR**

Sprinkle some dry gelatin over your favorite fruit.

**OR**

Prepare waffles, following package directions. Butter waffles with table knife while they are still warm. Immediately sprinkle some dry gelatin over waffles. The more you sprinkle on, the brighter the color.

If you have leftover gelatin, fold up package to use another time.

# EASY PUDDING MILKSHAKE

| INGREDIENTS | EQUIPMENT |
|---|---|
| 1 cup cold milk<br>2 tablespoons JELL-O Instant Pudding, any flavor<br>1 scoop (½ cup) ice cream, any flavor, softened | Measuring cup<br>1-quart shaker with a tight lid<br>Measuring spoons<br>Ice cream scoop or ½ cup measure<br>Drinking glass |

**1** **POUR** 1 cup of cold milk into shaker. Add 2 tablespoons of pudding mix and the ice cream. Put lid on shaker very tightly.

**2** **SHAKE** very hard for at least 1 minute. (Be sure to hold top and bottom of shaker tightly.)

**3** **OPEN** shaker. Pour into glass. Drink right away.

Makes 1 serving

If you have leftover pudding mix, fold up package to use another time.

# FAVORITE FUN TOPPINGS

Top off your JELL-O Pudding and JELL-O Gelatin recipes with all kinds of fun toppings. These are some of JELL-O MAN's and WOBBLY's favorites. You may want to add some of your own.

| | | |
|---|---|---|
| **chocolate chips** | **gum drops** | **nuts** |
| **jelly beans** | **miniature marshmallows** | **red hot candies** |
| **string licorice** | **nonpareils** | **gummy bears** |
| **butterscotch chips** | **candy corn** | **jellied fruit slices** |
| **peanut butter chips** | **plain or toasted** | **multi-colored milk** |
| | **coconut** | **chocolate candies** |

# JIGGLERS Mania

*What's more fun than making and eating JIGGLERS?
Going crazy over "JIGGLERS Surprises," "JIGGLERS
Pineapple Snacks" and more!*

**JIGGLERS "SURPRISES"**
*(recipe on page 372)*

# JIGGLERS
Gelatin Snacks

<table>
<tr><td>

## INGREDIENTS

4 packages (4-serving size each) OR 2 packages (8-serving size each) JELL-O Gelatin, any flavor

2½ cups boiling water

</td><td>

## EQUIPMENT

Medium mixing bowl
Measuring cup
Rubber scraper or large spoon
13 x 9-inch pan
Small cookie cutters or table knife

</td></tr>
</table>

**1** **POUR** gelatin into bowl. Add 2½ cups boiling water to gelatin. Stir with rubber scraper until gelatin is completely dissolved, about 2 minutes.

**2** **POUR** into 13 x 9-inch pan. Put pan into refrigerator to chill until firm, about 3 hours.

**3** **TAKE** pan out of refrigerator. Put about 1 inch of warm water in sink. Dip **just bottom** of pan into warm water for 15 seconds.

**4** **USE** cookie cutters to cut gelatin into any shapes you wish. (If you do not have cookie cutters, cut gelatin into squares with a table knife.)

**5** **LIFT** shapes out of pan with your fingers.

Makes about 24 small shapes

Use any leftover pieces to make "Scrap Happy" (see page 376).

# JIGGLERS "SURPRISES"

## INGREDIENTS

4 packages (4-serving size each) OR 2 packages (8-serving size each) JELL-O Gelatin, any flavor

2½ cups boiling water

36 "surprises," such as: banana slices, strawberry halves, canned pineapple chunks

## EQUIPMENT

Medium mixing bowl
Measuring cup
Rubber scraper or large spoon
13 x 9-inch pan
Table knife

**1** **POUR** gelatin into bowl. Add 2½ cups boiling water to gelatin. Stir with rubber scraper until gelatin is completely dissolved, about 2 minutes. Pour into 13 x 9-inch pan.

**2** **LET** pan of gelatin stand on counter for 30 minutes. Gelatin will become thickened.

**3** **ARRANGE** "surprises" in rows in thickened gelatin so that, when cut, each square will have a surprise. Put pan into refrigerator to chill until firm, about 3 hours. Take pan out of refrigerator.

**4** **PUT** about 1 inch of warm water in sink. Dip **just bottom** of pan into warm water for 15 seconds. With table knife, cut gelatin into shapes, making sure you have a piece of fruit in each shape. Lift shapes out of pan with your fingers.

Makes about 36 small shapes

Use any leftover pieces to make "Scrap Happy" (see page 376).

# JIGGLERS PINEAPPLE SNACKS

<table>
<tr><th>INGREDIENTS</th><th>EQUIPMENT</th></tr>
</table>

| INGREDIENTS | EQUIPMENT |
|---|---|
| 4 packages (4-serving size each) OR 2 packages (8-serving size each) JELL-O Gelatin, any flavor<br><br>2 cups boiling water<br><br>1 can (8 ounces) crushed pineapple with juice, undrained | Medium mixing bowl<br>Measuring cup<br>Rubber scraper or large spoon<br>13 x 9-inch pan<br>Small cookie cutters or table knife |

**1** **POUR** gelatin into bowl. Add 2 cups boiling water to gelatin. Stir with rubber scraper until gelatin is completely dissolved, about 2 minutes. Add crushed pineapple with juice. Stir. Pour into 13 x 9-inch pan.

**2** **PUT** pan into refrigerator to chill until firm, about 3 hours. Take pan out of refrigerator. Put about 1 inch of warm water in sink. Dip **just bottom** of pan into warm water for 15 seconds.

**3** **USE** cookie cutters to cut gelatin into shapes. (If you do not have cookie cutters, cut gelatin into shapes with a table knife.) Lift shapes out of pan with your fingers or table knife.

Makes about 36 small shapes

Use any leftover pieces to make "Scrap Happy" (see page 376).

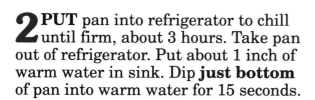

# SCRAP HAPPY

After you have made JELL-O JIGGLERS, you can use the leftovers to make a delicious snack—"Scrap Happy."

Make a "dish" by spreading thawed COOL WHIP Whipped Topping over the bottom and up the sides of a small bowl. Tear the scraps from your JIGGLERS into little pieces with your fingers. Then fill each bowl with the JIGGLERS scraps. Put bowls into refrigerator to chill until serving time.

# Rainy Day Fun

*Being stuck in the house on a rainy day doesn't have to be boring. Whip up a few "Dirt Cups," a "Gelatin Pizza" or some "Colorful Candy Popcorn Balls" and have your own little party.*

**COLORFUL CANDY POPCORN BALLS**
*(recipe on page 384)*

# DIRT CUPS

<table>
<tr><th>INGREDIENTS</th><th>EQUIPMENT</th></tr>
<tr><td>

2 cups cold milk

1 package (4-serving size) JELL-O Instant Pudding, Chocolate Flavor

3½ cups (8-ounce container) COOL WHIP Whipped Topping, thawed

1 package (16 ounces) chocolate sandwich cookies, crushed, divided

</td><td>

Measuring cup

Medium mixing bowl

Wire whisk

Rubber scraper or large spoon

Measuring spoons

8 to 10 paper or plastic cups (8 ounces each)

Baseball decorations, if you wish

</td></tr>
</table>

**1** **POUR** 2 cups of cold milk into bowl. Add pudding mix. Beat with wire whisk until well blended, about 2 minutes. Let pudding stand 5 minutes.

**2** **STIR** whipped topping and ½ of the crushed cookies into pudding **very gently** with rubber scraper until mixture is all the same color. Place about 1 tablespoon of the remaining crushed cookies into bottom of each paper or plastic cup.

**3** **FILL** cups about ¾ full with pudding mixture. Top each cup with the rest of the crushed cookies. Put cups into refrigerator to chill until set, about 1 hour. Add baseball decorations, if you wish.

Makes 8 to 10 Dirt Cups

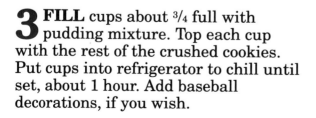

Make your favorite baseball pennants out of paper and toothpicks. You can make a baseball diamond out of licorice and candies. If you have small plastic baseball players, use them too!

# GELATIN PIZZA

<table>
<tr><td>

## INGREDIENTS

4 packages (4-serving size
   each) OR 2 packages
   (8-serving size each)
   JELL-O Gelatin, any flavor
2½ cups boiling water
   No-stick cooking spray
1 cup thawed COOL WHIP
   Whipped Topping
2 cups cut-up fruit

</td><td>

## EQUIPMENT

Medium mixing bowl
Measuring cup
Rubber scraper or large spoon
12-inch pizza pan with
 ½-inch sides
Table knife or pizza cutter
Metal spatula

</td></tr>
</table>

**1** **POUR** gelatin into bowl. Add 2½ cups boiling water to gelatin. Stir with rubber scraper until gelatin is completely dissolved, about 2 minutes. Spray inside of pizza pan with no-stick cooking spray. Pour gelatin mixture into pizza pan. Put pan into refrigerator to chill until firm, about 3 hours.

**2** **TAKE** pan out of refrigerator when ready to serve. Put about 1 inch of warm water in sink. Carefully dip **just bottom** of pan into warm water for 15 seconds. Spread whipped topping over gelatin with rubber scraper, leaving about 1 inch of space around outside edge of gelatin for pizza "crust."

**3** **TOP** pizza with fruit, arranging fruit in whatever design you like. Cut pizza into wedges with table knife. Lift pizza wedges from pan with spatula.

Makes 10 to 12 servings

# CHOCOLATE PUDDING COOKIES

<table>
<tr><td>

## INGREDIENTS

1 package (4-serving size)
   JELL-O Instant Pudding,
   Chocolate Flavor
1 cup buttermilk baking mix
¼ cup oil
1 egg
   Peanut butter chips or
   other assorted candies

</td><td>

## EQUIPMENT

Measuring cups
Large mixing bowl
Wooden spoon
Tablespoon
Cookie sheet
Metal or plastic spatula
Wire cooling racks

</td></tr>
</table>

**1 PREHEAT** oven to 350⁰. Put pudding mix and baking mix in bowl. Mix together with wooden spoon. Add oil and egg. Mix together until mixture forms a ball.

**2 TAKE** a small spoonful of dough and shape it into a ½-inch ball. Place ball on ungreased cookie sheet. Shape rest of dough into ½-inch balls. Place balls about 2 inches apart on ungreased cookie sheet.

**3 PRESS** your thumb into middle of each ball to make a thumbprint. Put peanut butter chips or candies in thumbprint. Bake at 350⁰ for 5 to 8 minutes or until lightly browned. Remove cookies from cookie sheet with spatula. Place on wire racks; cool.

Makes about 36 cookies

# COLORFUL CANDY POPCORN BALLS

<table>
<tr><th>INGREDIENTS</th></tr>
</table>

## INGREDIENTS

12  cups popped popcorn
 1  cup peanuts
 ¾  cup multi-colored milk
    chocolate candies
 ¼  cup (½ stick) margarine
 1  bag (10 ½ ounces) KRAFT
    Miniature Marshmallows
 1  package (4-serving size)
    JELL-O Gelatin, any flavor
    Margarine for greasing
    your hands

## EQUIPMENT

Measuring cups
Huge bowl or very large pot
Wooden spoon
Large microwavable bowl
Pot holders
Waxed paper

**1** **POUR** popcorn into huge bowl. Add peanuts and milk chocolate candies. Mix together with spoon.

**2** **PUT** margarine and marshmallows in large **microwavable** bowl. Microwave on HIGH 1½ to 2 minutes or until marshmallows are puffed. Using pot holders, take bowl out of microwave. **(Careful! Bowl will be hot.)** Mix together with spoon.

**3** **ADD** gelatin to marshmallow mixture. Stir with spoon until mixture is all the same color.

**4** **POUR** marshmallow mixture over popcorn mixture in huge bowl. Quickly stir with spoon until marshmallow mixture evenly covers popcorn mixture. Let mixture cool slightly. **Grease your hands well** with some margarine. Shape mixture into balls with your hands. Place balls on waxed paper until completely cool.

Makes about 24 popcorn balls

# ICE CREAM SHOP PIES

Now that you are a super cook, invent your very own pie. Use the "Toffee Bar Crunch Pie" on page 392 as your basic recipe. Change the crust, the sauce, the pudding flavor and the candies and you have a new pie! Here are 2 changes to the "Toffee Bar Crunch Pie" to get you started. Now make up your own! Fill in the chart so you have a record of your recipe.

|  | Toffee Bar Crunch Pie | Pistachio Chocolate Bar Pie | Rocky Road Pie | *My Pie* |
|---|---|---|---|---|
| **Sauce** | Butterscotch | Chocolate | Chocolate | |
| **Crust** | Graham Cracker | Chocolate Crumb | Chocolate Crumb | |
| **JELL-O Instant Pudding Flavor** | Vanilla | Pistachio | Chocolate | |
| **Candy Add-Ins** | 1 cup chopped chocolate-covered English toffee bars | 1 cup chopped chocolate candy bars | ½ cup chocolate chips and ½ cup KRAFT Miniature Marshmallows | |

# Family Dinners.

*You will be the star of the family when you make one of these super recipes for dinner. Whether you choose "Strawberry-Banana Salad" or "Pudding Poke Cake," your whole family will be impressed.*

**STRAWBERRY-BANANA SALAD**
*(recipe on page 388)*

# STRAWBERRY-BANANA SALAD

## INGREDIENTS

2 packages (4-serving size each) JELL-O Gelatin, Strawberry or Strawberry-Banana Flavor

1½ cups boiling water

1 cup cold water
Ice cubes

2 medium bananas, sliced
No-stick cooking spray
Mixed fresh fruit, such as: strawberry halves, banana slices, grapes (about 2 cups)

## EQUIPMENT

Large mixing bowl
2-cup measuring cup
Rubber scraper or large spoon
4-cup mold
Serving plate

**1** POUR gelatin into bowl. Add 1½ cups boiling water to gelatin. Stir with rubber scraper until gelatin is completely dissolved, about 2 minutes.

**2** POUR 1 cup cold water into 2-cup measuring cup. Add enough ice cubes to make 1¾ cups in all. Add the ice cubes and water to gelatin mixture. Stir until slightly thickened. Remove any unmelted ice.

**3** **LET** gelatin stand until thickened, 5 to 10 minutes. Gently stir in sliced bananas. Spray inside of mold with no-stick cooking spray. Pour gelatin mixture into mold. Put mold into refrigerator to chill until firm, about 2 hours. Take mold out of refrigerator.

**4** **PUT** about 4 inches of warm water in sink. Dip mold into warm water **just to top** of mold for 10 seconds. Dip your fingers in warm water. Gently pull gelatin from edge of mold with wet fingers.

**5** **PUT** plate upside down on top of mold. Holding tightly, turn mold and plate over so mold is on top and plate is on bottom. (Have an adult help you.) Shake gently to loosen gelatin. Take mold off. Arrange fresh fruit inside or around mold, as you wish.

Makes 8 servings

# PUDDING POKE CAKE

<table>
<tr><td>

## INGREDIENTS

1 **pound cake loaf (about 12 ounces)**

1½ **cups cold milk**

1 **package (4-serving size) JELL-O Instant Pudding, Chocolate Flavor**

**Candy decorations, if you wish**

</td><td>

## EQUIPMENT

**Serving plate**
**Wooden spoon**
**Measuring cups**
**1-quart shaker with a tight lid**
**Table knife**

</td></tr>
</table>

**1 REMOVE** cake from wrapper and place it on plate. Poke 25 to 30 holes into top of cake with handle of wooden spoon.

**2 POUR** 1½ cups of cold milk into shaker. Add pudding mix. Put lid on shaker very tightly. Shake very hard for at least 45 seconds. (Be sure to hold top and bottom of shaker tightly.)

**3 POUR** about ¼ of the pudding mixture quickly over holes in cake. Tap cake lightly on counter so pudding will go down holes. Pour about ⅓ of the rest of the pudding over holes. Tap cake again.

**4** **LET** rest of pudding stand 2 minutes to thicken. Frost sides and top of cake with remaining pudding using table knife. Put cake into refrigerator to chill until serving time. Sprinkle with candy decorations, if you wish.

Makes 8 to 10 servings

# TOFFEE BAR CRUNCH PIE

<table>
<tr><th>INGREDIENTS</th><th>EQUIPMENT</th></tr>
</table>

**INGREDIENTS**

$^{1}/_{3}$ cup butterscotch sauce

1 packaged graham cracker crust

1$^{1}/_{2}$ cups cold half-and-half or milk

1 package (4-serving size) JELL-O Instant Pudding, Vanilla Flavor

3$^{1}/_{2}$ cups (8-ounce container) COOL WHIP Whipped Topping, thawed

1 cup chopped chocolate-covered English toffee bars (about 6 bars)

Additional toffee bars, chopped, if you wish

**EQUIPMENT**

Measuring cups

Tablespoon

Large mixing bowl

Wire whisk

Rubber scraper

**1 POUR** butterscotch sauce onto bottom of pie crust. Spread gently with back of spoon to cover evenly.

**2 POUR** 1$^{1}/_{2}$ cups of cold half-and-half into bowl. Add pudding mix. Beat with wire whisk until well blended, about 2 minutes. Let pudding stand until slightly thickened, about 5 minutes.

**3** **STIR** whipped topping and chopped toffee bars into pudding **very gently** with rubber scraper until mixture is all the same color. Spoon mixture into crust.

**4** **PUT** pie in freezer for 6 hours or overnight. Remove pie from freezer. Let pie stand at room temperature about 10 minutes before serving. Decorate with chopped toffee bars, if you wish.

Makes 8 servings

Store any leftover pie in the freezer.

# Cookies & Pies

Includes
**PRIZE-WINNING**
Recipes

# CONTENTS

Tips for Cookie Success
From the Crisco Kitchen     **396**

Cookie Classics     **398**

Delicious Bar Cookies     **412**

Extra Special Cookies     **420**

Down-Home Pies     **432**

Party-Time Pies     **446**

Left to right: Chocolate Peanut Butter Cup Cookies (*page 430*);
Lola's Apple Pie (*page 432*)

# TIPS FOR COOKIE SUCCESS FROM THE CRISCO KITCHEN

★★★★

## General guidelines

• Read the entire recipe before beginning to make sure you have all the necessary ingredients and baking utensils.

• Measure all the ingredients accurately and assemble them in the order called for in the recipe.

• Prepare pans and baking sheets according to the recipe directions. Adjust the oven racks and heat the oven before starting to bake. Check the oven temperature for accuracy with a mercury oven thermometer.

• Follow the recipe directions and baking times exactly. Check for doneness using the test given in the recipe.

• Add 1 tablespoon milk or water for each ½ cup Butter Flavor Crisco when converting a recipe calling for butter or margarine.

## Measuring

• Use standardized graduated measuring cups for measuring all dry ingredients and ingredients like Butter Flavor Crisco, peanut butter, sour cream, yogurt, nuts, dried fruit, marshmallow creme, coconut, chopped fresh fruit, preserves and jams. Fill the correct measuring cup to overflowing and level it off with the straight edge of metal spatula or knife.

• Use standardized glass or plastic liquid measuring cups with a pouring spout to measure all liquid ingredients. Place the cup on a flat surface, fill to the desired mark and check the measurement at eye level.

• Use standardized graduated measuring spoons, not eating or serving spoons, for measuring small amounts of ingredients. For dry ingredients, fill the correct measuring spoon to overflowing and level it off with the straight edge of a metal spatula or knife.

- Lightly spoon flour into the correct measuring cup and then level it off with the straight edge of a metal spatula or knife. Do not tap or bang the measuring cup or dip the measuring cup into the bag as this will pack the flour. Too much flour can make cookies dry.

- Press brown sugar into the correct measuring cup and level it off with the straight edge of a metal spatula or knife. It should hold the shape of the cup when turned out. Use light brown sugar unless otherwise stated.

- Press Butter Flavor Crisco into the correct measuring cup. Cut through with a metal spatula or knife and press again to eliminate air pockets. Level with the straight edge of a metal spatula or knife.

- Use large eggs unless stated otherwise.

## Baking

- Use shiny, sturdy aluminum baking sheets with little or no sides. They allow the heat to circulate easily during baking and promote even browning. Cookies baked on insulated baking sheets may need 1 to 2 minutes longer baking time.

- Bake only one baking sheet at a time in the center of the oven. If the cookies brown unevenly, rotate the baking sheet from front to back halfway through the baking time. If you do use more than one sheet at a time, rotate the baking sheets from top to bottom halfway through the baking time. Space oven racks 6 inches apart. Allow baking sheets to cool between batches; the dough will spread if placed on a hot baking sheet.

- Watch cookies carefully to avoid overbaking. Check them at the minimum baking time, then check them often to make sure they don't overbake. Follow the recipe for yield and size since the baking time is determined for that size cookie.

- Remove cookies from the baking sheets immediately after baking and place in a single layer on wire racks to cool, unless otherwise specified. Always cool cookies completely before stacking and storing. Bar cookies may be cooled and stored in the baking pan.

## Storage

- Store cooled cookies at room temperature in airtight containers unless otherwise specified in the recipe. Store each kind separately to prevent changes in flavor and texture. Freeze baked cookies in airtight containers or freezer bags for up to six months.

# Cookie Classics

## ★ CHILD'S CHOICE ★

**Debbie and Garret Smith, Cascade, Montana**
*Garret (age 8) and his mom, Debbie, filled these cookies with every kind of goodie they could think of.*

2⅓ cups all-purpose flour
1 cup Butter Flavor Crisco®
1 teaspoon baking soda
½ teaspoon baking powder
1 cup granulated sugar
1 cup firmly packed brown sugar
2 eggs
1 teaspoon maple flavor

2 cups Quaker® Oats (quick or old fashioned), uncooked
¾ cup Hershey's Semi-Sweet Chocolate Chips
¾ cup Reese's® Peanut Butter Chips
¾ cup miniature marshmallows

1. Heat oven to 350°F. Grease baking sheet with Butter Flavor Crisco.

2. Combine flour, Butter Flavor Crisco, baking soda and baking powder in large bowl. Beat at low speed of electric mixer until blended. Increase speed to medium. Mix thoroughly. Beat in granulated sugar, brown sugar, eggs and maple flavor. Add oats. Stir in chocolate chips, peanut butter chips and marshmallows with spoon until well blended.

3. Shape dough into 1½-inch balls. Flatten slightly. Place 2 inches apart on greased baking sheet.

4. Bake at 350°F for 9 to 10 minutes or until light golden brown. Cool 1 minute on baking sheet before removing to cooling rack.

*Makes 3½ dozen cookies*

*Child's Choice*

# ★ BUTTER-FLAVORED ★ BRICKLE DRIZZLES

**Judy and John Repplinger, Sheridan, Oregon**
*Judy and her son John, 15, decided their cookies won the blue ribbon at the Oregon State Fair because they are moist and chewy, yet at the same time crunchy.*

## COOKIES

1 cup Butter Flavor Crisco®
1 cup granulated sugar
1 cup firmly packed brown sugar
1 can (14 ounces) sweetened condensed milk (not evaporated milk)
1 teaspoon vanilla

1¾ cups all-purpose flour
1 teaspoon salt
½ teaspoon baking soda
3 cups Quick Quaker® Oats, uncooked
1 cup almond brickle chips

## DRIZZLE

1 cup Hershey's Milk Chocolate Chips

1. Heat oven to 350°F. Grease baking sheet with Butter Flavor Crisco.

2. **For cookies,** combine Butter Flavor Crisco, granulated sugar and brown sugar in large bowl. Stir with spoon until well blended and creamy. Stir in condensed milk and vanilla. Mix well.

3. Combine flour, salt and baking soda. Stir into creamed mixture. Stir in oats.

4. Shape dough into 1-inch balls. Press tops into brickle chips. Place brickle side up 2 inches apart on greased baking sheet.

5. Bake at 350°F for 9 to 10 minutes or until set but not browned. Remove to cooling rack. Cool completely.

6. **For drizzle,** place chocolate chips in heavy resealable sandwich bag. Seal. Microwave at 50% (MEDIUM). Knead bag after 1 minute. Repeat until smooth (or melt by placing in bowl of hot water). Cut tiny tip off corner of bag. Squeeze out and drizzle over cookies. *Makes 6 dozen cookies*

*Butter-Flavored Brickle Drizzles*

# ★ OATMEAL COOKIES ★

**Joan and Karlie Pagano, Tulsa, Oklahoma**
*Joan and seven-year-old Karlie really had a third member of the family on their team at the Tulsa State Fair; Joan's mother provided inspiration, support and guidance during the creation of this prize-winning cookie.*

1¼ cups Butter Flavor Crisco®
¾ cup firmly packed brown sugar
3 tablespoons milk
1 teaspoon water
½ teaspoon vanilla
½ teaspoon coconut flavor
1 egg

1¼ cups all-purpose flour
1 teaspoon baking soda
¾ teaspoon salt
3 cups Quaker® Oats (quick or old fashioned), uncooked
½ cup pecan pieces
½ cup raisins

1. Heat oven to 325°F.

2. Combine Butter Flavor Crisco, brown sugar, milk, water, vanilla and coconut flavor in large bowl. Beat at medium speed of electric mixer until well blended. Beat in egg.

3. Combine flour, baking soda and salt. Add gradually to creamed mixture at low speed. Mix until well blended. Stir in oats, nuts and raisins with spoon. Drop by rounded teaspoonfuls 2 inches apart onto ungreased baking sheet.

4. Bake at 325°F for 10 to 12 minutes or until slightly browned and slightly moist in center. Cool 2 minutes on baking sheet before removing to cooling rack.

*Makes 5 dozen cookies*

# SNICKERDOODLES

2 cups sugar, divided
1 cup Butter Flavor Crisco®
2 eggs
2 tablespoons milk
1 teaspoon vanilla

2¾ cups all-purpose flour
2 teaspoons cream of tartar
1 teaspoon baking soda
¾ teaspoon salt
2 teaspoons cinnamon

1. Heat oven to 400°F.

2. Combine 1½ cups sugar, Butter Flavor Crisco, eggs, milk and vanilla in large bowl. Beat at medium speed of electric mixer until well blended.

3. Combine flour, cream of tartar, baking soda and salt. Add gradually to creamed mixture at low speed. Mix just until blended. Shape dough into 1-inch balls.

4. Combine remaining ½ cup sugar and cinnamon in small bowl. Roll balls of dough in mixture. Place 2 inches apart on ungreased baking sheet.

5. Bake at 400°F for 7 to 8 minutes. Remove to cooling rack.

*Makes 6 dozen cookies*

**Hint:** Cinnamon-sugar mixture can be put in resealable plastic bag. Put 2 to 3 dough balls at a time in bag. Seal. Shake to sugar-coat dough.

**VARIATION**
**Colored Sugar Snickerdoodles:** Add the 2 teaspoons cinnamon to flour mixture in Step 3. Combine 3 tablespoons colored sugar and 3 tablespoons granulated sugar. Use for coating instead of cinnamon-sugar mixture.

# ★ PEANUT BUTTER CHOCOLATE ★ CHIP COOKIES

**Teri and Nicholas Redding, Sibley, Louisiana**
*It was 12-year-old Nicholas who convinced his mother, Teri, to join him in a mother/son baking team, which produced this prize-winning cookie.*

1 cup plus 1 tablespoon Butter Flavor Crisco®, divided
1 cup slivered almonds
¾ cup granulated sugar
¾ cup firmly packed brown sugar
¾ cup Jif® Creamy Peanut Butter
1 teaspoon vanilla
½ teaspoon almond extract
1 teaspoon water
2 eggs
2¼ cups all-purpose flour
1 teaspoon baking powder
1 teaspoon salt
1 package (12 ounces) Hershey's Semi-Sweet Chocolate Chips (2 cups)

1. Heat oven to 350°F.

2. Place 1 tablespoon Butter Flavor Crisco and nuts in baking pan. Place in 350°F oven to melt shortening. Stir well. Stir every 2 minutes until nuts are light golden brown. Remove from oven. Cool completely.

3. Combine remaining 1 cup Butter Flavor Crisco, granulated sugar, brown sugar, peanut butter, vanilla, almond extract and water in large bowl. Beat at medium speed of electric mixer until well blended. Add eggs. Beat until blended.

4. Combine flour, baking powder and salt. Add gradually to creamed mixture at low speed. Mix just until blended. Stir in nuts and chocolate chips with spoon. Drop by rounded tablespoonfuls 2 inches apart onto ungreased baking sheet.

5. Bake at 350°F for 10 to 12 minutes or until light golden brown. Remove to cooling rack.

*Makes 3½ to 4 dozen cookies*

# ★ BRIAN'S BUFFALO COOKIES ★

**Vickie and Brian Vaughan, Sparks, Nevada**
*Brian's Buffalo Cookies were named the Chocolate Chip National Winner at the 1991 Butter Flavor Crisco American Cookie Celebration.*

1 cup Butter Flavor Crisco®, melted
1 cup granulated sugar
1 cup firmly packed brown sugar
2 tablespoons milk
1 teaspoon vanilla
2 eggs
2 cups all-purpose flour
1 teaspoon baking powder
1 teaspoon baking soda
½ teaspoon salt
1 cup Quaker® Oats (quick or old fashioned), uncooked
1 cup corn flakes, crushed to about ½ cup
1 cup Hershey's Semi-Sweet Chocolate Chips
½ cup chopped pecans
½ cup flake coconut

1. Heat oven to 350°F. Grease baking sheet with Butter Flavor Crisco.

2. Combine Butter Flavor Crisco, granulated sugar, brown sugar, milk and vanilla in large bowl. Beat at low speed of electric mixer until well blended. Add eggs. Beat at medium speed until well blended.

3. Combine flour, baking powder, baking soda and salt. Add gradually to creamed mixture at low speed. Stir in oats, corn flakes, chocolate chips, nuts and coconut with spoon. Fill ice cream scoop that holds ¼ cup with dough (or use ¼ cup measure). Level with knife. Drop 3 inches apart onto greased baking sheet.

4. Bake at 350°F for 13 to 15 minutes or until lightly browned around edges but still slightly soft in center. Cool 3 minutes on baking sheet before removing to cooling rack with wide, thin pancake turner. *Makes 2 to 2½ dozen cookies*

*Brian's Buffalo Cookies*

# ★ DREAMY CHOCOLATE CHIP ★ COOKIES

**Alieen Reed and Alissia Harmon, Pine Bluff, Arkansas**
*Alieen and Alissia may be newcomers to Pine Bluff, but the mother-daughter team obviously knows its way around a kitchen.*

1¼ cups firmly packed brown sugar
¾ cup Butter Flavor Crisco®
3 eggs, lightly beaten
2 teaspoons vanilla
1 package (4 ounces) German's sweet chocolate, melted, cooled
3 cups all-purpose flour
1 teaspoon baking soda
½ teaspoon salt
1 package (11½ ounces) Hershey's Milk Chocolate Chips
1 package (10 ounces) Hershey's Premium Semi-Sweet Chocolate Chunks
1 cup coarsely chopped macadamia nuts

1. Heat oven to 375°F.

2. Combine brown sugar, Butter Flavor Crisco, eggs and vanilla in large bowl. Beat at low speed of electric mixer until blended. Increase speed to high. Beat 2 minutes. Add melted chocolate. Mix until well blended.

3. Combine flour, baking soda and salt. Add gradually to creamed mixture at low speed.

4. Stir in chocolate chips, chocolate chunks and nuts with spoon. Drop by rounded tablespoonfuls 3 inches apart onto ungreased baking sheet.

5. Bake at 375°F for 9 to 11 minutes or until set. Cool 2 minutes on baking sheet before removing to cooling rack. *Makes 3 dozen cookies*

*Dreamy Chocolate Chip Cookies*

# ★ CHOCO-SCUTTERBOTCH ★

**Mary Fran and Rachelle Nelson,
Plymouth, New Hampshire**
*Mary Fran and her daughter, Rachelle, just recently moved from a
city of 60,000 to the small farm community of Plymouth.*

⅔ cup Butter Flavor Crisco®
½ cup firmly packed brown sugar
2 eggs
1 package (18.25 ounces)
    Duncan Hines® Moist Deluxe
    Yellow Cake Mix
1 cup toasted rice cereal

½ cup milk chocolate chunks
½ cup Hershey's Butterscotch
    Chips
½ cup Hershey's Semi-Sweet
    Chocolate Chips
½ cup coarsely chopped walnuts
    or pecans

1. Heat oven to 375°F.

2. Combine Butter Flavor Crisco and brown sugar in large bowl. Beat at medium speed of electric mixer until well blended. Beat in eggs.

3. Add cake mix gradually at low speed. Mix until well blended. Stir in cereal, chocolate chunks, butterscotch chips, chocolate chips and nuts with spoon. Stir until well blended. Shape dough into 1¼-inch balls. Place 2 inches apart on ungreased baking sheet. Flatten slightly. Shape sides to form circle, if necessary.

4. Bake at 375°F for 7 to 9 minutes or until lightly browned around edges. Cool 2 minutes before removing to paper towels.    *Makes 3 dozen cookies*

# ★ OATMEAL HONEY COOKIES ★

**Sherry and Ashlie Willis, Memphis, Tennessee**
*Sherry and Ashlie had one advantage in the Mid-South Fair in
Memphis — they had based their recipe on an old family recipe for
"grandma's cookies."*

1 cup Butter Flavor Crisco®
1 cup firmly packed dark brown
    sugar
1 egg
½ cup honey
¼ cup granulated sugar
¼ cup water
1½ teaspoons vanilla

1½ cups all-purpose flour
1 teaspoon cinnamon
½ teaspoon baking soda
½ teaspoon salt
3 cups Quaker® Oats (quick or
    old fashioned), uncooked
1 cup raisins
½ cup coarsely chopped pecans

*continued*

*Choco-Scutterbotch*

1. Heat oven to 350°F. Grease baking sheet with Butter Flavor Crisco.

2. Combine Butter Flavor Crisco, brown sugar, egg, honey, granulated sugar, water and vanilla in large bowl. Beat at low speed of electric mixer until blended. Increase speed to medium. Beat until light and creamy.

3. Combine flour, cinnamon, baking soda and salt. Add gradually to creamed mixture at low speed. Increase speed to medium. Beat until well blended. Stir in oats with spoon. Mix until well blended. Stir in raisins and nuts. Drop by heaping tablespoonfuls onto greased baking sheet.

4. Bake at 350°F for 11 to 12 minutes or until golden brown. Cool 3 to 5 minutes on baking sheet before removing to flat surface.

*Makes 3 dozen cookies*

**Note:** For small cookies, drop dough by heaping teaspoonfuls onto greased baking sheet. Bake at 350°F for 9 to 11 minutes. Makes 4 to 5 dozen small cookies.

# ★ OATMEAL TOFFEE LIZZIES ★

**Jan and Elizabeth Whitaker, Crofton, Kentucky**
*Although Jan considers herself an accomplished chef, she had never entered a cooking competition before.*

1 cup Butter Flavor Crisco®
1 cup granulated sugar
1 cup firmly packed brown sugar
2 eggs, beaten
1 tablespoon milk
1 teaspoon vanilla
2 cups all-purpose flour
1 teaspoon baking soda

1 teaspoon salt
2 cups Quick Quaker® Oats, uncooked
1 package (12 ounces) Hershey's Semi-Sweet Chocolate Chips (2 cups)
3/4 cup almond brickle chips
1/2 cup finely chopped pecans

1. Heat oven to 350°F. Grease baking sheet with Butter Flavor Crisco.

2. Combine Butter Flavor Crisco, granulated sugar and brown sugar in large bowl. Beat with spoon until well blended. Add eggs, milk and vanilla. Mix well.

3. Combine flour, baking soda and salt. Add to creamed mixture. Mix well. Stir in oats, chocolate chips, brickle chips and nuts until well blended. Shape dough into 1¼- to 1½-inch balls with lightly floured hands. Place 2 inches apart on greased baking sheet. Flatten slightly.

4. Bake at 350°F for 12 to 15 minutes or until cookies begin to brown around edges. Remove to flat surface to cool.

*Makes 4½ dozen cookies*

# ★ PEANUT BUTTER AND JELLY ★ THUMBPRINT COOKIES

**Terry and Mandy Moore, Oaklyn, New Jersey**
*This mother-daughter team has been entering baking contests
together for four years.*

## COOKIES

½ cup **Butter Flavor Crisco®**
½ cup **Jif® Creamy Peanut Butter**
½ cup **granulated sugar**
½ cup **firmly packed brown sugar**
1½ teaspoons **vanilla**
1 **egg**
¼ cup **toasted wheat germ**
¾ cup **all-purpose flour**

½ cup **whole wheat flour**
¾ teaspoon **baking soda**
½ teaspoon **baking powder**
½ teaspoon **salt**
1 **egg white, lightly beaten**
1 cup **chopped cocktail peanuts**
¼ cup **strawberry spreadable fruit**\*

## DRIZZLE

3 tablespoons **Hershey's Semi-Sweet Chocolate Chips**

1. **For cookies,** combine Butter Flavor Crisco, peanut butter, granulated sugar, brown sugar and vanilla in large bowl. Beat with spoon until well blended. Beat in egg and wheat germ.

2. Combine all-purpose flour, whole wheat flour, baking soda, baking powder and salt. Stir into creamed mixture. Cover. Refrigerate 3 hours or overnight.

3. Heat oven to 375°F. Grease baking sheet with Butter Flavor Crisco.

4. Shape dough into ¾-inch balls. Roll in egg white and then nuts. Place 2 inches apart on greased baking sheet. Press thumb in center of each ball.

5. Bake at 375°F for 8 to 10 minutes or until set and just beginning to brown. Remove to cooling rack. Spoon ¼ teaspoon spreadable fruit into center of each hot cookie. Cool completely.

6. **For drizzle,** place chocolate chips in heavy resealable sandwich bag. Seal. Microwave at 50% (MEDIUM). Knead bag after 1 minute. Repeat until smooth (or melt by placing in bowl of hot water). Cut tiny tip off corner of bag. Squeeze out and drizzle over cookies.            *Makes 5½ to 6 dozen cookies*

\*Substitute strawberry jam for spreadable fruit, if desired.

# *Delicious Bar Cookies*

## ★ EMILY'S DREAM BARS ★

**Michael and Emily Cacia, Indianapolis, Indiana**
*Emily credits teamwork between her and father, Michael, for the success of these cookies. Both teammates credit the chocolate-covered peanuts for the extra-special flavor.*

1 cup Jif® Extra Crunchy Peanut Butter
½ cup Butter Flavor Crisco®
½ cup firmly packed brown sugar
½ cup light corn syrup
1 egg
1 teaspoon vanilla
1 cup all-purpose flour
½ teaspoon baking powder
¼ cup milk

2 cups 100% natural oats, honey and raisins cereal
1 package (12 ounces) Hershey's Mini Chips Semi-Sweet Chocolate (2 cups), divided
1 cup almond brickle chips
1 cup milk chocolate covered peanuts
1 package (2 ounces) nut topping (⅓ cup)

1. Heat oven to 350°F. Grease 13×9×2-inch pan with Butter Flavor Crisco.

2. Combine peanut butter, Butter Flavor Crisco, brown sugar and corn syrup in large bowl. Beat at medium speed of electric mixer until creamy. Add egg and vanilla. Beat well.

3. Combine flour and baking powder. Add alternately with milk to creamed mixture at medium speed. Stir in cereal, 1 cup chocolate chips, almond brickle chips and chocolate covered nuts with spoon. Spread in greased pan.

4. Bake at 350°F for 20 to 26 minutes or until golden brown and toothpick inserted in center comes out clean. Sprinkle remaining 1 cup chocolate chips over top immediately after removing from oven. Let stand about 3 minutes or until chips become shiny and soft. Spread over top. Sprinkle with nut topping. Cool completely. Cut into bars about 2×1 inch.      *Makes 4½ dozen bars*

*Emily's Dream Bars*

# ★ CHIPPY CHEESEYS ★

**Virginia and Peter Spina, Jamesville, New York**
*Both Virginia and her 12-year-old son, Peter, claim they invented
the name of this winner, chewy chocolate chip cookies with a creamy
cheesecake layer.*

**BASE**

1¼ cups firmly packed brown
    sugar
¾ cup Butter Flavor Crisco®
1 egg
2 tablespoons milk
1 tablespoon vanilla

2 cups all-purpose flour
1 teaspoon salt
¾ teaspoon baking soda
1 cup Hershey's Mini Chips
    Semi-Sweet Chocolate
1 cup finely chopped walnuts

**FILLING**

2 packages (8 ounces each) cream
    cheese, softened
2 eggs

¾ cup granulated sugar
1 teaspoon vanilla

1. Heat oven to 375°F. Grease 13×9×2-inch pan with Butter Flavor Crisco.

2. **For base,** combine brown sugar and Butter Flavor Crisco in large bowl. Beat at medium speed of electric mixer until creamy. Beat in 1 egg, milk and 1 tablespoon vanilla.

3. Combine flour, salt and baking soda. Add gradually to creamed mixture at low speed. Stir in chocolate chips and nuts with spoon. Spread half of dough in greased pan.

4. Bake at 375°F for 8 minutes.

5. **For filling,** combine cream cheese, 2 eggs, granulated sugar and 1 teaspoon vanilla in medium bowl. Beat at medium speed of electric mixer until smooth. Pour over hot crust.

6. Roll remaining dough into 13×9-inch rectangle between sheets of waxed paper. Remove top sheet. Flip dough over onto filling. Remove waxed paper.

7. Bake at 375°F for 40 minutes or until top is set and light golden brown. Cool to room temperature. Cut into bars about 2 × 1¾ inches. Refrigerate.

*Makes 2½ dozen bars*

# ★ PEANUT BUTTER BARS ★

**Lois and Ryan Mahoney, Casper, Wyoming**
*Ryan, 8, claims his mother is the family chocoholic, but Lois insists that it was Ryan's idea to use chocolate in their prize-winning entry.*

## BASE
⅔ cup Jif® Creamy Peanut Butter
½ cup Butter Flavor Crisco®
¾ cup firmly packed brown sugar
½ cup granulated sugar
2 eggs
1 teaspoon vanilla

1½ cups all-purpose flour
½ teaspoon baking soda
¼ teaspoon salt
1 cup Quick Quaker® Oats, uncooked

## PEANUT BUTTER LAYER
1½ cups confectioners sugar
2 tablespoons Jif® Creamy Peanut Butter

1 tablespoon butter or margarine, softened
3 tablespoons milk

## CHOCOLATE GLAZE
2 squares (1 ounce each) Hershey's® Unsweetened Baking Chocolate

2 tablespoons butter or margarine

1. Heat oven to 350°F. Grease 13×9×2-inch pan with Butter Flavor Crisco.

2. **For base,** combine ⅔ cup peanut butter and Butter Flavor Crisco in large bowl. Beat at medium speed of electric mixer until blended. Add brown sugar and granulated sugar. Beat until well blended. Add eggs and vanilla. Beat until well blended.

3. Combine flour, baking soda and salt. Stir into creamed mixture with spoon. Stir in oats. Press into bottom of greased pan.

4. Bake at 350°F for 20 minutes or until golden brown. Cool to room temperature.

5. **For peanut butter layer,** combine confectioners sugar, 2 tablespoons peanut butter, 1 tablespoon butter and milk. Mix with spoon until smooth. Spread on base. Refrigerate 30 minutes.

6. **For chocolate glaze,** combine chocolate and 2 tablespoons butter in microwave-safe measuring cup. Microwave at 50% (MEDIUM). Stir after 1 minute. Repeat until smooth (or melt on rangetop in small saucepan on very low heat). Cool slightly. Spread over peanut butter layer. Cut into bars about 3×1½ inches. Refrigerate about 1 hour or until set. Let stand 15 to 20 minutes at room temperature before serving.

*Makes 2 dozen bars*

*Peanut Butter Bars*

# ★ CHEWY OATMEAL-APRICOT-DATE ★ BARS

**Nina and Louise Bevilacqua, Haverhill, Massachusetts**
*This artistic mother-and-daughter team believes that "there is no better art form than fine food" and proved it by creating a masterpiece that won the blue ribbon.*

## COOKIES
1¼ cups firmly packed brown sugar
¾ cup plus 4 teaspoons Butter Flavor Crisco®
3 eggs
2 teaspoons vanilla
2 cups Quick Quaker® Oats, uncooked, divided
½ cup all-purpose flour
2 teaspoons baking powder

1 teaspoon cinnamon
¼ teaspoon nutmeg
¼ teaspoon salt
1 cup finely grated carrots
1 cup finely minced dried apricots
1 cup minced dates
1 cup finely chopped walnuts
⅔ cup Hershey's Vanilla Milk Chips

## FROSTING
1 package (3 ounces) cream cheese, softened
¼ cup Butter Flavor Crisco®
2½ cups confectioners sugar
1 to 2 teaspoons milk

¾ teaspoon lemon extract
½ teaspoon vanilla
½ teaspoon finely grated lemon peel
⅓ cup finely chopped walnuts

1. Heat oven to 350°F. Grease 13×9×2-inch pan with Butter Flavor Crisco. Flour lightly.

2. **For cookies,** combine brown sugar and ¾ cup plus 4 teaspoons Butter Flavor Crisco in large bowl. Beat at medium speed of electric mixer until fluffy. Add eggs, one at a time, and vanilla. Beat until well blended and fluffy.

3. Process ½ cup oats in food processor or blender until finely ground. Combine with flour, baking powder, cinnamon, nutmeg and salt. Add gradually to creamed mixture at low speed. Add remaining 1½ cups oats, carrots, apricots, dates, 1 cup nuts and vanilla milk chips. Mix until partially blended. Finish mixing with spoon. Spread in greased pan.

4. Bake at 350°F for 35 to 45 minutes or until center is set and cookie starts to pull away from sides of pan. Toothpick inserted in center should come out clean. *Do not overbake.* Cool completely.

5. **For frosting,** combine cream cheese, ¼ cup Butter Flavor Crisco, confectioners sugar, milk, lemon extract, vanilla and lemon peel in medium bowl. Beat at low speed until blended. Increase speed to medium-high. Beat until fluffy. Spread on baked surface. Sprinkle with ⅓ cup nuts. Cut into bars about 2¼×2 inches. Refrigerate.

*Makes 2 dozen bars*

*Chewy Oatmeal-Apricot-Date Bars*

# Extra Special Cookies

## ★ OATMEAL SHAGGIES ★

**Carolyn McPharlin and Jessica Hoffmann,**
**Salt Lake City, Utah**
*Ten-year-old Jessica grew the carrots for these chewy cookies in her*
*part of the family garden.*

### COOKIES
2 cups Quick Quaker® Oats,
   uncooked
1 cup finely shredded carrots
1 cup firmly packed brown sugar
1 cup raisins
1 cup all-purpose flour
1 teaspoon baking powder
1 teaspoon baking soda
1 teaspoon salt

½ teaspoon cinnamon
½ teaspoon cloves
2 eggs, beaten
½ cup Butter Flavor Crisco®,
   melted and cooled
⅓ cup milk
1 cup shredded coconut
½ cup finely chopped walnuts

### FROSTING
1 cup confectioners sugar
2 tablespoons butter or
   margarine, softened

2 teaspoons grated orange peel
1 tablespoon plus 1 teaspoon
   Citrus Hill® Orange Juice

1. Heat oven to 350°F. Grease baking sheet with Butter Flavor Crisco.

2. **For cookies,** combine oats, carrots, brown sugar and raisins in large bowl.

3. Combine flour, baking powder, baking soda, salt, cinnamon and cloves. Stir into oat mixture with spoon.

4. Combine eggs, Butter Flavor Crisco and milk. Stir into carrot mixture. Stir in coconut and nuts. Drop by rounded tablespoonfuls 2½ inches apart onto greased baking sheet.

5. Bake at 350°F for 10 to 12 minutes or until lightly browned. Remove to cooling rack. Cool completely.

6. **For frosting,** combine confectioners sugar, butter, orange peel and orange juice in small bowl. Stir until smooth and good spreading consistency. Frost cookies.
*Makes 2½ to 3 dozen cookies*

*Oatmeal Shaggies*

# ★ FROSTED PEANUT BUTTER ★ PEANUT BRITTLE COOKIES

**Claudia and Verne Cysensky, Tacoma, Washington**
*These peanutty treats were the Grand Prize Winner at the 1991 Butter Flavor Crisco American Cookie Celebration.*

### PEANUT BRITTLE
1½ cups granulated sugar
1½ cups shelled unroasted Spanish peanuts
¾ cup light corn syrup
½ teaspoon salt

1 tablespoon Butter Flavor Crisco®
1½ teaspoons vanilla
1½ teaspoons baking soda

### COOKIES
½ cup Butter Flavor Crisco®
½ cup granulated sugar
½ cup firmly packed brown sugar
½ cup Jif® Creamy Peanut Butter
1 tablespoon milk

1 egg
1⅓ cups all-purpose flour
¾ teaspoon baking soda
½ teaspoon baking powder
¼ teaspoon salt

### FROSTING
1¼ cups Reese's® Peanut Butter Chips

Reserved 1 cup crushed peanut brittle

1. **For peanut brittle,** grease 15½ × 12-inch baking sheet with Butter Flavor Crisco.

2. Combine 1½ cups granulated sugar, nuts, corn syrup and 1½ teaspoon salt in 3-quart saucepan. Cook and stir on medium-low heat until 240°F on candy thermometer.

3. Stir in 1 tablespoon Butter Flavor Crisco and vanilla. Cook and stir until 300°F on candy thermometer. Watch closely so mixture does not burn.

4. Remove from heat. Stir in 1½ teaspoons baking soda. Pour onto greased baking sheet. Spread to ¼-inch thickness. Cool. Break into pieces. Crush into medium-fine pieces to measure 1 cup. Set aside.

5. Heat oven to 375°F.

6. **For cookies,** combine ½ cup Butter Flavor Crisco, ½ cup granulated sugar, brown sugar, peanut butter and milk in large bowl. Beat at medium speed of electric mixer until well blended. Beat in egg.

7. Combine flour, ¾ teaspoon baking soda, baking powder and ¼ teaspoon salt. Add gradually at low speed. Mix until well blended.

*continued*

*Frosted Peanut Butter Peanut Brittle Cookies*

8. Shape dough into 1¼-inch balls. Place 3½ inches apart on ungreased baking sheet. Flatten into 3-inch circle.

9. Bake at 375°F for 8 to 9 minutes or until light brown. Cool 2 minutes on baking sheet before removing to flat surface. Cool completely.

10. **For frosting,** place peanut butter chips in microwave-safe measuring cup or bowl. Microwave at 50% (MEDIUM). Stir after 1 minute. Repeat until smooth (or melt in saucepan on very low heat). Spread frosting on half of each cookie.

11. Sprinkle reserved crushed peanut brittle over frosting. Refrigerate to set quickly or let stand at room temperature.          *Makes 2 dozen cookies*

# ★ PEACH-STUFFED OATMEAL ★ ALMOND COOKIES

**Sherry and Christina Kemp, Elk Grove, California**
*Sherry says she's always been drawn by the creative possibilities in baking but admits that she and her daughter, Christina, were surprised to take top honors in this, their first baking competition.*

## COOKIES

½ cup plus 2 tablespoons butter or margarine, softened, divided
2½ cups Quaker® Oats (quick or old fashioned), uncooked
1 cup sugar
½ cup Butter Flavor Crisco®

1 can (12½ ounces) almond filling, divided
1 egg, lightly beaten
1 tablespoon plus 1½ teaspoons Citrus Hill® Orange Juice
1 tablespoon half-and-half
1½ cups all-purpose flour

## FILLING

1 large fresh peach, peeled and mashed
½ cup sugar

1 tablespoon peach schnapps
½ teaspoon fresh lemon juice
Reserved almond filling

## GARNISH

1 cup Hershey's® Semi-Sweet Chocolate Chips

1 package (2 ounces) blanched almonds, ground (½ cup)

1. **For cookies,** melt 2 tablespoons butter in large skillet on medium heat. Add oats. Stir until oats are lightly browned. Turn out onto paper towels. Cool completely.

2. Combine 1 cup sugar, Butter Flavor Crisco and remaining ½ cup butter in large bowl. Beat at low speed of electric mixer until fluffy.

3. Place ⅔ cup almond filling in small bowl. Stir in, one at a time, egg, orange juice and half-and-half. Stir until well blended. Add to creamed mixture at low speed.

4. Stir one fourth of flour at a time into creamed mixture with spoon. Stir in oats. Cover. Place in freezer until dough is very firm.

5. **For filling,** combine peach, $1/2$ cup sugar, schnapps and lemon juice in small saucepan. Cook and stir on medium heat until thick and glossy. Reserve 2 tablespoons. Cool mixture in saucepan completely. Add remaining almond filling (about $1/2$ cup) to saucepan. Stir until well blended.

6. Heat oven to 350°F. Line baking sheet with parchment paper.

7. Shape dough into 1-inch balls. Place 2 inches apart on parchment paper. Flatten slightly.

8. Bake at 350°F for 9 to 12 minutes or just until barely golden. Cool 2 minutes on baking sheet before removing to cooling rack. Cool completely.

9. Place $1/4$ teaspoon peach filling on each bottom of half of the cookies. Top with remaining cookies. Press together gently. Press outside edges of cookies together. Brush one side of all sandwiched cookies with reserved 2 tablespoons peach mixture.*

10. **For garnish,** place chocolate chips in microwave-safe cup or bowl. Microwave at 50% (MEDIUM). Stir after 1 minute. Repeat until smooth (or melt by placing in small saucepan on very low heat). Spread edge of cookies with chocolate and then roll lightly in nuts. Place on waxed paper, glazed side up, until chocolate is set.                    *Makes 4 dozen sandwich cookies*

*Stir $1/4$ teaspoon water into peach mixture if too thick.

# PEANUT BUTTER SENSATIONS

1 cup Jif® Creamy Peanut Butter
$3/4$ cup granulated sugar
$1/2$ cup firmly packed brown sugar
$1/2$ cup Butter Flavor Crisco®
1 tablespoon milk
1 teaspoon vanilla

1 egg
$1 1/4$ cups all-purpose flour
$3/4$ teaspoon baking soda
$1/2$ teaspoon baking powder
$1/4$ teaspoon salt

1. Heat oven to 375°F.

2. Combine peanut butter, granulated sugar, brown sugar, Butter Flavor Crisco, milk and vanilla in large bowl. Beat at medium speed of electric mixer until well blended. Beat in egg.

3. Combine flour, baking soda, baking powder and salt. Add gradually to creamed mixture at low speed. Mix just until blended. Drop by rounded tablespoonfuls 2 inches apart onto ungreased baking sheet. Make crisscross marks on top with floured fork tines.

4. Bake at 375°F for 8 to 10 minutes. Cool 2 minutes on baking sheet before removing to cooling rack.                    *Makes 2 dozen cookies*

# ★ HEAVENLY OATMEAL HEARTS ★

**Mary and Nicole Severson, Minot, North Dakota**
*Six-year-old Nicole loves to help her mom in the kitchen and says
baking and playing golf are two of her favorite activities.*

## COOKIES
1 cup plus 2 tablespoons Butter
    Flavor Crisco®
1 cup firmly packed brown sugar
½ cup granulated sugar
2 eggs
1 teaspoon vanilla
1½ cups plus ⅓ cup all-purpose
    flour
1½ teaspoons baking soda
¾ teaspoon salt

3 cups Quaker® Oats (quick or
    old fashioned), uncooked
1 cup Hershey's Milk Chocolate
    Chips
1 cup Hershey's Vanilla Milk
    Chips
1 cup plus 2 tablespoons
    cinnamon roasted peanuts,*
    chopped

## DRIZZLE
½ cup Hershey's Milk Chocolate
    Chips
½ cup Hershey's Vanilla Milk
    Chips

1 teaspoon Butter Flavor Crisco®,
    divided

1. Heat oven to 375°F.

2. **For cookies,** combine 1 cup plus 2 tablespoons Butter Flavor Crisco, brown sugar and granulated sugar in large bowl. Beat at medium speed of electric mixer until light and fluffy. Beat in eggs and vanilla.

3. Combine flour, baking soda and salt. Add gradually to creamed mixture at low speed. Mix until well blended. Stir in oats, 1 cup chocolate chips, 1 cup vanilla milk chips and nuts with spoon.

4. Place 3-inch heart-shaped cookie cutter on ungreased baking sheet. Place ⅓ cup dough inside cutter. Press to edges and level. Remove cutter. Repeat to form remaining cookies. Space 2½ inches apart.

5. Bake at 375°F for 9 minutes or until light golden brown. Cool on baking sheet until slightly warm before removing to cooling rack. Cool completely.

6. **For drizzle,** place ½ cup chocolate chips and ½ cup vanilla milk chips in separate heavy resealable sandwich bags. Add ½ teaspoon Butter Flavor Crisco to each bag. Seal. Microwave at 50% (MEDIUM). Knead bag after 1 minute. Repeat with each bag until smooth (or melt by placing each in bowl of hot water). Cut tiny tip off corner of each bag. Squeeze out and drizzle over cookies. To serve, cut in half, if desired. *Makes 22 heart cookies*

*Substitute honey roasted peanuts and 1½ teaspoons cinnamon if cinnamon roasted peanuts are unavailable.

*Heavenly Oatmeal Hearts*

# ★ JEREMY'S FAMOUS TURTLES ★

**Louise and Jeremy Kopasz, Pueblo, Colorado**
*Jeremy and his grandmother made these cookies which were named the Oatmeal National Winner at the 1991 Butter Flavor Crisco American Cookie Celebration.*

## COOKIES

3 egg whites
1 egg yolk
1¼ cups Butter Flavor Crisco®
¾ cup firmly packed brown sugar
½ cup granulated sugar
1 teaspoon vanilla
1¾ cups all-purpose flour
1 teaspoon baking soda
¾ teaspoon salt
½ cup Hershey®s Butterscotch Chips
½ cup Hershey®s Semi-Sweet Chocolate Chips

½ cup chopped dates
½ cup chopped pecans
½ cup diced dried fruit bits
⅓ cup cinnamon applesauce
¼ cup toasted wheat germ
¼ cup ground shelled sunflower seeds
2 tablespoons honey
3 cups Quaker® Oats (quick or old fashioned), uncooked
8 ounces pecan halves (2 cups)

## COATING

1 to 2 egg whites, lightly beaten          ½ cup granulated sugar

1. **For cookies,** place 3 egg whites in medium bowl. Beat at medium speed of electric mixer until frothy. Beat in egg yolk until well blended.

2. Combine Butter Flavor Crisco, brown sugar and granulated sugar in large bowl. Beat at medium speed until well blended. Add egg mixture and vanilla. Beat until well blended.

3. Combine flour, baking soda and salt. Add gradually to creamed mixture at low speed. Stir in with spoon, one at a time, butterscotch chips, chocolate chips, dates, chopped nuts, fruit bits, applesauce, wheat germ, sunflower seeds, honey and oats. Cover. Refrigerate dough 1 hour.

4. Heat oven to 350°F. Grease baking sheet with Butter Flavor Crisco.

5. Shape dough into 1½-inch balls. Cut pecan halves into 4 lengthwise pieces for legs. Save broken pieces for heads and tails

6. **For coating,** dip top of cookie ball in beaten egg white, then dip in sugar. Place sugar side up 2½ inches apart on greased baking sheet. Insert lengthwise nut pieces for legs. Flatten slightly. Place nut sliver for tail and rounded nut piece for head.

7. Bake at 350°F for 9 to 11 minutes or until lightly browned. Reposition nuts, if necessary. Cool 30 seconds on baking sheet before removing to paper towels.
*Makes 7½ dozen cookies*

*Jeremy's Famous Turtles*

# ★ CHOCOLATE PEANUT BUTTER ★ CUP COOKIES

**Maria and Jenna Baldwin, Mesa, Arizona**
*Jenna and her mother, Maria, won the blue ribbon at the Arizona State Fair over a number of other competitors, including Jenna's nine-year-old sister, Kathryn.*

## COOKIES
1 cup Hershey's Semi-Sweet Chocolate Chips
2 squares (1 ounce each) Hershey's Unsweetened Baking Chocolate
1 cup sugar
½ cup Butter Flavor Crisco®
2 eggs

1 teaspoon salt
1 teaspoon vanilla
1½ cups plus 2 tablespoons all-purpose flour
½ teaspoon baking soda
¾ cup finely chopped peanuts
36 miniature Reese's® Peanut Butter Cups, unwrapped

## DRIZZLE
1 cup Reese's® Peanut Butter Chips

1. Heat oven to 350°F.

2. **For cookies,** combine chocolate chips and chocolate squares in microwave-safe measuring cup or bowl. Microwave at 50% (MEDIUM). Stir after 2 minutes. Repeat until smooth (or melt on rangetop in small saucepan on very low heat). Cool slightly.

3. Combine sugar and Butter Flavor Crisco in large bowl. Beat at medium speed of electric mixer until blended and crumbly. Beat in eggs, one at a time, then salt and vanilla. Reduce speed to low. Add chocolate slowly. Mix until well blended. Stir in flour and baking soda with spoon until well blended. Shape dough into 1¼-inch balls. Roll in nuts. Place 2 inches apart on ungreased baking sheet.

4. Bake at 350°F for 8 to 10 minutes or until set. Press peanut butter cup into center of each cookie immediately. Press cookie against cup. Cool 2 minutes on baking sheet before removing to cooling rack. Cool completely.

5. **For drizzle,** place peanut butter chips in heavy resealable sandwich bag. Seal. Microwave at 50% (MEDIUM). Knead bag after 1 minute. Repeat until smooth (or melt by placing bag in hot water). Cut tiny tip off corner of bag. Squeeze out and drizzle over cookies.

*Makes 3 dozen cookies*

*Chocolate Peanut Butter Cup Cookies*

# Down~Home Pies

## ★ LOLA'S APPLE PIE ★

*Lola Mefferd, Bellflower, California*
*Lola has always considered baking pies her "virtuoso performance."*

**CRUST**
> 10-inch Classic Crisco® Double
> Crust

**FILLING**
> 8 to 9 cups thinly sliced, peeled
> Granny Smith or other tart
> apples (about 3 pounds or
> 9 medium)
> ¾ to 1 cup sugar
> 2 tablespoons all-purpose flour

> 1 teaspoon cinnamon
> ⅛ teaspoon allspice
> ⅛ teaspoon cloves
> ⅛ teaspoon salt
> 2 tablespoons butter or
> margarine

**TOPPING**
> Sugar

1. **For crust,** prepare (see pages 436–437). Roll and press bottom crust into 10-inch pie plate. Do not bake. Heat oven to 400°F.

2. **For filling,** place apples in large bowl. Combine ¾ to 1 cup sugar, flour, cinnamon, allspice, cloves and salt. Sprinkle over apples. Toss to coat. Spoon into unbaked pie crust. Dot with butter. Moisten pastry edge with water.

3. Roll top crust same as bottom. Lift onto filled pie. Trim ½ inch beyond edge of pie plate. Fold top edge under bottom crust. Flute. Cut slits or shapes in top crust to allow steam to escape.

4. **For topping,** sprinkle with sugar.

5. Bake at 400°F for 50 to 55 minutes or until filling in center is bubbly and crust is golden brown. Cover edge with foil, if necessary, to prevent overbrowning. Serve barely warm or at room temperature. *One 10-inch pie*

*Lola's Apple Pie*

# ★ DELAWARE BLUEBERRY PIE ★

*Loretta Wootten, Velton, Deleware*
*"I give away pies for every occasion," says Loretta, "they are my trademark."*

**CRUST**
9-inch Classic Crisco® Double Crust

**FILLING**
4½ cups fresh blueberries, divided
½ cup granulated sugar
½ cup firmly packed brown sugar
2 tablespoons plus 1½ teaspoons cornstarch
½ teaspoon cinnamon
⅛ teaspoon salt

1 tablespoon butter or margarine
1 teaspoon peach schnapps
2 tablespoons quick-cooking tapioca
4 to 5 drops red food color (optional)

**DECORATIONS (optional)**
Reserved dough

2 tablespoons melted vanilla frozen yogurt

1. **For crust,** prepare (see pages 436–437). Roll and press bottom crust into 9-inch pie plate. Do not bake. Reserve dough scraps for decorations, if desired. Heat oven to 425°F.

2. **For filling,** place ½ cup blueberries in resealable plastic sandwich bag. Crush berries. Pour juice and berries into strainer over liquid measuring cup. Press berries to extract all juice. Pour water over berries until juice measures ½ cup.

3. Combine granulated sugar, brown sugar, cornstarch, cinnamon and salt in large saucepan. Add blueberry juice mixture. Cook and stir on medium heat until mixture comes to a boil. Remove from heat. Stir in butter and schnapps. Set pan in cold water about 5 minutes to cool. Stir in tapioca. Add food color, if desired. Stir in remaining blueberries carefully. Spoon into unbaked pie crust. Moisten pastry edge with water.

4. Roll top crust same as bottom. Lift onto filled pie. Trim ½ inch beyond edge of pie plate. Fold top edge under bottom crust. Flute.

5. **For decorations,** cut stars and diamonds from reserved dough. Dip cutouts in melted yogurt. Place on top of pie and around edge. Cut slits in top crust to allow steam to escape.

6. Bake at 425°F for 15 minutes. Cover cutouts and edge of pie with foil, if necessary, to prevent overbrowning. *Reduce oven temperature to 375°F. Bake* 20 to 25 minutes or until filling in center is bubbly and crust is golden brown. Cool to room temperature before serving.

*One 9-inch Pie*

*Delaware Blueberry Pie*

# CLASSIC CRISCO CRUST

## 8-, 9- OR 10-INCH SINGLE CRUST

1⅓ cups all-purpose flour
 ½ teaspoon salt
 ½ cup Crisco® Shortening
 3 tablespoons cold water

## 8- OR 9-INCH DOUBLE CRUST

2 cups all-purpose flour
1 teaspoon salt
¾ cup Crisco® Shortening
5 tablespoons cold water

## 10-INCH DOUBLE CRUST

2⅔ cups all-purpose flour
 1 teaspoon salt
 1 cup Crisco® Shortening
 7 to 8 tablespoons cold water

1. Spoon flour into measuring cup and level. Combine flour and salt in medium bowl.

2. Cut in Crisco using pastry blender (or 2 knives) until all flour is blended to form pea-size chunks.

3. Sprinkle with water, 1 tablespoon at a time. Toss lightly with fork until dough will form a ball.

## For Single Crust Pies

4. Press dough between hands to form a 5- to 6-inch "pancake." Flour rolling surface and rolling pin lightly. Roll dough into circle.

## For Baked Pie Crusts

1. For recipes using a baked pie crust, heat oven to 425°F. Prick bottom and sides thoroughly with fork (50 times) to prevent shrinkage.

2. Bake at 425°F for 10 to 15 minutes or until lightly browned.

## For Unbaked Pie Crusts

1. For recipes using an unbaked pie crust, follow baking directions given in that recipe.

5. Trim 1 inch larger than upside-down pie plate. Loosen dough carefully.

## For Double Crust Pies

1. Divide dough in half. Roll each half separately. Transfer bottom crust to pie plate. Trim edge even with pie plate.

6. Fold dough into quarters. Unfold and press into pie plate. Fold edge under. Flute.

2. Add desired filling to unbaked pie crust. Moisten pastry edge with water. Lift top crust onto filled pie. Trim 1/2 inch beyond edge of pie plate. Fold top edge under bottom crust. Flute. Cut slits in top crust to allow steam to escape. Bake according to specific recipe directions.

# CONTEMPORARY TECHNIQUES

## Food Processor Method

1. Place Crisco, water and flour in processor bowl. Sprinkle salt over flour.

2. Process 3 to 5 seconds until dough just forms. Shape into ball.

Note: For flakier crust, freeze Crisco in tablespoon-size chunks before processing.

## Waxed Paper Method

1. Flour "pancake" lightly on both sides.

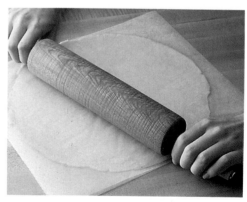

2. Roll between sheets of waxed paper (or plastic wrap) on dampened countertop. Peel off top sheet.

3. Flip dough into pie plate. Remove other sheet.

# DECORATIVE TIPS

## Rope Edge

Fold overhang under and make stand-up edge. Press thumb into pastry at an angle. Pinch pastry between thumb and knuckle of index finger, rolling knuckle toward thumb. Place thumb in groove left by finger and repeat.

## Cutouts

Trim edge even with pie plate. Cut desired shapes (about 3/4 inch in size) from remaining pastry using tiny cookie cutter, thimble or bottlecap. Moisten pastry edge. Place cutouts on pastry edge, slightly overlapping. Press into place.

## Woven Lattice Top

1. Leave overhang on bottom crust. Cut top crust into ten 1/2-inch strips. Place 5 strips evenly across filling. Fold every other strip back. Lay first strip across in opposite direction.

2. Continue in this pattern, folding back every other strip each time you add a cross strip.

3. Trim ends of lattice strips even with crust overhang. Press together. Fold edge under. Flute.

# ★ PEACH DELIGHT PIE ★

*Michelle Neumiller, Casper, Wyoming*
*Championship cooking must run in this family's blood because*
*Michelle is the daughter of last year's Wyoming winner, Joan*
*Neumiller.*

**FILLING**
2½ cups sliced, peeled peaches
    (about 1¼ pounds or
    2 to 3 large)
¾ cup granulated sugar

¼ cup quick-cooking tapioca
1 teaspoon lemon juice
1 teaspoon peach-flavored brandy

**CRUMB MIXTURE**
¼ cup all-purpose flour
¼ cup firmly packed brown sugar
¼ cup chopped almonds

3 tablespoons butter or
    margarine, melted

**CRUST**
9-inch Classic Crisco® Double
    Crust

**GLAZE**
1 egg white, lightly beaten

Granulated sugar

1. **For filling,** combine peaches, granulated sugar, tapioca, lemon juice and brandy in medium bowl. Stir well. Let stand while making crumb mixture and crust.

2. **For crumb mixture,** combine flour, brown sugar, nuts and butter. Mix until crumbly.

3. Heat oven to 425°F.

4. **For crust,** prepare (see pages 436–437). Roll and press bottom crust into 9-inch pie plate. Do not bake. Sprinkle half of crumb mixture over unbaked pie crust. Add filling. Top with remaining crumbs.

5. Roll top crust same as bottom. Cut out heart shapes with cookie cutter. Place on filling around edge of pie.

6. **For glaze,** brush cutouts with egg white. Sprinkle with granulated sugar. Cover edge of pie with foil to prevent overbrowning.

7. Bake at 425°F for 10 minutes. *Reduce oven temperature to 350°F. Bake 25 minutes. Remove foil. Bake 5 minutes. Serve barely warm or at room temperature.*

*One 9-inch Pie*

*Peach Delight Pie*

# ★ OHIO SOUR CHERRY PIE ★

**Diane Cordial, Powell, Ohio**
*Diane's pie was the national winner at the 1991 Crisco American Pie Celebration.*

## FILLING
1¼ cups sugar
¼ cup cornstarch
1 bag (20 ounces) frozen dry pack pitted red tart cherries (4 cups)

2 tablespoons butter or margarine
¾ teaspoon vanilla
½ teaspoon almond extract
1 or 2 drops red food color (optional)

## CRUST
3 cups all-purpose flour
1 tablespoon plus 1½ teaspoons sugar
1 teaspoon salt
1 cup plus 2 tablespoons Crisco® Shortening

½ cup water
1 egg, lightly beaten
1 tablespoon vinegar

## GLAZE
1 tablespoon milk

½ teaspoon sugar

1. **For filling,** combine 1¼ cups sugar and cornstarch in medium saucepan. Stir in cherries gently. Cook and stir on medium or medium-high heat about 10 minutes or until mixture comes to a boil and is thickened and clear. Remove from heat. Stir in butter, vanilla, almond extract and red food color, if desired. Cool 1 hour.

2. **For crust,** combine flour, 1 tablespoon plus 1½ teaspoons sugar and salt in large bowl. Cut in Crisco using pastry blender (or 2 knives) until all flour is blended to form pea-size chunks.

3. Combine water, egg and vinegar in small bowl. Sprinkle over flour mixture, 1 tablespoon at a time. Toss lightly with fork until dough will form a ball. (You may not use all of liquid.) Divide dough into thirds. Form three 5- to 6-inch "pancakes." Wrap 1 in plastic wrap. Refrigerate or freeze for later use.

4. Heat oven to 375°F.

5. Roll and press bottom crust into 9-inch pie plate (see pages 436–437). Spoon filling into unbaked pie crust. Moisten pastry edge with water.

6. Roll top crust same as bottom. Cut the word OHIO or other design in center of crust. Lift crust onto filled pie. Trim ½ inch beyond edge of pie plate. Fold top edge under bottom crust. Flute. Add leaf cutouts.

7. **For glaze,** brush with milk. Sprinkle with ½ teaspoon sugar.

8. Bake at 375°F for 35 to 40 minutes or until filling in center is bubbly and crust is golden brown. Serve warm or at room temperature.          *One 9-inch Pie*

*Ohio Sour Cherry Pie*

# ★ PEANUT SUPREME PIE ★

*Violet La Breque, Leesburg, Virginia*
*This is the second consecutive win for Violet in Crisco's American*
*Pie Celebration.*

CRUST
    9-inch Classic Crisco® Single
    Crust

PEANUT LAYER
    ½ cup chopped peanuts    ½ cup confectioners sugar
    ½ cup Jif® Creamy Peanut Butter    ½ cup half-and-half

FILLING
    1 can (14 ounces) sweetened    1 package (6-serving size) vanilla
        condensed milk        flavor instant pudding and
    ½ cup Jif® Creamy Peanut Butter        pie filling mix (not sugar-free)
    1 cup milk

TOPPING
    ¾ cup chopped peanuts

1. **For crust,** prepare (see pages 436–437). Do not bake. Heat oven to 400°F.

2. **For peanut layer,** combine ½ cup nuts, peanut butter, confectioners sugar and half-and-half in medium bowl. Stir until well blended. Pour into unbaked pie crust.

3. Bake at 400°F for 20 to 25 minutes or until crust is golden brown. Cool completely.

4. **For filling,** combine sweetened condensed milk and peanut butter in large bowl. Beat at low speed of electric mixer until well blended. Add milk slowly. Add pudding mix. Increase speed to medium. Beat 2 minutes. Pour over cooled peanut layer.

5. **For topping,** sprinkle ¾ cup nuts over filling. Refrigerate 1 hour or more.

*One 9-inch Pie*

*Peanut Supreme Pie*

# Party~Time Pies

## ★ LUSCIOUS CRANBERRY AND ★ BLUEBERRY PIE

*Michele Delanty, Sunrise Beach, Missouri*
*In addition to baking daily for family and friends, Michele supplies*
*her husband's volunteer fire department meetings with cookies.*

**CRUST**
    9-inch Classic Crisco® Double
    Crust

**FILLING**
    1 can (16 ounces) whole berry
    cranberry sauce
    1/3 cup firmly packed brown sugar
    1/4 cup granulated sugar
    2 tablespoons all-purpose flour
    2 tablespoons cornstarch
    2 tablespoons Citrus Hill®
    Orange Juice

    1/2 teaspoon mace

    1/2 teaspoon dried grated orange
    peel
    1/8 teaspoon salt
    2 cups fresh or frozen blueberries
    2 tablespoons butter or
    margarine
    1 egg, beaten

1. **For crust,** prepare (see pages 436–437) adding mace to flour mixture. Roll and press bottom crust into 9-inch pie plate. Do not bake. Reserve dough scraps for decorations, if desired. Heat oven to 425°F.

2. **For filling,** combine cranberry sauce, brown sugar, granulated sugar, flour, cornstarch, orange juice, orange peel and salt in large bowl. Stir in blueberries. Spoon into unbaked pie crust. Dot with butter. Moisten pastry edge with water.

3. Roll top crust same as bottom. Lift onto filled pie. Trim 1/2 inch beyond edge of pie plate. Fold top edge under bottom crust. Flute. Cut dogwood blossoms in top crust to allow steam to escape.

4. Cut flower or other shapes from reserved dough. Place on top of pie. Brush crust with egg.

5. Bake at 425°F for 40 minutes or until filling in center is bubbly and crust is golden brown. Cover edge with foil during last 10 minutes to prevent overbrowning. Cool to room temperature before serving. *One 9-inch Pie*

*Luscious Cranberry and Blueberry Pie*

# ★ CHERRY CITY AMARETTO ★ CHERRY CREAM PIE

*Florence Neavoll, Salem, Oregon*
*This outstanding pie gets its name from Salem's nickname, The Cherry City.*

CRUST
  10-inch Classic Crisco® Single
  Crust

CREAM LAYER
  ⅔ cup granulated sugar
  ¼ cup cornstarch
  ¼ teaspoon salt
  2 cups half-and-half

  1 cup milk
  3 egg yolks, lightly beaten
  1 tablespoon butter or margarine
  ½ teaspoon almond extract

FILLING
  1 can (16 ounces) pitted red tart
    cherries in water
  ½ cup reserved cherry liquid
  ⅔ cup granulated sugar
  2 tablespoons cornstarch
  2 tablespoons all-purpose flour
  ⅛ teaspoon salt

  1 tablespoon amaretto
  1 teaspoon red food color
    (optional)
  ½ teaspoon fresh lemon juice
  ½ teaspoon vinegar
  1 tablespoon butter or margarine

TOPPING
  1½ teaspoons unflavored gelatin
  2 tablespoons plus 2 teaspoons
    water
  1½ cups whipping cream
  6 tablespoons confectioners sugar

  1 teaspoon almond extract
  1 bar (1¼ ounces) white
    chocolate with almonds,
    shaved
  Slivered almonds

1. **For crust,** prepare and bake (see pages 436–437). Cool completely.

2. **For cream layer,** combine ⅔ cup granulated sugar, ¼ cup cornstarch and salt in medium saucepan. Stir in half-and-half and milk. Cook and stir on medium heat until mixture comes to a boil. Boil 1 minute. Remove from heat. Stir half of mixture into beaten egg yolks. Mix well. Return mixture to saucepan. Blend well. Boil and stir 1 minute. Remove from heat. Stir in butter and almond extract. Cool to room temperature. Refrigerate.

3. **For filling,** drain cherries, reserving ½ cup liquid. Pat cherries with paper towels. Combine ⅔ cup granulated sugar, 2 tablespoons cornstarch, flour and salt in medium saucepan. Mix until smooth. Cook and stir on medium heat until mixture is thickened and clear. Add cherries. Cook and stir on low heat 10 to 15 minutes. Remove from heat. Stir in amaretto, food color, lemon juice, vinegar and butter. Cool to room temperature. *continued*

4. **For topping,** combine gelatin and water in very small saucepan. Cook and stir on low heat until gelatin dissolves. Cool until warm, but still liquid.

5. Beat whipping cream in medium bowl at high speed of electric mixer until soft peaks form. Beat in gelatin slowly. Beat in confectioners sugar and almond extract.

6. **To assemble pie,** spread cream layer in cooled pie crust. Cover with cherry filling. Pipe topping over filling in decorative fashion. Sprinkle with shaved chocolate and slivered nuts. Refrigerate.

*One 10-inch Pie*

# ★ CHOCOLATE CHIP PECAN PIE ★

*Janice Kyle, Oklahoma City, Oklahoma*
*Janice was encouraged to enter her pie in Crisco's American Pie Celebration by her prize-winning sister, Rosalie Seebeck. Rosalie won the national contest in 1989.*

**CRUST**
9-inch Classic Crisco® Single
Crust

**FILLING**
4 eggs
1 cup sugar
1 cup light corn syrup
3 tablespoons butter or
   margarine, melted
1 teaspoon vanilla

¼ teaspoon salt
2 cups pecan halves
½ cup Hershey®'s Semi-Sweet
   Chocolate Chips
1 tablespoon plus 1½ teaspoons
   bourbon, optional

1. **For crust,** prepare (see pages 436–437). Do not bake. Heat oven to 375°F.

2. **For filling,** beat eggs in large bowl at low speed of electric mixer until blended. Stir in sugar, corn syrup, butter, vanilla and salt with spoon until blended. Stir in nuts, chocolate chips and bourbon. Pour into unbaked pie crust.

3. Bake at 375°F for 55 to 60 minutes or until set. Cover edge with foil, if necessary, to prevent overbrowning. Cool to room temperature before serving. Refrigerate leftover pie.

*One 9-inch Pie*

*Chocolate Chip Pecan Pie*

# ★ CIDER APPLE PIE IN ★ CHEDDAR CRUST

*Mary Lou Tuckwiller, Lewisburg, West Virginia*
*Mary Lou has taken the traditional taste of sweet and succulent apple pie and contrasted it with the sharp taste of Cheddar cheese in this terrific pie.*

**CRUST**

| | |
|---|---|
| 2 cups sifted all-purpose flour | ⅔ cup Crisco® Shortening |
| 1 cup shredded Cheddar cheese | 5 to 6 tablespoons ice water |
| ½ teaspoon salt | |

**FILLING**

| | |
|---|---|
| 6 cups sliced, peeled apples (about 2 pounds or 6 medium) | 2 tablespoons cornstarch |
| | 2 tablespoons water |
| 1 cup apple cider | ½ teaspoon cinnamon |
| ⅔ cup sugar | 1 tablespoon butter or margarine |

**GLAZE**

| | |
|---|---|
| 1 egg yolk | 1 tablespoon water |

1. Heat oven to 400°F.

2. **For crust,** place flour, cheese and salt in food processor bowl. Add Crisco. Process 15 seconds. Sprinkle water through food chute, 1 tablespoon at a time, until dough just forms (process time not to exceed 20 seconds). Shape into ball. Divide dough in half. Press between hands to form two 5- to 6-inch "pancakes." Roll and press bottom crust into 9-inch pie plate.

3. **For filling,** combine apples, apple cider and sugar in large saucepan. Cook and stir on medium-high heat until mixture comes to a boil. Reduce heat to low. Simmer 5 minutes. Combine cornstarch, 2 tablespoons water and cinnamon. Stir into apples. Cook and stir until mixture comes to a boil. Remove from heat. Stir in butter. Spoon into unbaked pie crust. Moisten pastry edge with water.

4. Roll top crust same as bottom. Lift onto filled pie. Trim ½ inch beyond edge of pie plate. Fold top edge under bottom crust. Flute. Cut slits or design in top crust to allow steam to escape.

5. **For glaze,** beat egg yolk with fork. Stir in 1 tablespoon water. Brush over top.

6. Bake at 400°F for 35 to 40 minutes or until filling in center is bubbly and crust is golden brown. Cover edge with foil, if necessary, to prevent overbrowning. Cool to room temperature before serving.     *One 9-inch Pie*

**Note:** Golden Delicious, Granny Smith and Jonathan apples are all suitable for pie baking.

*Cider Apple Pie in Cheddar Crust*

# ★ CITRUS DREAM PIE ★

*Gloria Norton, Jacksonville, Florida*
*Gloria is a 2-time winner of Crisco's American Pie Celebration in Florida.*

## CRUST

9-inch Classic Crisco® Single Crust

3 to 4 tablespoons sesame seed, toasted

## LEMON-ORANGE BUTTER FILLING

1½ cups sugar
¼ cup all-purpose flour
¼ cup cornstarch
⅛ teaspoon salt
1 cup Citrus Hill® Orange Juice
¼ cup water

3 egg yolks, lightly beaten
2 tablespoons butter or margarine
1 teaspoon grated lemon peel
1 teaspoon grated orange peel
⅓ cup fresh lemon juice

## LIME CREAM FILLING

1 envelope (about 1 tablespoon) unflavored gelatin
¾ cup cold water, divided
3 egg yolks
¾ cup sugar

2 packages (8 ounces each) cream cheese, softened
2 teaspoons grated lime peel
¼ cup fresh lime juice

## TOPPING AND GARNISH

1 cup whipping cream, whipped
½ cup reserved lemon-orange butter filling (optional)

1. **For crust,** prepare (see pages 436–437) adding sesame seed to flour mixture. Bake and cool completely.

2. **For lemon-orange butter filling,** combine 1½ cups sugar, flour, cornstarch and salt in medium saucepan. Stir orange juice and ¼ cup water into sugar mixture gradually. Cook and stir on medium heat until mixture comes to a boil. Reduce heat to low. Cook and stir 8 minutes. Stir ½ cup hot filling into egg yolks slowly. Mix well. Return mixture to saucepan. Cook and stir on medium heat until mixture comes to a boil. Reduce heat to low. Cook and stir 4 minutes. Remove from heat. Add butter. Stir well. Add lemon peel, orange peel and lemon juice. Stir until blended. Cool.

3. **For lime cream filling,** sprinkle gelatin over ¼ cup water in small bowl. Beat egg yolks lightly in small saucepan. Stir in ¾ cup sugar gradually. Add remaining ½ cup water gradually. Stir well. Cook and stir on medium heat 5 minutes. Remove from heat. Add gelatin mixture, stirring until dissolved. Cool 2 to 3 minutes.

4. Beat cream cheese at medium speed of electric mixer until light and fluffy. Add slightly cooled gelatin mixture gradually. Beat at low speed until blended. Stir in lime peel and lime juice. Place in freezer 1 hour to set filling.

*continued*

*Citrus Dream Pie*

5. **To assemble pie,** spread half of lemon-orange butter filling in bottom of baked pie crust. Spoon lime cream filling over lemon-orange butter filling. Place in freezer 1 hour. Drop teaspoonfuls of remaining lemon-orange butter filling over lime filling, reserving ½ cup for garnish, if desired. Spread gently to cover.

6. **For garnish,** spread whipped cream carefully over top. Use reserved lemon-orange butter filling to pipe lattice strips across top, if desired. Refrigerate several hours or until firm.

*One 9-inch Pie*

# ★ SHOO-FLY PIE ★

*Patricia S. Ziegler, Allentown, Pennsylvania*
*Long ago, Pennsylvania farmers developed the Shoo-Fly Pie, so named because it was so sweet one had to "shoo away" the flies.*

## CRUST
　2 nine-inch Classic Crisco® Single
　　Crusts

## FILLING
| | |
|---|---|
| 2 cups all-purpose flour | ⅓ cup light or dark molasses |
| 1 cup sugar | 1 egg |
| ½ cup Crisco® Shortening | 1 teaspoon baking soda |
| ⅔ cup dark corn syrup | 1 cup warm water |

1. **For crusts,** prepare (see pages 436–437). Do not bake. Heat oven to 400°F.

2. **For filling,** combine flour and sugar in large bowl. Cut in Crisco using pastry blender (or 2 knives) until mixture is crumbly.

3. Combine corn syrup, molasses and egg in medium bowl. Beat at low speed of electric mixer until blended.

4. Stir baking soda into water. Stir into molasses mixture. Stir in half of crumb mixture. Divide molasses mixture equally into 2 unbaked pie crusts. Sprinkle each with half of remaining crumbs.

5. Bake at 400°F for 10 minutes. *Reduce oven temperature to 350°F.* Bake 25 to 30 minutes or until set.

6. Serve warm or at room temperature. Refrigerate leftover pie.

*Two 9-inch Pies*

# ★ NEW HAMPSHIRE WHITE ★ MOUNTAIN PUMPKIN PIE

*Nancy Labrie, Rye, New Hampshire*
*A self-taught cook, Nancy finds cooking to be a creative outlet.*

**CRUST**
9-inch Classic Crisco® Single
Crust

**NUT FILLING**
2/3 cup chopped walnuts
1/3 cup firmly packed brown sugar
1/3 cup maple syrup

3 tablespoons butter or
margarine

**PUMPKIN FILLING**
2 1/2 cups mashed, cooked or canned
solid-pack pumpkin (not
pumpkin pie filling)
1 cup evaporated milk
3 egg yolks
1 cup granulated sugar

2 tablespoons butter or
margarine, melted
1 teaspoon cinnamon
1 teaspoon pumpkin pie spice
1 teaspoon vanilla
1/4 teaspoon salt

**MERINGUE**
3 egg whites
1/4 teaspoon cream of tartar
1/4 cup granulated sugar

2 tablespoons maple syrup, at
room temperature

1. **For crust,** prepare (see pages 436–437). Do not bake. Heat oven to 425°F.

2. **For nut filling,** combine nuts, brown sugar, 1/3 cup maple syrup and 3 tablespoons butter in small saucepan. Cook and stir on medium heat until sugar is dissolved and nuts are glazed.

3. **For garnish,** if desired dip 3 or 4 walnut halves in filling to glaze. Spread thin coating of glaze on pastry leaf cutouts. Place on sheet of foil. Bake at 425°F until lightly browned. Cool. Pour nut filling into unbaked pie crust.

4. **For pumpkin filling,** combine pumpkin, evaporated milk, egg yolks, 1 cup granulated sugar, 2 tablespoons butter, cinnamon, pumpkin pie spice, vanilla and salt in large bowl. Beat at medium speed of electric mixer until blended. Pour over nut filling.

5. Bake at 425°F for 10 minutes. *Reduce oven temperature to 350°F.* Bake 50 minutes or until knife inserted in center comes out clean.

6. **For meringue,** beat egg whites and cream of tartar in medium bowl at high speed until foamy. Beat in 1/4 cup granulated sugar and 2 tablespoons maple syrup, 1 tablespoon at a time. Beat until sugar is dissolved and stiff peaks form. Spread over filling, covering completely and sealing to edge of pie.

7. Bake at 350°F for 12 to 15 minutes or until golden. Cool to room temperature before serving. Refrigerate leftover pie.                    *One 9-inch Pie*

# HERSHEY'S®
# FABULOUS DESSERTS

# CONTENTS

Cakes & Cheesecakes     **460**

Cool Desserts     **476**

Pies     **486**

Breads, Muffins & Coffeecakes     **494**

Candies & Snacks     **502**

Cookies & Cookie Bars     **510**

Chocolatetown Special Cake (*page 472*)

# CAKES & CHEESECAKES

From elegant to easy, indulge yourself with any one of these wonderful cakes.

From left to right: Devil's Delight Cake, Peanut Butter-Fudge Marble Cake (recipes page 462) and Chocolate Sour Cream Cake (recipe page 465)

## Devil's Delight Cake

1 package (18.25 ounces) devil's food cake mix (with pudding in the mix)
4 eggs
1 cup water
1/2 cup vegetable oil
1 cup chopped nuts
1 cup miniature marshmallows
1 cup HERSHEY'S Semi-Sweet Chocolate Chips
1/2 cup raisins
Confectioners' sugar or Chocolate Chip Glaze (recipe follows)

Heat oven to 350°. Grease and flour 12-cup Bundt pan. In large mixer bowl combine cake mix, eggs, water and oil; beat on low speed just until blended. Increase speed to medium; beat 2 minutes. Stir in nuts, marshmallows, chocolate chips and raisins. Pour batter into prepared pan. Bake 45 to 50 minutes or until wooden pick inserted in center comes out clean. Cool 10 minutes; remove from pan to wire rack. Cool completely. Sprinkle confectioners' sugar over top or drizzle Chocolate Chip Glaze over top.

*12 to 16 servings*

## Chocolate Chip Glaze

In small saucepan combine 2 tablespoons butter or margarine, 2 tablespoons light corn syrup and 2 tablespoons water. Cook over low heat, stirring constantly, until mixture begins to boil. Remove from heat; add 1 cup HERSHEY'S Semi-Sweet Chocolate Chips. Stir until chips are melted and mixture is smooth. Continue stirring until glaze is desired consistency.

*About 1 cup glaze*

## Peanut Butter-Fudge Marble Cake

1 package (18.25 or 19.75 ounces) fudge marble cake mix
3 eggs
1/3 cup plus 2 tablespoons vegetable oil, divided
Water
1 cup REESE'S Peanut Butter Chips

Heat oven to 350°. Grease and flour two 8- or 9-inch round baking pans. Prepare cake batters according to package directions using eggs, 1/3 cup oil and water. In top of double boiler over hot, not boiling, water melt peanut butter chips with remaining 2 tablespoons oil, stirring constantly. OR, in small microwave-safe bowl place chips and oil. Microwave at HIGH (100%) 45 seconds; stir. (If necessary, microwave at HIGH additional 15 seconds or until melted and smooth when stirred.) Gradually add peanut butter mixture to vanilla batter, blending well. Pour peanut butter batter into prepared pans. Randomly place spoonfuls of chocolate batter on top; swirl as directed on package. Bake 30 to 40 minutes or until wooden pick inserted in center comes out clean. Cool 15 minutes; remove from pans. Cool completely on wire rack; frost as desired.

*10 to 12 servings*

## Collector's Cocoa Cake

3/4 cup butter or margarine
1 3/4 cups sugar
  2 eggs
  1 teaspoon vanilla extract
  2 cups all-purpose flour
3/4 cup HERSHEY'S Cocoa
1 1/4 teaspoons baking soda
1/2 teaspoon salt
1 1/3 cups water
    Creamy Peanut Butter Frosting
    (recipe follows)

Heat oven to 350°. Grease and flour two 8- or 9-inch round baking pans. In large mixer bowl cream butter and sugar. Add eggs and vanilla; beat 1 minute at medium speed. Combine flour, cocoa, baking soda and salt; add alternately with water to creamed mixture, beating after each addition. Pour batter into prepared pans. Bake 35 to 40 minutes for 8-inch rounds, 30 to 35 minutes for 9-inch rounds, or until wooden pick inserted in center comes out clean. Cool 10 minutes; remove from pans. Cool completely. Frost with Creamy Peanut Butter Frosting. Cover; refrigerate frosted cake.         *8 to 10 servings*

## Creamy Peanut Butter Frosting

  1 package (8 ounces) cream
    cheese, softened
1/2 cup REESE'S Peanut Butter
1/4 cup butter or margarine,
    softened
3 2/3 cups (1-pound box)
    confectioners' sugar
  1 teaspoon vanilla extract

In large mixer bowl beat cream cheese, peanut butter and butter until creamy. Gradually add confectioners' sugar and vanilla, beating until well blended.
        *About 3 cups frosting*

Hershey's Fabulous Desserts    463

# Cocoa Cheesecake

Graham Crust (recipe follows)
2 packages (8 ounces each)
cream cheese, softened
3/4 cup plus 2 tablespoons sugar,
divided
1/2 cup HERSHEY'S Cocoa
2 teaspoons vanilla extract,
divided
2 eggs
1 cup dairy sour cream

Prepare Graham Crust; set aside. Heat oven to 375°. In large mixer bowl beat cream cheese, 3/4 cup sugar, cocoa and 1 teaspoon vanilla until light and fluffy. Add eggs; blend well. Pour batter into prepared crust. Bake 20 minutes. Remove from oven; cool 15 minutes. Increase oven temperature to 425°. In small bowl combine sour cream, remaining 2 tablespoons sugar and remaining 1 teaspoon vanilla; stir until smooth. Spread evenly over baked filling. Bake 10 minutes. Cool; chill several hours or overnight.

*10 to 12 servings*

## Graham Crust

In small bowl combine 1 1/2 cups graham cracker crumbs, 1/3 cup sugar and 1/3 cup melted butter or margarine. Press mixture onto bottom and halfway up side of 9-inch springform pan.

**Chocolate Lover's Cheesecake:**
Prepare as above, adding 1 cup HERSHEY'S Semi-Sweet Chocolate Chips after eggs have been blended into mixture. Bake and serve as directed.

# Chocolate Sour Cream Cake

1 3/4 cups all-purpose flour
1 3/4 cups sugar
3/4 cup HERSHEY'S Cocoa
1 1/2 teaspoons baking soda
1 teaspoon salt
2/3 cup butter or margarine,
softened
2 cups dairy sour cream
2 eggs
1 teaspoon vanilla extract
Fudge Frosting (recipe follows)

Heat oven to 350°. Grease and flour 13 x 9 x 2-inch baking pan. In large mixer bowl combine flour, sugar, cocoa, baking soda and salt. Blend in butter, sour cream, eggs and vanilla. Beat 3 minutes on medium speed. Pour batter into prepared pan. Bake 40 to 45 minutes or until wooden pick inserted in center comes out clean. Cool completely in pan on wire rack. Frost with Fudge Frosting.

*12 to 15 servings*

## Fudge Frosting

3 tablespoons butter or
margarine
1/3 cup HERSHEY'S Cocoa
1 1/3 cups confectioners' sugar
2 to 3 tablespoons milk
1/2 teaspoon vanilla extract

In small saucepan over low heat melt butter. Add cocoa; cook, stirring constantly, just until mixture begins to boil. Pour mixture into small mixer bowl; cool completely. To cocoa mixture, add confectioners' sugar alternately with milk, beating to spreading consistency. Blend in vanilla.

*About 1 cup frosting*

*Cocoa Cheesecake*

# Black Forest Torte

Deep Dark Chocolate Cake
(recipe page 468)
1 can (21 ounces) cherry pie
  filling, chilled
1 container (4 ounces) frozen
  whipped topping, thawed

Bake cake in two 9-inch round baking pans as directed. Cool 10 minutes; remove from pans to wire rack. Cool completely. Place one layer on serving plate. Spoon half of pie filling in center and spread to within 1/2 inch of edge. Spoon or pipe border of whipped topping around edge. Top with second layer. Spoon remaining pie filling to within 1/2 inch of edge. Make border around top edge with remaining topping. Chill.           *10 to 12 servings*

# Triple Layer Chocolate Mousse Cake

Deep Dark Chocolate Cake
  (recipe page 468)
Chocolate Mousse, Double
  Recipe (recipe page 483)
Sliced almonds (optional)
Chocolate curls (optional)

Bake cake in three 8-inch round baking pans at 350° for 30 to 35 minutes. Cool 10 minutes; remove from pans to wire rack. Cool completely. Prepare Chocolate Mousse, Double Recipe, as directed. Fill and frost layers with mousse. Garnish with sliced almonds and chocolate curls, if desired. Chill at least 1 hour. Cover; refrigerate frosted cake.

*10 to 12 servings*

# Chocolate Chip Orange Pound Cake

1/2 cup butter, softened
4 ounces (1/2 of 8-ounce
  package) cream cheese,
  softened
3/4 cup granulated sugar
2 eggs
1 teaspoon vanilla extract
1/4 teaspoon grated orange peel
1 cup all-purpose flour
1 teaspoon baking powder
1 cup HERSHEY'S MINI CHIPS Semi-
  Sweet Chocolate
Confectioners' sugar

Heat oven to 325°. Grease and flour 9 x 5 x 3-inch loaf pan. Cut butter and cream cheese into 1-inch slices; place in bowl of food processor. Add granulated sugar; process until smooth, about 30 seconds. Add eggs, vanilla and orange peel; process until blended, about 10 seconds. Add flour and baking powder; process until blended, about 10 seconds. Stir in MINI CHIPS Chocolate. Pour batter into prepared pan. Bake 45 to 50 minutes or until cake pulls away from sides of pan. Cool 10 minutes; remove from pan. Cool completely on wire rack. Sprinkle confectioners' sugar over cake.           *About 10 servings*

*Black Forest Torte (top) and Triple Layer Chocolate Mousse Cake*

*Deep Dark Chocolate Cake*

# Deep Dark Chocolate Cake

    2 cups sugar
 1³/₄ cups all-purpose flour
    ³/₄ cup HERSHEY'S Cocoa
 1¹/₂ teaspoons baking powder
 1¹/₂ teaspoons baking soda
    1 teaspoon salt
    2 eggs
    1 cup milk
    ¹/₂ cup vegetable oil
    2 teaspoons vanilla extract
    1 cup boiling water
       One-Bowl Buttercream Frosting
       (recipe page 472)

Heat oven to 350°. Grease and flour two 9-inch round baking pans or 13 × 9 × 2-inch baking pan. In large mixer bowl combine sugar, flour, cocoa, baking powder, baking soda and salt. Add eggs, milk, oil and vanilla; beat on medium speed 2 minutes. Remove from mixer; stir in boiling water (batter will be thin). Pour into prepared pan(s). Bake 30 to 35 minutes for round pans, 35 to 40 minutes for rectangular pan, or until wooden pick inserted in center comes out clean. Cool 10 minutes; remove from pan(s) to wire rack. Cool completely. (Cake may be left in rectangular pan, if desired.) Frost with One-Bowl Buttercream Frosting.

*10 to 12 servings*

**VARIATION**

**Chocolate Cupcakes:** Prepare Deep Dark Chocolate Cake as directed. Fill paper-lined muffin cups (2¹/₂ inches in diameter) ²/₃ full with batter. Bake at 350° for 18 to 22 minutes or until wooden pick inserted in center comes out clean. Cool; frost as desired.

*About 3 dozen cupcakes*

# Hot Fudge Pudding Cake

 1¹/₄ cups granulated sugar, divided
    1 cup all-purpose flour
    7 tablespoons HERSHEY'S Cocoa, divided
    2 teaspoons baking powder
    ¹/₄ teaspoon salt
    ¹/₂ cup milk
    ¹/₃ cup butter or margarine, melted
 1¹/₂ teaspoons vanilla extract
    ¹/₂ cup packed light brown sugar
 1¹/₄ cups hot water
       Whipped topping

Heat oven to 350°. In large mixer bowl combine ³/₄ cup granulated sugar, flour, 3 tablespoons cocoa, baking powder and salt. Stir in milk, butter and vanilla; beat until smooth. Pour into 8- or 9-inch square baking pan. Combine remaining ¹/₂ cup granulated sugar, brown sugar and remaining 4 tablespoons cocoa; sprinkle mixture evenly over batter. Pour hot water over top; *do not stir.* Bake 35 to 40 minutes or until center is almost set. Let stand 15 minutes; spoon into dessert dishes, spooning sauce from bottom of pan over top. Garnish with whipped topping.

*About 8 servings*

## *N*o-Bake Chocolate Cheesecake

1 1/2 cups HERSHEY'S Semi-Sweet
　　　Chocolate Chips
　　1 package (8 ounces) cream
　　　cheese, softened
　　1 package (3 ounces) cream
　　　cheese, softened
　1/2 cup sugar
　1/4 cup butter or margarine,
　　　softened
　　2 cups frozen non-dairy whipped
　　　topping, thawed
　　　8-inch (6 ounces) packaged
　　　graham cracker crumb crust

**Microwave Directions:** In small microwave-safe bowl place chocolate chips. Microwave at HIGH (100%) 1 to 1 1/2 minutes or until chips are melted and mixture is smooth when stirred. Set aside to cool. In large mixer bowl beat cream cheese, sugar and butter until smooth. On low speed blend in melted chocolate. Fold in whipped topping until blended; spoon into crust. Cover; chill until firm. Garnish as desired.　　*About 8 servings*

## All-Chocolate Boston Cream Pie

1 cup all-purpose flour
1 cup sugar
1/3 cup HERSHEY'S Cocoa
1/2 teaspoon baking soda
6 tablespoons butter or margarine, softened
1 cup milk
1 egg
1 teaspoon vanilla extract
Chocolate Filling (recipe follows)
Satiny Chocolate Glaze (recipe follows)

Heat oven to 350°. Grease and flour 9-inch round baking pan. In large mixer bowl combine flour, sugar, cocoa and baking soda. Add butter, milk, egg and vanilla. Blend on low speed until all ingredients are moistened. Beat on medium speed 2 minutes or until mixture is smooth. Pour into prepared pan. Bake 30 to 35 minutes or until wooden pick inserted in center comes out clean. Cool 10 minutes; remove from pan. Cool completely. Meanwhile, prepare Chocolate Filling. Cut cake horizontally into two thin layers. Spread filling over one cake layer; top with remaining layer. Cover; chill. Pour Satiny Chocolate Glaze on top of cake, allowing some to drizzle down side. Cover; chill several hours. Garnish as desired. *8 servings*

### Chocolate Filling

1/2 cup sugar
1/4 cup HERSHEY'S Cocoa
2 tablespoons cornstarch
1 1/2 cups light cream or half-and-half
1 tablespoon butter or margarine
1 teaspoon vanilla extract

In medium saucepan combine sugar, cocoa and cornstarch; gradually add light cream. Cook and stir over medium heat until mixture thickens and begins to boil; boil and stir 1 minute. Remove from heat; blend in butter and vanilla. Press plastic wrap directly onto surface. Cool completely.

### Satiny Chocolate Glaze

2 tablespoons butter or margarine
3 tablespoons HERSHEY'S Cocoa
2 tablespoons water
1/2 teaspoon vanilla extract
1 cup confectioners' sugar

In small saucepan over low heat melt butter. Add cocoa and water. Cook, stirring constantly, until mixture thickens; *do not boil*. Remove from heat; add vanilla. Gradually add confectioners' sugar, beating with wire whisk until smooth. Add additional water, 1/2 teaspoon at a time, until desired consistency.
*About 3/4 cup glaze*

## Marble Cheesecake

Chocolate Crumb Crust (recipe follows)
3 packages (8 ounces each) cream cheese, softened
1 cup sugar, divided
1/2 cup dairy sour cream
2 1/2 teaspoons vanilla extract, divided
3 tablespoons all-purpose flour
3 eggs
1/4 cup HERSHEY'S Cocoa
1 tablespoon vegetable oil

Prepare Chocolate Crumb Crust; set aside. Heat oven to 450°. In large mixer bowl combine cream cheese, 3/4 cup sugar, sour cream and 2 teaspoons vanilla; beat on medium speed until smooth. Gradually add flour; blend well. Add eggs and beat well; set aside. In small bowl combine cocoa and remaining ¹/₄ cup sugar. Add oil, remaining ¹/₂ teaspoon vanilla and 1¹/₂ cups of cream cheese mixture; blend well. Spoon plain and chocolate mixtures alternately into cooled crust, ending with dollops of chocolate on top. Swirl gently with metal spatula or knife to marble. Bake 10 minutes. Without opening oven door, decrease temperature to 250° and continue to bake 30 minutes. Turn off oven; leave cheesecake in oven 30 minutes without opening door. Remove from oven; loosen cake from side of pan. Cool completely. Cover; chill.                    *10 to 12 servings*

### Chocolate Crumb Crust

> 1 cup vanilla wafer crumbs
> (about 30 wafers)
> ¹/₄ cup confectioners' sugar
> ¹/₄ cup HERSHEY'S Cocoa
> ¹/₄ cup butter or margarine,
>    melted

Heat oven to 350°. In medium bowl stir together crumbs, confectioners' sugar and cocoa. Stir in butter. Press mixture onto bottom and ¹/₂ inch up side of 9-inch springform pan. Bake 8 minutes; cool.

*Marble Cheesecake*

# Chocolatetown Special Cake

- ½ cup HERSHEY'S Cocoa
- ½ cup boiling water
- ⅔ cup shortening
- 1¾ cups sugar
- 1 teaspoon vanilla extract
- 2 eggs
- 2¼ cups all-purpose flour
- 1½ teaspoons baking soda
- ½ teaspoon salt
- 1⅓ cups buttermilk or sour milk*
  One-Bowl Buttercream Frosting (recipe follows)

In small bowl stir together cocoa and boiling water until smooth; set aside. Heat oven to 350°. Grease and flour two 9-inch round baking pans. In large mixer bowl cream shortening, sugar and vanilla until light and fluffy. Add eggs; beat well. Combine flour, baking soda and salt; add alternately with buttermilk to creamed mixture. Blend in cocoa mixture. Pour into prepared pans. Bake 35 to 40 minutes or until wooden pick inserted in center comes out clean. Cool 10 minutes; remove from pans. Cool completely; frost with One-Bowl Buttercream Frosting. Garnish as desired.

*10 to 12 servings*

*To sour milk: Use 1 tablespoon plus 1 teaspoon white vinegar plus milk to equal 1⅓ cups.

## One-Bowl Buttercream Frosting

- 6 tablespoons butter or margarine, softened
  HERSHEY'S Cocoa:
  - ⅓ cup for light flavor
  - ½ cup for medium flavor
  - ¾ cup for dark flavor
- 2⅔ cups confectioners' sugar
- ⅓ cup milk
- 1 teaspoon vanilla extract

In small mixer bowl cream butter. Add cocoa and confectioners' sugar alternately with milk; beat to spreading consistency (additional milk may be needed). Blend in vanilla.

*About 2 cups frosting*

## *C*hocolate Cherry *Upside-Down Cake*

    1 tablespoon cold water
    1 tablespoon cornstarch
  1/4 to 1/2 teaspoon almond extract
      (optional)
    1 can (21 ounces) cherry pie
      filling
1²/3 cups all-purpose flour
    1 cup sugar
  1/4 cup HERSHEY'S Cocoa
    1 teaspoon baking soda
  1/2 teaspoon salt
    1 cup water
  1/3 cup vegetable oil
    1 teaspoon white vinegar
  1/2 teaspoon vanilla extract

Heat oven to 350°. In medium bowl combine cold water, cornstarch and almond extract, if desired. Stir in cherry pie filling; blend well. Spread evenly on bottom of ungreased 9-inch square baking pan; set aside. In medium bowl combine flour, sugar, cocoa, baking soda and salt. Add water, oil, vinegar and vanilla; beat with spoon or wire whisk until batter is smooth and well blended. Pour evenly over cherries. Bake 40 to 45 minutes or until wooden pick inserted in center comes out clean. Cool 10 minutes; invert onto serving plate. Serve warm.

*About 9 servings*

# Chocolate Stripe Cake

1 package (about 18.25 ounces)
   white cake mix
1 envelope unflavored gelatin
¼ cup cold water
¼ cup boiling water
1 cup HERSHEY'S Syrup
   Whipped topping

Heat oven to 350°F. Line 13 × 9 × 2-inch baking pan with foil; grease and flour foil. Prepare cake batter and bake according to package directions. Cool 15 minutes; do *not* remove cake from pan. With end of drinking straw, carefully pierce down through cake to bottom of pan, making rows about 1 inch apart covering length and width of cake. In small bowl, sprinkle gelatin over cold water; let stand 1 minute to soften. Add boiling water; stir until gelatin is completely dissolved and mixture is clear. Stir in syrup. Pour chocolate mixture evenly over cooled cake, making sure entire top is covered and mixture has flowed into holes. Cover; refrigerate about 5 hours or until set. Remove cake from pan; peel off foil. Spread with whipped topping. Cover; refrigerate leftovers.

*12 to 15 servings*

# Cocoa Bundt Cake

1²/₃ cups all-purpose flour
1½ cups sugar
½ cup HERSHEY'S Cocoa
1½ teaspoons baking soda
1 teaspoon salt
½ teaspoon baking powder
2 eggs
½ cup shortening
1½ cups buttermilk or sour milk*
1 teaspoon vanilla extract
   Cocoa Glaze (recipe follows)

Heat oven to 350°. Generously grease and flour 12-cup Bundt pan. In large mixer bowl blend flour, sugar, cocoa, baking soda, salt and baking powder; add remaining ingredients except Cocoa Glaze. Beat on low speed 1 minute, scraping bowl constantly. Beat on high speed 3 minutes, scraping bowl occasionally. Pour into prepared pan. Bake 50 to 55 minutes or until wooden pick inserted in center comes out clean. Cool 10 minutes; remove from pan to wire rack. Cool completely. Drizzle with Cocoa Glaze. Garnish as desired.

*12 to 16 servings*

*To sour milk: Use 1 tablespoon plus 1½ teaspoons white vinegar plus milk to equal 1½ cups.

# Cocoa Glaze

2 tablespoons butter or
   margarine
2 tablespoons HERSHEY'S Cocoa
2 tablespoons water
1 cup confectioners' sugar
½ teaspoon vanilla extract

In small saucepan over low heat melt butter; add cocoa and water, stirring constantly, until mixture thickens. *Do not boil.* Remove from heat; gradually add confectioners' sugar and vanilla, beating with wire whisk until smooth. Add additional water, ½ teaspoon at a time, until desired consistency.

*About ¾ cup glaze*

**VARIATION**
**Cocoa Sheet Cake:** Prepare batter as directed; pour into greased and floured 13×9×2-inch baking pan. Bake at 350° for 35 to 40 minutes or until wooden pick inserted in center comes out clean. Cool completely; frost with One-Bowl Buttercream Frosting (recipe page 472).

*Cocoa Bundt Cake*

# Cool DESSERTS

Soothing, refreshing desserts for everyday or for entertaining guests.

From left to right: Easy Double Chocolate Ice Cream, Creamy Smooth Choco-Blueberry Parfaits and Chocolate Mint Dessert (recipes page 478).

## Chocolate Mint Dessert

1 cup all-purpose flour
1 cup sugar
1/2 cup butter or margarine, softened
4 eggs
1 1/2 cups (16-ounce can) HERSHEY'S Syrup
Mint Cream Center (recipe follows)
Chocolate Topping (recipe follows)

Heat oven to 350°. Grease 13 x 9 x 2-inch baking pan. In large mixer bowl combine flour, sugar, butter, eggs and syrup; beat until smooth. Pour into prepared pan; bake 25 to 30 minutes or until top springs back when touched lightly. Cool completely in pan. Spread Mint Cream Center on cake; cover and chill. Pour Chocolate Topping over chilled dessert. Cover; chill at least 1 hour before serving. Garnish as desired. *About 12 servings*

### Mint Cream Center

2 cups confectioners' sugar
1/2 cup butter or margarine, softened
2 tablespoons green creme de menthe*

In small mixer bowl combine confectioners' sugar, butter and creme de menthe; beat until smooth.

*1 tablespoon water, 1/2 to 3/4 teaspoon mint extract and 3 drops green food color may be substituted for creme de menthe.

### Chocolate Topping

6 tablespoons butter or margarine
1 cup HERSHEY'S Semi-Sweet Chocolate Chips

In small saucepan over very low heat melt butter and chocolate chips. Remove from heat; stir until smooth. Cool slightly.

## Creamy Smooth Choco-Blueberry Parfaits

1 package (6 ounces) instant chocolate pudding and pie filling
2 cups milk
1/2 cup HERSHEY'S Syrup
3 1/2 cups (8-ounce container) frozen non-dairy whipped topping, thawed
1 3/4 cups canned blueberry pie filling, chilled

In large mixer bowl combine pudding mix, milk and syrup; mix well. In separate bowl fold whipped topping into blueberry pie filling; reserve about 1 cup for garnish. Beginning with chocolate mixture, alternately layer with blueberry topping in parfait glasses. Cover and chill. Top with reserved blueberry topping. Garnish as desired. *6 to 8 parfaits*

## Easy Double Chocolate Ice Cream

2 cups chilled whipping cream
2 tablespoons HERSHEY'S Cocoa
1 can (14 ounces) sweetened condensed milk
1/3 cup HERSHEY'S Syrup

Line 9 x 5 x 3-inch loaf pan with foil. In large mixer bowl beat whipping cream and cocoa until stiff. Combine sweetened condensed milk and syrup; fold into whipped cream mixture. Pour into prepared pan. Cover; freeze 6 hours or until firm. *About 6 servings*

## *P*eanut Butter Sundae Pie

No-Bake Chocolate Crumb
   Crust (recipe follows)
1 quart vanilla ice cream
   Peanut Butter Chip Ice Cream
   Sauce (recipe follows)

Prepare No-Bake Chocolate Crumb
Crust. Cover; freeze. Place scoops of
ice cream into crust. Cover; freeze
until just before serving. Serve with
Peanut Butter Chip Ice Cream Sauce.
*8 servings*

### *No-Bake Chocolate Crumb Crust*

In small bowl combine 1 cup
graham cracker crumbs, 1/4 cup
HERSHEY'S Cocoa, 1/4 cup sugar and
1/3 cup melted butter or margarine.
Press mixture onto bottom and up
sides of buttered 9-inch pie plate.

### *Peanut Butter Chip Ice Cream Sauce*

1 cup REESE'S Peanut Butter Chips
1/3 cup evaporated milk
2 tablespoons light corn syrup
1 tablespoon butter or
   margarine
1 teaspoon vanilla extract

**Microwave Directions:** In small
microwave-safe bowl combine
peanut butter chips, evaporated
milk, corn syrup and butter; stir.
Microwave at HIGH (100%) 1 to 1 1/2
minutes or until chips are softened;
stir with whisk until chips are melted
and mixture is smooth. Stir in vanilla.
Cool slightly.
*About 3/4 cup sauce*

**Conventional Directions:** In small
saucepan combine all ingredients
except vanilla. Cook over low heat,
stirring constantly, until chips are
melted and mixture is smooth. Stir in
vanilla. Cool slightly.

*Chocolate Rum Ice Cream*

## *C*hocolate Rum Ice Cream

1 cup sugar
2 tablespoons all-purpose flour
1 cup milk
1 egg, slightly beaten
2 bars (2 ounces) HERSHEY'S
   Unsweetened Baking
   Chocolate, broken into
   pieces
1/2 teaspoon rum extract
2 cups chilled light cream

**Microwave Directions:** In large
microwave-safe bowl combine sugar
and flour; gradually stir in milk. Blend
in egg and baking chocolate
pieces. Microwave at HIGH (100%) 2
to 2 1/2 minutes, stirring frequently, just
until mixture boils and thickens. Add
rum extract; blend with wire whisk
until mixture is smooth. Chill
thoroughly. Add light cream to
chilled mixture; blend well. Freeze in
2-quart ice cream freezer according
to manufacturer's directions.
*About 8 servings*

## No-Bake Chocolate Cake Roll

1 package (3½ ounces) instant vanilla pudding and pie filling
3 tablespoons HERSHEY'S Cocoa, divided
1 cup milk
3½ cups (8-ounce container) frozen non-dairy whipped topping, thawed and divided
1 package (8½ ounces) crisp chocolate wafers (about 36)

In small mixer bowl combine pudding mix and 2 tablespoons cocoa. Add milk; beat on low speed until smooth and thickened. Fold in 1 cup whipped topping; blend well. Spread about 1 tablespoon pudding mixture onto each chocolate wafer. On foil, stack wafers on edges to form one long roll. Wrap tightly; chill at least 5 hours or overnight. Sift remaining 1 tablespoon cocoa over remaining 2½ cups whipped topping; blend well. Cover; refrigerate until just before serving. Unwrap roll; place on serving tray. Spread reserved whipped topping mixture over entire roll. To serve, cut diagonally in slices. Store, covered, in refrigerator. Garnish as desired.

*About 8 servings*

## Chocolate-Marshmallow Mousse

1 bar (7 ounces) HERSHEY'S Milk Chocolate Bar
1½ cups miniature marshmallows
⅓ cup milk
1 cup chilled whipping cream

**Microwave Directions:** Break chocolate bar into pieces; place in medium microwave-safe bowl with marshmallows and milk. Microwave at HIGH (100%) 1 to 1½ minutes or just until mixture is smooth when stirred; cool to room temperature. In small mixer bowl beat whipping cream until stiff; fold into cooled chocolate mixture. Pour into dessert dishes. Cover; chill 1 to 2 hours or until set.

*6 servings*

### VARIATIONS

**Chocolate-Marshmallow Mousse Parfaits:** Prepare Chocolate-Marshmallow Mousse according to directions. Alternately spoon mousse and sweetened whipped cream or whipped topping into parfait glasses. Cover; chill about 1 hour.

*4 to 6 servings*

**Chocolate-Marshmallow Mousse Pie:** Prepare Microwave Chocolate Crumb Crust (recipe follows) or use 8-inch (6 ounces) packaged chocolate flavored crumb crust. Prepare Chocolate-Marshmallow Mousse according to directions. Pour into crust. Cover; chill 2 to 3 hours or until firm. Garnish as desired.

*8 servings*

## Microwave Chocolate Crumb Crust

Grease microwave-safe 9-inch pie plate. In small microwave-safe bowl place ½ cup butter or margarine. Microwave at HIGH (100%) about 1 minute or until melted. Stir in 1½ cups graham cracker crumbs, 6 tablespoons HERSHEY'S Cocoa and ⅓ cup confectioners' sugar until well blended. Press onto bottom and up sides of prepared pie plate. Microwave at HIGH 1 to 1½ minutes or until blistered; *do not overcook.* Cool completely before filling.

*No-Bake Chocolate Cake Roll*

*Choco-Berry Frozen Dessert (left) and Cherry-Crowned Cocoa Pudding*

# Choco-Berry Frozen Dessert

3 packages (3 ounces each) cream cheese, softened and divided
1 cup HERSHEY'S Syrup
1/2 cup water
4 1/2 cups (about 12 ounces) frozen non-dairy whipped topping, thawed and divided
3/4 cup pureed strawberries (fresh, sweetened OR frozen, thawed and drained berries)

Line 9 x 5 x 3-inch loaf pan with foil. In large mixer bowl beat 2 packages cream cheese. Blend in syrup and water; beat until smooth. Fold in 3 cups whipped topping. Spoon half of chocolate mixture into prepared pan; freeze 15 minutes. Chill remaining chocolate mixture. In small mixer bowl beat remaining package cream cheese. Blend in strawberries until smooth. Fold in remaining 1 1/2 cups whipped topping. Spoon strawberry mixture over chocolate layer in pan. Top with chilled chocolate mixture. Cover; freeze several hours or overnight until firm. Unmold about 10 minutes before serving. Peel off foil before slicing.

*About 10 servings*

## Chocolate Mousse

1 teaspoon unflavored gelatin
1 tablespoon cold water
2 tablespoons boiling water
1/2 cup sugar
1/4 cup HERSHEY'S Cocoa
1 cup chilled whipping cream
1 teaspoon vanilla extract

In custard cup sprinkle gelatin over cold water; let stand 1 minute to soften. Add boiling water; stir until gelatin is completely dissolved and mixture is clear. Cool slightly. In small mixer bowl stir together sugar and cocoa; add whipping cream and vanilla. Beat at medium speed, scraping bottom of bowl occasionally, until stiff peaks form; pour in gelatin mixture and beat until well blended. Spoon into serving dishes. Chill about 1/2 hour.

*Four 1/2 cup servings*

**Double Recipe:** Use 1 envelope gelatin; double remaining ingredients. Follow directions above; use large mixer bowl.

## Cherry-Crowned Cocoa Pudding

1 cup sugar
1/2 cup HERSHEY'S Cocoa
1/3 cup all-purpose biscuit baking mix
2 cups milk
1 cup water
1 can (21 ounces) cherry pie filling, chilled

In medium saucepan combine sugar, cocoa and baking mix. Stir in milk and water. Cook over medium heat, stirring constantly, until mixture comes to full boil; remove from heat. Pour into dessert dishes. Press plastic wrap directly onto surface. Chill several hours or until set. Garnish with cherry pie filling.       *6 servings*

## Fruited Chocolate Sorbet

1 ripe, medium banana
1 1/2 cups orange juice
1/2 cup sugar
1/4 cup HERSHEY'S Cocoa
1 cup chilled whipping cream

Slice banana into blender container. Add orange juice; blend until smooth. Add sugar and cocoa; blend until thoroughly combined. Add whipping cream; blend well. Pour mixture into 9-inch square pan. Freeze until hard around edges. Spoon mixture into large mixer bowl or blender container; blend until smooth. Pour into 1-quart mold. Freeze 4 to 6 hours or until firm. To serve, unmold onto chilled plate; cut into slices.       *About 8 servings*

## Fast Fudge Pots de Creme

1 package (3 1/2 ounces) chocolate pudding and pie filling
2 cups milk
1 cup HERSHEY'S Semi-Sweet Chocolate Chips or MINI CHIPS

In medium saucepan combine pudding mix and milk. Cook over medium heat, stirring constantly, until mixture comes to full boil; remove from heat. Stir in chocolate chips until melted and mixture is smooth. Spoon into 8 creme pots or demitasse cups. Press plastic wrap directly onto surface. Serve slightly warm or chilled. Garnish as desired.

*8 servings*

Peel bananas; cut each into thirds. Insert wooden stick into each banana piece; place on wax paper-covered tray. Cover; freeze until firm. In top of double boiler over hot, not boiling, water melt chocolate chips and shortening. Remove bananas from freezer just before dipping. Dip each piece into warm chocolate, covering completely; allow excess to drip off. Immediately roll in peanuts. Cover; return to freezer. Serve frozen.

*9 pops*

## Chocolate Cream Squares

    Chocolate Graham Crust
      (recipe follows)
  1 package (3 ounces) cream
      cheese, softened
  2/3 cup sugar
  1 teaspoon vanilla extract
  1/3 cup HERSHEY'S Cocoa
  1/3 cup milk
  1 container (8 ounces) frozen
      non-dairy whipped topping,
      thawed

Prepare Chocolate Graham Crust; reserve 1/4 cup crumb mixture. Press remaining crumbs onto bottom of 9-inch square pan; set aside. In small mixer bowl beat cream cheese, sugar and vanilla until well blended. Add cocoa alternately with milk, beating until smooth. Gradually fold in whipped topping until well combined. Spoon mixture over crust. Sprinkle reserved crumbs over top. Cover; chill 6 to 8 hours or until set. Cut into squares.        *6 to 9 servings*

### Chocolate Graham Crust
In medium bowl, stir together 1 1/4 cups graham cracker crumbs, 1/4 cup HERSHEY'S Cocoa, 1/4 cup sugar and 1/3 cup melted butter or margarine.

*Chocolate-Covered Banana Pops*

## Chocolate-Covered Banana Pops

  3 ripe, large bananas
  9 wooden ice cream sticks or
      skewers
  2 cups (12-ounce package)
      HERSHEY'S Semi-Sweet
      Chocolate Chips
  2 tablespoons shortening
  1 1/2 cups coarsely chopped
      unsalted, roasted peanuts

# Three-In-One Chocolate Pudding & Pie Filling

³/₄ cup sugar
¹/₃ cup HERSHEY'S Cocoa
2 tablespoons cornstarch
2 tablespoons all-purpose flour
¹/₄ teaspoon salt
2 cups milk
2 egg yolks, slightly beaten
2 tablespoons butter or
   margarine
1 teaspoon vanilla extract

In medium saucepan combine sugar, cocoa, cornstarch, flour and salt; blend in milk and egg yolks. Cook over medium heat, stirring constantly, until mixture boils; boil and stir 1 minute. Remove from heat; blend in butter and vanilla. Pour into medium bowl or individual serving dishes; press plastic wrap directly onto surface. Cool; chill.

*4 servings*

**Pie:** Reduce milk to 1³/₄ cups; cook as directed. Pour hot pudding into 8-inch (6 ounces) packaged graham crumb crust; press plastic wrap onto surface. Chill; top with sweetened whipped cream or whipped topping before serving.          *6 servings*

**Parfaits:** Alternate layers of cold pudding and sweetened whipped cream in parfait glasses.
*4 to 6 servings*

**Microwave Directions:** In 2-quart microwave-safe bowl combine sugar, cocoa, cornstarch, flour and salt; blend in milk and egg yolks. Microwave at HIGH (100%) 5 minutes, stirring several times, or until mixture boils. Microwave at HIGH 1 to 2 additional minutes or until mixture is smooth and thickened. Stir in butter and vanilla. Cool as directed above.

# PIES

A tantalizing
selection of pies—
all easy to make,
and easy to enjoy.

Chocolate Grasshopper Pie (recipe
page 488)

# Chocolate Grasshopper Pie

Microwave Chocolate Crumb
  Crust (recipe follows) or
  8-inch (6 ounces) packaged
  chocolate flavored crumb
  crust
3 cups miniature marshmallows
1/2 cup milk
1/4 cup HERSHEY'S Cocoa
2 tablespoons white creme de
  menthe
2 tablespoons white creme de
  cacao
1 cup chilled whipping cream
2 tablespoons confectioners'
  sugar

Prepare crust, if desired; set aside. In
medium saucepan combine
marshmallows, milk and cocoa. Stir
constantly over low heat until
marshmallows are melted; remove
from heat. Stir in creme de menthe
and creme de cacao; cool to room
temperature. In small mixer bowl
beat whipping cream with
confectioners' sugar until stiff. Fold in
cooled chocolate mixture. Spoon
into crust. Cover and freeze several
hours or overnight. Garnish as
desired.                *6 to 8 servings*

## Microwave Chocolate Crumb Crust

Grease microwave-safe 9-inch pie
plate. In small microwave-safe bowl
place 1/2 cup butter or margarine.
Microwave at HIGH (100%) about 1
minute or until melted. Stir in 1 1/2
cups graham cracker crumbs, 6
tablespoons HERSHEY'S Cocoa and
1/3 cup confectioners' sugar until well
blended. Press onto bottom and up
sides of prepared pie plate.
Microwave at HIGH 1 to 1 1/2 minutes
or until blistered; *do not overcook.*
Cool completely before filling.

# Chocolatetown Pie

9-inch unbaked pastry shell
1/2 cup butter or margarine,
  softened
2 eggs, beaten
2 teaspoons vanilla extract or
  2 tablespoons bourbon
1 cup sugar
1/2 cup all-purpose flour
1 cup HERSHEY'S Semi-Sweet
  Chocolate Chips or MINI
  CHIPS
1 cup chopped pecans or
  walnuts
Festive Whipped Cream
  (optional, recipe follows)

Prepare pastry shell; set aside. Heat
oven to 350°. In small mixer bowl
cream butter; add eggs and vanilla.
Combine sugar and flour; add to
creamed mixture. Stir in chocolate
chips and nuts; pour into unbaked
pastry shell. Bake 45 to 50 minutes or
until golden. Cool about 1 hour.
Serve warm with Festive Whipped
Cream, if desired. Garnish as
desired.                *8 to 10 servings*

## Festive Whipped Cream

1/2 cup chilled whipping cream
2 tablespoons confectioners'
  sugar
1/4 teaspoon vanilla extract or
  1 teaspoon bourbon

In small mixer bowl combine all
ingredients; beat until stiff.
                *About 1 cup topping*

## Chocolate Mousse Pie with Rum Cream Topping

Chocolate Mousse (recipe page 483)
8-inch baked pastry shell or 8-inch (6 ounces) packaged chocolate flavored crumb crust
1 cup chilled whipping cream
2 tablespoons confectioners' sugar
2 teaspoons light rum or 1/4 teaspoon rum extract

Prepare Chocolate Mousse. Pour mixture into pastry shell. In small mixer bowl beat cream, confectioners' sugar and rum until stiff. Spread topping over mousse. Cover; chill at least 2 hours. Garnish as desired.　　　*6 to 8 servings*

## Chocolate Cream Pie

1 package (3 ounces) cream cheese, softened
1/2 cup sugar
1 teaspoon vanilla extract
1/3 cup HERSHEY'S Cocoa
1/3 cup milk
1 container (8 ounces) frozen non-dairy whipped topping, thawed
8-inch (6 ounces) packaged graham crumb crust

In small mixer bowl combine cream cheese, sugar and vanilla until blended. Add cocoa alternately with milk, beating until smooth. Gradually fold in whipped topping until well combined. Spoon into crust. Cover; chill 4 to 6 hours or until set.
*6 to 8 servings*

*Chocolate Mousse Pie with Rum Cream Topping*

## Cocoa Cloud Pie

2 packages (3 ounces each)
    cream cheese, softened
1 cup confectioners' sugar
2 teaspoons vanilla extract
1/2 cup HERSHEY'S Cocoa
1/4 cup milk
2 cups chilled whipping cream
8-inch (6 ounces) packaged
    crumb crust

In large mixer bowl beat cream
cheese, confectioners' sugar and
vanilla until well blended. Add
cocoa alternately with milk, beating
until smooth. Gradually add
whipping cream, beating until stiff.
Spoon into crust. Cover; chill several
hours or overnight. Garnish as
desired.                    *6 to 8 servings*

## Peanut Butter Tarts

1 package (3 1/2 ounces) instant
    vanilla pudding and pie
    filling
1 1/2 cups milk, divided
1 cup REESE'S Peanut Butter Chips
6 (4-ounce package) single
    serve graham crusts
Whipped topping
Fresh fruit

In small mixer bowl blend pudding
mix and 1 cup milk; set aside. In top
of double boiler over hot, not boiling,
water melt peanut butter chips with
remaining 1/2 cup milk, stirring
constantly to blend. (OR in small
microwave-safe bowl place chips
and 1/2 cup milk. Microwave at HIGH
(100%) 45 seconds; stir. If necessary,
microwave at HIGH additional 15
seconds or until melted and smooth
when stirred.)  Gradually add to

pudding, blending well. Spoon into
crusts. Cover; chill until set. Garnish
with whipped topping and fruit.
                                    *6 servings*

## Individual Chocolate Cream Pies

1 1/2 ounces (1/2 of 3-ounce
    package) cream cheese,
    softened
6 tablespoons sugar
1/2 teaspoon vanilla extract
2 1/2 tablespoons HERSHEY'S Cocoa
2 1/2 tablespoons milk
1 cup chilled whipping cream
6 (4-ounce package) single
    serve graham crusts
Whipped topping
HERSHEY'S MINI CHIPS Semi-
    Sweet Chocolate

In small mixer bowl beat cream
cheese, sugar and vanilla until well
blended. Add cocoa alternately with
milk, beating until smooth. In
separate bowl beat whipping cream
until stiff; fold into chocolate mixture.
Spoon into crusts. Cover; chill until
set. Garnish with whipped topping
and MINI CHIPS Chocolate.

                                    *6 servings*

*From top to bottom: Cocoa Cloud Pie,
Peanut Butter Tarts and Individual
Chocolate Cream Pies*

## Hershey's Syrup Pie

9-inch baked pastry shell
2 egg yolks
1/3 cup cornstarch
1/4 teaspoon salt
1 3/4 cups milk
1 cup HERSHEY'S Syrup
1 teaspoon vanilla extract
Syrup Whipped Topping
   (recipe follows)
Fresh fruit

**Microwave Directions:** In medium microwave-safe bowl beat egg yolks. Add cornstarch, salt, milk and syrup; blend well. Microwave at MEDIUM-HIGH (70%) 6 to 8 minutes, stirring every 2 minutes with whisk, or until mixture is smooth and very thick. Stir in vanilla. Pour into baked pastry shell. Press plastic wrap directly onto surface; chill several hours or overnight. Garnish with Syrup Whipped Topping and fresh fruit.

*6 to 8 servings*

### Syrup Whipped Topping

In small mixer bowl combine 1 cup chilled whipping cream, 1/2 cup HERSHEY'S Syrup, 2 tablespoons confectioners' sugar and 1/2 teaspoon vanilla extract. Beat just until cream holds definite shape; *do not overbeat.*

*About 2 1/4 cups topping*

## Fudge Brownie Pie

2 eggs
1 cup sugar
1/2 cup butter or margarine, melted
1/2 cup all-purpose flour
1/3 cup HERSHEY'S Cocoa
1/4 teaspoon salt
1 teaspoon vanilla extract
1/2 cup chopped nuts (optional)
Ice Cream
Hot Fudge Sauce (recipe follows)

Heat oven to 350°. Lightly grease 8-inch pie plate. In small mixer bowl beat eggs; blend in sugar and butter. Combine flour, cocoa and salt; add to butter mixture. Stir in vanilla and nuts, if desired. Pour into prepared pie plate. Bake 25 to 30 minutes or until almost set. (Pie will not test done in center.) Cool; cut into wedges. Serve topped with scoop of ice cream and drizzled with Hot Fudge Sauce. *6 to 8 servings*

## Hot Fudge Sauce

3/4 cup sugar
1/2 cup HERSHEY'S Cocoa
1/2 cup plus 2 tablespoons (5-ounce can) evaporated milk
1/3 cup light corn syrup
1/3 cup butter or margarine
1 teaspoon vanilla extract

In small saucepan combine sugar and cocoa; blend in evaporated milk and corn syrup. Cook over medium heat, stirring constantly, until mixture boils; boil and stir 1 minute. Remove from heat; stir in butter and vanilla. Serve warm.
*About 1 3/4 cups sauce*

**Microwave Directions:** In medium microwave-safe bowl combine all sauce ingredients except butter and vanilla. Microwave at HIGH (100%) 1 to 3 minutes, stirring often, until mixture boils. Stir in butter and vanilla. Cool slightly; serve warm.

# Breads, Muffins & Coffeecakes

Let the irresistible aroma of these breads and coffeecakes fill your kitchen.

Chocolate Chip Banana Bread (top) and Cocoa Oatmeal Mufins (recipes page 496)

## Cocoa Oatmeal Muffins

1 cup quick-cooking rolled oats
1 cup buttermilk or sour milk*
1/3 cup butter or margarine, softened
1/2 cup packed light brown sugar
1 egg
1 cup all-purpose flour
1/4 cup HERSHEY'S Cocoa
1 teaspoon baking powder
1 teaspoon salt
1/2 teaspoon baking soda
1 cup raisins
1/2 cup chopped walnuts (optional)

Heat oven to 400°. Grease or paper-line muffin cups (2½ inches in diameter). In small bowl stir together oats and buttermilk; let stand 20 minutes. In large bowl beat butter, sugar and egg until fluffy. Stir together flour, cocoa, baking powder, salt and baking soda; add to butter mixture alternately with oats mixture. Stir in raisins and walnuts, if desired. Fill prepared muffin cups 2/3 full with batter. Bake 18 to 20 minutes or until wooden pick inserted in center comes out clean.

*About 14 muffins*

*To sour milk: Use 1 tablespoon white vinegar plus milk to equal 1 cup.

## Chocolate Chip Banana Bread

2 cups all-purpose flour
1 cup sugar
1 teaspoon baking powder
1/2 teaspoon baking soda
1 teaspoon salt
1 cup mashed ripe bananas (about 3 small)
1/2 cup shortening
2 eggs
1 cup HERSHEY'S Semi-Sweet Chocolate Chips
1/2 cup chopped walnuts

Heat oven to 350°. Grease bottoms only of two 8½ x 4½ x 2½-inch loaf pans. In large mixer bowl combine all ingredients except chocolate chips and walnuts; blend well on medium speed. Stir in chips and walnuts. Pour into prepared pans. Bake 45 to 50 minutes or until wooden pick inserted in center comes out clean. Cool 10 minutes; remove from pans. Cool completely on wire rack.

*2 loaves*

## Chocolate Almond Braided Coffeecake

1/3 cup HERSHEY'S Semi-Sweet Chocolate Chips, melted and cooled
1/3 cup sugar
1/4 cup dairy sour cream
2 tablespoons chopped, toasted almonds*
1 can (8 ounces) refrigerated quick crescent dinner rolls

Heat oven to 350°. In small mixer bowl combine melted chocolate, sugar and sour cream; stir in almonds. On ungreased cookie sheet unroll dough into 2 long rectangles. Overlap long sides to form 13 x 7-inch rectangle; press perforations to seal. Spread chocolate mixture in 2-inch strip lengthwise down center of dough. Make cuts 1 inch apart on each side just to edge of filling. Fold strips at an angle across filling, alternating from side to side. Fold under ends to seal. Bake 20 to 25 minutes or until browned. Cool; cut into slices. Serve warm.

*8 servings*

*To toast almonds: Toast in shallow baking pan in 350° oven, stirring occasionally, 8 to 10 minutes or until golden brown.

## Chocolate Dessert Waffles

1/2 cup HERSHEY'S Cocoa
1/4 cup butter or margarine, melted
3/4 cup sugar
2 eggs
2 teaspoons vanilla extract
1 cup all-purpose flour
1/2 teaspoon baking soda
1/2 teaspoon salt
1/2 cup buttermilk or sour milk*
1/2 cup chopped nuts (optional)
   Hot Fudge Sauce (recipe page 493)
   Strawberry Dessert Cream (recipe follows)

In small mixer bowl blend cocoa and butter until smooth; stir in sugar. Add eggs and vanilla; beat well. Combine flour, baking soda and salt; add alternately with buttermilk to cocoa mixture. Stir in nuts, if desired. Bake in waffle iron according to manufacturer's directions. Carefully remove waffle from iron. Serve warm with Hot Fudge Sauce and Strawberry Dessert Cream.
*About ten 4-inch waffles*

*To sour milk: Use 1 1/2 teaspoons white vinegar plus milk to equal 1/2 cup.

## Strawberry Dessert Cream
In small mixer bowl beat 1 cup chilled whipping cream until stiff. Fold in 1/3 cup strawberry preserves and 3 drops red food color, if desired.    *About 2 cups topping*

# Mini Chips Blueberry Bread

2 packages (14.5 ounces each)
  blueberry nut quick bread
  mix
2 eggs, slightly beaten
3/4 cup buttermilk or sour milk*
1/2 cup vegetable oil
1 1/2 cups HERSHEY'S MINI CHIPS
  Semi-Sweet Chocolate
  Mini Chips Glaze (recipe
  follows)

Heat oven to 350°. Grease and flour
12-cup Bundt pan. In large bowl
combine bread mix, eggs, buttermilk
and oil. Beat with spoon 1 minute. Stir
in MINI CHIPS Chocolate. Pour into
prepared pan. Bake 45 to 50 minutes
or until wooden pick inserted in
center comes out clean. Cool 10
minutes; remove from pan. Wrap
tightly in foil. Cool completely. Glaze
with Mini Chips Glaze.     *12 servings*

*To sour milk: Use 2 teaspoons white
vinegar plus milk to equal 3/4 cup.

**Loaf Version:** Prepare half of batter
as directed above using 1 package
blueberry nut quick bread mix, 1
egg, 6 tablespoons buttermilk or sour
milk, 1/4 cup vegetable oil and 3/4
cup MINI CHIPS Semi-Sweet
Chocolate. Pour batter into greased
and floured 9 x 5 x 3-inch loaf pan.
Bake; cool as directed above.

*1 loaf*

## Mini Chips Glaze
In small saucepan bring 2
tablespoons sugar and 2
tablespoons water to boil, stirring
until sugar dissolves. Remove from
heat; add 1/2 cup HERSHEY'S MINI
CHIPS Semi-Sweet Chocolate. Stir with
wire whisk until chips are melted and
mixture is smooth; use immediately.
*About 1/2 cup glaze*

# Mini Chips Blueberry Breakfast Cake

1 package (14.5 ounces)
  blueberry nut quick bread
  mix
1 cup dairy sour cream
1/4 cup water
1 egg
1/2 cup HERSHEY'S MINI CHIPS Semi-
  Sweet Chocolate
  Topping (recipe follows)

Heat oven to 350°. Grease bottom
only of 9-inch square baking pan. In
medium bowl combine bread mix,
sour cream, water, egg and MINI
CHIPS Chocolate; stir until well
moistened and blended. Spread into
prepared pan. Sprinkle Topping over
batter. Bake 40 to 45 minutes or until
golden brown. Cool; cut into
squares.              *9 servings*

## Topping
In small bowl combine 1/4 cup all-
purpose flour, 1/4 cup sugar and 2
tablespoons softened butter or
margarine until crumbly. Stir in 1/4
cup HERSHEY'S MINI CHIPS Semi-Sweet
Chocolate.

*Mini Chips Blueberry Bread (top) and
Mini Chips Blueberry Breakfast Cake*

## Mini Chips Surprise Muffins

1 package (16.1 ounces) nut
    quick bread mix
1 egg, slightly beaten
1 cup milk
¼ cup vegetable oil
1 cup HERSHEY'S MINI CHIPS Semi-
    Sweet Chocolate
⅓ cup fruit preserves, any flavor

Heat oven to 400°. Grease or paper-line 18 muffin cups (2½ inches in diameter). In large bowl combine bread mix, egg, milk and oil. Beat with spoon 1 minute. Stir in MINI CHIPS Chocolate. Fill muffin cups ¼ full with batter. Spoon about ½ teaspoon preserves onto center of batter. Fill muffin cups ¾ full with batter. Bake 20 to 22 minutes or until lightly browned. Serve warm.

*About 1½ dozen muffins*

*Mini Chips Surprise Muffins*

## Easy Chocolate Zucchini Cake

1 package (16.1 ounces) nut
    quick bread mix
½ cup granulated sugar
1 teaspoon ground cinnamon
¾ cup vegetable oil
3 eggs, slightly beaten
1½ cups shredded zucchini
1 cup HERSHEY'S Semi-Sweet
    Chocolate Chips
    Confectioners' sugar (optional)

Heat oven to 350°. Grease and flour 9-inch square baking pan. In large bowl combine bread mix, granulated sugar, cinnamon, oil and eggs; mix until well blended. Stir in zucchini and chocolate chips; pour into prepared pan. Bake 40 to 45 minutes or until wooden pick inserted in center comes out clean. Cool. Sprinkle confectioners' sugar over top, if desired. Cover; refrigerate leftovers.
*9 servings*

## Mini Chips Pancakes

1 carton (16 ounces) frozen
    pancake batter, thawed
½ cup HERSHEY'S MINI CHIPS Semi-
    Sweet Chocolate
    Fruit syrup or pancake syrup

Lightly grease griddle; heat to 375°. In small bowl combine pancake batter and MINI CHIPS Chocolate. Pour about 2 tablespoons batter onto hot griddle. Turn when surface is bubbly; cook until lightly browned. Serve warm with syrup.

*About 14 four-inch pancakes*

## Chocolate Upside Down Coffeecake

3/4 cup apple jelly
1 package (16 ounces) pound cake mix
1 cup HERSHEY'S Milk Chocolate Chips, divided

Heat oven to 325°. Grease and flour 9-inch square baking pan. Spread jelly evenly onto bottom of prepared pan. Prepare cake batter according to package directions. Stir in 1/2 cup milk chocolate chips. Pour batter over jelly layer, spreading gently and evenly. Sprinkle remaining 1/2 cup chips over top. Bake 50 to 55 minutes or until cake springs back when touched lightly. Cool 5 minutes in pan; invert onto serving plate. Cool at least 15 minutes; serve warm.

*About 9 servings*

## Cocoa-Nut Bread

2 1/4 cups all-purpose flour
1 1/2 cups sugar
1/3 cup HERSHEY'S Cocoa
3 1/2 teaspoons baking powder
1 teaspoon salt
1 egg
1 1/4 cups milk
1/2 cup vegetable oil
1 cup finely chopped nuts

Heat oven to 350°. Grease and flour 9 x 5 x 3-inch loaf pan. In large bowl combine all ingredients except nuts. Beat with spoon 30 seconds; stir in nuts. Pour into prepared pan. Bake 65 to 70 minutes or until wooden pick inserted in center comes out clean. Cool 10 minutes; remove from pan. Wrap tightly in foil. Cool completely.

*1 loaf*

*Mini Chips Cinnamon Crescents*

## Mini Chips Cinnamon Crescents

1 can (8 ounces) refrigerated quick crescent dinner rolls
Ground cinnamon
1/2 cup HERSHEY'S MINI CHIPS Semi-Sweet Chocolate
Confectioners' sugar

Heat oven to 375°. On ungreased cookie sheet unroll dough to form 8 triangles. Lightly sprinkle cinnamon and 1 tablespoon MINI CHIPS Chocolate on top of each. Gently press into dough to adhere. Starting at shortest side of triangle, roll dough to opposite point. Bake 10 to 12 minutes or until golden brown. Sprinkle confectioners' sugar over top. Serve warm.

*8 crescents*

# CANDIES & SNACKS

Easiest-ever candies for holiday gift giving, plus plenty of great treats for anytime snacking.

Clockwise from far left: Easy Rocky Road, Pastel-Coated Cocoa Bonbons, Easy Double Decker Fudge (recipes page 504) and Coconut Honey Bars (recipe 506).

## Pastel-Coated Cocoa Bonbons

2 packages (3 ounces each)
    cream cheese, softened
2 cups confectioners' sugar
1/2 cup HERSHEY'S Cocoa
2 tablespoons butter, melted
1 teaspoon vanilla extract
    Pastel Coating (recipe follows)

In small mixer bowl beat cream cheese. Add confectioners' sugar, cocoa, butter and vanilla; blend well. Cover; chill several hours or until firm enough to handle. Shape into 1-inch balls; place on wax paper-covered tray. Refrigerate, uncovered, 3 to 4 hours or until dry. Using long fork dip cold centers into very warm Pastel Coating. Quickly remove. Place on wax paper-covered tray; swirl coating on top of bonbon. Refrigerate until firm. Store in airtight container in refrigerator.

*2 dozen bonbons*

### Pastel Coating

6 tablespoons butter
3 cups confectioners' sugar
1/4 cup milk
1 teaspoon vanilla extract
    Red or green food color

**Microwave Directions:** In medium microwave-safe bowl combine all ingredients except food color. Microwave at HIGH (100%) 1 to 1 1/2 minutes or until smooth when stirred. Tint pastel pink or green with several drops food color.

## Easy Rocky Road

2 cups (12-ounce package)
    HERSHEY'S Semi-Sweet
    Chocolate Chips
1/4 cup butter or margarine
2 tablespoons shortening
3 cups miniature marshmallows
1/2 cup coarsely chopped nuts

**Microwave Directions:** Butter 8-inch square pan. In large microwave-safe bowl place chocolate chips, butter and shortening; microwave at MEDIUM (50%) 5 to 7 minutes or until chips are melted and mixture is smooth when stirred. Add marshmallows and nuts; blend well. Spread evenly into prepared pan. Cover; chill until firm. Cut into 2-inch squares.

*16 squares*

## Easy Double Decker Fudge

1 cup REESE'S Peanut Butter Chips
1 can (14 ounces) sweetened
    condensed milk, divided
2 tablespoons butter or
    margarine, softened
1 cup HERSHEY'S Semi-Sweet
    Chocolate Chips
1 teaspoon vanilla extract,
    divided

**Microwave Directions:** Line 9-inch square pan or 9 x 5 x 3-inch loaf pan with foil; lightly butter foil. In medium microwave-safe bowl, place peanut butter chips, 2/3 cup sweetened condensed milk and butter. In second medium microwave-safe bowl, place chocolate chips and remaining sweetened condensed milk. Microwave bowl with peanut butter chips at HIGH (100%) 1 minute or until chips are melted and mixture is smooth when stirred; stir in 1/2 teaspoon vanilla. Immediately pour and spread evenly into prepared pan. Microwave bowl with chocolate chips at HIGH 1 minute or until chips are melted and mixture is smooth when stirred; stir in remaining 1/2 teaspoon vanilla. Immediately pour and spread over peanut butter layer; cool. Cover; refrigerate until firm. Cut into 1-inch squares. Store in airtight container in refrigerator.

*About 2 dozen squares*

## Cherries 'n Chocolate Fudge

1 can (14 ounces) sweetened
   condensed milk
2 cups (12-ounce package)
   HERSHEY'S Semi-Sweet
   Chocolate Chips
1/2 cup coarsely chopped
   almonds
1/2 cup chopped candied
   cherries
1 teaspoon almond extract
   Candied cherry halves
   (optional)

Line 8-inch square pan with foil. In medium microwave-safe bowl combine sweetened condensed milk and chocolate chips; stir lightly. Microwave at HIGH (100%) 1½ to 2 minutes or until chips are melted and mixture is smooth when stirred. Stir in almonds, chopped cherries and almond extract. Spread evenly in prepared pan. Cover; chill until firm. Cut into 1-inch squares. Garnish with cherry halves, if desired. Cover; store in refrigerator.

*About 4 dozen squares*

## Chocolate Dipped Fruit

1 cup HERSHEY'S Semi-Sweet
   Chocolate Chips
1 tablespoon shortening (not
   butter, margarine or oil)
   Assorted fresh fruit, washed
   and chilled

In top of double boiler over hot, not boiling, water melt chocolate chips and shortening; stir until smooth. Allow mixture to cool slightly. Dip fruit or fruit slices about 2/3 of the way into chocolate mixture. Shake gently to remove excess chocolate. Place on wax paper-covered tray. Chill, uncovered, about 30 minutes or until chocolate is firm.

*About ½ cup coating*

*Fudge Caramels*

## Fudge Caramels

2 cups sugar
2/3 cup HERSHEY'S Cocoa
1/8 teaspoon salt
1 cup light corn syrup
1 cup evaporated milk
1/2 cup water
1/4 cup butter or margarine
1 teaspoon vanilla extract

Butter 9-inch square pan; set aside. In heavy 3-quart saucepan combine sugar, cocoa, salt and corn syrup; stir in evaporated milk and water. Cook over medium heat, stirring constantly, until mixture boils. Cook, stirring frequently, to 245°F on a candy thermometer (firm-ball stage) or until syrup, when dropped into very cold water, forms a firm ball that does not flatten when removed from water. Remove from heat; stir in butter and vanilla, blending well. Pour into prepared pan; cool. With buttered scissors cut into 1-inch squares. Wrap individually.

*About 6 dozen candies*

## Fast Chocolate-Pecan Fudge

½ cup butter or margarine
¾ cup HERSHEY'S Cocoa
4 cups confectioners' sugar
1 teaspoon vanilla extract
½ cup evaporated milk
1 cup pecan pieces
Pecan halves (optional)

**Microwave Directions:** Line 8-inch square pan with foil. In medium microwave-safe bowl place butter. Microwave at HIGH (100%) 1 to 1½ minutes or until melted. Add cocoa; stir until smooth. Stir in confectioners' sugar and vanilla; blend well (mixture will be dry and crumbly). Stir in evaporated milk. Microwave at HIGH 1 minute; stir. Microwave additional 1 minute or until mixture is hot. Beat with wooden spoon until smooth; add pecans. Pour into prepared pan. Cool. Cover; chill until firm. Cut into 1-inch squares. Garnish with pecan halves, if desired. Cover; store in refrigerator.
*About 4 dozen squares*

## Coconut Honey Bars

⅓ cup butter or margarine
⅓ cup packed light brown sugar
⅓ cup honey
½ teaspoon vanilla extract
2 cups quick-cooking rolled oats
1⅓ cups flaked coconut
½ cup raisins
1 cup REESE'S Peanut Butter Chips

Heat oven to 400°. Line 8-inch square baking pan with foil; grease foil. In large saucepan melt butter; remove from heat. Add remaining ingredients; stir until blended. Press mixture into prepared pan. Bake 15 to 20 minutes or just until golden brown. Cool completely; cut into bars. *About 2 dozen bars*

## Mint 'n Chocolate Fudge

½ cup butter or margarine
¾ cup HERSHEY'S Cocoa
4 cups confectioners' sugar
1 teaspoon vanilla extract
½ cup evaporated milk
Pastel Mint Topping (recipe follows)

**Microwave Directions:** Line 8-inch square pan with foil. In medium microwave-safe bowl place butter. Microwave at HIGH (100%) 1 to 1½ minutes or until melted. Add cocoa; stir until smooth. Stir in confectioners' sugar and vanilla; blend well (mixture will be dry and crumbly). Stir in evaporated milk. Microwave at HIGH 1 to 2 minutes or until mixture is hot. Beat with wire whisk until smooth. Immediately pour into prepared pan. Cover; chill until firm. Spread Pastel Mint Topping evenly over fudge; chill until firm. Cut into 1-inch squares. Cover; store in refrigerator.
*About 4 dozen squares*

### Pastel Mint Topping
In small mixer bowl beat 3 tablespoons softened butter or margarine, 1 tablespoon water and ⅛ to ¼ teaspoon mint extract until blended. Gradually add 1½ cups confectioners' sugar and 2 drops green or red food color. Beat until smooth.

*From top to bottom: Cherries 'n Chocolate Fudge (recipe page 505), Fast Chocolate-Pecan Fudge and Mint 'n Chocolate Fudge*

In large mixer bowl beat cream cheese and milk until fluffy. Add confectioners' sugar, cocoa and vanilla; blend well. Stir in nuts, if desired. Cover; chill several hours or until firm enough to handle. To form centers shape into 1-inch balls. Place on wax paper-covered tray. Refrigerate, uncovered, 3 to 4 hours or until dry. Using long fork, dip cold centers into Peanut Butter Coating. (To remove excess coating, slide fork across rim of pan and tap a few times.) Place on wax paper-covered tray; swirl coating on top of bonbon. If coating becomes too thick, reheat over hot water. OR reheat in microwave at HIGH (100%) 30 seconds. Refrigerate, uncovered, 1 hour. Store in airtight container in refrigerator.

*About 10 dozen bonbons*

## Peanut Butter Coating

In top of double boiler over hot, not boiling, water melt 3⅓ cups (two 10-ounce packages) REESE'S Peanut Butter Chips and ¼ cup shortening (not butter, margarine or oil), stirring constantly to blend. Set aside; cool slightly.

**Microwave Directions:** Make centers as directed. In 2-quart microwave-safe bowl place peanut butter chips and shortening. Microwave at HIGH (100%) 1 to 2 minutes, stirring once, or just until chips are melted and mixture is smooth when stirred. Coat and store bonbons as directed.

## Peanutty-Cocoa Bonbons

2 packages (3 ounces each) cream cheese, softened
1 tablespoon milk
4 cups confectioners' sugar
⅓ cup HERSHEY'S Cocoa
1 teaspoon vanilla extract
1 cup finely chopped nuts (optional)
Peanut Butter Coating (recipe follows)

# *C*hocolate Truffles

³/₄ cup butter
³/₄ cup HERSHEY'S Cocoa
1 can (14 ounces) sweetened
   condensed milk
1 tablespoon vanilla extract
   Cocoa or confectioners' sugar

In heavy saucepan over low heat
melt butter. Add cocoa; stir until
smooth. Blend in sweetened
condensed milk; stir constantly until
mixture is thick, smooth and glossy,
about 4 minutes. Remove from heat;
stir in vanilla. Chill 3 to 4 hours or
until firm. Shape into 1¹/₄-inch balls;
roll in cocoa or confectioners' sugar.
Chill until firm, 1 to 2 hours. Store,
covered, in refrigerator.
*About 2¹/₂ dozen candies*

**VARIATIONS**
**Nut Truffles:** Add ³/₄ cup coarsely
chopped toasted pecans to
chocolate mixture when adding
vanilla. (To toast pecans: Toast ³/₄ cup
pecan halves in shallow baking pan
in 350° oven, stirring occasionally, 6
to 8 minutes or until golden brown.
Cool.)

**Rum Nut Truffles:** Decrease vanilla
to 1 teaspoon. Stir in 2 to 3
tablespoons rum or 1 teaspoon rum
extract and ³/₄ cup coarsely
chopped toasted nuts.

**Espresso Truffles:** Decrease vanilla
to 1 teaspoon. Stir in 1¹/₄ teaspoons
instant espresso coffee with vanilla.
Roll balls in cocoa or chopped nuts.

**Nut-Coated Truffles:** Roll balls in
chopped nuts.

# COOKIES & COOKIE BARS

Here's all kinds of cookies to choose from— all made delicious with chocolate.

Five Layer Bars (left) and Cocoa Cherry Drops (recipes page 512)

## Cocoa Cherry Drops

1/2 cup plus 2 tablespoons butter
    or margarine
1 cup sugar
1 egg
1 teaspoon vanilla extract
1 1/4 cups all-purpose flour
6 tablespoons HERSHEY'S Cocoa
1/2 teaspoon baking soda
1/2 teaspoon salt
1 cup chopped maraschino
    cherries, well drained
1/2 cup chopped walnuts
    Walnut pieces (optional)

Heat oven to 350°. In large mixer bowl cream butter and sugar. Beat in egg and vanilla. Combine flour, cocoa, baking soda and salt; blend into creamed mixture. Stir in cherries and chopped walnuts. Drop by rounded teaspoonfuls onto ungreased cookie sheet. Press walnut piece into each cookie, if desired. Bake 10 to 12 minutes or until set. Cool slightly; remove from cookie sheet to wire rack. Cool completely.

*About 4 dozen cookies*

## Five Layer Bars

3/4 cup butter or margarine
1 3/4 cups graham cracker crumbs
1/4 cup HERSHEY'S Cocoa
2 tablespoons sugar
1 can (14 ounces) sweetened
    condensed milk
1 cup HERSHEY'S Semi-Sweet
    Chocolate Chips
1 cup raisins or chopped dried
    apricots or miniature
    marshmallows
1 cup chopped nuts

Heat oven to 350°. In 13 x 9 x 2-inch baking pan melt butter in oven. Combine crumbs, cocoa and sugar; sprinkle over butter. Pour sweetened condensed milk evenly over crumbs. Sprinkle chocolate chips and raisins over sweetened condensed milk. Sprinkle nuts on top; press down firmly. Bake 25 to 30 minutes or until lightly browned. Cool completely; cover with aluminum foil. Let stand at room temperature about 8 hours before cutting into bars.

*About 3 dozen bars*

### VARIATION

**Golden Bars:** Substitute 1 cup REESE'S Peanut Butter Chips for chocolate chips. Sprinkle 1 cup golden raisins or chopped dried apricots over chips. Proceed as above.

## Chewy Chocolate Macaroons

1 package (14 ounces) flaked
    coconut (about 5 1/3 cups)
1/2 cup HERSHEY'S Cocoa
1 can (14 ounces) sweetened
    condensed milk
2 teaspoons vanilla extract
    Red candied cherries, halved

Heat oven to 350°. In large bowl thoroughly combine coconut and cocoa; stir in sweetened condensed milk and vanilla. Drop by rounded teaspoonfuls onto generously greased cookie sheet. Press cherry half into each cookie. Bake 8 to 10 minutes or until almost set. Immediately remove from cookie sheet to wire rack. Cool completely. Store loosely covered at room temperature.

*About 4 dozen cookies*

# Buried Cherry Cookies

Chocolate Frosting (recipe
  follows)
1/2 cup butter or margarine
1 cup sugar
1 egg
1 1/2 teaspoons vanilla extract
1 1/2 cups all-purpose flour
1/3 cup HERSHEY'S Cocoa
1/4 teaspoon baking powder
1/4 teaspoon baking soda
1/4 teaspoon salt
1 jar (10 ounces) small
  maraschino cherries
  (about 44)

Prepare Chocolate Frosting; set
aside. Heat oven to 350°. In large
mixer bowl cream butter, sugar, egg
and vanilla until light and fluffy.
Combine flour, cocoa, baking
powder, baking soda and salt;
gradually add to creamed mixture
until well blended. Shape dough into
1-inch balls. Place about 2 inches
apart on ungreased cookie sheet.
Press thumb gently in center of each
cookie. Drain cherries; place one
cherry in center of each cookie.
Bake 10 minutes or until edges are
set; remove from cookie sheet to wire
rack. Spoon scant teaspoonful
frosting over cherry, spreading to
cover cherry.
*About 3 1/2 dozen cookies*

## Chocolate Frosting

2/3 cup sweetened condensed
  milk
1/2 cup HERSHEY'S Semi-Sweet
  Chocolate Chips

In small saucepan combine
sweetened condensed milk and
chocolate chips. Stir constantly over
low heat until chips are melted and
mixture is smooth, about 5 minutes.
Remove from heat; cool thoroughly.

## No-Bake Cocoa Haystacks

1½ cups sugar
½ cup butter or margarine
½ cup milk
½ cup HERSHEY'S Cocoa
1 teaspoon vanilla extract
3½ cups quick-cooking rolled oats
1 cup flaked coconut
½ cup chopped nuts

In medium saucepan combine sugar, butter, milk and cocoa. Cook over medium heat, stirring constantly, until mixture comes to a full boil; remove from heat. Stir in remaining ingredients. Immediately drop by rounded teaspoonfuls onto wax paper. Cool completely. Store in cool, dry place.

*About 4 dozen cookies*

## Spiced Chip Cookies

1 package (18.25 or 18.5 ounces) spice cake mix
1 cup quick-cooking rolled oats
¾ cup butter or margarine, softened
2 eggs
2 cups (11.5-ounce package) HERSHEY'S Milk Chocolate Chips
½ cup coarsely chopped nuts

Heat oven to 350°. In large mixer bowl combine cake mix, oats, butter and eggs; mix well. Stir in milk chocolate chips and nuts. Drop by rounded teaspoonfuls onto ungreased cookie sheet. Bake 10 to 12 minutes or until very lightly browned. Cool slightly; remove from cookie sheet to wire rack. Cool completely.

*About 4 dozen cookies*

## Cut Out Chocolate Cookies

½ cup butter or margarine
¾ cup sugar
1 egg
1 teaspoon vanilla extract
1½ cups all-purpose flour
⅓ cup HERSHEY'S Cocoa
½ teaspoon baking powder
½ teaspoon baking soda
¼ teaspoon salt
**Satiny Chocolate Glaze or Vanilla Glaze (recipes follow)**

In large mixer bowl cream butter, sugar, egg and vanilla until light and fluffy. Combine flour, cocoa, baking powder, baking soda and salt; add to butter mixture, blending well. Chill dough about 1 hour or until firm enough to roll. Heat oven to 325°. On lightly floured board or between 2 pieces of wax paper, roll small portions of dough to ¼-inch thickness. Cut into desired shapes with cookie cutters; place on ungreased cookie sheet. Bake 5 to 7 minutes or until no indentation remains when touched. Cool slightly; remove from cookie sheet to wire rack. Cool completely. Frost with Satiny Chocolate Glaze or Vanilla Glaze. *About 3 dozen cookies*

*Cut Out Chocolate Cookies*

## Satiny Chocolate Glaze

- 2 tablespoons butter or margarine
- 3 tablespoons HERSHEY'S Cocoa
- 2 tablespoons water
- 1/2 teaspoon vanilla extract
- 1 cup confectioners' sugar

In small saucepan over low heat, melt butter. Add cocoa and water. Cook, stirring constantly, until mixture thickens; *do not boil*. Remove from heat; add vanilla. Gradually add confectioners' sugar, beating with wire whisk until smooth. Add additional water, 1/2 teaspoon at a time, until desired consistency.

*About 3/4 cup glaze*

## Vanilla Glaze

- 3 tablespoons butter or margarine
- 2 cups confectioners' sugar
- 1 teaspoon vanilla extract
- 2 to 3 tablespoons milk
- 2 to 4 drops food color (optional)

In small saucepan over low heat, melt butter. Remove from heat; blend in confectioners' sugar and vanilla. Gradually add milk, beating with wire whisk until smooth. Blend in food color, if desired.

*About 1 cup glaze*

*English Toffee Bars*

# English Toffee Bars

   2 cups all-purpose flour
   1 cup packed light brown sugar
 1/2 cup butter
   1 cup pecan halves
     Toffee Topping (recipe follows)
   1 cup HERSHEY'S Milk Chocolate
     Chips

Heat oven to 350°. In large mixer bowl combine flour, sugar and butter; mix until fine crumbs form. (A few large crumbs may remain.) Press into ungreased 13 x 9 x 2-inch baking pan. Sprinkle pecans over crust. Drizzle Toffee Topping evenly over pecans and crust. Bake 20 to 22 minutes or until topping is bubbly and golden. Remove from oven. Immediately sprinkle chocolate chips over top; press gently onto surface. Cool completely. Cut into bars.          *About 3 dozen bars*

## Toffee Topping
In small saucepan combine 2/3 cup butter and 1/3 cup packed light brown sugar. Cook over medium heat, stirring constantly, until mixture comes to boil; boil and stir 30 seconds. Use immediately.

# Butter Pecan Squares

 1/2 cup butter, softened
 1/2 cup packed light brown sugar
   1 egg
   1 teaspoon vanilla extract
 3/4 cup all-purpose flour
   2 cups HERSHEY'S Milk Chocolate
     Chips, divided
 3/4 cup chopped pecans, divided

Heat oven to 350°. Grease 8- or 9-inch square baking pan. In small mixer bowl cream butter, sugar, egg and vanilla until light and fluffy. Blend in flour. Stir in 1 cup milk chocolate chips and 1/2 cup pecans. Spread into prepared pan. Bake 25 to 30 minutes or until lightly browned. Remove from oven. Immediately sprinkle remaining 1 cup chips over surface. Let stand 5 to 10 minutes or until chips soften; spread evenly. Immediately sprinkle remaining 1/4 cup pecans over top; press gently onto chocolate. Cool completely. Cut into squares.          *About 16 squares*

*Butter Pecan Squares*

Drizzle Topped Brownies

## Drizzle Topped Brownies

1¼ cups all-purpose biscuit baking
    mix
1 cup sugar
½ cup HERSHEY'S Cocoa
½ cup butter or margarine,
    melted
2 eggs
1 teaspoon vanilla extract
1 cup HERSHEY'S Semi-Sweet
    Chocolate Chips or MINI
    CHIPS
    Quick Vanilla Glaze (recipe
    follows)

Heat oven to 350°. Grease 8- or 9-inch square baking pan. In medium bowl combine baking mix, sugar and cocoa; mix with spoon or fork until thoroughly blended. Add butter, eggs and vanilla, mixing well. Stir in chocolate chips. Spread into prepared pan. Bake 25 to 30 minutes or until wooden pick inserted in center comes out clean. Cool completely. Drizzle Quick Vanilla Glaze over cooled brownies. Cut into bars.          *About 20 brownies*

### Quick Vanilla Glaze
In small bowl combine ½ cup confectioners' sugar, 1 tablespoon water and ¼ teaspoon vanilla extract; blend well.

## Signature Brownies

1 package (15 ounces) golden
    sugar cookie mix
½ cup HERSHEY'S Cocoa
½ cup HERSHEY'S Syrup
¼ cup butter or margarine,
    melted
1 egg
½ cup coarsely chopped nuts
    No-Cook Fudge Frosting
    (recipe follows)

Heat oven to 350°. Grease 8- or 9-inch square baking pan. In medium bowl combine cookie mix (and enclosed flavor packet) and cocoa. Stir in syrup, butter and egg, blending well. Stir in nuts. Spread into prepared pan. Bake 25 to 30 minutes or until wooden pick inserted in center comes out clean. Cool completely. Frost with No-Cook Fudge Frosting. Cut into bars.          *About 20 brownies*

### No-Cook Fudge Frosting
In small bowl combine 2 cups confectioners' sugar, ½ cup HERSHEY'S Syrup, ¼ cup HERSHEY'S Cocoa, ¼ cup melted butter or margarine and ½ teaspoon vanilla extract; blend well. Use immediately.

# Chocolate Teddy Bears

²/₃ cup butter or margarine
  1 cup sugar
  2 teaspoons vanilla extract
  2 eggs
2¹/₂ cups all-purpose flour
  ¹/₂ cup HERSHEY'S Cocoa
  ¹/₂ teaspoon baking soda
  ¹/₄ teaspoon salt

In large mixer bowl cream butter, sugar and vanilla until light and fluffy. Add eggs; blend well. Combine flour, cocoa, baking soda and salt; gradually add to creamed mixture, blending thoroughly. Chill until dough is firm enough to handle. Heat oven to 350°.

To shape teddy bears: For each cookie, form a portion of the dough into 1 large ball for body (1 to 1¹/₂ inches), 1 medium-size ball for head (³/₄ to 1 inch), 4 small balls for arms and legs (¹/₂ inch), 2 smaller balls for ears, 1 tiny ball for nose and 4 tiny balls for paws (optional). On ungreased cookie sheet flatten large ball slightly for body. Attach medium-size ball for head by overlapping slightly onto body. Place balls for arms, legs and ears, and a tiny ball on head for nose. Arrange other tiny balls atop ends of legs and arms for paws, if desired. With wooden pick, draw eyes and mouth; pierce small hole at top of cookie for use as hanging ornament, if desired. Bake 6 to 8 minutes or until set. Cool 1 minute; remove from cookie sheet to wire rack. Cool completely. Store in covered container. If cookies will be used as ornaments, allow to dry on wire rack at least 6 hours before hanging. Decorate with ribbon or pull ribbon through hole for hanging, if desired.          *About 14 cookies*

## Peanut Butter Chips and Jelly Bars

1 1/2 cups all-purpose flour
1/2 cup sugar
3/4 teaspoon baking powder
1/2 cup butter or margarine
1 egg, beaten
3/4 cup grape jelly
1 cup REESE'S Peanut Butter Chips, divided

Heat oven to 375°. Grease 9-inch square baking pan. In medium bowl combine flour, sugar and baking powder; cut in butter with pastry blender or fork to form coarse crumbs. Add egg; blend well. Reserve half of mixture; press remaining mixture onto bottom of prepared pan. Spread jelly evenly over crust. Sprinkle 1/2 cup peanut butter chips over jelly. Combine remaining crumb mixture with remaining 1/2 cup chips; sprinkle over top. Bake 25 to 30 minutes or until lightly browned. Cool completely. Cut into bars.

*About 1 1/2 dozen bars*

## Chocolate Crinkle Cookies

2 cups sugar
3/4 cup vegetable oil
3/4 cup HERSHEY'S Cocoa
4 eggs
2 teaspoons vanilla extract
2 1/3 cups all-purpose flour
2 teaspoons baking powder
1/2 teaspoon salt
Confectioners' sugar

In large mixer bowl combine sugar and oil; add cocoa, blending well. Beat in eggs and vanilla. Combine flour, baking powder and salt; add to cocoa mixture, blending well. Cover; chill at least 6 hours. Heat oven to 350°. Shape dough into 1-inch balls; roll in confectioners' sugar. Place 2 inches apart on greased cookie sheet. Bake 12 to 14 minutes or until almost no indentation remains when touched. Remove from cookie sheet to wire rack. Cool completely.

*About 4 dozen cookies*

*Peanut Butter Chips and Jelly Bars*

# Duncan Hines®

# BAKING
## FOR
## SPECIAL OCCASIONS

# CONTENTS

Breakfast Buffet                         **522**

Packed Lunch Goodies                     **530**

Fabulous After Dinner Desserts           **538**

No-Cholesterol Anytime Treats            **546**

Special Celebrations                     **554**

Picnic Sweets                            **562**

Children's Party Delights                **572**

Double Berry Layer Cake (*page 538*)

# *B*REAKFAST BUFFET

❖

## Peachy Blueberry Crunch                9 Servings

1 package Duncan Hines®
    Bakery Style Blueberry
    Muffin Mix
4 cups peeled, sliced
    peaches (about 4 large)
½ cup water

3 tablespoons brown sugar
½ cup chopped pecans
⅓ cup butter or margarine,
    melted
    Whipped topping or ice
    cream (optional)

1. Preheat oven to 350°F.

2. Rinse blueberries from Mix with cold water and drain.

3. Arrange peach slices in ungreased 9-inch square pan. Sprinkle blueberries over peaches. Combine water and brown sugar in liquid measuring cup. Pour over fruit.

4. Combine muffin mix, pecans and melted butter in large bowl. Stir until thoroughly blended. (Mixture will be crumbly.) Sprinkle crumb mixture over fruit. Sprinkle contents of topping packet from Mix over crumb mixture. Bake at 350°F for 50 to 55 minutes or until lightly browned and bubbly. Serve warm with whipped topping, if desired.

> **Tip:** *If peaches are not fully ripened when purchased, place several peaches in a paper bag at room temperature; loosely close and check daily. Peaches are ripe when they give to slight pressure.*

# Orange Cinnamon Swirl Bread

**1 Loaf (12 Slices)**

**BREAD**
- 1 package Duncan Hines® Bakery Style Cinnamon Swirl Muffin Mix
- 1 egg
- ⅔ cup orange juice
- 1 tablespoon grated orange peel

**ORANGE GLAZE**
- ½ cup confectioners sugar
- 2 to 3 teaspoons orange juice
- 1 teaspoon grated orange peel
- Quartered orange slices, for garnish (optional)

1. Preheat oven to 350°F. Grease and flour 8½×4½×2½-inch loaf pan.

2. **For bread,** combine muffin mix and contents of topping packet from Mix in large bowl. Break up any lumps. Add egg, ⅔ cup orange juice and 1 tablespoon orange peel. Stir until moistened, about 50 strokes. Knead swirl packet from Mix for 10 seconds before opening. Squeeze contents on top of batter. Swirl into batter with knife or spatula, folding from bottom of bowl to get an even swirl. (Do not completely mix into batter.) Pour into pan. Bake at 350°F for 55 to 60 minutes or until toothpick inserted in center comes out clean. Cool in pan 10 minutes. Loosen loaf from pan. Invert onto cooling rack. Turn right-side up. Cool completely.

3. **For orange glaze,** place confectioners sugar in small bowl. Add orange juice, 1 teaspoon at a time, stirring until smooth and desired consistency. Stir in 1 teaspoon orange peel. Drizzle over loaf. Garnish with orange slices, if desired.

---

**Tip:** *If glaze becomes too thin, add more confectioners sugar. If glaze is too thick, add more orange juice.*

---

**Orange Cinnamon Swirl Bread**

# Spring Break Blueberry Coffeecake

**9 Servings**

## TOPPING

½ cup flaked coconut
¼ cup firmly packed brown
    sugar
2 tablespoons butter or
    margarine, softened

1 tablespoon all-purpose
    flour

## CAKE

1 package Duncan Hines®
    Blueberry Muffin Mix
1 can (8 ounces) crushed
    pineapple with juice,
    undrained

1 egg

1. Preheat oven to 350°F. Grease 9-inch square pan.

2. **For topping,** combine coconut, brown sugar, butter and flour in small bowl. Mix with fork until well blended. Set aside.

3. Rinse blueberries from Mix with cold water and drain.

4. **For cake,** place muffin mix in medium bowl. Break up any lumps. Add pineapple with juice and egg. Stir until moistened, about 50 strokes. Fold in blueberries. Spread in pan. Sprinkle reserved topping over batter. Bake at 350°F for 25 to 30 minutes or until toothpick inserted in center comes out clean. Serve warm or cool completely.

---

**Tip:** *To keep blueberries from discoloring batter, drain on paper towels after rinsing.*

---

# Cinnamon Rolls

**24 Rolls**

## ROLLS

1 package Duncan Hines®
  Moist Deluxe Yellow
  Cake Mix
5 cups all-purpose flour
2 packages (¼ ounce each)
  active dry yeast

2½ cups hot water
  Butter or margarine,
    softened
  Ground cinnamon
  Granulated sugar

## TOPPING

½ cup butter or margarine,
  melted
¼ cup firmly packed brown
  sugar

¼ cup light corn syrup
1 cup chopped nuts

1. Grease two 13×9×2-inch pans.

2. **For rolls,** combine cake mix, flour and yeast in large bowl. Stir until well blended. Stir in hot water. Cover and let rise in warm place for 1 hour or until doubled.

3. Divide dough in half. Roll half the dough into large rectangle on floured surface. Spread with generous amount of softened butter. Sprinkle with cinnamon and granulated sugar. Roll up jelly-roll fashion and cut into 12 slices. Place rolls in one pan. Repeat with remaining dough. Cover and let rise in pans for 30 to 40 minutes or until doubled.

4. Preheat oven to 375°F.

5. **For topping,** combine melted butter, brown sugar, corn syrup and nuts in liquid measuring cup. Pour evenly over rolls. Bake at 375°F for 25 minutes or until light golden brown. Serve warm or cool completely.

---

**Tip:** *For a special touch, place 1 cup confectioners sugar in small bowl. Add 1 to 2 tablespoons water, stirring until smooth and desired consistency. Drizzle glaze over baked rolls.*

---

# PACKED *Lunch* GOODIES

✠

## Triple Treat Cookies

**3 Dozen Cookies**

2 packages Duncan Hines®
  Golden Sugar
  Cookie Mix
2 eggs
2 tablespoons water

¾ cup semi-sweet mini
  chocolate chips
½ cup chopped pecans
½ cup flaked coconut

1. Preheat oven to 375°F.

2. Combine cookie mixes, contents of buttery flavor packets from Mixes, eggs and water in large bowl. Stir until thoroughly blended.

3. Place chocolate chips, pecans and coconut on 3 individual plates. Shape 3 measuring teaspoonfuls dough into 3 balls. Roll 1 ball in chocolate chips, 1 ball in pecans and 1 ball in coconut. Place balls together with sides touching on ungreased baking sheets. Repeat with remaining dough, placing cookies 2 inches apart. Bake at 375°F for 8 to 10 minutes or until light golden brown. Cool 1 minute on baking sheets. Carefully remove to cooling racks. Cool completely. Store in airtight container.

> **Tip:** *To save time when forming dough into balls, use a 1-inch spring-operated cookie scoop. Spring-operated cookie scoops are available at kitchen specialty shops.*

**Triple Treat Cookies**

## Cindy's Fudgy Brownies

24 Brownies

1 package Duncan Hines® Fudge Brownie Mix, Family Size
1 egg
⅓ cup water
⅓ cup Crisco® Oil or Crisco® Puritan® Oil
¾ cup semi-sweet chocolate chips
½ cup chopped pecans

1. Preheat oven to 350°F. Grease bottom of 13×9×2-inch pan.

2. Combine brownie mix, egg, water and oil in large bowl. Stir with spoon until well blended, about 50 strokes. Stir in chocolate chips. Spread in pan. Sprinkle with pecans. Bake at 350°F for 25 to 28 minutes or until set. Cool completely. Cut into bars.

> **Tip:** *Overbaking brownies will cause them to become dry. Follow the recommended baking times given in recipes closely.*

## Irresistible Lemon Bars

24 Bars

1 package Duncan Hines® Golden Sugar Cookie Mix
1½ cups granulated sugar
3 tablespoons all-purpose flour
¾ teaspoon baking powder
¼ teaspoon salt
3 eggs, slightly beaten
3 tablespoons lemon juice
1 tablespoon grated lemon peel
Confectioners sugar

1. Preheat oven to 350°F.

2. Combine cookie mix and contents of buttery flavor packet from Mix in large bowl. Stir with fork until thoroughly blended. Press evenly into ungreased 13×9×2-inch pan. Bake at 350°F for 14 to 16 minutes or until lightly browned.

3. Combine granulated sugar, flour, baking powder and salt in large bowl. Add eggs, lemon juice and lemon peel. Stir until thoroughly blended. Pour over hot cookie crust. Bake at 350°F for 16 to 18 minutes longer or until lightly browned. Cool completely. Dust with confectioners sugar. Refrigerate until ready to serve. Cut into bars.

> **Tip:** *For an 8- or 9-inch square pan, bake cookie crust at 350°F for 18 to 20 minutes. Pour topping over hot crust. Bake at 350°F for 20 to 22 minutes longer or until lightly browned.*

**Cindy's Fudgy Brownies**

Duncan Hines Baking for Special Occasions    533

# Lemon Poppy Seed Cupcakes     30 Cupcakes

**CUPCAKES**

1 package Duncan Hines®
  Moist Deluxe Lemon
  Supreme Cake Mix
3 eggs

1⅓ cups water
⅓ cup Crisco® Oil or
  Crisco® Puritan® Oil
3 tablespoons poppy seed

**LEMON FROSTING**

1 container (16 ounces)
  Duncan Hines® Creamy
  Homestyle Vanilla
  Frosting
1 teaspoon grated lemon
  peel

¼ teaspoon lemon extract
3 to 4 drops yellow food
  coloring
Yellow and orange
  gumdrops, for garnish

1. Preheat oven to 350°F. Place 30 (2½-inch) paper liners in muffin cups.

2. **For cupcakes,** combine cake mix, eggs, water, oil and poppy seed in large bowl. Beat at medium speed with electric mixer for 2 minutes. Fill paper liners about half full. Bake at 350°F for 18 to 21 minutes or until toothpick inserted in center comes out clean. Cool in pans 5 minutes. Remove to cooling racks. Cool completely.

3. **For lemon frosting,** combine Vanilla frosting, lemon peel and lemon extract in small bowl. Tint with yellow food coloring to desired color. Frost cupcakes with lemon frosting. Decorate with gumdrops.

> **Tip:** *Store poppy seed in an airtight container in the refrigerator or freezer.*

# Special Chocolate Chip Sandwiches

**18 Sandwich Cookies**

1 package Duncan Hines®
    Chocolate Chip
    Cookie Mix
1 egg
2 teaspoons water

8 ounces chocolate-flavored
    candy coating
¼ cup chopped sliced
    natural almonds

1. Preheat oven to 375°F.

2. Combine cookie mix, contents of buttery flavor packet from Mix, egg and water in large bowl. Stir until thoroughly blended. Drop by rounded teaspoonfuls 2 inches apart onto ungreased baking sheets. Bake at 375°F for 8 to 10 minutes or until light golden brown. Cool 1 minute on baking sheets. Remove to cooling racks. Cool completely.

3. Place chocolate candy coating in small saucepan. Melt on low heat, stirring frequently until smooth.

4. To assemble, spread about ½ teaspoon melted coating on bottom of one cookie; top with second cookie. Press together to make sandwiches. Repeat with remaining cookies. Dip one-third of each sandwich cookie in remaining melted coating and sprinkle with chopped almonds. Place on cooling racks until coating is set. Store between layers of waxed paper in airtight container.

> **Tip:** *Place waxed paper under cooling racks to catch chocolate coating drips and to make clean-up easier.*

# FABULOUS *After Dinner* DESSERTS

✢

## Double Berry Layer Cake                    12 Servings

1 package Duncan Hines® Moist Deluxe Strawberry Supreme Cake Mix
⅔ cup strawberry jam, divided
2½ cups fresh blueberries, rinsed, drained and divided

1 container (8 ounces) frozen whipped topping, thawed and divided
Fresh strawberry slices, for garnish

1. Preheat oven to 350°F. Grease and flour two 9-inch round cake pans.

2. Prepare, bake and cool cake following package directions for basic recipe.

3. Place one cake layer on serving plate. Spread with ⅓ cup strawberry jam. Arrange 1 cup blueberries on jam. Spread half the whipped topping to within ½ inch of cake edge. Place second cake layer on top. Repeat with remaining ⅓ cup strawberry jam, 1 cup blueberries and remaining whipped topping. Garnish with strawberry slices and remaining ½ cup blueberries. Refrigerate until ready to serve.

> **Tip:** *For best results, cut cake with serrated knife; clean knife after each slice.*

**Double Berry Layer Cake**

# Triple Orange Delight

**12 to 16 Servings**

1 package Duncan Hines®
   Angel Food Cake Mix
2 cans (11 ounces each)
   mandarin orange
   segments, undrained
2 packages (4-serving size
   each) orange flavored
   gelatin

1 quart orange sherbet
1 container (12 ounces)
   frozen whipped topping,
   thawed
Additional whipped
   topping, for garnish
Mint leaves, for garnish

1. Preheat oven to 375°F.

2. Prepare, bake and cool cake following package directions.

3. Drain mandarin oranges, reserving juice. Set mandarin oranges aside. Bring 1 cup reserved juice to boil. Stir in gelatin until dissolved. Pour into large bowl. Add sherbet, stirring until melted. Fold in whipped topping.

4. To assemble, brush loose crust from cake with paper towel. Trim bottom crust from cake. Tear cake into bite-size pieces. Place half the cake pieces in ungreased 13×9×2-inch pan. Reserve 12 to 16 mandarin oranges in refrigerator for garnish. Cut remaining mandarin oranges into pieces. Place half the orange pieces over cake pieces. Cover with half the sherbet mixture. Repeat with remaining cake pieces, orange pieces and sherbet mixture. Refrigerate overnight.

5. To serve, cut dessert into squares. Garnish servings with reserved mandarin oranges, dollops of additional whipped topping and mint leaves.

---

**Tip:** *Drain orange segments on paper towels to absorb excess moisture.*

---

**Triple Orange Delight**

# Chiffon Cake with Citrus Sauce and Fresh Fruit

**12 to 16 Servings**

## CAKE

1 package Duncan Hines® Angel Food Cake Mix
1 cup water
¾ cup Crisco® Oil or Crisco® Puritan® Oil

3 eggs
¼ cup all-purpose flour
2 tablespoons grated lemon peel
½ teaspoon vanilla extract

## CITRUS SAUCE

1 cup sugar
⅓ cup orange juice
1 egg, lightly beaten
1 tablespoon lemon juice
1 teaspoon grated lemon peel
1 cup whipping cream, whipped

Fresh strawberries, sliced, for garnish
Fresh blueberries, for garnish
Kiwifruit, peeled and sliced, for garnish

1. Preheat oven to 350°F.

2. **For cake,** combine Egg White Packet (blue "A" packet) from Mix and water in large bowl. Beat at low speed with electric mixer for 1 minute. Beat at high speed until very stiff peaks form; set aside. Combine Cake Flour Mixture (red "B" packet) from Mix, oil, 3 eggs, flour, 2 tablespoons lemon peel and vanilla extract in large bowl. Beat at low speed with electric mixer until blended. Beat at medium speed for 3 minutes. Fold beaten egg white mixture into lemon batter. Pour batter into ungreased 10-inch tube pan. Run knife through batter to remove air bubbles. Bake at 350°F for 40 to 45 minutes or until toothpick inserted in center comes out clean. Cool following package directions.

3. **For citrus sauce,** combine sugar, orange juice, 1 egg, lemon juice and 1 teaspoon lemon peel in heavy 1-quart saucepan. Cook on medium heat for 10 minutes, stirring constantly, until mixture just comes to a boil. Remove from heat. Refrigerate until chilled. Fold in whipped cream.

4. To serve, cut cake into individual servings. Spoon sauce over cake slices. Garnish with strawberry slices, blueberries and kiwifruit slices.

> **Tip:** *To obtain the most juice from lemons, bring them to room temperature, then roll them on the countertop before squeezing.*

**Chiffon Cake with Citrus Sauce and Fresh Fruit**

# Raspberry Sherbet Brownie Dessert

**12 to 16 Servings**

1 package Duncan Hines®
   Chocolate Lovers'
   Double Fudge
   Brownie Mix
2 eggs
⅓ cup water
¼ cup Crisco® Oil or
   Crisco® Puritan® Oil
½ gallon raspberry sherbet,
   softened

1 package (12 ounces)
   frozen dry pack red
   raspberries, thawed and
   undrained
⅓ cup sugar
   Fresh raspberries, for
   garnish

1. Preheat oven to 350°F. Grease bottom of 13×9×2-inch pan.

2. Combine brownie mix, contents of fudge packet from Mix, eggs, water and oil in large bowl. Stir with spoon until well blended, about 50 strokes. Spread in pan. Bake and cool brownies following package directions. Spread softened sherbet over cooled brownies. Cover and freeze for 3 to 4 hours or overnight until firm.

3. For raspberry sauce, combine thawed raspberries with juice and sugar in small saucepan. Bring to a boil. Simmer until berries are soft. Push mixture through sieve into small bowl to remove seeds. Cool completely.

4. To serve, cut dessert into squares. Spoon raspberry sauce over each serving. Garnish with fresh raspberries.

> **Tip:** *Raspberries are most plentiful during June and July. They should be plump with a hollow core. Plan to use them within 1 or 2 days after purchase.*

# NO-CHOLESTEROL
## *Anytime*
# TREATS

❖

## Cinnamon Ripple Cake                    12 to 16 Servings

1 package Duncan Hines®
    Angel Food Cake Mix
1 tablespoon *plus*
    ¼ teaspoon ground
    cinnamon, divided

1½ cups frozen lite whipped
    topping, thawed

1. Preheat oven to 375°F.

2. Prepare cake following package directions. Spoon one-fourth of batter into ungreased 10-inch tube pan. Spread evenly. Sprinkle 1 teaspoon cinnamon over batter with small fine sieve. Repeat layering 2 more times. Top with remaining cake batter. Bake and cool following package directions.

3. Combine whipped topping and remaining ¼ teaspoon cinnamon in small bowl. Serve with cake slices.

> **Tip:** *For angel food cakes, always use a totally grease-free cake pan to get the best volume.*

**Cinnamon Ripple Cake**

# Glazed Ribbon Dessert

**24 Servings**

1 package Duncan Hines®
    Moist Deluxe White
    Cake Mix
¾ cup strawberry preserves
6 strawberries, halved

1 to 2 peaches, thinly sliced
1 cup peach preserves
    Mint leaves, for garnish
    (optional)

1. Preheat oven to 350°F. Grease and flour 13×9×2-inch pan.

2. Prepare, bake and cool cake following package directions for No Cholesterol recipe. Remove from pan.

3. Split cake in half horizontally (see Tip). Place bottom cake layer on serving plate. Spread with strawberry preserves. Place top cake layer on top of strawberry preserves. Score top with knife to make 24 servings. Alternate strawberry halves and peach slices to form desired design. Heat peach preserves; press through sieve. Brush fruit and top of cake with warmed preserves to glaze. Garnish with mint leaves, if desired.

> **Tip:** *Lift top cake layer with foil-covered, cardboard rectangle.*

# Banana Blueberry Muffins

**12 Muffins**

1 package Duncan Hines®
    Bakery Style Blueberry
    Muffin Mix
2 egg whites

½ cup water
1 medium-size ripe banana,
    mashed (about ½ cup)

1. Preheat oven to 400°F. Place 12 (2½-inch) paper liners in muffin cups.

2. Rinse blueberries from Mix with cold water and drain.

3. Empty muffin mix into bowl. Break up any lumps. Add egg whites, water and mashed banana. Stir until moistened, about 50 strokes. Fold in blueberries. Fill paper liners two-thirds full. Sprinkle with contents of topping packet from Mix. Bake at 400°F for 18 to 22 minutes or until toothpick inserted in center comes out clean. Cool in pan 5 to 10 minutes. Serve warm or cool completely.

> **Tip:** *To reheat leftover muffins, wrap muffins tightly in foil. Place in 400°F oven for 10 to 15 minutes.*

# Strawberry Bars

**16 Bars**

1 package Duncan Hines®
Golden Sugar
Cookie Mix
1 teaspoon grated lemon
peel

¼ teaspoon ground
cinnamon
1 egg white
¾ cup strawberry preserves
Confectioners sugar

1. Preheat oven to 350°F. Grease sides of 9-inch square pan (see Tip).

2. Combine cookie mix, lemon peel and cinnamon in large bowl. Add contents of buttery flavor packet from Mix and egg white. Stir until thoroughly blended. Press half the dough into bottom of pan. Spread with preserves. Make ropes with remaining dough to form lattice top over preserves (see Photo). Bake at 350°F for 30 to 32 minutes or until golden. Cool completely. Dust with confectioners sugar. Cut into bars.

> **Tip:** *Strawberry Bars will be easier to remove from the pan if the sides have been greased.*

# Chocolate Banana Cake

**12 to 16 Servings**

1 package Duncan Hines®
Moist Deluxe Swiss
Chocolate Cake Mix
1½ cups light vanilla nonfat
yogurt, divided

2 medium bananas, sliced
and divided
1 tablespoon chopped
pecans

1. Preheat oven to 350°F. Grease and flour 10-inch tube pan.

2. Prepare, bake and cool cake following package directions for No Cholesterol recipe.

3. Split cake into thirds horizontally. Place bottom cake layer on serving plate. Spread ½ cup yogurt on cake. Arrange half the banana slices on yogurt. Place middle cake layer on top of bananas. Repeat with ½ cup yogurt and remaining banana slices. Place top cake layer on top of bananas. Glaze with remaining ½ cup yogurt. Sprinkle with pecans. Refrigerate until ready to serve.

> **Tip:** *To save time, simply cut cake into serving slices, top with yogurt and garnish with banana slices and chopped pecans.*

# Lemon Raspberry Chocolate Delight

**12 to 16 Servings**

1 package Duncan Hines® Moist Deluxe Lemon Supreme Cake Mix
3 tablespoons margarine
¼ cup *plus* 2 tablespoons sugar
2 tablespoons unsweetened cocoa

2 tablespoons light corn syrup
¼ cup water
1 teaspoon vanilla extract
2 pints lemon sorbet
1 pint fresh raspberries, for garnish
Mint leaves, for garnish

1. Preheat oven to 350°F. Grease and flour 13×9×2-inch pan.

2. Prepare, bake and cool cake following package directions for No Cholesterol recipe.

3. Melt margarine on low heat in small saucepan. Remove from heat. Add sugar, cocoa, corn syrup and water. Cook on low heat, stirring constantly, until sauce is smooth and begins to boil. Remove from heat. Stir in vanilla extract. Cool slightly.

4. To serve, cut cake into squares. Top each square with scoop of lemon sorbet. Drizzle with 1 tablespoon cocoa sauce. Garnish with fresh raspberries and mint leaves.

---

**Tip:** *To save time, purchase chocolate syrup to use in place of cocoa sauce.*

---

# SPECIAL CELEBRATIONS

✠

## May Day Cake

1 package Duncan Hines® Moist Deluxe Strawberry Supreme Cake Mix

2 containers (16 ounces each) Duncan Hines® Creamy Homestyle Cream Cheese Frosting

Fresh flowers (roses, pansies or daisies), for garnish (see Tip)

1. Preheat oven to 350°F. Grease and flour two 8-inch round cake pans.

2. Prepare, bake and cool cake following package directions for basic recipe.

3. Fill and frost cake with Cream Cheese frosting. Garnish with fresh flowers just before serving.

---

**Tip:** *Be sure to use only non-toxic flowers. Rinse fresh flowers with cool water and dry with paper towels. Place small piece of plastic wrap under flowers that rest on cake.*

**May Day Cake**

# Strawberry Meringue Cakes

**12 to 16 Servings**

1 package Duncan Hines®
    Moist Deluxe Yellow
    Cake Mix
4 eggs, separated
1⅓ cups orange juice
¼ teaspoon cream of tartar

1¼ cups sugar, divided
1 quart fresh strawberries,
    divided
2 cups whipping cream,
    chilled
Mint leaves, for garnish

1. Preheat oven to 350°F. Cut two 14-inch circles of heavy duty aluminum foil; line two 9-inch round cake pans. Grease bottoms and sides of foil; leave 1-inch overhang to form handles.

2. Combine cake mix, egg yolks and orange juice in large bowl. Beat at medium speed with electric mixer for 4 minutes. Pour into pans.

3. Place egg whites and cream of tartar in large bowl. Beat at high speed with electric mixer until soft peaks form. Add 1 cup sugar gradually; beat until stiff peaks form. Spread meringue gently over batter. Bake at 350°F for 35 to 40 minutes or until meringue is golden brown. Cool completely.

4. To assemble, lift edges of aluminum foil to remove cake layers from pans. Carefully remove foil, keeping meringue-side up. Place cakes on serving plates. Reserve several strawberries for garnish. Slice remaining strawberries. Combine whipping cream and remaining ¼ cup sugar in large bowl. Beat at high speed with electric mixer until stiff peaks form. Spread whipped cream mixture on meringue. Arrange strawberry slices in circular pattern on top. Garnish with mint leaves and reserved strawberries. Refrigerate until ready to serve.

---

**Tip:** *For ease in lining cake pan, shape aluminum foil to fit by forming over bottom and sides of pan. Remove and place inside pan.*

---

**Strawberry Meringue Cake**

# Fudgy Pistachio Cake

**12 to 16 Servings**

### CAKE

1 package Duncan Hines®
   Moist Deluxe White
   Cake Mix
1 package (4-serving size)
   pistachio instant
   pudding and pie
   filling mix
4 eggs

1 cup water
⅓ cup Crisco® Oil or
   Crisco® Puritan® Oil
1 can (16 ounces) chocolate
   syrup
Confectioners sugar, for
   garnish

### FUDGE SAUCE

1 can (12 ounces)
   evaporated milk
1¾ cups granulated sugar
4 squares (1 ounce each)
   unsweetened chocolate

¼ cup butter or margarine
1½ teaspoons vanilla extract
¼ teaspoon salt
Chopped pistachio nuts,
   for garnish

1. Preheat oven to 350°F. Grease and flour 10-inch Bundt® pan.

2. **For cake,** combine cake mix, pudding mix, eggs, water and oil in large bowl. Beat at medium speed with electric mixer for 2 minutes. Pour half the batter into pan. Combine remaining batter and chocolate syrup until blended. Pour over batter in pan. Bake at 350°F for 65 to 70 minutes or until toothpick inserted in center comes out clean. Cool in pan 25 minutes. Invert onto serving plate. Cool completely. Dust with confectioners sugar.

3. **For fudge sauce,** combine evaporated milk and granulated sugar in medium saucepan. Stir constantly on medium heat until mixture comes to a rolling boil. Boil and stir for 1 minute. Add unsweetened chocolate; stir until melted. Beat until smooth. Remove from heat. Stir in butter, vanilla extract and salt.

4. To serve, pour several tablespoons warm fudge sauce on each serving plate. Place cake slices on fudge sauce. Garnish with chopped pistachio nuts. Dust with confectioners sugar.

> **Tip:** *To keep pistachio nuts fresh, store in the freezer.*

**Fudgy Pistachio Cake**

# Easter Basket Cake

**12 to 16 Servings**

1 package Duncan Hines®
    Moist Deluxe Cake Mix
    (any flavor)
1 container (16 ounces)
    Duncan Hines® Creamy
    Homestyle Chocolate
    Frosting

Green food coloring
½ teaspoon water
1 cup flaked coconut
    Assorted Easter candies
2 (12-inch) chenille stems
    Pastel ribbon

1. Preheat oven to 350°F. Grease and flour two 9-inch round cake pans.

2. Prepare, bake and cool cake following package directions for basic recipe.

3. Place one cake layer on serving plate. Spread with Chocolate frosting. Top with second cake layer. Frost top with thin layer of frosting. Frost sides and outer 1-inch of cake top with remaining frosting. Make basketweave pattern in frosting with fork tines (see Photo).

4. Combine several drops green food coloring and water in small bowl. Add coconut. Toss with fork until evenly tinted. Place tinted coconut on top of basket for grass. Arrange candies on top.

5. Make handle with chenille stem ends twisted together. Wrap handle with ribbon. Insert in cake. Tie bow on side of handle.

> **Tip:** *To stiffen ribbon for a pretty bow, place ribbon between sheets of waxed paper. With iron set on low heat, press for several seconds.*

# PICNIC SWEETS

❖

## Everyone's Favorite Cake
### 12 to 16 Servings

1 package Duncan Hines®
  Moist Deluxe Yellow
  Cake Mix
1 package (4-serving size)
  vanilla instant pudding
  and pie filling mix
4 eggs
1 cup dairy sour cream
½ cup Crisco® Oil or
  Crisco® Puritan® Oil

2 teaspoons vanilla extract
2 containers (16 ounces
  each) Duncan Hines®
  Creamy Homestyle
  Chocolate Frosting
1 chocolate-covered nougat,
  caramel, peanut candy
  bar, sliced, for garnish

1. Preheat oven to 350°F. Grease and flour two 9-inch square pans.

2. Combine cake mix, pudding mix, eggs, sour cream, oil and vanilla extract in large bowl. Beat at medium speed with electric mixer for 2 minutes. Pour into pans. Bake at 350°F for 33 to 38 minutes or until toothpick inserted in center comes out clean. Cool in pans 15 minutes. Invert onto cooling racks. Cool completely. Place cakes on serving plates.

3. Frost sides and top of each cake with Chocolate frosting. Swirl frosting in diagonal pattern on top. Pull tip of knife through frosting 5 to 7 times to form fan shape. Garnish each cake with slices of candy bar.

> **Tip:** *Store leftover frosting tightly covered in refrigerator. Spread frosting between graham crackers for a quick snack.*

# Creamy Nectarine Torte

**12 to 16 Servings**

1 package Duncan Hines®
    Moist Deluxe Yellow
    Cake Mix
½ cup sugar
¼ cup cornstarch
½ teaspoon ground
    cinnamon
½ cup water
3¾ cups fresh peeled and
    chopped nectarines
    (about 6 to 8 medium)
¼ teaspoon almond extract

1 cup dairy sour cream,
    divided
¾ cup sliced toasted
    almonds, divided
    (see Tip)
1 container (16 ounces)
    Duncan Hines® Creamy
    Homestyle Cream
    Cheese Frosting
Nectarine slices, for
    garnish

1. Preheat oven to 350°F. Grease and flour two 8-inch round cake pans.

2. Prepare, bake and cool cake following package directions for basic recipe.

3. Combine sugar, cornstarch and cinnamon in large saucepan. Stir in water. Add chopped nectarines. Cook on medium heat, stirring constantly, until clear and thickened. Stir in almond extract. Cool completely.

4. Split each cake layer in half horizontally. Place one cake layer on serving plate. Spread one-third nectarine filling (about 1 cup) to within ½ inch of cake edge. Spread ⅓ cup sour cream over filling. Sprinkle 2 tablespoons almonds over sour cream. Repeat layering 2 more times. Top with remaining cake layer. Frost sides and top with Cream Cheese frosting. Press remaining almonds into frosting on sides of cake. Refrigerate several hours. Garnish with nectarine slices before serving.

> **Tip:** *Toast almonds in 350°F oven on baking sheet for 5 to 7 minutes or until fragrant and light golden brown.*

**Creamy Nectarine Torte**

# Peanut Butter Spritz Sandwiches

**2½ to 3 Dozen Sandwich Cookies**

1 package Duncan Hines®
   Peanut Butter
   Cookie Mix

1 egg
3 bars (1.55 ounces each)
   milk chocolate

1. Preheat oven to 375°F.

2. Combine cookie mix, contents of peanut butter packet from Mix and egg in large bowl. Stir until thoroughly blended. Fill cookie press with dough. Press desired shapes 2 inches apart onto ungreased baking sheets. Bake at 375°F for 7 to 9 minutes or until set, but not browned. Cool 1 minute on baking sheets.

3. Cut each milk chocolate bar into 12 sections by following division marks on bars.

4. To assemble, carefully remove one cookie from baking sheet. Place one milk chocolate section on bottom of warm cookie; top with second cookie. Press together to make sandwich. Repeat with remaining cookies. Place sandwich cookies on cooling rack until chocolate is set. Store in airtight container.

---

**Tip:** *For best appearance, use cookie press plates that give solid shapes.*

---

**Peanut Butter Spritz Sandwiches**

# Orange Coconut Cake

**16 Servings**

1 package Duncan Hines®
  Moist Deluxe Orange
  Supreme Cake Mix
2 eggs
¾ cup water
½ cup orange juice

⅓ cup Crisco® Oil or
  Crisco® Puritan® Oil
1 cup finely chopped pecans
1 cup flaked coconut,
  divided
1 jar (12 ounces) orange
  marmalade, warmed

1. Preheat oven to 350°F. Grease and flour 13×9×2-inch pan.

2. Combine cake mix, eggs, water, orange juice and oil in large bowl. Beat at medium speed with electric mixer for 2 minutes. Stir in pecans and ½ cup coconut. Pour into pan. Bake at 350°F for 35 to 40 minutes or until toothpick inserted in center comes out clean. Cool completely.

3. To serve, cut cake into squares. Spoon warmed marmalade over cake. Sprinkle servings with remaining ½ cup coconut.

> **Tip:** *The flavor of this tender cake is even better the second day.*

# Outrageous Angel Food Cake

**12 to 16 Servings**

**CAKE**

1 package Duncan Hines®
  Angel Food Cake Mix

1 envelope unsweetened
  drink mix (any flavor),
  divided (see Tip)

**GLAZE**

1 cup confectioners sugar

1 to 2 tablespoons milk

1. Preheat oven to 375°F.

2. **For cake,** combine Cake Flour Mixture (red "B" packet) from Mix and ½ teaspoon dry drink mix in large bowl. Prepare, bake and cool cake following package directions.

3. **For glaze,** combine confectioners sugar and remaining dry drink mix in small bowl. Add milk, 1 teaspoon at a time, stirring until smooth and desired consistency. Drizzle over cake.

> **Tip:** *Let your children choose their favorite color and flavor.*

Orange Coconut Cake

# Chocolate Confection Cake    20 to 24 Servings

**1 package Duncan Hines®**
   **Moist Deluxe Devil's**
   **Food Cake Mix**

## FILLING
   1 cup evaporated milk
   1 cup granulated sugar
   24 large marshmallows

   1 package (14 ounces)
      flaked coconut

## TOPPING
   ½ cup butter or margarine
   ¼ cup *plus* 2 tablespoons
      milk
   ⅓ cup unsweetened cocoa

   1 pound confectioners sugar
      (3½ to 4 cups)
   1 teaspoon vanilla extract
   ¾ cup sliced almonds

1. Preheat oven to 350°F. Grease and flour 15½×10½×1-inch jelly-roll pan.

2. Prepare cake following package directions for basic recipe. Pour into pan. Bake at 350°F for 20 to 25 minutes or until toothpick inserted in center comes out clean.

3. **For filling,** combine evaporated milk and granulated sugar in large saucepan. Bring mixture to a boil. Add marshmallows and stir until melted. Stir in coconut. Spread on warm cake.

4. **For topping,** combine butter, milk and cocoa in medium saucepan. Stir on low heat until butter is melted. Add confectioners sugar and vanilla extract, stirring until smooth. Stir in almonds (see Tip). Pour over filling. Spread evenly to edges. Cool completely.

---

**Tip:** *For a pretty presentation, sprinkle the ¾ cup almond slices over topping instead of stirring almonds into topping.*

---

# CHILDREN'S *Party* DELIGHTS

❦

## Banana Split Cake                    12 to 16 Servings

1 package Duncan Hines® Moist Deluxe Banana Supreme Cake Mix
3 eggs
1⅓ cups water
½ cup all-purpose flour
⅓ cup Crisco® Oil or Crisco® Puritan® Oil
1 cup semi-sweet mini chocolate chips

2 to 3 bananas
1 can (16 ounces) chocolate syrup
1 container (8 ounces) frozen whipped topping, thawed
½ cup chopped walnuts
Colored sprinkles
Maraschino cherries with stems, for garnish

1. Preheat oven to 350°F. Grease and flour 13×9×2-inch pan.

2. Combine cake mix, eggs, water, flour and oil in large bowl. Beat at medium speed with electric mixer for 2 minutes. Stir in chocolate chips. Pour into pan. Bake at 350°F for 32 to 35 minutes or until toothpick inserted in center comes out clean. Cool completely.

3. Slice bananas. Cut cake into squares; top with banana slices. Drizzle with chocolate syrup. Top with whipped topping, walnuts and sprinkles. Garnish with maraschino cherries.

> **Tip:** *Dip bananas in diluted lemon juice to prevent darkening.*

**Banana Split Cake**

# Butterfly Cakes

**16 Servings**

1 package Duncan Hines® Moist Deluxe Cake Mix (any flavor)

1 container (16 ounces) Duncan Hines® Creamy Homestyle Vanilla Frosting, divided

Assorted candies such as chocolate chips, peanut butter chips, vanilla milk chips, halved gumdrops, halved jelly beans and candy-coated chocolate pieces

4 bars (2 to 2½ ounces each) chocolate-covered crunchy peanut butter candy

4 chocolate-covered peanut butter cups

Spaghetti (uncooked)

1. Preheat oven to 350°F. Grease and flour two 9-inch round cake pans.

2. Prepare, bake and cool cake following package directions for basic recipe.

3. To assemble, cut each cake in half to form 2 semicircles (see Tip). Arrange on serving platters (see Photo). Reserve 1 tablespoon Vanilla frosting for candies. Frost sides and tops of cakes with remaining frosting. Use tip of knife to mark sections of wings. Decorate each section with candy pieces. Spread reserved frosting on flat side of one candy bar. Top with second candy bar; press together. Repeat with remaining candy bars. Place between cake semicircles for bodies. Spread reserved frosting on flat side of one peanut butter cup. Top with second peanut butter cup; press together. Repeat with remaining peanut butter cups. Place at top end of candy bars for heads. Use vanilla milk chips for eyes and spaghetti for antennas.

> **Tip:** *Cakes are easier to frost when completely frozen. After cutting into semicircles, return to freezer while organizing candies for decorations.*

**Butterfly Cake**

# Peanut Butter Pizza Cookies

**18 (3-Inch) Cookies**

2 packages Duncan Hines®
   Peanut Butter
   Cookie Mix
2 eggs
1 tablespoon water
   Sugar
1 container (16 ounces)
   Duncan Hines® Creamy
   Homestyle Chocolate
   Frosting

Cashews
Candy-coated chocolate
   pieces
Gumdrops, halved
Flaked coconut
1 bar (2 ounces) white
   chocolate baking bar
1 tablespoon Crisco®
   Shortening

1. Preheat oven to 375°F.

2. For cookies, place cookie mixes in large bowl. Break up any lumps. Add eggs, contents of peanut butter packets from Mixes and water. Stir until thoroughly blended. Shape into 18 (2-inch) balls (about 3 level tablespoons each). Place 3½ inches apart on ungreased baking sheets. Flatten with bottom of large glass dipped in sugar to make 3-inch circles. Bake at 375°F for 9 to 11 minutes or until set. Cool 1 minute on baking sheets. Remove to cooling racks. Cool completely.

3. Frost cookies with Chocolate frosting. Decorate with cashews, candy pieces, gumdrops and coconut. Melt white chocolate and shortening in small saucepan on low heat, stirring constantly, until smooth. Drizzle over cookies. Store between layers of waxed paper in airtight container.

---

**Tip:** *To melt white chocolate in microwave, place in microwave-safe bowl. Add shortening. Microwave at DEFROST (30% power) for 5 minutes. Stir well. Microwave at DEFROST (30% power) for 1 to 2 minutes longer, stirring every minute until smooth.*

---

# Turtle Cake

1 package Duncan Hines®
   Moist Deluxe Fudge
   Marble Cake Mix
6 fun size chocolate-covered
   nougat, caramel, peanut
   candy bars
1 container (16 ounces)
   Duncan Hines® Creamy
   Homestyle Cream
   Cheese Frosting, divided

Green food coloring
2 tablespoons slivered
   almonds
Candy-coated chocolate
   pieces
Vanilla milk chips

1. Preheat oven to 350°F. Grease and flour 2½-quart ovenproof glass bowl with rounded bottom.

2. Prepare cake following package directions for basic recipe. Pour into bowl. Bake at 350°F for 55 to 60 minutes or until toothpick inserted in center comes out clean. Cool in bowl 20 minutes. Invert onto cooling rack. Cool completely.

3. To assemble, place cake on serving plate. Remove 1-inch cake square from upper side of cake for head. Insert 2 fun size candy bars, flat sides together, into square hole for head. Position remaining 4 candy bars under cake for feet. Reserve 1 teaspoon Cream Cheese frosting. Tint remaining Cream Cheese frosting with green food coloring; frost cake. Sprinkle almonds on top. Place candy-coated chocolate pieces around bottom edge of shell. Attach vanilla milk chips to head with reserved frosting for eyes.

> **Tip:** *For a brighter green frosting, use green paste food color available from cake decorating and specialty shops.*

Turtle Cake

# Lemon Sunshine Cake

**12 to 16 Servings**

1 package Duncan Hines®
   Moist Deluxe Lemon
   Supreme Cake Mix
5 cups confectioners sugar
¾ cup Crisco® Shortening
⅓ cup non-dairy powdered
   creamer
¼ cup lemon juice
¼ cup *plus* ¾ teaspoon
   water, divided

½ teaspoon salt
   Yellow food coloring
1½ cups flaked coconut
2 mandarin orange
   segments
2 small blue candies
1 maraschino cherry,
   drained
½ orange slice
   Red licorice lace

1. Preheat oven to 350°F. Grease and flour two 8-inch round cake pans.

2. Prepare, bake and cool cake following package directions for basic recipe. Freeze one layer.

3. For frosting, combine confectioners sugar, shortening, non-dairy powdered creamer, lemon juice, ¼ cup water and salt in large bowl. Beat at medium speed with electric mixer for 3 minutes. Beat at high speed for 5 minutes. Add more confectioners sugar to thicken or more water to thin, as needed. Tint frosting with yellow food coloring to desired color. To tint coconut, combine several drops yellow food coloring and remaining ¾ teaspoon water in small bowl. Add coconut. Toss with fork.

4. To assemble, place unfrozen cake layer in center of 16-inch round serving plate. Frost sides and top with 1 cup frosting. Cut frozen cake layer into 8 equal wedges (see Diagram). Trim curved side of each wedge to fit round layer. Place wedges around cake to form sun as shown. Frost cake wedges. Press coconut on sides of wedges. Arrange mandarin oranges and small blue candies for eyes, cherry for nose, orange slice for mouth and licorice for eyebrows.

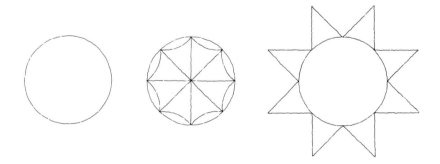

**Tip:** *For variety, choose your own assortment of candy.*

# ACKNOWLEDGMENTS

The publishers would like to thank the companies and organizations listed below for the use of their recipes in this publication.

Bel Paese Sales Company
Bongrain Cheese U.S.A.
Borden Kitchens, Borden, Inc.
California Date
   Administrative Committee
California Table Grape
   Commission
Canned Food Information
   Council
Checkerboard Kitchens,
   Ralston Purina Company
Cookin' Good
The Creamette Company
Delmarva Poultry
   Industry, Inc.
Del Monte Foods
Dole Food Company, Inc.
Hershey Chocolate U.S.A.
Kellogg Company
Kikkoman International Inc.

The Kingsford Products
   Company
Kraft General Foods, Inc.
Lawry's® Foods, Inc.
Thomas J. Lipton Co.
M.J.B. Rice Company
Nabisco Foods Group
National Dairy Board
Nestlé Food Company
Perdue Farms
Pet Incorporated
The Procter & Gamble
   Company
Reckitt & Colman, Inc.
StarKist Seafood Company
The Sugar Association, Inc.
Wampler–Longacre, Inc.
Washington Apple
   Commission

# PHOTO CREDITS

The publishers would like to thank the companies and organizations listed below for the use of their photographs in this publication.

Bel Paese Sales Company
Bongrain Cheese U.S.A.
California Date
   Administrative Committee
Canned Food Information
   Council
Cookin' Good
The Creamette Company
Delmarva Poultry
   Industry, Inc.
Dole Food Company, Inc.
Hershey Chocolate U.S.A.
Kikkoman International Inc.
The Kingsford
   Products Company

Kraft General Foods, Inc.
Lawry's® Foods, Inc.
M.J.B. Rice Company
Nabisco Foods Group
National Dairy Board
Nestlé Food Company
The Procter & Gamble
   Company
Reckitt & Colman, Inc.
StarKist Seafood Company
The Sugar Association, Inc.
Washington Apple
   Commission

# INDEX

## A

Acapulco Salad, 286
Albondigas Soup, 252
All-American Barbecue Sauce and
    Marinade, 19
All-Chocolate Boston Cream Pie, 470
**Almonds**
    Cherry City Amaretto Cherry
        Cream Pie, 449
    Chocolate Almond Braided
        Coffeecake, 496
    Dijon Almond Chicken, 24
    Peach-Stuffed Oatmeal Almond
        Cookies, 424
Amigo Pita Pocket Sandwiches, 260
Angel Hair Stir-Fry, 334
**Appetizers & Snacks**
    Baha Roll, 168
    Beef and Fruit Skewers, 307
    Beef Kushisashi, 311
    Bits O' Teriyaki Chicken, 306
    Crispy Tortellini Bites, 240
    Crispy Wontons, 300
    Deluxe Fajita Nachos, 242
    Empandillas, 242
    Empress Chicken Wings, 302
    Garlic Chicken Bundles, 308
    Glazed Ginger Chicken, 309
    Mariachi Drumsticks, 238
    Marinated Mushrooms, 311
    Meat-Filled Oriental Pancakes,
        298
    Molletes, 241
    Oriental Pancakes, 300
    Polenta Strips with Creamy Salsa
        Spread, 244
    Polynesian Kabobs, 307
    Prawns-in-Shell, 305
    Saucy Shrimp, 311
    Scandinavian Smörgåsbord, 158
    Seafood Wontons, 172
    Sesame Pork Tidbits with Sweet
        & Sour Sauce, 305
    Shrimp Teriyaki, 303
    Shrimp with Sweet & Sour Sauce,
        300
    South-of-the-Border Meatballs, 241
    Southwestern Potato Skins, 244
    Spicy Pork Strips, 311
    Spring Rolls, 303
    Tacos Botanas, 246
    Teriyaki Lamb Riblets, 305

**Apples**
    Apple & Rice-Stuffed Chicken, 33
    Chicken-Apple Stuffed Pita, 18
    Cider Apple Pie in Cheddar Crust,
        452
    Grilled Chicken and Apple with
        Fresh Rosemary, 24
    Lola's Apple Pie, 432
    Tuna-Waldorf Salad Mold, 134
**Apricots**
    Apricot Glazed Chicken, 29
    Chewy Oatmeal-Apricot-Date
        Bars, 418
Arroz con Pollo Burritos, 258
**Artichokes**
    Artichoke Chicken Pilaf, 44
    Seafood Kabobs, 226
    Tuna-Stuffed Artichokes, 154
**Asparagus**
    Tuna & Asparagus au Gratin, 178
    Tuna Salad Elegante, 162
    Scandinavian Smörgåsbord, 158
    Superb Fillet of Sole &
        Vegetables, 98
**Avocados**
    Avocado-Corn Salsa, 216
    Avocado Raspberry Spice Salad,
        282
    Southwestern Guacamole, 235
    Tostada Salad, 288
Aztec Chili Salad, 278

## B

**Bacon**
    Buffet Bean Bake, 121
    Chicken-Mac Casserole, 90
    Home-Style Chicken 'n Biscuits, 92
    Hot German-Style Potato Salad,
        120
    New Year Chicken, 59
    Polynesian Kabobs, 307
Baha Roll, 168
Baja Fruited Salmon, 272
Bake & Glaze Teri Ribs, 323
Baked Ham & Cheese Monte Cristo,
    116
**Bananas**
    Banana Blueberry Muffins, 548
    Banana Split Cake, 572
    Chocolate Banana Cake, 550

**Bananas,** *continued*
    Chocolate Chip Banana Bread, 496
    Chocolate-Covered Banana Pops, 484
    Fruited Chocolate Sorbet, 483
    Strawberry-Banana Salad, 388
**Barbecue** (*see* **Grilled Recipes**)
BBQ Baby Back Ribs, 196
Barbecue Basics, direct heat cooking, 185
Barbecue Basics, fish grilling pointers, 220
Barbecue Basics, indirect heat cooking, 185
Barbecue Basics, meat grilling chart, 190
Barbecue Basics, turkey grilling pointers, 206
Barbecued Turkey Breast, 211
Barbecued Turkey with Herbs, 207
**Bar Cookies** (*see also* **Brownies**)
    Butter Pecan Squares, 516
    Chewy Oatmeal-Apricot-Date Bars, 418
    Chippy Cheeseys, 414
    Emily's Dream Bars, 412
    English Toffee Bars, 516
    Five Layer Bars, 512
    Golden Bars, 512
    Irresistible Lemon Bars, 532
    Peanut Butter Bars, 417
    Peanut Butter Chips and Jelly Bars, 519
    Strawberry Bars, 550
**Beans**
    Aztec Chili Salad, 278
    Brunswick Stew, 55
    Buffet Bean Bake, 121
    California-Style Chicken, 90
    Chicken and Vegetable Couscous, 56
    Chop Suey Casserole, 108
    Classic Hamburger Casserole, 108
    Eight Layer Fiesta Dip, 246
    Fiesta Ranch Bean Dip, 235
    Mexican Lasagna, 70
    Molletes, 241
    Original Green Bean Casserole, 122
    Rio Grande Quesadillas, 266
    Sausage Succotash, 114
    Simply Green Beans, 282
    Spicy Burrito Bonanza, 250
    Sweet and Spicy Chicken Stir-Fry, 67

**Beans,** *continued*
    Sweet Chicken Risotto, 67
    Tacos Botanas, 246
    Toluca Taters, 264
    Tostada Salad, 288
**Bean Sprouts**
    Bean Sprout & Spinach Salad, 346
    Lotus Chicken Chop Suey, 333
    Shantung Chicken, 331
    Spring Rolls, 303
    Steamed Chinese Buns, 347
**Beef** (*see also* **Beef, Ground; Burgers**)
    Beef and Fruit Skewers, 307
    Beef Kushisashi, 311
    Beef Tenderloin with Dijon-Cream Sauce, 202
    Beef with Dry Spice Rub, 188
    Broccoli & Beef Stir-Fry, 317
    Cancun Steak Sandwiches, 254
    Carne Asada, 248
    Cheese-Stuffed Beef Rolls, 104
    Chop Suey Casserole, 108
    Classic Chinese Pepper Steak, 312
    Countdown Casserole, 102
    Dragon Beef Kabobs, 314
    Fruited Beef Kabobs, 252
    Korean Beef & Vegetable Salad, 317
    Mongolian Beef, 318
    Sichuan Beef & Snow Peas, 314
    Teriyaki Glazed Beef Kabobs, 200
    Thai Beef Salad, 319
    Veal Tonnato, 130
    Wine Country Steak, 198
    Yangtze Stir-Fry, 314
**Beef, Ground** (*see also* **Burgers**)
    Albondigas Soup, 252
    Aztec Chili Salad, 278
    Classic Hamburger Casserole, 108
    Eight Layer Fiesta Dip, 246
    Empandillas, 242
    Meat-Filled Oriental Pancakes, 298
    Mexicali Pizza, 256
    Mini Meat Loaves & Vegetables, 106
    South-of-the-Border Meatballs, 241
    Southwestern Potato Skins, 244
    Spicy Burrito Bonanza, 250
    Tex-Mex Lasagna, 109
    Tostada Salad, 288
    Twisty Beef Bake, 106
**Beverages**
    Easy Pudding Milkshake, 366

Bits O' Teriyaki Chicken, 306
Black Forest Torte, 466
**Blueberries**
    Banana Blueberry Muffins, 548
    Creamy Smooth Choco-Blueberry
      Parfaits, 478
    Delaware Blueberry Pie, 435
    Double Berry Layer Cake, 538
    Luscious Cranberry and
      Blueberry Pie, 446
    Mini Chips Blueberry Bread,
      498
    Mini Chips Blueberry Breakfast
      Cake, 498
    Peachy Blueberry Crunch, 522
    Spring Break Blueberry
      Coffeecake, 526
Braised Chinese Duckling, 332
Braised Duckling and Pears, 334
**Breads** (*see also* **Muffins**)
    Chocolate Chip Banana Bread,
      496
    Cocoa-Nut Bread, 501
    Knepp, 45
    Mini Chips Blueberry Bread, 498
    Orange Cinnamon Swirl Bread,
      524
    Steamed Chinese Buns, 347
**Breakfast Foods**
    Baked Ham & Cheese Monte
      Cristo, 116
    Breakfast Magic, 364
    Chocolate Almond Braided
      Coffeecake, 496
    Chocolate Dessert Waffles, 497
    Chocolate Upside Down
      Coffeecake, 501
    Cinnamon Rolls, 528
    Make-Ahead Brunch Bake, 112
    Mini Chips Blueberry Breakfast
      Cake, 498
    Mini Chips Cinnamon Crescents,
      501
    Mini Chips Pancakes, 500
    Peachy Blueberry Crunch, 522
    Spring Break Blueberry
      Coffeecake, 526
Breakfast Magic, 364
Brian's Buffalo Cookies, 404
**Broccoli**
    Baked Ham & Cheese Monte
      Cristo, 116
    Broccoli & Beef Stir-Fry, 317
    Cheesy Pork Chops 'n Potatoes,
      116

**Broccoli,** *continued*
    Chicken à la Divan, 10
    Chicken, Broccoli & Rice Soup, 42
    Chicken to the Macs, 54
    Creamy Turkey & Broccoli, 84
    Ham & Macaroni Twists, 114
    Herb-Baked Fish & Rice, 94
    No Fuss Tuna Quiche, 136
    Shanghai Shrimp Stir-Fry, 342
    Tex-Mex Stir-Fry, 270
    Tuna Tortilla Roll-Ups, 96
Broccoli & Beef Stir-Fry, 317
**Brownies**
    Cindy's Fudgy Brownies, 532
    Drizzle Topped Brownies, 517
    Signature Brownies, 517
Brunswick Stew, 55
Buffet Bean Bake, 121
**Burgers**
    Gourmet Olé Burgers, 256
    Nutty Burgers, 196
    Tarragon Chicken Burgers, 22
Buried Cherry Cookies, 513
Butter Pecan Squares, 516
Butter-Flavored Brickle Drizzles, 401
Butterfly Cakes, 574

# C

**Cakes & Cupcakes** (*see also*
    **Cheesecakes**)
    All-Chocolate Boston Cream Pie,
      470
    Banana Split Cake, 572
    Black Forest Torte, 466
    Butterfly Cakes, 574
    Chiffon Cake with Citrus Sauce
      and Fresh Fruit, 542
    Chocolate Banana Cake, 550
    Chocolate Cherry Upside-Down
      Cake, 473
    Chocolate Chip Orange Pound
      Cake, 466
    Chocolate Confection Cake, 570
    Chocolate Cupcakes, 468
    Chocolate Mint Dessert, 478
    Chocolate Sour Cream Cake, 465
    Chocolate Stripe Cake, 474
    Chocolatetown Special Cake, 472
    Cinnamon Ripple Cake, 546
    Cocoa Bundt Cake, 474
    Cocoa Sheet Cake, 474
    Collector's Cocoa Cake, 463

**Cakes & Cupcakes,** *continued*
Creamy Nectarine Torte, 564
Deep Dark Chocolate Cake, 468
Devil's Delight Cake, 462
Double Berry Layer Cake, 538
Easter Basket Cake, 560
Easy Chocolate Zucchini Cake, 500
Everyone's Favorite Cake, 562
Fudgy Pistachio Cake, 558
Glazed Ribbon Dessert, 548
Hot Fudge Pudding Cake, 468
Lemon Poppy Seed Cupcakes, 534
Lemon Sunshine Cake, 580
May Day Cake, 554
Orange Coconut Cake, 568
Outrageous Angel Food Cake, 568
Peanut Butter-Fudge Marble
Cake, 462
Pudding Poke Cake, 390
Strawberry Meringue Cakes, 556
Triple Layer Chocolate Mousse
Cake, 466
Turtle Cake, 578
California Date-Chicken Salad, 23
California-Style Chicken, 90
Cancun Steak Sandwiches, 254
**Candies**
Butterfly Cakes, 574
Cherries 'n Chocolate Fudge, 505
Chocolate Dipped Fruit, 505
Chocolate Truffles, 509
Coconut Honey Bars, 506
Colorful Candy Popcorn Balls,
384
Easy Double Decker Fudge, 504
Easy Rocky Road, 504
Espresso Truffles, 509
Fast Chocolate-Pecan Fudge, 506
Mint 'n Chocolate Fudge, 506
Nut-Coated Truffles, 509
Nut Truffles, 509
Pastel-Coated Cocoa Bonbons,
504
Peanutty-Cocoa Bonbons, 508
Rum Nut Truffles, 509
Cantonese Chicken Salad, 330
**Caramels**
Fudge Caramels, 505
Caribbean Chicken Paella, 68
Carne Asada, 248
**Carrots**
Celebration Pork & Rice, 323
Chewy Oatmeal-Apricot-Date
Bars, 418
Garlic Chicken Bundles, 308

**Carrots,** *continued*
Hot & Spicy Glazed Carrots, 348
Oatmeal Shaggies, 420
Pineapple Chicken Packets, 55
Superb Fillet of Sole &
Vegetables, 98
Tuna & Wild Rice Amandine, 158
**Casseroles**
Baked Ham & Cheese Monte
Cristo, 116
California-Style Chicken, 90
Cheesy Pasta Swirls, 118
Cheesy Pork Chops 'n Potatoes,
116
Chicken Enchilada Casserole, 64,
266
Chicken-Mac Casserole, 90
Chicken to the Macs, 54
Chili-Chicken Sombreros, 84
Chop Suey Casserole, 108
Classic Hamburger Casserole, 108
Countdown Casserole, 102
Creamy Turkey & Broccoli, 84
Crunchy-Topped Fish &
Vegetables, 101
Dreamy Creamy Chicken
Lasagna, 73
El Dorado Rice Casserole, 288
Foolproof Clam Fettucine, 100
Ham & Macaroni Twists, 114
Hearty Chicken Bake, 91
Home-Style Chicken 'n Biscuits, 92
Italian Antipasto Bake, 92
Lattice-Top Chicken, 82
Louisiana Seafood Bake, 98
Make-Ahead Brunch Bake, 112
Mexican Lasagna, 70
Mini Meat Loaves & Vegetables,
106
Monterey Spaghetti Casserole,
120
Mustard Chicken & Vegetables,
86
Original Green Bean Casserole,
122
Saucy Garden Patch Vegetables,
124
Sausage Succotash, 114
Sour Cream Tortilla Casserole,
290
Spaghetti Squash Medley, 286
Spicy Ravioli and Cheese, 284
Squash Olé, 292
Superb Fillet of Sole &
Vegetables, 98

**Casseroles,** *continued*
Swiss Vegetable Medley, 122
Tex-Mex Lasagna, 109
Tomato-Bread Casserole, 280
Tortilla Stack Tampico, 260
Tuna & Asparagus au Gratin, 178
Tuna & Wild Rice Amandine, 158
Tuna & Zucchini-Stuffed
 Manicotti, 160
Twisty Beef Bake, 106
Zesty Chicken & Rice, 88
Celebration Pork & Rice, 323
Celery Sauce, 37
Celery Sauté, 292
**Cereal**
Apricot Glazed Chicken, 29
Brian's Buffalo Cookies, 404
Chicken Enchilada Casserole, 64
Chicken Italian, 12
Choco-Scutterbotch, 408
Crispy Chicken Drummettes, 15
Emily's Dream Bars, 412
Hawaiian Chicken Salad, 22
New Year Chicken, 59
Sesame Seed Chicken, 26
Chawan Mushi, 347
**Cheese**
Aztec Chili Salad, 278
Baked Ham & Cheese Monte
 Cristo, 116
Cancun Steak Sandwiches, 254
Cheese-Stuffed Beef Rolls, 104
Cheesy Pasta Swirls, 118
Cheesy Pork Chops 'n Potatoes,
 116
Chicken, Broccoli & Rice Soup, 42
Chicken Cordon Doux®, 59
Chicken Cutlets Classica®
 Fontina, 28
Chicken Cutlets Parmesan, 44
Chicken Enchilada Casserole, 64,
 266
Chicken-Mac Casserole, 90
Chicken Rellenos, 72
Chicken Royale, 26
Chicken to the Macs, 54
Chile con Queso Spread, 240
Chili-Chicken Sombreros, 84
Cider Apple Pie in Cheddar Crust,
 452
Countdown Casserole, 102
Creamy Herbed Chicken, 46
Crunchy-Topped Fish &
 Vegetables, 101
Curried Chicken Pot Pie, 82

**Cheese,** *continued*
Deluxe Fajita Nachos, 242
Dreamy Creamy Chicken
 Lasagna, 73
Eight Layer Fiesta Dip, 246
El Dorado Rice Casserole, 288
Fettucine à la Tuna, 142
Fiesta Chicken Sandwiches, 63
Gourmet Olé Burgers, 256
Grilled Chicken and Vegetable
 Sandwiches, 13
Grilled Pizza, 232
Ham & Macaroni Twists, 114
Home-Style Chicken 'n Biscuits,
 92
Individual Pizza, 144
Italian Antipasto Bake, 92
Lattice-Top Chicken, 82
Make-Ahead Brunch Bake, 112
Mexicali Pizza, 256
Mexican Lasagna, 70
Molletes, 241
Monterey Potatoes, 280
Monterey Spaghetti Casserole, 120
New Year Chicken, 59
Polenta Strips with Creamy Salsa
 Spread, 244
Pork Chops O'Brien, 112
Rio Grande Quesadillas, 266
Saucy Garden Patch Vegetables,
 124
Sausage Succotash, 114
Sour Cream Tortilla Casserole,
 290
Southwestern Potato Skins, 244
Spaghetti Squash Medley, 286
Spicy Burrito Bonanza, 250
Spicy Ravioli and Cheese, 284
Spinach-Onion Stuffing Balls, 121
Superb Fillet of Sole &
 Vegetables, 98
Surprisingly Simple Chicken
 Cacciatore, 58
Swiss Vegetable Medley, 122
Tacos Botanas, 246
Tamale Pie, 68
Tex-Mex Lasagna, 109
Toluca Taters, 264
Tomato-Bread Casserole, 280
Tortellini with Three-Cheese
 Tuna Sauce, 166
Tortilla Stack Tampico, 260
Tostada Salad, 288
Tuna & Zucchini-Stuffed
 Manicotti, 160

**Cheese,** *continued*
Tuna Chilies Rellenos, 166
Tuna Lasagna Bundles, 100
Tuna Poor-Boy, 144
Tuna-Stuffed Bakers, 180
Tuna Tortilla Roll-Ups, 96
Turkey Cordon Bleu, 88
Turkey Picatta on Grilled Rolls, 210
Twisty Beef Bake, 106
Zesty Chicken en Papillote, 21
Zucchini Mexicana, 284

**Cheesecakes**
Chocolate Lover's Cheesecake, 465
Cocoa Cheesecake, 465
Marble Cheesecake, 470
No-Bake Chocolate Cheesecake, 469

Cheese-Stuffed Beef Rolls, 104
Cheesy Pasta Swirls, 118
Cheesy Pork Chops 'n Potatoes, 116

**Cherries**
Black Forest Torte, 466
Buried Cherry Cookies, 513
Cherries 'n Chocolate Fudge, 505
Cherry City Amaretto Cherry Cream Pie, 449
Cherry-Crowned Cocoa Pudding, 483
Chocolate Cherry Upside-Down Cake, 473
Cocoa Cherry Drops, 512
Ohio Sour Cherry Pie, 442

Chewy Chocolate Macaroons, 512
Chewy Oatmeal-Apricot-Date Bars, 418

**Chicken**
All-American Barbecue Sauce and Marinade, 19
Angel Hair Stir-Fry, 334
Apple & Rice-Stuffed Chicken, 33
Apricot Glazed Chicken, 29
Arroz con Pollo Burritos, 258
Artichoke Chicken Pilaf, 44
Bits O' Teriyaki Chicken, 306
Brunswick Stew, 55
California Date-Chicken Salad, 23
California-Style Chicken, 90
Cantonese Chicken Salad, 330
Caribbean Chicken Paella, 68
Chawan Mushi, 347
Chicken Adobo, 334
Chicken à la Divan, 10
Chicken and Vegetable Couscous, 56

**Chicken,** *continued*
Chicken-Apple Stuffed Pita, 18
Chicken, Broccoli & Rice Soup, 42
Chicken Cordon Doux®, 59
Chicken Cutlets Classica® Fontina, 28
Chicken Cutlets Parmesan, 44
Chicken Enchilada Casserole, 64, 266
Chicken Fajitas, 70
Chicken Fried Rice, 351
Chicken in French Onion Sauce, 80
Chicken Italian, 12
Chicken Jambalaya, 71
Chicken-Mac Casserole, 90
Chicken Pasta Salad, 15
Chicken Picadillo, 73
Chicken Rellenos, 72
Chicken Ribbons Satay, 204
Chicken Royale, 26
Chicken Spinach Stracciatella, 45
Chicken Thighs and Vegetables Lyonnaise, 48
Chicken to the Macs, 54
Chicken with Mediterranean Salsa, 212
Chicken with Sherry Sauce, 48
Chicken with Snow Peas and Walnuts, 40
Chicken with Sweet and Sour Grape Sauce, 33
Chili-Chicken Sombreros, 84
Chinese-Style Pot Roast Chicken, 332
Cilantro-Lime Chicken and Mango Kabobs, 16
Citrus Chicken, 42
Citrus Marinated Chicken, 208
Classic Sweet & Sour Chicken, 337
Colache con Pollo, 264
Cold Lime Chicken and Couscous, 60
Creamy Herbed Chicken, 46
Crispy Chicken Drummettes, 15
Curried Chicken Pot Pie, 82
Deluxe Fajita Nachos, 242
Dijon Almond Chicken, 24
Double-Coated Chicken, 30
Dreamy Creamy Chicken Lasagna, 73
Empress Chicken Wings, 302
Fiesta Chicken Sandwiches, 63
Fried Rice, 74

**Chicken,** *continued*

Garlic Chicken Bundles, 308
Glazed Ginger Chicken, 309
Golden Glazed Chicken Breasts, 40
Green Chile Chicken, 75
Grilled Chicken and Apple with
　Fresh Rosemary, 24
Grilled Chicken and Vegetable
　Sandwiches, 13
Grilled Chicken and Ziti Salad, 14
Grilled Rosemary Chicken, 30
Hawaiian Chicken Salad, 22
Hearty Chicken Bake, 91
Hearty Chicken Stir-Fry with
　Noodles, 336
Hearty Lancaster Chicken,
　Vegetable and Dumpling Soup,
　45
Hollywood Chicken, 35
Home-Style Chicken 'n Biscuits,
　92
Honey-Mustard Glazed Chicken,
　29
Hot, Spicy, Tangy, Sticky
　Chicken, 211
Italian Antipasto Bake, 92
Italian Vegetable Chicken, 61
Kung Pao Stir-Fry, 333
Lattice-Top Chicken, 82
Lemon Chicken Broil, 268
Lemon-Dilled Chicken, 10
Lemon-Garlic Roasted Chicken,
　214
Lemon Herbed Chicken, 207
Lotus Chicken Chop Suey, 333
Macaroni and Chicken Salad, 16
Mariachi Drumsticks, 238
Mexican Lasagna, 70
Molé Sauce for Chicken or
　Turkey, 262
Mustard Chicken & Vegetables,
　86
New Delhi Chicken Thighs, 74
New England Chicken 'n' Corn
　Chowder, 51
New Year Chicken, 59
No-Peek Chicken and Rice, 46
One Skillet Spicy Chicken 'n
　Rice, 262
Orange-Cashew Chicken, 333
Orange-Dijon Chicken, 210
Paella, 65
Pecan-Coated Wingettes, 21
Pineapple Chicken Packets, 55
Pineapple Chicken Rice Bowl, 37

**Chicken,** *continued*

Quick Arroz con Pollo, 49
Rio Grande Quesadillas, 266
Roast Chicken with Savory
　Cornbread Stuffing, 38
Romance® Chicken Marinara, 75
Sausage-Chicken Creole, 110
Sesame Seed Chicken, 26
Shantung Chicken, 331
Sierra Chicken Bundles, 268
Southwestern Grilled Chicken
　with Yogurt Salsa, 32
Spicy Chicken, 328
Spicy Fruited Chicken, 53
Surprisingly Simple Chicken
　Cacciatore, 58
Sweet 'n Sour, 51
Sweet and Spicy Chicken Stir-
　Fry, 67
Sweet Chicken Risotto, 67
Szechuan Chicken, 64
Tamale Pie, 68
Tandoori Style Grilled Chicken, 38
Tangy Chicken Walnut Salad, 12
Tarragon Chicken Burgers, 22
Tortilla Stack Tampico, 260
West Indies Curried Drumsticks,
　66
Zesty Chicken & Rice, 88
Zesty Chicken en Papillote, 21
Chiffon Cake with Citrus Sauce and
　Fresh Fruit, 542
Child's Choice, 398
Chile con Queso Spread, 240
Chili-Chicken Sombreros, 84
Chinese Noodle Cakes, 340
Chinese Porcupine Meatballs, 340
Chinese-Style Pot Roast Chicken,
　332
Chippy Cheeseys, 414
Choco-Berry Frozen Dessert, 482
**Chocolate** (*see also* **Chocolate
　Chips; Cocoa**)
Banana Split Cake, 572
Black Forest Torte, 466
Butter-Flavored Brickle Drizzles,
　401
Cherries 'n Chocolate Fudge, 505
Choco-Berry Frozen Dessert, 482
Chocolate Almond Braided
　Coffeecake, 496
Chocolate Banana Cake, 550
Chocolate Chip Glaze, 462
Chocolate-Covered Banana Pops,
　484

**Chocolate,** *continued*
Chocolate Dipped Fruit, 505
Chocolate Frosting, 513
Chocolate Lover's Cheesecake, 465
Chocolate-Marshmallow Mousse, 481
Chocolate-Marshmallow Mousse Parfaits, 481
Chocolate-Marshmallow Mousse Pie, 481
Chocolate Mint Dessert, 478
Chocolate Mousse Pie with Rum Cream Topping, 489
Chocolate Peanut Butter Cup Cookies, 430
Chocolate Pudding Cookies, 382
Chocolate Rum Ice Cream, 479
Chocolate Stripe Cake, 474
Chocolate Topping, 478
Chocolatetown Pie, 488
Creamy Smooth Choco-Blueberry Parfaits, 478
Devil's Delight Cake, 462
Dreamy Chocolate Chip Cookies, 407
Easter Basket Cake, 560
Easy Double Chocolate Ice Cream, 478
Easy Double Decker Fudge, 504
Easy Rocky Road, 504
Everyone's Favorite Cake, 562
Fast Fudge Pots de Creme, 483
Fudgy Pistachio Cake, 558
Hershey's Syrup Pie, 492
Microwave Chocolate Crumb Crust, 481
Mini Chips Blueberry Breakfast Cake, 498
Mini Chips Glaze, 498
No-Bake Chocolate Cheesecake, 469
No-Bake Chocolate Crumb Crust, 479
Peach-Stuffed Oatmeal Almond Cookies, 424
Peanut Butter Bars, 417
Peanut Butter-Fudge Marble Cake, 462
Peanut Butter Pizza Cookies, 576
Peanut Butter Spritz Sandwiches, 566
Pistachio Chocolate Bar Pie, 386
Raspberry Sherbet Brownie Dessert, 544
Rocky Road Pie, 386

**Chocolate,** *continued*
Syrup Whipped Topping, 492
Triple Layer Chocolate Mousse Cake, 466
Turtle Cake, 578
**Chocolate Chips**
Banana Split Cake, 572
Brian's Buffalo Cookies, 404
Butter Pecan Squares, 516
Child's Choice, 398
Chippy Cheeseys, 414
Chocolate Chip Banana Bread, 496
Chocolate Chip Orange Pound Cake, 466
Chocolate Chip Pecan Pie, 450
Chocolate Upside Down Coffeecake, 501
Choco-Scutterbotch, 408
Cindy's Fudgy Brownies, 532
Devil's Delight Cake, 462
Dreamy Chocolate Chip Cookies, 407
Drizzle Topped Brownies, 517
Easy Chocolate Zucchini Cake, 500
Emily's Dream Bars, 412
English Toffee Bars, 516
Five Layer Bars, 512
Heavenly Oatmeal Hearts, 426
Jeremy's Famous Turtles, 429
Mini Chips Blueberry Bread, 498
Mini Chips Cinnamon Crescents, 501
Mini Chips Pancakes, 500
Mini Chips Surprise Muffins, 500
Oatmeal Toffee Lizzies, 410
Peanut Butter Chocolate Chip Cookies, 403
Special Chocolate Chip Sandwiches, 536
Spiced Chip Cookies, 514
Triple Treat Cookies, 530
Chocolate Confection Cake, 570
Chocolate Cream Pie, 489
Chocolate Cream Squares, 484
Chocolate Crinkle Cookies, 519
Chocolate Crumb Crust, 471
Chocolate Cupcakes, 468
Chocolate Dessert Waffles, 497
Chocolate Filling, 470
Chocolate Graham Crust, 484
Chocolate Grasshopper Pie, 488
Chocolate Lover's Cheesecake, 465
Chocolate Mousse, 483
Chocolate Sour Cream Cake, 465

Chocolate Teddy Bears, 518
Chocolatetown Special Cake, 472
Chocolate Upside Down Coffeecake, 501
Choco-Scutterbotch, 408
Chop Suey Casserole, 108
Cider Apple Pie in Cheddar Crust, 452
Cilantro-Lime Chicken and Mango Kabobs, 16
Cindy's Fudgy Brownies, 532
Cinnamon Ripple Cake, 546
Cinnamon Rolls, 528
Citrus Chicken, 42
Citrus Dream Pie, 454
Citrus Marinated Chicken, 208
Citrus Tarragon Butter, 208
Classic Chinese Pepper Steak, 312
Classic Crisco Crust, 436
Classic Hamburger Casserole, 108
Classic Sweet & Sour Chicken, 337
**Cocoa**
    All-Chocolate Boston Cream Pie, 470
    Buried Cherry Cookies, 513
    Cherry-Crowned Cocoa Pudding, 483
    Chewy Chocolate Macaroons, 512
    Chocolate Cherry Upside-Down Cake, 473
    Chocolate Confection Cake, 570
    Chocolate Cream Pie, 489
    Chocolate Cream Squares, 484
    Chocolate Crinkle Cookies, 519
    Chocolate Crumb Crust, 471
    Chocolate Cupcakes, 468
    Chocolate Dessert Waffles, 497
    Chocolate Filling, 470
    Chocolate Graham Crust, 484
    Chocolate Grasshopper Pie, 488
    Chocolate Lover's Cheesecake, 465
    Chocolate Mousse, 483
    Chocolate Sour Cream Cake, 465
    Chocolate Teddy Bears, 518
    Chocolatetown Special Cake, 472
    Chocolate Truffles, 509
    Cocoa Bundt Cake, 474
    Cocoa Cheesecake, 465
    Cocoa Cherry Drops, 512
    Cocoa Cloud Pie, 490
    Cocoa Glaze, 474
    Cocoa-Nut Bread, 501
    Cocoa Oatmeal Muffins, 496
    Cocoa Sheet Cake, 474

**Cocoa,** *continued*
    Collector's Cocoa Cake, 463
    Cut Out Chocolate Cookies, 514
    Deep Dark Chocolate Cake, 468
    Espresso Truffles, 509
    Fast Chocolate-Pecan Fudge, 506
    Fruited Chocolate Sorbet, 483
    Fudge Brownie Pie, 493
    Fudge Caramels, 505
    Fudge Frosting, 465
    Hot Fudge Pudding Cake, 468
    Hot Fudge Sauce, 493
    Individual Chocolate Cream Pies, 490
    Lemon Raspberry Chocolate Delight, 552
    Marble Cheesecake, 470
    Microwave Chocolate Crumb Crust, 488
    Mint 'n Chocolate Fudge, 506
    No-Bake Chocolate Cake Roll, 481
    No-Bake Cocoa Haystacks, 514
    No-Cook Fudge Frosting, 517
    Nut-Coated Truffles, 509
    Nut Truffles, 509
    One-Bowl Buttercream Frosting, 472
    Pastel-Coated Cocoa Bonbons, 504
    Peanutty-Cocoa Bonbons, 508
    Rum Nut Truffles, 509
    Satiny Chocolate Glaze, 470, 515
    Signature Brownies, 517
    Three-in-One Chocolate Pudding & Pie Filling, 485
**Coconut**
    Chewy Chocolate Macaroons, 512
    Chocolate Confection Cake, 570
    Coconut Honey Bars, 506
    Easter Basket Cake, 560
    No-Bake Cocoa Haystacks, 514
    Oatmeal Shaggies, 420
    Orange Coconut Cake, 568
    Triple Treat Cookies, 530
Colache con Pollo, 264
Cold Lime Chicken and Couscous, 60
Collector's Cocoa Cake, 463
Colored Sugar Snickerdoodles, 403
Colorful Candy Popcorn Balls, 384
Compound Butters for Grilled Fish or Chicken, 221
**Cookies** (*see also* **Bar Cookies; Brownies**)
    Brian's Buffalo Cookies, 404
    Buried Cherry Cookies, 513
    Butter-Flavored Brickle Drizzles, 401

**Cookies,** *continued*
  Chewy Chocolate Macaroons, 512
  Child's Choice, 398
  Chocolate Crinkle Cookies, 519
  Chocolate Peanut Butter Cup Cookies, 430
  Chocolate Pudding Cookies, 382
  Chocolate Teddy Bears, 518
  Choco-Scutterbotch, 408
  Cocoa Cherry Drops, 512
  Colored Sugar Snickerdoodles, 403
  Cut Out Chocolate Cookies, 514
  Dreamy Chocolate Chip Cookies, 407
  Frosted Peanut Butter Peanut Brittle Cookies, 423
  Heavenly Oatmeal Hearts, 426
  Jeremy's Famous Turtles, 429
  No-Bake Cocoa Haystacks, 514
  Oatmeal Cookies, 402
  Oatmeal Honey Cookies, 408
  Oatmeal Shaggies, 420
  Oatmeal Toffee Lizzies, 410
  Peach-Stuffed Oatmeal Almond Cookies, 424
  Peanut Butter and Jelly Thumbprint Cookies, 411
  Peanut Butter Chocolate Chip Cookies, 403
  Peanut Butter Pizza Cookies, 576
  Peanut Butter Sensations, 425
  Peanut Butter Spritz Sandwiches, 566
  Snickerdoodles, 402
  Special Chocolate Chip Sandwiches, 536
  Spiced Chip Cookies, 514
  Triple Treat Cookies, 530
**Corn**
  Amigo Pita Pocket Sandwiches, 260
  Avocado-Corn Salsa, 216
  Chicken Rellenos, 72
  Colache con Pollo, 264
  Ensalada Simplese, 290
  Mexican-Style Corn Salad, 235
  New England Chicken 'n' Corn Chowder, 51
  Santa Fe Potato Salad, 294
  Sausage Succotash, 114
  Squash Olé, 292

Countdown Casserole, 102
**Cranberries**
  Luscious Cranberry and Blueberry Pie, 446
**Cream Cheese** (*see also* **Cheesecakes**)
  Chewy Oatmeal-Apricot-Date Bars, 418
  Chippy Cheeseys, 414
  Choco-Berry Frozen Dessert, 482
  Chocolate Chip Orange Pound Cake, 466
  Chocolate Cream Pie, 489
  Chocolate Cream Squares, 484
  Citrus Dream Pie, 454
  Cocoa Cloud Pie, 490
  Creamy Peanut Butter Frosting, 463
  Fresh Pineapple with Sesame Dip, 303
  Marble Cheesecake, 470
  No-Bake Chocolate Cheesecake, 469
  Pastel-Coated Cocoa Bonbons, 504
  Peanutty-Cocoa Bonbons, 508
Creamy Herbed Chicken, 46
Creamy Nectarine Torte, 564
Creamy Peanut Butter Frosting, 463
Creamy Smooth Choco-Blueberry Parfaits, 478
Creamy Turkey & Broccoli, 84
Crispy Chicken Drummettes, 15
Crispy Lite Spareribs, 326
Crispy Tortellini Bites, 240
Crispy Wontons, 300
Crunchy-Topped Fish & Vegetables, 101
**Crusts**
  Chocolate Crumb Crust, 471
  Chocolate Graham Crust, 484
  Classic Crisco Crust, 436
  Graham Crust, 465
  Microwave Chocolate Crumb Crust, 481, 488
  No-Bake Chocolate Crumb Crust, 479
Crusts, Cutouts, 439
Crusts, Rope Edge, 439
Crusts, Woven Lattice Top, 439
Cucumber Dill Dip, 235
Cucumber Fan Salad, 348
Curried Chicken Pot Pie, 82
Cut Out Chocolate Cookies, 514

# D

**Dates**
    California Date-Chicken Salad, 23
    Chewy Oatmeal-Apricot-Date Bars, 418
Deep Dark Chocolate Cake, 468
Delaware Blueberry Pie, 435
Deluxe Fajita Nachos, 242
**Desserts** (*see also* **Bar Cookies; Brownies; Cakes & Cupcakes; Cheesecakes; Cookies; Frozen Desserts; Gelatin Desserts; Pies & Tarts; Pies, Frozen**)
    Cherry-Crowned Cocoa Pudding, 483
    Chocolate Cream Squares, 484
    Chocolate Dessert Waffles, 497
    Chocolate-Marshmallow Mousse, 481
    Chocolate-Marshmallow Mousse Parfaits, 481
    Chocolate Mousse, 483
    Creamy Smooth Choco-Blueberry Parfaits, 478
    Dirt Cups, 378
    Fast Fudge Pots de Creme, 483
    Funny Face Desserts, 362
    Lemon Raspberry Chocolate Delight, 552
    No-Bake Chocolate Cake Roll, 481
    Raspberry Sherbet Brownie Dessert, 544
    Three-in-One Chocolate Pudding & Pie Filling, 485
    Triple Orange Delight, 540
Devil's Delight Cake, 462
Dijon Almond Chicken, 24
Dijon-Cream Sauce, 202
**Dips** (*see* **Spreads & Dips**)
Dirt Cups, 378
Double Berry Layer Cake, 538
Double-Coated Chicken, 30
Dragon Beef Kabobs, 314
Dreamy Chocolate Chip Cookies, 407
Dreamy Creamy Chicken Lasagna, 73
Drizzle Topped Brownies, 517
**Duck**
    Braised Chinese Duckling, 332
    Braised Duckling and Pears, 334

# E

Easter Basket Cake, 560
East Meets West Salad, 349
Easy Chocolate Zucchini Cake, 500
Easy Double Chocolate Ice Cream, 478
Easy Double Decker Fudge, 504
Easy Niçoise Salad, 130
Easy Paella, 170
Easy Pudding Milkshake, 366
Easy Rocky Road, 504
Easy Seafood Salad, 156
**Egg Dishes**
    Make-Ahead Brunch Bake, 112
    No Fuss Tuna Quiche, 136
    Oriental Tea Eggs, 351
    Puffy Tuna Omelet, 138
    Scrambled Eggs with Tuna & Onions, 152
    Tuna Frittata, 150
Egg Drop Soup, 300
Eight Layer Fiesta Dip, 246
Elaine's Tuna Tetrazzini, 132
El Dorado Rice Casserole, 288
Emily's Dream Bars, 412
Empandillas, 242
Empress Chicken Wings, 302
English Toffee Bars, 516
Ensalada Simplese, 290
Espresso Truffles, 509
Everyone's Favorite Cake, 562

# F

Fast Chocolate-Pecan Fudge, 506
Fast Fudge Pots de Creme, 483
Festive Whipped Cream, 488
Fettucine à la Tuna, 142
Fiesta Chicken Sandwiches, 63
Fiesta Ranch Bean Dip, 235
Firecracker Salad, 350
**Fish** (*see also* **Shellfish**)
    Baha Roll, 168
    Baja Fruited Salmon, 272
    Crunchy-Topped Fish & Vegetables, 101
    Easy Niçoise Salad, 130
    Easy Paella, 170
    Easy Seafood Salad, 156
    Elaine's Tuna Tetrazzini, 132
    Fettucine à la Tuna, 142

**Fish,** *continued*
  Gazpacho Tuna Salad, 142
  Ginger Fish Fillets, 341
  Grilled Fish Steaks with Tomato Basil Butter Sauce, 224
  Grilled Oriental Fish Steaks, 341
  "Grilled" Tuna with Vegetables in Herb Butter, 152
  Herb-Baked Fish & Rice, 94
  Individual Pizza, 144
  Jade Salad with Sesame Vinaigrette, 172
  Louisiana Seafood Bake, 98
  Mediterranean Fish & Pasta, 96
  No Fuss Tuna Quiche, 136
  Pescado Borracho, 274
  Pescado Viejo, 276
  Puffy Tuna Omelet, 138
  Santa Fe Tuna Salad with Chili-Lime Dressing, 170
  Scandinavian Smörgåsbord, 158
  Scrambled Eggs with Tuna & Onions, 152
  Sea Breeze Fish Salad, 342
  Seafood Wontons, 172
  Seviche, 272
  Shanghai Sweet & Sour Fish, 340
  Snapper with Pesto Butter, 218
  Southern-Style Fish Cassoulet, 176
  Spanish-Style Baked Catfish, 276
  Spiral Pasta Salad, 156
  Superb Fillet of Sole & Vegetables, 98
  Sweet 'n' Sour Tuna with Pineapple, 176
  Swordfish with Honey-Lime Glaze, 226
  Tortellini with Three-Cheese Tuna Sauce, 166
  Tuna & Asparagus au Gratin, 178
  Tuna & Fresh Fruit Salad, 148
  Tuna & Mushroom Stroganoff, 136
  Tuna & Shrimp Fajitas, 164
  Tuna & Vegetables à la Grecque, 146
  Tuna & Wild Rice Amandine, 158
  Tuna & Zucchini-Stuffed Manicotti, 160
  Tuna Chilies Rellenos, 166
  Tuna-Citrus Salad with Honey Dressing, 140
  Tuna Frittata, 150
  Tuna in Red Pepper Sauce, 150
  Tuna Lasagna Bundles, 100

**Fish,** *continued*
  Tuna-Lettuce Bundles, 140
  Tuna Poor-Boy, 144
  Tuna Provençale on French Bread, 178
  Tuna Salad Elegante, 162
  Tuna-Stuffed Artichokes, 154
  Tuna-Stuffed Bakers, 180
  Tuna-Stuffed Sole with Lime Sauce, 174
  Tuna Tortilla Roll-Ups, 96
  Tuna-Vegetable Chowder, 148
  Tuna Veronique, 132
  Tuna-Waldorf Salad Mold, 134
  Veal Tonnato, 130
  West Coast Bouillabaisse, 134
  Wisconsin Tuna Cake with Lemon-Dill Sauce, 12
Five Layer Bars, 512
Foolproof Clam Fettucine, 100
Fresh Pineapple with Sesame Dip, 303
Fresh Plum Sauce, 197
Fried Rice, 74
Frosted Peanut Butter Peanut Brittle Cookies, 423
**Frostings & Glazes**
  Chocolate Chip Glaze, 462
  Chocolate Frosting, 513
  Cocoa Glaze, 474
  Creamy Peanut Butter Frosting, 463
  Fudge Frosting, 465
  Mini Chips Glaze, 498
  No-Cook Fudge Frosting, 517
  One-Bowl Buttercream Frosting, 472
  Quick Vanilla Glaze, 517
  Satiny Chocolate Glaze, 470, 515
  Vanilla Glaze, 515
**Frozen Desserts** (*see also* **Pies, Frozen**)
  Choco-Berry Frozen Dessert, 482
  Chocolate-Covered Banana Pops, 484
  Chocolate Rum Ice Cream, 479
  Easy Double Chocolate Ice Cream, 478
  Fruited Chocolate Sorbet, 483
**Fruit** (*see also individual listings*)
  Baja Fruited Salmon, 272
  Chicken with Sweet and Sour Grape Sauce, 33
  Chiffon Cake with Citrus Sauce and Fresh Fruit, 542
  Chocolate Dipped Fruit, 505

**Fruit,** *continued*
  Cilantro-Lime Chicken and
    Mango Kabobs, 16
  Citrus Chicken, 42
  Citrus Dream Pie, 454
  Creamy Nectarine Torte, 564
  Fresh Plum Sauce, 197
  Macaroni and Chicken Salad, 16
  Melon Butter, 221
  Salsa Shrimp in Papaya, 292
  Santa Fe Tuna Salad with Chili-
    Lime Dressing, 170
  Sea Breeze Fish Salad, 342
  Tropical Fruit Salsa, 222
  Tuna & Fresh Fruit Salad, 148
  Tuna-Citrus Salad with Honey
    Dressing, 140
  Tuna Veronique, 132
Fruited Beef Kabobs, 252
Fruited Chocolate Sorbet, 483
Fudge Brownie Pie, 493
Fudge Caramels, 505
Fudge Frosting, 465
Fudgy Pistachio Cake, 558
Funny Face Desserts, 362

# G

Game Hens, Grilled, 208
Garlic Chicken Bundles, 308
Garlic Sauce, 214
Gazpacho Tuna Salad, 142
**Gelatin** (*see also* **Gelatin Desserts;
    Gelatin Salads**)
  Colorful Candy Popcorn Balls, 384
  Jigglers, 370
  Jigglers Pineapple Snacks, 374
  Jigglers "Surprises," 372
  Plain Gelatin, 360
**Gelatin Desserts**
  Gelatin Pizza, 380
  Scrap Happy, 376
Gelatin Pizza, 380
**Gelatin Salads**
  Strawberry-Banana Salad, 388
  Tuna-Waldorf Salad Mold, 134
Ginger Fish Fillets, 341
Glazed Ginger Chicken, 309
Glazed Pork Roast, 326
Glazed Ribbon Dessert, 548
**Glazes** (*see* **Frostings & Glazes**)
Golden Bars, 512
Golden Glazed Chicken Breasts, 40

Gourmet Olé Burgers, 256
Graham Crust, 465
Green Chile Chicken, 75
Grilled Antipasto Platter, 230
Grilled Bread, 194
Grilled Chicken and Apple with
    Fresh Rosemary, 24
Grilled Chicken and Vegetable
    Sandwiches, 13
Grilled Chicken and Ziti Salad, 14
Grilled Fish Steaks with Tomato
    Basil Butter Sauce, 224
Grilled Game Hens, 208
Grilled Mushrooms, 188
Grilled New Potatoes, 188
Grilled Oriental Fish Steaks, 341
Grilled Pizza, 232
**Grilled Recipes**
  BBQ Baby Back Ribs, 196
  Barbecued Turkey Breast, 211
  Barbecued Turkey with Herbs,
    207
  Beef Tenderloin with Dijon-
    Cream Sauce, 202
  Beef with Dry Spice Rub, 188
  Chicken Ribbons Satay, 204
  Chicken with Mediterranean
    Salsa, 212
  Citrus Marinated Chicken, 208
  Grilled Antipasto Platter, 230
  Grilled Bread, 194
  Grilled Chicken and Apple with
    Fresh Rosemary, 24
  Grilled Chicken and Vegetable
    Sandwiches, 13
  Grilled Chicken and Ziti Salad, 14
  Grilled Fish Steaks with Tomato
    Basil Butter Sauce, 224
  Grilled Game Hens, 208
  Grilled Mushrooms, 188
  Grilled New Potatoes, 188
  Grilled Oriental Fish Steaks, 341
  Grilled Pizza, 232
  Grilled Rosemary Chicken, 30
  Grilled Smoked Sausage, 197
  "Grilled" Tuna with Vegetables
    in Herb Butter, 152
  Grilled Vegetables with Balsamic
    Vinaigrette, 228
  Ham & Pineapple Pizza, 234
  Hot, Spicy, Tangy, Sticky
    Chicken, 211
  Lemon-Garlic Roasted Chicken,
    214
  Lemon Herbed Chicken, 207

**Grilled Recipes,** *continued*
Nutty Burgers, 196
Orange-Dijon Chicken, 210
Pineapple Chicken Rice Bowl, 37
Pork Chops with Orange-Radish
Relish, 198
Pork Kabobs with Mustard-
Bourbon Glaze, 200
Pork Tenderloin with Fresh Plum
Sauce, 197
Pork Tenderloin with Orange
Glaze, 192
Seafood Kabobs, 226
Shrimp Skewers with Tropical
Fruit Salsa, 222
Skewered Vegetables, 234
Snapper with Pesto Butter, 218
Southwestern Grilled Chicken
with Yogurt Salsa, 32
Swordfish with Honey-Lime
Glaze, 226
Tandoori Style Grilled Chicken, 38
Teriyaki Glazed Beef Kabobs, 200
Tomato-Feta Pizza, 234
Turkey Burritos, 216
Turkey Picatta on Grilled Rolls,
210
Veggie-Herb Pizza, 234
Wine & Rosemary Lamb Skewers,
194
Wine Country Steak, 198
Grilled Rosemary Chicken, 30
Grilled Smoked Sausage, 197
Grilled Vegetables with Balsamic
Vinaigrette, 228

## H

Haleakala Rice, 350
**Ham**
Baked Ham & Cheese Monte
Cristo, 116
Caribbean Chicken Paella, 68
Chicken Cordon Doux®, 59
Fried Rice, 74
Ham & Macaroni Twists, 114
Ham & Pineapple Pizza, 234
Paella, 65
Polynesian Kabobs, 307
Turkey Cordon Bleu, 88
Hawaiian Chicken Salad, 22
Hawaiian Pork Stew, 326
Hearty Chicken Bake, 91

Hearty Chicken Stir-Fry with
Noodles, 336
Hearty Lancaster Chicken,
Vegetable and Dumpling Soup,
45
Heavenly Oatmeal Hearts, 426
Herb-Baked Fish & Rice, 94
Hershey's Syrup Pie, 492
Hollywood Chicken, 35
Home-Style Chicken 'n Biscuits, 92
Honey-Lime Butter, 221
Honey-Mustard Glazed Chicken, 29
Hot & Sour Soup, 306
Hot & Spicy Glazed Carrots, 348
Hot Fudge Pudding Cake, 468
Hot Fudge Sauce, 493
Hot German-Style Potato Salad,
120
Hot Oriental Salad, 349
Hot, Spicy, Tangy, Sticky Chicken,
211
Hunan Stir-Fry with Tofu, 327

## I

**Ice Cream** (*see* **Frozen Desserts**)
Individual Chocolate Cream Pies,
490
Individual Pizza, 144
Irresistible Lemon Bars, 532
Italian Antipasto Bake, 92
Italian Vegetable Chicken, 61

## J

Jade Salad with Sesame
Vinaigrette, 172
Japanese Rice Salad, 344
Jeremy's Famous Turtles, 429
Jigglers, 370
Jigglers Pineapple Snacks, 374
Jigglers "Surprises," 372

## K

**Kabobs**
Beef and Fruit Skewers, 307
Cilantro-Lime Chicken and
Mango Kabobs, 16

**Kabobs,** *continued*
    Dragon Beef Kabobs, 314
    Fruited Beef Kabobs, 252
    Grilled Antipasto Platter, 230
    Polynesian Kabobs, 307
    Pork Kabobs with Mustard-
      Bourbon Glaze, 200
    Seafood Kabobs, 226
    Shrimp Skewers with Tropical
      Fruit Salsa, 222
    Skewered Vegetables, 234
    Teriyaki Glazed Beef Kabobs, 200
    Wine & Rosemary Lamb Skewers,
      194
Knepp, 45
Korean Beef & Vegetable Salad, 317
Korean Dressing, 317
Kung Pao Stir-Fry, 333

# L

**Lamb**
    Teriyaki Lamb Riblets, 305
    Wine & Rosemary Lamb Skewers,
      194
Lattice-Top Chicken, 82
Lawry's Fiesta Dip, 241
**Lemon**
    Citrus Tarragon Butter, 208
    Irresistible Lemon Bars, 532
    Lemon Baste, 230
    Lemon Chicken Broil, 268
    Lemon-Dilled Chicken, 10
    Lemon-Garlic Roasted Chicken,
      214
    Lemon Herbed Chicken, 207
    Lemon Poppy Seed Cupcakes, 534
    Lemon Raspberry Chocolate
      Delight, 552
    Lemon Sunshine Cake, 580
    Wisconsin Tuna Cake with
      Lemon-Dill Sauce, 12
**Lime**
    Cilantro-Lime Chicken and
      Mango Kabobs, 16
    Cold Lime Chicken and Couscous,
      60
    Honey-Lime Butter, 221
    Swordfish with Honey-Lime
      Glaze, 226
    Tuna-Stuffed Sole with Lime
      Sauce, 174
Lola's Apple Pie, 432

Lotus Chicken Chop Suey, 333
Louisiana Seafood Bake, 98
Luscious Cranberry and Blueberry
    Pie, 446

# M

Macaroni and Chicken Salad, 16
Make-Ahead Brunch Bake, 112
Mandarin Peach Sauce, 326
Marble Cheesecake, 470
Mariachi Drumsticks, 238
Marinated Mushrooms, 311
May Day Cake, 554
Meat-Filled Oriental Pancakes, 298
Mediterranean Fish & Pasta, 96
Mediterranean Salsa, 212
Melon Butter, 221
Mexicali Pizza, 256
Mexican Lasagna, 70
Mexican Sauce/Marinade, 19
Mexican-Style Corn Salad, 235
**Microwave Recipes**
    Brunswick Stew, 55
    Cheese-Stuffed Beef Rolls, 104
    Cheesy Pasta Swirls, 118
    Cheesy Pork Chops 'n Potatoes,
      116
    Cherries 'n Chocolate Fudge, 505
    Chicken Adobo, 334
    Chicken in French Onion Sauce,
      80
    Chocolate-Marshmallow Mousse,
      481
    Chocolate Rum Ice Cream, 479
    Chop Suey Casserole, 108
    Countdown Casserole, 102
    Creamy Turkey & Broccoli, 84
    Crispy Chicken Drummettes, 15
    Crunchy-Topped Fish &
      Vegetables, 101
    Dragon Beef Kabobs, 314
    Easy Double Decker Fudge, 504
    Easy Rocky Road, 504
    Fast Chocolate-Pecan Fudge, 506
    Foolproof Clam Fettucine, 100
    Glazed Pork Roast, 326
    Ham & Macaroni Twists, 114
    Hawaiian Chicken Salad, 22
    Herb-Baked Fish & Rice, 94
    Hershey's Syrup Pie, 492
    Home-Style Chicken 'n Biscuits,
      92

**Microwave Recipes,** *continued*
Hot Fudge Sauce, 493
Italian Antipasto Bake, 92
Lattice-Top Chicken, 82
Lotus Chicken Chop Suey, 333
Louisiana Seafood Bake, 98
Make-Ahead Brunch Bake, 112
Mariachi Drumsticks, 238
Mediterranean Fish & Pasta, 96
Microwave Chocolate Crumb
Crust, 488
Mini Meat Loaves & Vegetables,
106
Mint 'n Chocolate Fudge, 506
Monterey Potatoes, 280
Monterey Spaghetti Casserole,
120
Mustard Chicken & Vegetables,
86
No-Bake Chocolate Cheesecake,
469
Original Green Bean Casserole,
122
Pastel Coating, 504
Peanut Butter Chip Ice Cream
Sauce, 479
Peanut Butter Coating, 508
Pork Chops O'Brien, 112
Saucy Garden Patch Vegetables,
124
Sausage Succotash, 114
Shanghai Sweet & Sour Fish, 340
Simply Green Beans, 282
Simply Special Vegetable Pie, 124
Southern-Style Fish Cassoulet, 176
Spaghetti Squash Medley, 286
Steamed Chinese Buns, 347
Superb Fillet of Sole &
Vegetables, 98
Sweet 'n' Sour Tuna with
Pineapple, 176
Swiss Vegetable Medley, 122
Three-in-One Chocolate Pudding
& Pie Filling, 485
Tuna & Asparagus au Gratin, 178
Tuna Lasagna Bundles, 100
Tuna Provençale on French
Bread, 178
Tuna-Stuffed Bakers, 180
Tuna-Stuffed Sole with Lime
Sauce, 174
Tuna Tortilla Roll-Ups, 96
Turkey Cordon Bleu, 88
Twisty Beef Bake, 106
Zesty Chicken & Rice, 88

Mini Chips Blueberry Bread, 498
Mini Chips Blueberry Breakfast
Cake, 498
Mini Chips Cinnamon Crescents,
501
Mini Chips Glaze, 498
Mini Chips Pancakes, 500
Mini Chips Surprise Muffins, 500
Mini Meat Loaves & Vegetables,
106
Mint 'n Chocolate Fudge, 506
Mint Cream Center, 478
Molé Sauce for Chicken or Turkey,
262
Molletes, 241
Mongolian Beef, 318
Monterey Potatoes, 280
Monterey Spaghetti Casserole, 120
**Muffins**
Banana Blueberry Muffins, 548
Cocoa Oatmeal Muffins, 496
Mini Chips Surprise Muffins, 500
**Mushrooms**
Chicken Cutlets Classica®
Fontina, 28
Elaine's Tuna Tetrazzini, 132
Grilled Mushrooms, 188
Marinated Mushrooms, 311
Tuna & Mushroom Stroganoff,
136
Tuna & Wild Rice Amandine, 158
Tuna-Stuffed Artichokes, 154
Mu Shu-Style Fajitas, 250
Mustard Chicken & Vegetables, 86

# N

New Delhi Chicken Thighs, 74
New England Chicken 'n' Corn
Chowder, 51
New Hampshire White Mountain
Pumpkin Pie, 457
New Year Chicken, 59
New Year Fried Rice, 346
Niçoise Butter, 221
No-Bake Chocolate Cake Roll, 481
No-Bake Chocolate Cheesecake, 469
No-Bake Chocolate Crumb Crust,
479
No-Bake Cocoa Haystacks, 514
No-Cook Fudge Frosting, 517
No Fuss Tuna Quiche, 136
No-Peek Chicken and Rice, 46

**Nuts** (*see also* **Almonds; Peanuts; Pecans; Walnuts**)
Cinnamon Rolls, 528
Cocoa-Nut Bread, 501
Devil's Delight Cake, 462
Dreamy Chocolate Chip Cookies, 407
Emily's Dream Bars, 412
Five Layer Bars, 512
Fudgy Pistachio Cake, 558
New Hampshire White Mountain Pumpkin Pie, 457
Nut-Coated Truffles, 509
Nutty Burgers, 196
Orange-Cashew Chicken, 333
Peanutty-Cocoa Bonbons, 508
Rum Nut Truffles, 509
Tuna-Waldorf Salad Mold, 134
Nutty Burgers, 196


# O

Oatmeal Cookies, 402
Oatmeal Honey Cookies, 408
Oatmeal Shaggies, 420
Oatmeal Toffee Lizzies, 410
**Oats**
Brian's Buffalo Cookies, 404
Butter-Flavored Brickle Drizzles, 401
Chewy Oatmeal-Apricot-Date Bars, 418
Child's Choice, 398
Cocoa Oatmeal Muffins, 496
Coconut Honey Bars, 506
Heavenly Oatmeal Hearts, 426
Jeremy's Famous Turtles, 429
No-Bake Cocoa Haystacks, 514
Oatmeal Cookies, 402
Oatmeal Honey Cookies, 408
Oatmeal Shaggies, 420
Oatmeal Toffee Lizzies, 410
Peach-Stuffed Oatmeal Almond Cookies, 424
Peanut Butter Bars, 417
Spiced Chip Cookies, 514
Ohio Sour Cherry Pie, 442
One-Bowl Buttercream Frosting, 472
One Skillet Spicy Chicken 'n Rice, 262
**Orange**
Acapulco Salad, 286
BBQ Baby Back Ribs, 196
California Date-Chicken Salad, 23

**Orange,** *continued*
Chocolate Chip Orange Pound Cake, 466
Citrus Marinated Chicken, 208
Citrus Tarragon Butter, 208
Classic Sweet & Sour Chicken, 337
Fruited Beef Kabobs, 252
Hollywood Chicken, 35
Orange-Cashew Chicken, 333
Orange Cinnamon Swirl Bread, 524
Orange Coconut Cake, 568
Orange-Dijon Chicken, 210
Orange Glaze, 192
Pork Chops with Orange-Radish Relish, 198
Pork Tenderloin with Orange Glaze, 192
Spicy Fruited Chicken, 53
Sweet 'n' Sour Tuna with Pineapple, 176
Triple Orange Delight, 540
West Indies Curried Drumsticks, 66
Oriental Pancakes, 300
Oriental Pork Bundles, 320
Oriental Sauce/Marinade, 19
Oriental Tea Eggs, 351
Oriental Toss, 348
Original Green Bean Casserole, 122
Outrageous Angel Food Cake, 568


# P

Paella, 65
Pagoda Fried Rice, 349
**Pancakes & Waffles**
Chocolate Dessert Waffles, 497
Mini Chips Pancakes, 500
**Pasta**
Angel Hair Stir-Fry, 334
Cheesy Pasta Swirls, 118
Chicken and Vegetable Couscous, 56
Chicken-Mac Casserole, 90
Chicken Pasta Salad, 15
Chicken to the Macs, 54
Chinese Noodle Cakes, 340
Colache con Pollo, 264
Creamy Herbed Chicken, 46
Crispy Tortellini Bites, 240

**Pasta,** *continued*
  Dreamy Creamy Chicken
    Lasagna, 73
  Elaine's Tuna Tetrazzini, 132
  Fettucine à la Tuna, 142
  Foolproof Clam Fettucine, 100
  Grilled Chicken and Ziti Salad, 14
  Ham & Macaroni Twists, 114
  Hearty Chicken Stir-Fry with
    Noodles, 336
  Italian Antipasto Bake, 92
  Macaroni and Chicken Salad, 16
  Mediterranean Fish & Pasta, 96
  Monterey Spaghetti Casserole, 120
  Mustard Chicken & Vegetables,
    86
  Romance® Chicken Marinara, 75
  Spicy Ravioli and Cheese, 284
  Spiral Pasta Salad, 156
  Surprisingly Simple Chicken
    Cacciatore, 58
  Tortellini with Three-Cheese
    Tuna Sauce, 166
  Tuna & Zucchini-Stuffed
    Manicotti, 160
  Tuna in Red Pepper Sauce, 150
  Tuna Lasagna Bundles, 100
  Twisty Beef Bake, 106
Pastel-Coated Cocoa Bonbons, 504
Pastel Coating, 504
Pastel Mint Topping, 506
**Peaches**
  Glazed Ribbon Dessert, 548
  Mandarin Peach Sauce, 326
  Peach Delight Pie, 440
  Peach-Stuffed Oatmeal Almond
    Cookies, 424
  Peachy Blueberry Crunch, 522
**Peanut Butter**
  Chicken Ribbons Satay, 204
  Chocolate Peanut Butter Cup
    Cookies, 430
  Coconut Honey Bars, 506
  Creamy Peanut Butter Frosting,
    463
  Easy Double Decker Fudge, 504
  Emily's Dream Bars, 412
  Frosted Peanut Butter Peanut
    Brittle Cookies, 423
  Golden Bars, 512
  Peanut Butter and Jelly
    Thumbprint Cookies, 411
  Peanut Butter Bars, 417
  Peanut Butter Chip Ice Cream
    Sauce, 479

**Peanut Butter,** *continued*
  Peanut Butter Chips and Jelly
    Bars, 519
  Peanut Butter Chocolate Chip
    Cookies, 403
  Peanut Butter Coating, 508
  Peanut Butter-Fudge Marble
    Cake, 462
  Peanut Butter Pizza Cookies, 576
  Peanut Butter Sensations, 425
  Peanut Butter Spritz Sandwiches,
    566
  Peanut Butter Sundae Pie, 479
  Peanut Butter Tarts, 490
  Peanut Supreme Pie, 445
  Peanutty-Cocoa Bonbons, 508
**Peanuts**
  Chocolate-Covered Banana Pops,
    484
  Colorful Candy Popcorn Balls, 384
  Frosted Peanut Butter Peanut
    Brittle Cookies, 423
  Heavenly Oatmeal Hearts, 426
  Peanut Butter and Jelly
    Thumbprint Cookies, 411
  Peanut Supreme Pie, 445
Peanutty-Cocoa Bonbons, 508
**Pears**
  Braised Duckling and Pears, 334
**Pecans**
  Butter Pecan Squares, 516
  Chocolate Chip Pecan Pie, 450
  Chocolatetown Pie, 488
  English Toffee Bars, 516
  Fast Chocolate-Pecan Fudge, 506
  Jeremy's Famous Turtles, 429
  Nut Truffles, 509
  Orange Coconut Cake, 568
  Pecan-Coated Wingettes, 21
  Triple Treat Cookies, 530
**Peppers**
  Chicken Rellenos, 72
  Chili-Chicken Sombreros, 84
  Classic Chinese Pepper Steak, 312
  Fruited Beef Kabobs, 252
  Green Chile Chicken, 75
  Southwestern Grilled Chicken
    with Yogurt Salsa, 32
  Spicy Ravioli and Cheese, 284
  Spicy-Sweet Pineapple Pork, 254
  Sweet 'n' Sour Tuna with
    Pineapple, 176
  Tuna & Shrimp Fajitas, 164
  Tuna Chilies Rellenos, 166
  Tuna in Red Pepper Sauce, 150

Pescado Borracho, 274
Pescado Viejo, 276
**Pies & Tarts** (*see also* **Pies, Frozen; Pies, Savory**)
Cherry City Amaretto Cherry Cream Pie, 449
Chocolate Chip Pecan Pie, 450
Chocolate Cream Pie, 489
Chocolate Grasshopper Pie, 488
Chocolate-Marshmallow Mousse Pie, 481
Chocolate Mousse Pie with Rum Cream Topping, 489
Chocolatetown Pie, 488
Cider Apple Pie in Cheddar Crust, 452
Citrus Dream Pie, 454
Cocoa Cloud Pie, 490
Delaware Blueberry Pie, 435
Fudge Brownie Pie, 493
Hershey's Syrup Pie, 492
Individual Chocolate Cream Pies, 490
Lola's Apple Pie, 432
Luscious Cranberry and Blueberry Pie, 446
New Hampshire White Mountain Pumpkin Pie, 457
Ohio Sour Cherry Pie, 442
Peach Delight Pie, 440
Peanut Butter Tarts, 490
Peanut Supreme Pie, 445
Pistachio Chocolate Bar Pie, 386
Rocky Road Pie, 386
Shoo-Fly Pie, 456
Three-in-One Chocolate Pudding & Pie Filling, 485
Toffee Bar Crunch Pie, 392
**Pies, Frozen**
Peanut Butter Sundae Pie, 479
**Pies, Savory**
Curried Chicken Pot Pie, 82
No Fuss Tuna Quiche, 136
Simply Special Vegetable Pie, 124
Tamale Pie, 68
**Pineapple**
Beef and Fruit Skewers, 307
Dragon Beef Kabobs, 314
Fresh Pineapple with Sesame Dip, 303
Fruited Beef Kabobs, 252
Haleakala Rice, 350
Hawaiian Chicken Salad, 22
Hawaiian Pork Stew, 326
Pineapple Chicken Packets, 55

**Pineapple,** *continued*
Pineapple Chicken Rice Bowl, 37
Polynesian Kabobs, 307
Pork Chops Teriyaki, 324
Spicy Fruited Chicken, 53
Spicy-Sweet Pineapple Pork, 254
Spring Break Blueberry Coffeecake, 526
Sweet 'n Sour, 51
Sweet 'n' Sour Tuna with Pineapple, 176
Sweet and Spicy Chicken Stir-Fry, 67
Pistachio Chocolate Bar Pie, 386
**Pizzas**
Grilled Pizza, 232
Ham & Pineapple Pizza, 234
Individual Pizza, 144
Mexicali Pizza, 256
Tomato-Feta Pizza, 234
Veggie-Herb Pizza, 234
Plain Gelatin, 360
Plum Sauce, 320
Polenta Strips with Creamy Salsa Spread, 244
Polynesian Kabobs, 307
**Pork** (*see also* **Ham; Sausage**)
Bake & Glaze Teri Ribs, 323
BBQ Baby Back Ribs, 196
Brunswick Stew, 55
Celebration Pork & Rice, 323
Cheesy Pork Chops 'n Potatoes, 116
Chinese Porcupine Meatballs, 340
Crispy Lite Spareribs, 326
Crispy Wontons, 300
Glazed Pork Roast, 326
Hawaiian Pork Stew, 326
Hunan Stir-Fry with Tofu, 327
Meat-Filled Oriental Pancakes, 298
Mu Shu-Style Fajitas, 250
Oriental Pork Bundles, 320
Pork Chops O'Brien, 112
Pork Chops Teriyaki, 324
Pork Chops with Orange-Radish Relish, 198
Pork Kabobs with Mustard-Bourbon Glaze, 200
Pork Tenderloin with Fresh Plum Sauce, 197
Pork Tenderloin with Orange Glaze, 192
Sesame Pork Tidbits with Sweet & Sour Sauce, 305
Sichuan Pork Salad, 324

**Pork,** *continued*
Spicy Pork Strips, 311
Spicy Sichuan Pork Stew, 324
Spicy-Sweet Pineapple Pork, 254
Spring Rolls, 303
Tofu & Vegetable Stir-Fry, 322
**Potatoes**
California-Style Chicken, 90
Cheesy Pork Chops 'n Potatoes, 116
Classic Hamburger Casserole, 108
Easy Niçoise Salad, 130
Easy Seafood Salad, 156
Grilled New Potatoes, 188
Hawaiian Pork Stew, 326
Hearty Chicken Bake, 91
Hot German-Style Potato Salad, 120
Mini Meat Loaves & Vegetables, 106
Monterey Potatoes, 280
New England Chicken 'n' Corn Chowder, 51
Pork Chops O'Brien, 112
Santa Fe Potato Salad, 294
Sausage Succotash, 114
Southwestern Potato Skins, 244
Toluca Taters, 264
Tuna-Stuffed Bakers, 180
Prawns-in-Shell, 305
Pudding Poke Cake, 390
Puffy Tuna Omelet, 138
**Pumpkin**
New Hampshire White Mountain Pumpkin Pie, 457

# Q

Quick Arroz con Pollo, 49
Quick Vanilla Glaze, 517

# R

**Raisins**
Cocoa Oatmeal Muffins, 496
Five Layer Bars, 512
Golden Bars, 512
Oatmeal Honey Cookies, 408
Oatmeal Shaggies, 420
Raspberry Sherbet Brownie Dessert, 544

**Rice**
Apple & Rice-Stuffed Chicken, 33
Arroz con Pollo Burritos, 258
Artichoke Chicken Pilaf, 44
Baha Roll, 168
Caribbean Chicken Paella, 68
Celebration Pork & Rice, 323
Chicken, Broccoli & Rice Soup, 42
Chicken Fried Rice, 351
Chicken Jambalaya, 71
Easy Paella, 170
El Dorado Rice Casserole, 288
Fried Rice, 74
Haleakala Rice, 350
Herb-Baked Fish & Rice, 94
Japanese Rice Salad, 344
Louisiana Seafood Bake, 98
New Year Fried Rice, 346
No-Peek Chicken and Rice, 46
One Skillet Spicy Chicken 'n Rice, 262
Paella, 65
Pagoda Fried Rice, 349
Pineapple Chicken Rice Bowl, 37
Quick Arroz con Pollo, 49
Sausage-Chicken Creole, 110
Savory Luau Rice, 351
Shrimp Fried Rice, 349
Sierra Chicken Bundles, 268
Sweet 'n Sour, 51
Sweet Chicken Risotto, 67
Szechuan Chicken, 64
Tangy Chicken Walnut Salad, 12
Tex-Mex Stir-Fry, 270
Tuna & Wild Rice Amandine, 158
Zesty Chicken & Rice, 88
Rio Grande Quesadillas, 266
Roast Chicken with Savory Cornbread Stuffing, 38
Rocky Road Pie, 386
Romance® Chicken Marinara, 75
Rum Nut Truffles, 509

# S

**Salad Dressings**
Korean Dressing, 317
**Salads** (*see also* **Gelatin Salads; Salad Dressings**)
Acapulco Salad, 286
Avocado Raspberry Spice Salad, 282
Aztec Chili Salad, 278

Bean Sprout & Spinach Salad, 346

California Date-Chicken Salad, 23

Cantonese Chicken Salad, 330

Chicken Pasta Salad, 15

Cucumber Fan Salad, 348

East Meets West Salad, 349

Easy Niçoise Salad, 130

Easy Seafood Salad, 156

Ensalada Simplese, 290

Firecracker Salad, 350

Gazpacho Tuna Salad, 142

Grilled Chicken and Ziti Salad, 14

Hawaiian Chicken Salad, 22

Hot German-Style Potato Salad, 120

Hot Oriental Salad, 349

Jade Salad with Sesame Vinaigrette, 172

Japanese Rice Salad, 344

Korean Beef & Vegetable Salad, 317

Macaroni and Chicken Salad, 16

Mexican-Style Corn Salad, 235

Oriental Toss, 348

Salsa Shrimp in Papaya, 292

Santa Fe Potato Salad, 294

Santa Fe Tuna Salad with Chili-Lime Dressing, 170

Sea Breeze Fish Salad, 342

Sichuan Pork Salad, 324

Spiral Pasta Salad, 156

Sunomono Salad, 346

Tangy Chicken Walnut Salad, 12

Thai Beef Salad, 319

Tostada Salad, 288

Tuna & Fresh Fruit Salad, 148

Tuna & Vegetables à la Grecque, 146

Tuna-Citrus Salad with Honey Dressing, 140

Tuna-Lettuce Bundles, 140

Tuna Salad Elegante, 162

Salsa Shrimp in Papaya, 292

**Sandwiches** (*see also* **Burgers**)

Amigo Pita Pocket Sandwiches, 260

Cancun Steak Sandwiches, 254

Chicken-Apple Stuffed Pita, 18

Fiesta Chicken Sandwiches, 63

**Sandwiches,** *continued*

Grilled Chicken and Vegetable Sandwiches, 13

Tuna Poor-Boy, 144

Turkey Picatta on Grilled Rolls, 210

Santa Fe Potato Salad, 294

Santa Fe Tuna Salad with Chili-Lime Dressing, 170

Satiny Chocolate Glaze, 470, 515

**Sauces**

All-American Barbecue Sauce and Marinade, 19

Celery Sauce, 37

Citrus Tarragon Butter, 208

Dijon-Cream Sauce, 202

Elaine's Tuna Tetrazzini, 132

Fresh Plum Sauce, 197

Garlic Sauce, 214

Honey-Lime Butter, 221

Lemon Baste, 230

Mandarin Peach Sauce, 326

Melon Butter, 221

Mexican Sauce/Marinade, 19

Molé Sauce for Chicken or Turkey, 262

Niçoise Butter, 221

Orange Glaze, 192

Oriental Sauce/Marinade, 19

Plum Sauce, 320

Sweet & Sour Sauce, 305

Tamale Sauce, 258

Tomato Basil Butter Sauce, 224

Tuna & Mushroom Stroganoff, 136

Tuna Veronique, 132

Saucy Garden Patch Vegetables, 124

Saucy Shrimp, 311

Saucy Shrimp over Chinese Noodle Cakes, 338

**Sausage**

Chicken Jambalaya, 71

Grilled Smoked Sausage, 197

Italian Vegetable Chicken, 61

Make-Ahead Brunch Bake, 112

Sausage-Chicken Creole, 110

Sausage Succotash, 114

Spicy Burrito Bonanza, 250

Savory Luau Rice, 351

Scandinavian Smörgåsbord, 158

Scrambled Eggs with Tuna & Onions, 152

Scrap Happy, 376

Sea Breeze Fish Salad, 342

**Seafood** (*see* **Fish; Shellfish**)
Seafood Kabobs, 226
Seafood Wontons, 172
Sesame Pork Tidbits with Sweet & Sour Sauce, 305
Sesame Seed Chicken, 26
Seviche, 272
Shanghai Shrimp Stir-Fry, 342
Shanghai Sweet & Sour Fish, 340
Shantung Chicken, 331
**Shellfish**
    Chinese Porcupine Meatballs, 340
    Easy Paella, 170
    Foolproof Clam Fettucine, 100
    Grilled Antipasto Platter, 230
    Jade Salad with Sesame Vinaigrette, 172
    Japanese Rice Salad, 344
    Louisiana Seafood Bake, 98
    Paella, 65
    Prawns-in-Shell, 305
    Salsa Shrimp in Papaya, 292
    Saucy Shrimp, 311
    Saucy Shrimp over Chinese Noodle Cakes, 338
    Scandinavian Smörgåsbord, 158
    Seafood Kabobs, 226
    Seviche, 272
    Shanghai Shrimp Stir-Fry, 342
    Shrimp Fried Rice, 349
    Shrimp Skewers with Tropical Fruit Salsa, 222
    Shrimp Teriyaki, 303
    Shrimp with Sweet & Sour Sauce, 300
    Sonora Shrimp, 274
    Steamed Chinese Buns, 347
    Tex-Mex Stir-Fry, 270
    Tuna & Shrimp Fajitas, 164
    West Coast Bouillabaisse, 134
Shoestring Jicama Sauté, 294
Shoo-Fly Pie, 456
Shrimp Fried Rice, 349
Shrimp Skewers with Tropical Fruit Salsa, 222
Shrimp Teriyaki, 303
Shrimp with Sweet & Sour Sauce, 300
Sichuan Beef & Snow Peas, 314
Sichuan Pork Salad, 324
**Side Dishes** (*see also* **Vegetables**)
    Buffet Bean Bake, 121
    Chawan Mushi, 347
    Chicken Fried Rice, 351
    El Dorado Rice Casserole, 288

**Side Dishes,** *continued*
    Grilled Bread, 194
    Haleakala Rice, 350
    New Year Fried Rice, 346
    Oriental Tea Eggs, 351
    Pagoda Fried Rice, 349
    Savory Luau Rice, 351
    Shrimp Fried Rice, 349
    Sour Cream Tortilla Casserole, 290
    Spinach-Onion Stuffing Balls, 121
Sierra Chicken Bundles, 268
Signature Brownies, 517
Simply Green Beans, 282
Simply Special Vegetable Pie, 124
Skewered Vegetables, 234
Snapper with Pesto Butter, 218
Snickerdoodles, 402
Sonora Shrimp, 274
**Soups & Stews**
    Albondigas Soup, 252
    Brunswick Stew, 55
    Chicken, Broccoli & Rice Soup, 42
    Chicken Spinach Stracciatella, 45
    Egg Drop Soup, 300
    Hawaiian Pork Stew, 326
    Hearty Lancaster Chicken, Vegetable and Dumpling Soup, 45
    Hot & Sour Soup, 306
    New England Chicken 'n' Corn Chowder, 51
    Pescado Viejo, 276
    Southern-Style Fish Cassoulet, 176
    Spicy Sichuan Pork Stew, 324
    Tuna-Vegetable Chowder, 148
    West Coast Bouillabaisse, 134
**Sour Cream**
    Chocolate Sour Cream Cake, 465
    Cocoa Cheesecake, 465
    Creamy Nectarine Torte, 564
    Crispy Tortellini Bites, 240
    Everyone's Favorite Cake, 562
    Lawry's Fiesta Dip, 241
    Sour Cream Tortilla Casserole, 290
Southern-Style Fish Cassoulet, 176
South-of-the-Border Meatballs, 241
Southwestern Grilled Chicken with Yogurt Salsa, 32
Southwestern Guacamole, 235
Southwestern Potato Skins, 244
Spaghetti Squash Medley, 286
Spanish-Style Baked Catfish, 276
Special Chocolate Chip Sandwiches, 536

Spiced Chip Cookies, 514
Spicy Burrito Bonanza, 250
Spicy Chicken, 328
Spicy Fruited Chicken, 53
Spicy Pork Strips, 311
Spicy Ravioli and Cheese, 284
Spicy Sichuan Pork Stew, 324
Spicy-Sweet Pineapple Pork, 254
**Spinach**
    Baha Roll, 168
    Bean Sprout & Spinach Salad, 346
    Chicken-Mac Casserole, 90
    Chicken Royale, 26
    Jade Salad with Sesame
      Vinaigrette, 172
    Monterey Spaghetti Casserole,
      120
    Puffy Tuna Omelet, 138
    Spinach-Onion Stuffing Balls, 121
    Tuna Lasagna Bundles, 100
Spiral Pasta Salad, 156
**Spreads & Dips**
    Chile con Queso Spread, 240
    Cucumber Dill Dip, 235
    Eight Layer Fiesta Dip, 246
    Fiesta Ranch Bean Dip, 235
    Fresh Pineapple with Sesame Dip,
      303
    Lawry's Fiesta Dip, 241
    Southwestern Guacamole, 235
Spring Break Blueberry Coffeecake,
    526
Spring Rolls, 303
Squash Olé, 292
Steamed Chinese Buns, 347
**Stews** (*see* **Soups & Stews**)
**Strawberries**
    Choco-Berry Frozen Dessert, 482
    Double Berry Layer Cake, 538
    Glazed Ribbon Dessert, 548
    Strawberry-Banana Salad, 388
    Strawberry Bars, 550
    Strawberry Dessert Cream, 497
    Strawberry Meringue Cakes, 556
Sunomono Salad, 346
Superb Fillet of Sole & Vegetables,
    98
Surprisingly Simple Chicken
    Cacciatore, 58
Sweet 'n Sour, 51
Sweet & Sour Sauce, 305
Sweet 'n' Sour Tuna with Pineapple,
    176
Sweet and Spicy Chicken Stir-Fry,
    67

Sweet Chicken Risotto, 67
Swiss Vegetable Medley, 122
Swordfish with Honey-Lime Glaze,
    226
Syrup Whipped Topping, 492
Szechuan Chicken, 64

# T

Tacos Botanas, 246
Tamale Pie, 68
Tamale Sauce, 258
Tandoori Style Grilled Chicken, 38
Tangy Chicken Walnut Salad, 12
Tarragon Chicken Burgers, 22
**Tarts** (*see* **Pies & Tarts**)
Teriyaki Glazed Beef Kabobs, 200
Teriyaki Lamb Riblets, 305
Tex-Mex Lasagna, 109
Tex-Mex Stir-Fry, 270
Thai Beef Salad, 319
Three-in-One Chocolate Pudding &
    Pie Filling, 485
Toffee Bar Crunch Pie, 392
Toffee Topping, 516
Tofu & Vegetable Stir-Fry, 322
Toluca Taters, 264
**Tomatoes**
    Albondigas Soup, 252
    Aztec Chili Salad, 278
    Brunswick Stew, 55
    Chicken Enchilada Casserole,
      266
    Chicken Jambalaya, 71
    Chicken Picadillo, 73
    El Dorado Rice Casserole, 288
    Grilled Fish Steaks with Tomato
      Basil Butter Sauce, 224
    Louisiana Seafood Bake, 98
    Mediterranean Fish & Pasta, 96
    Mediterranean Salsa, 212
    Mexican Lasagna, 70
    Molé Sauce for Chicken or
      Turkey, 262
    One Skillet Spicy Chicken 'n
      Rice, 262
    Paella, 65
    Pescado Borracho, 274
    Pescado Viejo, 276
    Polynesian Kabobs, 307
    Sonora Shrimp, 274
    Sour Cream Tortilla Casserole,
      290

**Tomatoes,** *continued*
    Tamale Sauce, 258
    Tex-Mex Lasagna, 109
    Toluca Taters, 264
    Tomato Basil Butter Sauce, 224
    Tomato-Bread Casserole, 280
    Tostada Salad, 288
    Tuna Provençale on French Bread, 178
    Twisty Beef Bake, 106
    West Coast Bouillabaisse, 134
    Zucchini Mexicana, 284
**Toppings**
    Chocolate Topping, 478
    Festive Whipped Cream, 488
    Hot Fudge Sauce, 493
    Pastel Mint Topping, 506
    Peanut Butter Chip Ice Cream Sauce, 479
    Strawberry Dessert Cream, 497
    Syrup Whipped Topping, 492
    Toffee Topping, 516
Tortellini with Three-Cheese Tuna Sauce, 166
Tortilla Stack Tampico, 260
Tostada Salad, 288
Triple Layer Chocolate Mousse Cake, 466
Triple Orange Delight, 540
Triple Treat Cookies, 530
Tropical Fruit Salsa, 222
Tuna & Asparagus au Gratin, 178
Tuna & Fresh Fruit Salad, 148
Tuna & Mushroom Stroganoff, 136
Tuna & Shrimp Fajitas, 164
Tuna & Vegetables à la Grecque, 146
Tuna & Wild Rice Amandine, 158
Tuna & Zucchini-Stuffed Manicotti, 160
Tuna Chilies Rellenos, 166
Tuna-Citrus Salad with Honey Dressing, 140
Tuna Frittata, 150
Tuna in Red Pepper Sauce, 150
Tuna Lasagna Bundles, 100
Tuna-Lettuce Bundles, 140
Tuna Poor-Boy, 144
Tuna Provençale on French Bread, 178
Tuna Salad Elegante, 162
Tuna-Stuffed Artichokes, 154
Tuna-Stuffed Bakers, 180
Tuna-Stuffed Sole with Lime Sauce, 174

Tuna Tortilla Roll-Ups, 96
Tuna-Vegetable Chowder, 148
Tuna Veronique, 132
Tuna-Waldorf Salad Mold, 134
**Turkey**
    Amigo Pita Pocket Sandwiches, 260
    Barbecued Turkey Breast, 211
    Barbecued Turkey with Herbs, 207
    Creamy Turkey & Broccoli, 84
    Molé Sauce for Chicken or Turkey, 262
    Toluca Taters, 264
    Turkey Burritos, 216
    Turkey Cordon Bleu, 88
    Turkey Picatta on Grilled Rolls, 210
Turtle Cake, 578
Twisty Beef Bake, 106

# V

Vanilla Glaze, 515
Veal Tonnato, 130
**Vegetables** (*see also individual listings*)
    Acapulco Salad, 286
    Caribbean Chicken Paella, 68
    Celery Sauté, 292
    Cheesy Pasta Swirls, 118
    Chicken and Vegetable Couscous, 56
    Chicken in French Onion Sauce, 80
    Chicken Spinach Stracciatella, 45
    Chicken Thighs and Vegetables Lyonnaise, 48
    Chicken with Snow Peas and Walnuts, 40
    Countdown Casserole, 102
    Creamy Herbed Chicken, 46
    Crunchy-Topped Fish & Vegetables, 101
    Cucumber Dill Dip, 235
    Cucumber Fan Salad, 348
    Curried Chicken Pot Pie, 82
    Easy Niçoise Salad, 130
    Easy Paella, 170
    Fettucine à la Tuna, 142
    Firecracker Salad, 350
    Gazpacho Tuna Salad, 142

**Vegetables,** *continued*
Grilled Antipasto Platter, 230
Grilled Chicken and Vegetable
Sandwiches, 13
Grilled Chicken and Ziti Salad, 14
"Grilled" Tuna with Vegetables
in Herb Butter, 152
Grilled Vegetables with Balsamic
Vinaigrette, 228
Hearty Chicken Bake, 91
Hearty Lancaster Chicken,
Vegetable and Dumpling Soup,
45
Home-Style Chicken 'n Biscuits,
92
Hot Oriental Salad, 349
Individual Pizza, 144
Italian Antipasto Bake, 92
Italian Vegetable Chicken, 61
Korean Beef & Vegetable Salad,
317
Lattice-Top Chicken, 82
Mini Meat Loaves & Vegetables,
106
Mu Shu-Style Fajitas, 250
Mustard Chicken & Vegetables,
86
Oriental Toss, 348
Pineapple Chicken Rice Bowl, 37
Saucy Garden Patch Vegetables,
124
Sausage-Chicken Creole, 110
Seafood Wontons, 172
Shoestring Jicama Sauté, 294
Sichuan Beef & Snow Peas, 314
Simply Special Vegetable Pie, 124
Skewered Vegetables, 234
Southern-Style Fish Cassoulet, 176
Spaghetti Squash Medley, 286
Spicy Chicken, 328
Spicy Fruited Chicken, 53
Spiral Pasta Salad, 156
Sunomono Salad, 346
Sweet 'n Sour, 51
Swiss Vegetable Medley, 122
Tofu & Vegetable Stir-Fry, 322
Tuna & Vegetables à la Grecque,
146
Tuna-Stuffed Bakers, 180
Tuna-Stuffed Sole with Lime
Sauce, 174
Tuna-Vegetable Chowder, 148
Yangtze Stir-Fry, 314
Zesty Chicken & Rice, 88
Veggie-Herb Pizza, 234

# W

**Walnuts**
Chewy Oatmeal-Apricot-Date
Bars, 418
Chippy Cheeseys, 414
Tangy Chicken Walnut Salad,
12
West Coast Bouillabaisse, 134
West Indies Curried Drumsticks,
66
Wine & Rosemary Lamb Skewers,
194
Wine Country Steak, 198
Wisconsin Tuna Cake with Lemon-
Dill Sauce, 128

# Y

Yangtze Stir-Fry, 314
**Yogurt**
Chicken Enchilada Casserole,
64
New Delhi Chicken Thighs, 74
Southwestern Grilled Chicken
with Yogurt Salsa, 32
Tandoori Style Grilled Chicken,
38
Tuna & Fresh Fruit Salad, 148

# Z

Zesty Chicken & Rice, 88
Zesty Chicken en Papillote, 21
**Zucchini**
Cheese-Stuffed Beef Rolls, 104
Easy Chocolate Zucchini Cake,
500
Hearty Chicken Stir-Fry with
Noodles, 336
Mediterranean Fish & Pasta,
96
Romance® Chicken Marinara,
75
Sichuan Pork Salad, 324
Squash Olé, 292
Tacos Botanas, 246
Tuna & Zucchini-Stuffed
Manicotti, 160
Tuna Frittata, 150
Zucchini Mexicana, 284

# METRIC CONVERSION CHART

## VOLUME MEASUREMENTS (dry)

⅛ teaspoon = 0.5 mL
¼ teaspoon = 1 mL
½ teaspoon = 2 mL
¾ teaspoon = 4 mL
1 teaspoon = 5 mL
1 tablespoon = 15 mL
2 tablespoons = 30 mL
¼ cup = 60 mL
⅓ cup = 75 mL
½ cup = 125 mL
⅔ cup = 150 mL
¾ cup = 175 mL
1 cup = 250 mL
2 cups = 1 pint = 500 mL
3 cups = 750 mL
4 cups = 1 quart = 1 L

## VOLUME MEASUREMENTS (fluid)

1 fluid ounce (2 tablespoons) = 30 mL
4 fluid ounces (½ cup) = 125 mL
8 fluid ounces (1 cup) = 250 mL
12 fluid ounces (1½ cups) = 375 mL
16 fluid ounces (2 cups) = 500 mL

## WEIGHTS (mass)

½ ounce = 15 g
1 ounce = 30 g
3 ounces = 90 g
4 ounces = 120 g
8 ounces = 225 g
10 ounces = 285 g
12 ounces = 360 g
16 ounces = 1 pound = 450 g

## DIMENSIONS

$\frac{1}{16}$ inch = 2 mm
⅛ inch = 3 mm
¼ inch = 6 mm
½ inch = 1.5 cm
¾ inch = 2 cm
1 inch = 2.5 cm

## OVEN TEMPERATURES

250°F = 120°C
275°F = 140°C
300°F = 150°C
325°F = 160°C
350°F = 180°C
375°F = 190°C
400°F = 200°C
425°F = 220°C
450°F = 230°C

## BAKING PAN SIZES

| Utensil | Size in Inches/Quarts | Metric Volume | Size in Centimeters |
|---|---|---|---|
| Baking or Cake Pan (square or rectangular) | 8×8×2 | 2 L | 20×20×5 |
| | 9×9×2 | 2.5 L | 22×22×5 |
| | 12×8×2 | 3 L | 30×20×5 |
| | 13×9×2 | 3.5 L | 33×23×5 |
| Loaf Pan | 8×4×3 | 1.5 L | 20×10×7 |
| | 9×5×3 | 2 L | 23×13×7 |
| Round Layer Cake Pan | 8×1½ | 1.2 L | 20×4 |
| | 9×1½ | 1.5 L | 23×4 |
| Pie Plate | 8×1¼ | 750 mL | 20×3 |
| | 9×1¼ | 1 L | 23×3 |
| Baking Dish or Casserole | 1 quart | 1 L | — |
| | 1½ quart | 1.5 L | — |
| | 2 quart | 2 L | — |